In Person

IN PERSON

*Reenactment in Postwar
and Contemporary Cinema*

Ivone Margulies

OXFORD
UNIVERSITY PRESS

OXFORD
UNIVERSITY PRESS

Oxford University Press is a department of the University of Oxford. It furthers the University's objective of excellence in research, scholarship, and education by publishing worldwide. Oxford is a registered trade mark of Oxford University Press in the UK and certain other countries.

Published in the United States of America by Oxford University Press
198 Madison Avenue, New York, NY 10016, United States of America.

© Oxford University Press 2019

All rights reserved. No part of this publication may be reproduced, stored in a retrieval system, or transmitted, in any form or by any means, without the prior permission in writing of Oxford University Press, or as expressly permitted by law, by license, or under terms agreed with the appropriate reproduction rights organization. Inquiries concerning reproduction outside the scope of the above should be sent to the Rights Department, Oxford University Press, at the address above.

You must not circulate this work in any other form and you must impose this same condition on any acquirer.

Library of Congress Cataloging-in-Publication Data
Names: Margulies, Ivone, author.
Title: In person : reenactment in postwar and contemporary cinema / Ivone Margulies.
Description: New York, NY : Oxford University Press, [2019] | Includes bibliographical references.
Identifiers: LCCN 2018014403| ISBN 9780190496821 (hardcover) | ISBN 9780190496838 (paperback) | ISBN 9780190496852 (companion website) | ISBN 9780190496845 (Updf) | ISBN 9780190914028 (Epub)
Subjects: LCSH: Realism in motion pictures. | Motion pictures—History—20th century.
Classification: LCC PN1995.9.R3 M36 2019 | DDC 791.43612—dc23 LC record available at https://lccn.loc.gov/2018014403

9 8 7 6 5 4 3 2 1

Paperback printed by Webcom Inc., Canada
Hardback printed by Bridgeport National Bindery, Inc., United States of America

CONTENTS

Acknowledgments   vii

Introduction—Estrangement and Exemplarity: In-Person Reenactment   1
    Exemplarity   8
    Stages of Actualization   11
    In Person Reenactment: The Book   13
1. Casting Relatives: The Spectrum of Substitution   19
    Orson Welles's *Four Men in a Raft (It's All True)*   25
    Endurance: Kinship and the Exceptional Body   29
    Reenacting Heredity: *Sons*   33
2. Neorealist Reenactment as Postwar Pedagogy   37
    Zavattini's "Last Judgment" Cinema   40
    The Story of Caterina   47
    Footprints: Streetwalkers and Maggiorani's Back   54
    Attempted Suicide: Antonioni's Singularities   57
    Anonymous Stars: Donatella Marrosu and Anna Magnani   67
3. Celebrity Reenactment, Biopic, and the Mortal Body   77
    Sophia: Her Own Story   84
    Bazin's Cine-mythographies   92
    Cinema's Existential Arena   94
    Torero! Replicants   98
    Mexican Ciné-verdad, Carlos Velo, Hugo Butler, and Zavattini   104
4. A Sort of Psychodrama: Verité Moments 58–61   113
    Role-play: The Real in Balance   120
    Provisional Closure: Reflexivity and Death in *The Human Pyramid*   124
    Chronicle of a Summer (1960–1961) as *Autocritique* (1958)   130
    A "Nascent" Register: Group Dynamics and the Worker   136
5. Ascetic Stages: Reenactment in Post-Holocaust Cinema   141
    Pedovision: Ritual, Wandering Words   147
    Marceline Loridan, Testimony With (out) an "I"   153
    Splitting: Oumarou Ganda's Solo   162
    The Karski Report—Of a Report   167
    Filming and Refilming: Phatic Reenactment   171
    Ascetic Stages, Next   178

6. Trial Stages: Rithy Panh's Parajuridical Cinema   183
    Solo Routines: The Critical Valence of Alienation   188
    Paintings, Desks, Files, and Faces: Reflexive Platforms   192
    S21's Judicial Context   200
    Parajuridical Scenarios and the Confessional Imperative   205
    An Internal Chorus: Files and Faces   209

7. Reenactment and A-filiation in *Serras da Desordem*   219
    "When Is Carapiru?"   221
    Twenty Years Later: Brazilian Films on "First" and Recurrent Contact   228
    Leading to *Serras*   236
    The Actor as Agent: Carapiru, Pereio, and Tonacci   240
    A-filiation   245
    Disrupted Transmission   249

Conclusion: Senseless Mimesis   253

Select Bibliography   263
Notes   269
Index   321

ACKNOWLEDGMENTS

This book's long gestation demands lengthy acknowledgments. Mark Cohen, who followed all of its sinews, from its impossible ambitions to its current incarnation, comes first. His intelligence, demand for clarity, love, and wit are essential—for the book, but mainly for all the life and time in between.

A number of friends helped with their support, scholarship, and insight: I thank, in particular, Sam DiIorio, Katherine Model, Joe McElhaney, Kaira Cabanas, Rebekah Rutkoff, and Alessandra Raengo for their intellectual generosity and extensive comments on particular chapters. Noa Steimatsky is a constant, much needed interlocutor. My writing group can be credited for helping me finish the book. Leah Anderst, Jill Stevenson, Jennifer Dixon, and Peter Schaeffer commented on multiple chapter versions, and the sense of process developed in our wonderful gatherings has become a model for my work.

Friends in the United States and abroad suggested additional objects of study and facilitated access to new materials: Elaine Charnov (as Margaret Mead Festival director) introduced me to Zhang Yuan's *Sons*; Bruni Burrest suggested pertinent titles (as Human Rights Film Festival director) and Patricia Mourão referred me to Tonacci's *Serras da Desordem*, the brilliant film whose analysis caps the book. Sylvie Lindeperg and Frederique Berthet helped me feel in tune with the historical scholarship around post-Holocaust cinema. Richard Peña facilitated my contact with Abbas Kiarostami and helped with access to Velo's *Torero!*; Ismail Xavier, whose work is a continuing inspiration, and conversations with the late Andrea Tonacci and with Cristina Amaral, gave me extra insight on the making of *Serras*.

In addition, I want to thank friends and family who helped in various stages of the book's research and writing: Sonia Dain Margulies, Aida Marques, Roberta Saraiva Coutinho, Bernardo Carvalho, Eduardo Viveiros de Castro, Deborah Danowski, Ella Shohat, Robert Stam, Immy Humes, Katherine Hurbis Cherrier, Mick Hurbis Cherrier, Sara Venosa and Angelo Venosa, Eduardo and Maristela Margulies, and Eliane Keane.

Tim Corrigan, Dudley Andrew, Natalia Brizuela, Jonathan Kahana, Antonia Lant, Romy Golan, Denilson Lopes, Jens Andermann, and Claudiu Turcus's invitations to speak at various symposia and conferences on cinematic temporality, realism, and corporeality in cinema led to reflections that are now integral to this book. The same is true of the "Powers of Cinema" workshops developed by Lynn Higgins, Steven Ungar, and Dalton Kraus. I thank in particular DiIorio, Ungar, Higgins, the late Philip Watts, and Nathalie Rachlin for their engagement with my work on Jean

Rouch and sociodrama. Corrigan and Karen Redrobe's invitation to teach a course on reenactment at the University of Pennsylvania provided a welcome chance for testing some of my ideas. Deborah Danowski's translation of an early version of this book's argument into coherent Portuguese facilitated my communication with Brazilian audiences.

A Mellon Resident fellowship to co-direct a seminar on "The Aftermath" at the Center for the Humanities at the CUNY Graduate Center in 2007–2008 helped focus my reflection on the relationship between memorials, trials, and performance, and I thank the director Aoebhiann Sweeney and Michael Washburn for their encouragement and logistical help in organizing the public programs: "The Trial: Stages of Truth," Interdisciplinary Conference on the Trial and Performance (with Stephanie Golob) and "Documenting Catharsis: A Series on War and Reckoning." The broader questions raised by the seminar participants and invitees were formative material for the book.

At Anthology Film Archives, Jed Rapfogel and John Mhiripiri have been wonderful, knowledgeable resources. The chapters on post-Holocaust cinema and Rithy Panh were developed out of research done in Paris at the Memorial du Shoah, an institution commendable for considering genocide as a global phenomenon. Bifi and the Bibliothèque Nationale were great sources for French materials, and I want to thank the São Paulo Cinemateca staff for their help with materials related to Tonacci and to Eduardo Coutinho. Rosa Gaiarsa at UCLA Archives as well as the staff at the National Library in Washington, DC, were instrumental in the viewing of various reenactment films, in particular sports and actors' biopics.

A number of CUNY and Hunter College research awards enriched this project, providing each of the chapters with a solid and broader context. PSCCUNY awards and Presidential travel awards made possible extensive research in France, Brazil, and the United States. The Fund for Academic Development at Hunter College supported much needed editorial help.

Erik Butler's fine editing and the book's wonderful cover, designed by Sula Danowski, make me especially proud of its presentation.

At Oxford University Press, Norm Hirschy has been a delight to work with. An attentive editor, he has efficiently steered the book along its various production stages. I want to thank as well Lauralee Yeary and Aishwarya Krishnamoorthy for their help with revision, marketing, and design.

I dedicate this book to Mark Cohen and Alex Margulies Cohen with all my love.

In Person

INTRODUCTION
Estrangement and Exemplarity

In-Person Reenactment

People understand themselves better than the social fabric; and to see themselves on the screen, performing their daily actions—remembering that to see oneself gives one the sense of being unlike oneself, like hearing one's own voice on the radio—can help them to fill up a void, a lack of knowledge of reality.

Cesare Zavattini[1]

Enlarged twenty times . . . revealed to be a neuropath by his psychiatrist, made public, bare and confused, man finds himself through the cinematic camera cut off in all his lies . . . shameful and perhaps truthful. Mental health, the judicial inquisition will someday use this confessing film where the subject sees himself as object. When will there be dramatists to do this?

Jean Epstein[2]

At the trial, in Abbas Kiarostami's *Close-Up*'s central scene, Hossein Sabzian reveals how he assumed the role of the known filmmaker Mohsen Makhmalbaf. Lacking the means to film—a crew and even a camera—he had to limit his impersonation to rehearsals and what he described as location scouting. After promising the Ahankahn family to make a film with them, he inspects all the rooms in the house. He has family members walk back and forth inside their residence, and he even proposes to cut down a tree that might block a shot of the facade.

These scenarios, in between minimalist performance acts and sketches, expose Sabzian's precarious hold as director. And yet after two days of commanding the Ahankahns to move about in their own house, Sabzian is brought to trial for impersonation. From Sabzian's passive resemblance to Makhmalbaf to his active impersonation[3]; from acting like a director, to having people from a higher social class act at his command, multiple modalities of acting and mimetic passing are subject to

Kiarostami's filmic modulation. Reenactment is his instrument to sift through and set in relief the fluid, social dimensions of individual identity.

The critical potential of in-person reenactment emerges in full force through *Close-Up*'s brilliant structure and argument. The film follows the actual trial brought up by the aggrieved family as it develops, but it strategically intercuts reenacted scenes of the impersonator in action as evidence of sorts. In one extended sequence we are privy to Sabzian's futile attempt to keep up the pretense while the family waits for the police to arrest him. Elaborate blocking and terse dialogue suggest the family's response to being duped. They act pretending as if they don't know he is an impostor. In the meantime, Sabzian mobilizes his skills as an actor in the symbolic atonement implied by reenactment, an expiatory performance that seems to motivate the ensuing acquittal.

In the last scene, the real Makhalbaf waits for Sabzian as he is released from prison. Sabzian cries, embarrassed; the two men embrace and climb onto Mahmalbaf's motorcycle to pay a visit to the Ahankahns. Filmed with the candid texture of direct cinema—in long shot and with a faltering microphone—the scene stands as an elaborate conceit. Since Makhmalbaf knew he was being filmed and Sabzian didn't, Kiarostami created the effect of a badly connected microphone in order to rebalance the power and articulation of their respective dialogue lines. Without this maneuver, Makhmalbaf would have turned into the protagonist and source of Sabzian's drama. With it, Kiarostami pulls these screen personae into the sphere of the *"semblable,"* the "like-being" who "resembles me in that I myself 'resemble' him" as Jean Luc Nancy writes: "we resemble together, if you will, in an 'acting alike' that is, implies, a relation of mutuality."[4]

The ride foregrounds the physiognomic similarity between the two men pointing to the impotence of representation to surmount real social distinctions (Fig. 0.1). In the meanwhile reenactment works as a poor vindicating mirror. It promotes the

Figure 0.1: Makhmalbaf and Sabzian ride together in *Close-Up* (Abbas Kiarostami, 1990).

awareness of the relation between impersonation (Sabzian posing as Makhmalbaf) and acting (Sabzian as Sabzian as Mahkbalbaf), along with the recognition of the absolute chasm enacted in this doubling. Through the frame of reenactment the film sifts through a series of semblances granting to the person of Sabzian, his own contour, his individuated dignity.

Kiarostami had significantly established his complicity with Sabzian's genuine desire to be another, providing him with a platform of expression. Possibly triggered by their common love of cinema, he warns Sabzian at the start of the film that one of the two cameras, mounted with close-up lens, was there for Sabzian to tell the audience facts and feelings that were legally unacceptable but were nevertheless true (Figs. 0.2 and 0.3).

Compare, then, Kiarostami's optics with Jean Epstein's advocacy of the close-up in a cinema imagined as normative apparatus. In his theoretical writings, Epstein warns about the camera's power to produce a radical rift in one's sense of identity but also to police the resulting alienation. The close-up's magnified revelations spark a series of controlling and critical metaphors. Cinema becomes a judicial machine delivering the alienated self as the true, legitimate self. The amplified image reframes the subject for scrutiny and judgment.

Altering the terms of the process from impersonation to in-person reenactment, Kiarostami transforms the trial from a fraud accusation into an exploration into the nature of belief. He shifts indictment into claim, third-person fiction into first-person agency.[5] Reconstituting a great part of the trial with the judge absent and continuing to interrogate the accused in close quarters for almost nine hours, he

Figure 0.2: First close-up, the confession (*Close-Up*, Abbas Kiarostami, 1990).

Figure 0.3: Sabzian talks to Kiarostami: "I'm interested in cinema" (*Close-Up*, Abbas Kiarostami, 1990).

amplifies cinematically Sabzian's voice. Using a setting with actual judicial impact as his backdrop, Kiarostami underlines the links between testimony and reenactment, hijacking for cinema the rhetorical power of a culprit's court appeal. Through this direct address Sabzian makes his plea not to the judge but to a cinephile audience (see Fig 0.4 in Color Insert, 1). As he explains his draw to cinema in a grainier footage, the film dramatizes through this frontal close-up and major verité trope, cinema's capacity to serve as a platform for testimony, for what may only be relayed *in person*.

In Person: Reenactment in Postwar and Contemporary Cinema considers what exactly *is* relayed once a person replays her own past on camera; what distinguishes in-person reenactment from other forms of mimetic, illustrative reconstructions of the past and what is its import in terms of social representativity and exemplarity.

Reenactment loosely denotes any practice restaging a historical or biographical event, or a typical traditional behavior. Various substitutes—actors, relatives, lookalikes, and members from a similar class, area, or expertise—may be enlisted to reconstruct unavailable aspects of reality in television docudramas, crime shows, and ethnographic documentaries. Tapping on redemptive and revisionist perspectives, in-person reenactment films foreground a different set of questions. The first relates to agency. The simplicity of the casting is especially tempting for activist filmmakers who might prefer to imagine that film gives transparent access to spontaneously generated modes of social reclamation. While one's performance of one's own life story is easily confused with a public reclamation of one's self and voice occluding all other factors that condition a film's address and critical interpellation, I am interested instead in how the ambiguous agency of the actual protagonist turned actor grants to these films their refractive, critical quality.

A second question relates to reenactment's belatedness. Reenactment is an explicitly after-the-fact practice that obviates the conventions ruling the adjustments between the different temporalities of the cinematic apparatus, narrative, and reality. A fictional strategy of actualization reenactment's temporality is as flexible as its potential functions. It works to ritually renew the bonds with an original event, to provide an exemplary image of conversion, or to create a form of embodied memorial. Still, the actual protagonist's replay always introduces a differential, a disturbance. The films push us to ask how the gap between past and present is configured within the work, what the force of the citation is in the political present, and how reenactment contributes, through embodied experience, to a future archive.

Acted by the original protagonist, in-person reenactment departs from the dramatization of habitual or shared realities to replay unique biographical or demarcated historical occurrences. The seeming self-evidence of this casting belies the deep implications the revenant has for cinema defined as a historical critical instrument. Most immediately, in-person reenactment responds to two noncongruent, nonexclusive orders. The first concerns appearances and verisimilitude—who better to embody one's past than its actual protagonist. The second is a performative move to make the past present, and its central question is why now. The person's status as living historical being, as actor and agent in the present, compels us to ask why this filmic "return," this present interpellation occurs. What sort of continuity with an original event is affirmed once the actual person reenacts her past and what function, psychic, exemplary, rhetorical, or ritual is at work in reenactment's belatedness?

Based on an embodied consciousness and its public transmission, the reenactment films I discuss help configure a new category in realist cinema promoting moral example (historical, biographies, cautionary tales); self-revision (neorealist cinema, cinema verité, activist tapes); and memorial, historiographical, and parajuridical testimonials.

Invested in the complexity of a theatrical representation that "acts" in the present, reenactment brings into the picture a foreign body, a changed presence that is transformative both in the film and for viewers. As a split figure, the real protagonist is suspended between past reference and present actualization. Bill Nichols aptly notes that "reenactment forfeits its indexical bond to the original event . . . paradoxically draw[ing] its phantasmic power from this very fact."[6] Always at odds with the time it represents the real/actor is an active and disturbing revenant whose surplus of presence generates a deep uncertainty regarding its status, its performative effectiveness, and its relation to an original experience.

However, the gap between a past self and a present self is essential to the confessional-performative dynamic animating the consciousness-raising and exemplarity purposes of reenactment.[7] Referring to this same dynamic in autobiographical writing, Jean Starobinski helps clarify the stakes of in-person reenactment, for acting in the first person has a necessary ethical dimension. Discussing St. Augustine and Rousseau's Confessions, he suggests that if there were no implicit changes in the development of one's character, the potential of a differential between narrator and narrative would hold no interest.[8] If no "life-conversion" event had occurred, "new developments would be treated as external (historical) events; we would then be in the presence of the conditions of what [Emile] Benveniste has named history and a narrator in the first person would hardly be necessary."[9] Ultimately a conversion authorizes the narrative, and "it is the internal transformation of the individual—and the exemplary character of this transformation—that furnishes a subject for a narrative discourse in which 'I' is both subject and object."[10]

At the same time, this basic narrative of conversion implies a distinction between a past and a present "I" that is hard for the viewer to manage, an ambiguity that ultimately informs the interest of in-person reenactment. Starobinski defines the difficulty when he states that "the deviation which establishes the autobiographical reflection is one of time and of identity . . . at the level of language the only intruding mark is that of time, [while] the personal mark, the 'I' remains constant."[11]

While the narrative is justified in terms of its conversion aim, it is precisely this difference that troubles, in turn, the autobiographical narrative. Since the narrator is no longer who he is today, the I has an "ambiguous constancy."[12] Conversely, "pronominal constancy is the index of a permanent responsibility," in narrative confessions since the "first person" embodies both the present reflection and the multiplicity of past states.[13]

The potential of in-person reenactment to rewrite the self is propped on the I's ambiguous constancy, as well as on its permanent responsibility. Besides engaging with the ethical horizon of in-person reenactment, this book explores the effects of this artificially created identity, its protean temporality and revising capabilities.

This study on in-person reenactment is part of a renewed engagement with the real apparent in contemporary art and cinema in the past decades.[14] Composites such as the actual/actor have become ubiquitous as artistic practice and critical category in order to stretch the reach of testimonials, to revise history and registers of authenticity.[15] They participate in a parafictional impulse in contemporary art, when for instance an expanded network of references and documents are used to validate an invented reality. Jumbling recreation and relic, reenactment and archive, works like Pierre Huyghe's *The Third Memory* (1999) or Omer Fast's *Spielberg's List* (2003) pursue in a distinct conceptual register questions raised more consequentially in 1980s documentaries such as Errol Morris's *The Thin Blue Line* and Claude Lanzmann's *Shoah*—that truth and history are subject to fissured and layered rewritings.[16] A repurposed biopic such as *Shulie*, Elisabeth Subrin's 1997 dramatized remake of a 1967 documentary on Shulamith Firestone, is an example of the kind of intervention made possible through reenactment's hybrid of fiction and actual reference. In *Shulie*, Subrin critically stretches the timeline of a known biography to revise patriarchal history. Seriously playing with plausibility, an actress stands in for a young Firestone prior to her development as a feminist theorist, opening a foreclosed fate to new potentialities.[17]

Despite insights gleaned from these conceptual practices, I distinguish the reenactment explored here from the experiences of past histories or lives discussed in the fields of affective history (recreational reconstitution of wars or past-centuries' everyday life) or participatory art. Even though many of these metafictional practices embed a redemptive promise into their recreations either by testing the activist reach of a political speech into different presents (in Mark Tribe's *The Huron Project*); by opening historical events to a new cast and dynamic configuration of forces as in Jeremy Deller's *Battle of Orgreave* recreation of a 1984 miner's strike; by adjudicating anew past legal cases as in parajudicial documentaries such as Joe Berliner and Bruce Sinofsky's *Paradise Lost: The Murder at the Robin Hood Hills* (1996) and Emilio de Antonio's *In the King of Prussia* (1982), or by bringing out a biography's alternate, virtual possibilities, my focus is more restricted.

My book theorizes the import of in-person reenactment through contextual readings of canonical postwar realist films: two omnibus films made at a moment marked by polemics in the definition of neorealism; two instances of cinema verité charged with pointed auto-critiques; and a Mexican biopic hailed as an early instance of docudrama by a jury composed by three major figures of realist cinema—Luchino Visconti, André Bazin, and John Grierson (Chapters 2–4). I follow these postwar instances of in-person reenactment as well as of transformative role-play with a discussion of contemporary films with explicit historiographical and traumatic dimensions (Chapters 5–7).

Tracing a verité arc that runs in parallel to established postwar realist cinemas, the book examines how reenactment films have become a forum for contested social realities, appropriating pedagogic, clinical, and legal models (such as talking cures, psychodrama, public testimony, and Truth and Reconciliation commissions) in their impetus to use this secondary stage to critically revise the past and to probe the interface between history and personal experience.

I delineate a historical shift from a redemptive use of exemplary reenactment in the fifties toward a critical stance evident in the unredemptive perspective promoted in post-*Shoah* reenactment films. Instead of guiding us for a predetermined fate as in exemplary versions of reenactment—Caterina (in Maselli and Zavattini's *The Story of Caterina*, 1953) who is shown abandoning her son, being pardoned, and finding work at the orphanage that has taken her child in—contemporary filmmakers represent stark realities that resist the notion of the protagonist's rehabilitation, or catharsis. Rather than serving as instrument of self-awareness or as a stage to reprocess one's identity, as in the cinema verité examples discussed (*Chronicle of a Summer*, 1961 or *The Human Pyramid*, 1959), the critical force of the revenant in contemporary post-*Shoah* cinema hangs instead on an ambiguous agency and problematic consciousness.

Still, independent of whether the films provide closure presenting images of self-awareness or not, all films examined consistently promote a categorical and temporal hesitation regarding the register and address of the actual person as actor: does the real/actor refer to past or present; does he function as claimant or a prop within a film's mise-en-scène and larger agenda? This density of motivation as well as its rhetorical force drives my interest in this particular mode of reenactment.

EXEMPLARITY

The patent instrumentality of in-person reenactment is especially evident in social activist documentary and ethnographic film. Even if the reconstituted events or situations originally affected only an individual or small group, by virtue of their "citation," these people's lives acquire a collective resonance that can then serve various didactic, parajuridical, and memorial agendas.

In Latin, *citare* means "calling someone out to the stand." In its first sense, citation is a summons to appear in court in the quality of witness or defendant, and only secondarily a passage from a text used to illustrate or support one's proposal. Filmic reenactment fuses the two meanings: since it is rhetorically motivated to submit a particular life or event to scrutiny and judgment, it needs to selectively represent those instances, those examples that will make the author's case. The person is summoned to the stand—in this case the camera/screen—to testify about her past, to enact both its evidence and perhaps its exculpation. His life, reenacted, is revised and becomes exemplary.

In grafting the notion of exemplarity onto reenactment films, I consider a range of meanings for "example." A person's action or conduct regarded as an object of imitation; appeals to precedents to authorize a course of action; a signal instance of punishment intended to have a deterrent effect, a cautionary function are significant because they serve a rhetorical purpose in pedagogic or militant films.[18]

Examples are concrete instances used to support a general statement, a means, according to Aristotle, of producing belief through induction.[19] In *Exemplum*, John Lyons notes a marked tendency to "fuse" or even "confuse" the cognitive/rhetorical functions of the example with its doctrinal and prescriptive function (the exemplum—in vernacular usage, a short narrative used to illustrate a moral point).[20] Example and exemplum are of course related in their intent to change the viewer.[21] In ancient rhetoric, the example had a broadly understood mimetic and persuasive range: not only does the example picture, it may also induce an imitative reproduction on the part of the audience."[22] The constant reference in sermons to the ultimate exemplar, the deeds and life of Christ, helps establish the status of the exemplum as an imitable model. Within this self-validating circle, *exemplum* means both the model to be copied and the copy or representation of that model—the exemplar.[23]

The exemplar, Timothy Hampton points out, "can be seen as a kind of textual node or point of juncture, where a given author's interpretation of the past overlaps with the desire to form and fashion readers."[24] A similar circularity between exemplary narratives and embodiment assures its believability and rhetorical force as future model. A "normative discourse 'operates' only if has already become A Story, a text articulated on something real and speaking in its name, i.e. a law made into a story and historicized, recounted by bodies," says Michel De Certeau.[25] In-person reenactment, I suggest, provides a particularly exemplary embodiment in that it confirms through replay one's story, its historicity, its value.

April Alliston's distinction between example and exemplum in literature helps rethink the exemplarity of realist cinema. She states that in the exemplary realism of the eighteenth century, "the text's status as exemplum takes precedence over its status as representation . . . the text asks to be read as an example capable of generating real action through imitation, rather than as an imitation of real action [as mimesis]."[26] The later "characters of mimetic realism [of the nineteenth century] are no longer presented as models for imitation, but they are example in the other evidentiary sense: they are particular instances that prove a maxim or precept, in this case an implicit statement of general truth about reality, by standing for it, representing it."[27]

This later model of evidentiary example, that of a mimetic realism, fits partial reenactment scenes because of their expositional logic. I therefore associate the "example" to fragmentary instances of reenactment used in social documentaries to bring to life a given practice (as in the instances discussed in Chapter 1) and to grant visual evidence to verbal demands. In *Janie's Janie* (Geri Ashur and Peter Varton, 1971), the protagonist irons clothes, an action staged to document what she typically does. Intercalated with talking head interviews or voice-over commentaries, such scenes introduce the concrete instance that stands for "an implicit statement of general truth" about domestic work. Such examples of specific actions or habitual behavior depend on their power to give specificity and force to a general claim while remaining sufficiently general to be applicable to other similar activist messages. Shabnam Vernani's *When Women Unite: The Story of an Uprising* (1996) shows women in rural India struggling against the alcoholism of their husbands. The film presents vignette reenactments strained with a pedagogic and political toll. Slow-motion images of the women on the road attacking the trucks and spilling the alcohol so their husbands can't drink gain an enhanced rhetorical quality. These scenes double as examples of the struggle and as models for future action. Detached from the film's texture, such reenactment scenes signal the desire to arrest contradictions and to provide idealized, exemplary models.

A number of consciousness-raising films of the early 1970s promote through such visual arrests and tableaus the ideal images for their activism. From evidentiary instances, examples that mimic, copy what happened, they are transformed through their cutout quality into paradigmatic images, exempla for future action. They have been cited, hence defamiliarized.

This cautionary function was present in Bertold Brecht's prospects for film. Brecht had envisioned extracting scenes from films for an archive classifying every known form of behavior.[28] Models not only of socially accepted actions—an after-dinner speech, for example—but of antisocial conduct could be taken out for viewing and studied. If, for instance, and this is Brecht's example, a man were tempted to beat his wife, he could go to the archive and study the action of wife beating, allowing him to distance himself from it and "adopt a more productive (sic) attitude to it."[29] Brecht didn't specify the practical format of this "pedagogium," as he called it, but it epitomizes an almost maniacal expansion of the didactic potential of film. Like reenactment, this theoretical archive's quotable images serve an exemplary realism.

The relation between reenactment, the Brechtian "pedagogium," and didactic plays (*Lehrstück*) is no accident. Brecht's definition of epic theater as one that promotes a critical audience helps to clarify pedagogic features of reenactment. In "The Street Scene: A Basic Model for an Epic Theatre," Brecht explains that an "example of a completely simple, 'natural' epic theatre" can be found in "an incident such as can be seen at any street corner: an eyewitness demonstrating to a collection of people how a traffic accident took place . . . the point is that the demonstrator acts out the behavior of driver or victim or both in such a way that the bystanders are able to form an opinion about the accident."[30] Brecht employs the quoted speech to avoid a transparent realism but also to create a critical, aware audience.[31] Thus, for the "street scene" to qualify as an epic, the "demonstration should have a socially practical significance."[32] The quotation excises, separates out an event to be looked at with greater attention.

As I define it, *reenactment* depends on the implied agency of a person's second act, which, verbally narrated or performed, is the main channel for exemplarity. An act is cited or quoted once the same person serves as demonstrator and example, or, better even as judge and evidence. Citation is essential to exemplarity, and throughout this book Brechtian pedagogical principles and making strange techniques permeate reenactment's rhetoric at its most basic self-reflexive articulation: placing oneself in a scene, displaying or designing its implications, providing a separate platform for judgment. If "reenactment has the distancing quality of a Brechtian gest, its main function is not to compel the acting out of original trauma," but, as Bill Nichols emphasizes in an essential article on reenactment, "to restore the lost object to a condition of visibility, so as to reclaim its significance."[33] Werner Herzog's *Little Dieter Needs to Fly* (1997) is a perfect example: "the recruited villagers stand listlessly around Dengler (little Dieter of the film's title), 'going through the motions' of guarding him as their prisoner . . . Their half-hearted . . . performance clearly conjures what Dengler went through, without compelling prisoner or guards to re-enter the psychic or emotional space of the original event."[34] Describing the protagonist's reenactment, Nichols uncovers an affect primarily relevant for in-person reenactment. For, in this case, "'going through the motions' takes on a formal ritualistic quality that nonetheless spans the moment between before—when need prevailed, and after—when these social gests function as signifiers of what was but is now, at the moment of signification, past."[35]

With the exception of biopics whose linear reconstruction can introduce unintentional fissures and discontinuities (e.g., an aged person representing herself at an earlier life moment), the examples I mention have an explicit reflexive structure. They are framed as experiments and they clearly state their goals to promote self-awareness, to publicize an individual tale refracting and amplifying a life's lesson. Exemplarity is the means for this amplification, the result of an intentional, asserted relation between a "story" and its recounted, historicized embodiment. Rowena Santos Aquino suggests that the "composite body," in reenactment (the social actor and the actor) is always already applicable to a collective since it narrates not only one's past and memories but also references others' experiences and memories. In this way, what she calls "social actor reenactment" extends public history's call for a "more participatory, historical, culture," and the replay of a contingent past activity raises it to a momentary universality, making its value discernible for the present.[36]

Two films on traumatic, national massacres during the 1960s introduce the intricate variables of social actor exemplarity. As Sylvie Jasen observes, each segment of Jorge Sanjines's *The Courage of the People* (also known as *The Night of San Juan*, 1971)—a reenactment of the 1967 massacre, by the Bolivian Army, of the indigenous community at the Siglo XX Mines—is introduced by a participant whose voice-over account of his experience grounds the dramatization performed by people who took part in the original events. Besides "titles identify[ing] the place, the number of the wounded and dead as well as the names of high ranking officials responsible along with their photos," the film makes reference to previous attacks on miners and their aftermath in other communities. These aggregated histories of abuse and their effects generate an evidentiary mass, assuring the film's role as exposé and record of collective memory.[37]

The Act of Killing (2012), Joshua Oppenheimer's intervention in Indonesia's national consciousness, differs in tone and target. Foregrounding perpetrators rather than victims, and individual imagination rather than a group logic, the film filters its topic—the massive killing of alleged communists in the mid-1960s under the Suharto regime—primarily through the chilling perspective of two killers who model their reenactment of the assassinations they committed on favorite Hollywood film genres. By presenting these extravaganzas alongside other demonstrated acts of killing some boastful others "sober," the filmmaker has tried to counter the characteristic exculpatory tone of testimonial documentary with a portrayal of the killer's present unrepentant state. And yet the lack of historical context, along with the intimate engagement with individual characters and their warped consciousness, seems to invite expectations of conversion. While I discuss contemporary reenactments that resist redemptive closure, *The Act of Killing* raises questions that bear directly on the notion of exemplarity: how are these characters' extreme behavior generalizable, and can a film focused on individualized self-narrative do without self-reflection? The film's difficulty in resolving this issue remains its most gripping effect.

STAGES OF ACTUALIZATION

Reenactment is a form of theater conjuring up a scene (through words or mimetic representation). I therefore engage willingly with the question of presence and theatricality in cinema. I study reenactment in its cinematic configuration, in its modes of address, and in its convocation of viewers as witnesses. To draw attention to recreated scenes is an integral part of the testimonial process: what is said is uniquely true not because it refers to actual events but because of its performative valence, and its co-presence with a viewer. Hence, aware that certain filmic maneuvers generate new relations between history, individual voices, and the presently addressed audiences, I rethink testimony through a theatrical trope—the monologue—as it is affectively enhanced through camera movement and framing.

Reenactment is understood here also as process and role-play. Activating a multidirectional temporality, both cinema and reenactment are effective stages for actualization, exemplary purposes, and critical analysis. These stages are understood here both as temporal pauses and as representational opportunities to process and display self-revision. These new configurations of the past take over entire narratives or discrete reenactment or testimony scenes, introducing problems both punctual and long ranging—for instance, the difficulties of employment for an unwed mother in the early 1950s; the lingering racism in an integrated high school in Abidjan, Ivory Coast; the unreadable results of indoctrination by the Khmer Rouge; or the precariousness of Indigenous existence in Brazil throughout its post-1964 coup history. Besides addressing these problematics, I explore how cinema stretches temporally and affectively to focus our attention to the protagonist's representation and to prod gestures and memories into newly created evidence.

Introducing his dossier on reenactment, Jonathan Kahana reminds us of the dual meanings of "enactment:" its reference to forms of making into an act . . . to effect "a permanent change in a social or institutional body with a singular utterance . . . enter[ing] among the acta or public records" but also its association with theater, the "staging of the announcement of the new [enacted] condition and its presentation to an effect upon the audience; to work in or upon to activate influence or inspire a feeling into a person, to represent a dramatic work."[38] These meanings correspond to the performative and the aesthetic dimensions of enactment, and this duality instantly engages with an act's value as both singular *and repeatable*. Reenactment merely invites an asserted intention to actualize the past *once again*, to stage and display it for reconsideration, while cinema, adds, as Kahana points out, an extra complication regarding the nature of immediacy and of recirculation. In-person reenactment films foreground these temporal and ontological quandaries through the embodied, existential nature of their actualizations. The assertion of one's voice and agency is compromised by the specter of inauthenticity and the belatedness of display, and the fixating qualities of cinema are in tension with the presence quotient needed for a proper enactment.

Diana Taylor and Rebecca Schneider have questioned the theoretical assumption shaping the early field of performance studies, that of an ephemeral, once-only event that disappears without a trace,[39] a conception of performance that grants primacy to the archive logic with written records recognized as *the* means to reproducibility and permanence. To support other forms of transmission (of a *repertoire* of cultural attitudes, ways of behaving), Taylor uses the notion of scenario, a "portable framework [that] bears the weight of accumulative repeats."[40] Her broad theorization of scenarios as "meaning-making paradigms" that "frame and activate social drama"[41] is pertinent to reenactment understood broadly as an activator of myths or attitudes needed for purposes of cultural continuity or political expediency (in her example, the frontier scenario in the United States).

However, it is the theatrical connotation of scenarios, as structures for repetition and a springboard for permutation and variations, that is most appropriate to discuss reenactment's critical replays. Recognizing that one needs to conjure up a "scene" and resort to a physical location "to recall, recount, or reactivate a scenario," Taylor underlines the fact that scenes "signal conscious strategies of display."[42] Regarding the actors' embodiment, the second vital element for display, scenarios afford the same critical possibility I ascribe to in-person reenactment. "Whether it's a question of mimetic representation (an actor assuming a role) or of performativity, of social actors assuming socially regulated patterns of appropriate behavior," the structural flexibility of scenarios makes possible a "generative critical distance between social actor and character,[43] ... more fully allow[ing] us to keep both the social actor and the role in view simultaneously, and thus recogniz[ing] areas of resistance and tension."[44]

Throughout, this book probes points of resistance and tension, loosely mapping them onto questions of presence and mediation, theater, and cinema. These tensions appear in the impossibility to match reenactment's chronological indeterminacy (a person standing for herself twenty years earlier) and the indexical precision of direct record evident in archival footage. In fact, reenactment's belatedness brushes against cinema's forward-thrusting temporality in two major ways: the passage of time affects the ability of people to represent a particular, past moment with verisimilitude. And more consequentially in films with a transformative agenda, the difficulty becomes one of creating closure to a developing narrative of process and consciousness raising.

I discuss the impossibility of reconciling therapeutic/juridical/activist pursuits with dramatic intent and narrative closure, but I admit these quandaries as intrinsic to the redemptive efforts of neorealist and verité narratives. So the metafictional shifts and ruptures that take place in Jean Rouch's *The Human Pyramid*, formally inspiring in their abrupt breaks with linear narrative, are an answer to the challenge of having film catch up with reality. These stunning reflexive ruptures as well as the narrators' commentary providing moral lessons (in the neorealist films discussed) point to the constant pressure to link text and reality, to make representation usable.

I have strategically placed my analyses of two contemporary films, Tonacci's *Ser* and Zhang Yuan's *Sons*, one at the concluding chapter, "Reenactment and A-filiation in *Serras da Desordem*," the other closing the first chapter "Casting Relatives: the Spectrum of Substitution," to stress the ways discontinuity and confrontations with myths of integration and affiliation typify contemporary reenactment's unredemptive aesthetics. The strikingly distinct aesthetics of these two films, *Sons'* hypernaturalist family melodrama and *Serras'* allegorical and hybrid intertextuality (intercutting documentary, reenactment and archive), indicate that the possibilities of in-person reenactment to challenge established affiliations do not depend on particular formal or narrative approaches. A major drive for this study is in fact the cinematic inventiveness in accommodating pedagogic, therapeutic or parajuridical agendas. In particular, I focus on the ways theatricality and performance are deployed to intensify co-presence and scrutiny in these films.

IN PERSON REENACTMENT: THE BOOK

In Person traces a genealogy of postwar realist cinema based on conceptions of casting and exemplarity, theorizes reenactment's split agency and elastic temporality as well as its potential as catalyst of self-revision, and clarifies the critical and historiographical dimension of unredemptive replay.

I believe that the activist impetus behind reenactment, the wish for a representation that corrects reality through a second act, has not been recognized as a central current in postwar cinema. A key objective of this book is to reassess the presentational, performative, and exemplary dimensions of this cinema; to note the interesting convergence between formal qualities of modern and contemporary realist cinema and their instrumental aspirations.

The valorization of anonymous everyday protagonists as well as the material, bodily realities of individuals and celebrities in neorealism, the emphasis on authenticity in cinema verité and New Wave cinemas, are core traits of postwar realist cinema magnified with in-person reenactment. Similarly, celebrated aesthetic aspects of modern and contemporary cinema—its hybridity, reflexivity, and performance ambiguity—have yet to be associated with the dynamic of estrangement and self-revision mobilized in reenactment's transformative ethos.

The book's restricted genealogy of in-person reenactment in the postwar casts a number of formal traits of modern (1950s) and contemporary cinema (1985–2010s) such as the New Wave's reflexive ruptures in diegesis or the lengthy shots and pressured address of slow cinema, in an alternate, instrumental light. The constitutive dualities of in-person reenactment, actor or person, past or present, representation or presentation, theatricality or authenticity, define new venues in thinking about an impure modern cinema, and the performance instability courted by contemporary cinema (Jia Zhangke, f.i.) [45] At stake in the early 1950s films (Chapter 2) is a modern cinema grappling with a neorealist heritage itself in flux, a challenge answered by Zavattini's proposal to closely retrace a person's life who reenacts her own story as a form of penance and example. The radicalization of the nonprofessional actor, who now becomes agent and actor of his own story, is advanced in two projects promoting the moral valence of anonymity and authenticity in 1953 Italian cinema: Zavattini and Maselli's *The Story of Caterina* and Antonioni's *Attempted Suicide* (episodes from *Love in the City, Amore in Città*) focus on anonymous women while Zavattini rephrases his antispectacle credo, producing a second omnibus film featuring major Italian stars exposing their "real" selves (*We the Women, Siamo Donne*: Alfredo Guarini's *Contest: 4 Actresses; 1 Hope*, Guido Franciolini's *Alida Valli*, Roberto Rossellini's *The Chicken*, Luigi Zampa's *Isa Miranda*, and Luchino Visconti's *Anna Magnani*). Dealing with suicide, a most individual gesture, *Attempted Suicides* brings to the fore existential and psychological questions that an earlier neorealist social agenda minimized.

I claim that much like Cesare Zavattini's vision of reenactment in one's own name as a public, anti-individualist lesson, Edgar Morin's statement that for cinema verité the main question is "making sure that the subject of the film will recognize themselves in their own roles" inaugurates a new paradigm for cinema: the camera and the projected image become conduits for an existential exercise, a moment-to-moment reprocessing of one's identity. "A Sort of Psychodrama: Verité Moments 58–61" (Chapter 4) addresses the political and cultural contours of this impetus for a transformative auto-critique, looking at two major experiments in self-awareness in late 1950s France: *The Human Pyramid* (Jean Rouch, 1959) and *Chronicle of a Summer* (Rouch and Edgar Morin, 1961). I contextualize Rouch and Morin's invocation of a therapeutic frame to refract France's anxiety over its identity and discuss the French reception of psychodrama and group dynamics as a move toward ethical self-reevaluation prompted by the end of colonialism and the postwar awareness of racism.

Reenactment, improvisation, and role-playing are instruments and *signifiers* of late neorealism's and of New Wave cinema's existentialist concern with theatricality and authenticity. Similarly, death, mortality, and age, unquestionable limits for in-person reenactment, emerge more broadly as major topics in this book.

In Chapter 3, I turn to the ontological and existential dimensions of reenactment by looking at two films: *Torero!* (Carlos Velo, 1956), a biopic featuring bullfighter Luis Procuna alongside newsreel footage of his youth; and *Sophia: Her Own Story* (Mel Stuart, 1984), in which Sophia Loren acts as herself from the age of thirty to forty-four and as her mother, Romilda Villani, at forty-six years old. These celebrity reenactments invite a phenomenological scrutiny as they foreground the contradiction between the autonomous temporality of reenactment and cinema's affinity for registering the flux of time.

From a theoretical perspective, the question of mortality in celebrity biopics is as relevant for considering the temporal specificity of reenactment as the urgency of testimonial recall or reenactment of events from twenty to forty years earlier is in the case of the passing of a generation of survivors and witnesses. And although the actor or sports-figure biopic seems out of place in the canonical postwar realist history tracked here, my interest in the tangency between the biographical film genre and reenactment stems from their shared logistical constraint, to cover a person's entire life span.

My emphasis on cinema's existential arena and star reenactment in between the discussion of neorealism's struggle for its continued relevance and Morin and Rouch's interest in role-play is doubly justified. Zavattini had a central role in the formulation of ciné-verdad in Mexico alongside Barbachano Ponce and Velo, the producer and director of *Torero!*. This particular biopic has, moreover, a pride of place in Bazin's reflections on cinema's existential and ontological quandaries, in writings on bullfighting and death. Bazin's considerations on the paradoxes of retroactivity and star aging are essential for understanding reenactment's recursive temporality and its import in activating different modalities and types of replay, from memory access to gestural scripts.

The retroactive stance of reenactment and its mimetic reconstruction of one's past would seem to contradict the seismographic emergence of the present promoted in the verité confessionals. I suggest, however, that cinema verité condenses the main requirements of self-revision theorized by Zavattini in a distinct psychoexistential register.[46] Cinema verité's predilection for its characters' contradictory subjectivity and tentative voice is key to understand the turning point instantiated in *Chronicle*'s "ethnographic-existential enterprise." Each individual gains a distinct testimonial autonomy, a voice that is, within the moralist structure of neorealist reenactment, still under control.[47]

Scaling down social dynamic themes to the chamber-drama dimensions of psychodrama, or of cinema, reflects a broader cultural turn from the concerns of social representativeness of 1930s documentaries and early neorealist cinema toward the vagaries of individual psychology. Thus, the chapter on cinema verité (Chapter 4) pivots between two cinemas propped on the link between self-performance and consciousness raising: the redemptive exemplarity of anonymous women's reenacted lives in neorealist films (Chapter 2) and staged testimonials where the literal or psychological return to past traumas and their original sites is complemented by a reanimated, actualized witnessing (as in *Shoah* or *S21*, discussed in Chapters 5 and 6).

"Ascetic Stages: Reenactment in Post-Holocaust Cinema" (Chapter 5) examines the transitional moment between modern and contemporary reenactment, and it considers the persistence of aesthetic configurations of ascesis and the empty site in existentialist inquiries of 1950s and 1960s European and French art films (*Night and Fog* and *L'avventura*) and their later, modified presence in the mise-en-scène of posttraumatic and testimonial cinemas. My discussion of Marceline and Ganda's monologue in this chapter makes clear the central role cinema verité plays in the confessional-performative arc of realist cinema. As Michael Rothberg, Joshua Hirsch, and others have pointed out, *Chronicle of a Summer* uniquely features a testimony spelling out the singular and Jewish status of Holocaust victimhood.[48] My intent in aligning some of the performative moves evident in Rouch and Morin's cinema with Lanzmann's has to do with their exfoliation of the self in their push for relived confessionals.

Reenactment and, in particular, testimonial monologues magnify the spectral temporality of posttraumatic stories conveying visually and dramatically the peculiar conditions of being in two places and times (imagined and real) at once. I examine these scenes/films' stark delineation of absence, their creation of an affective circuitry between the social actor and his listener/audience, through camera movement and monologue address. Rouch's "pedovision," the tracking of his characters' reflective state (Marceline, Oumarou Ganda) as they walk and talk through an insistent camera generates a phenomenological correlate for reenactment's affective charge, pushing viewers to relive a particular imagined reality as close, embodied following.

The verité pressure Jean Epstein envisioned for cinema (and expressed in the epigraph) finds its most direct correspondence in the juridical mise-en-scène and indicting impetus of post-Holocaust testimonials, in *Shoah* (Claude Lanzmann, 1984) and after. The performative efficacy of reenactment films dealing with mass atrocity depends on the actual return of original victims or perpetrators to former sites of physical or psychological trauma so their testimonials may serve parajuridical, evidentiary roles as well as a posttraumatic gauge of the presence of the past now.[49] This qualified "return" brings into scene the actual protagonist as actor, a dissonant presence. In a much-discussed scene from *Shoah*, the Holocaust survivor Simon Srebnik stands at the steps of a Catholic church, flanked by the Poles back in Chelmno, Poland.[50] In a sort of staging of violence Georges Didi-Huberman has called the "return despite everything," Srebnik's vacant look sets off, in the spatial harmony of a posed statement, the reality of a shattered past. A signal intersection of disrupted historical trajectories, Srebnik-returned becomes a charged historical index, a confronting question. *In Person* explores the modern and the contemporary contours of this cinematic relocation, asking what makes the "return" of the actual person as actor of his own story an uncanny incongruity but also an ethical and aesthetic necessity.

As we consider contemporary, post-*Shoah* cinema, other discourses based on reanimating the past, juridical and psychoanalytic, come to the fore. The first treats reenactment as supplemental evidence brought into court as a measure of plausibility to check the details of a crime or occurrence, and its evidentiary value is, as Louis George Schwartz notes in *Mechanical Witness*, contingent on other forms of witness corroboration.[51] Reenactment also describes the obsessive return of unresolved trauma in the form of a dramatic sequence of actions without the main actor's conscious mastery of the narrative. Largely unconscious, these traumatic repetitions point to a breakdown in the subject's ability to narrate what happened to him. In all these instances—of ritual and communal integration, of evidentiary explanation or of psychic dissociation—the individual's literal or imagined repetitions always signify more than just the story he or she tells. I examine this symptomatic dimension foregrounded with cinema verité, when I address the transition from modern to contemporary forms of in-person reenactment.

Reenactment, a mode defined by a supplementary relation to absence, is especially appropriate for a post-Holocaust context, matching closely Michael Rothberg's conception of a traumatic realist aesthetics, "an aesthetics of survival [which] meets its limits ... in the dilemma of belated temporality—the impossibility of reviving the dead."[52] Linda Williams identified in this posttraumatic cinema a new turn in verité documentary, where truth is no longer the assumed effect of a transparent expression but subject to a different excavation of the real, where speech wavers, indexing a memory and subjectivity that is constructed rather than revealed. As Janet Walker elegantly puts it, discussing documentaries of "return," reenactments "are powerful not just because they resurrect what was but because they constitute something that is not there."[53]

Straddling past and present, evidence and performative claim, reenactment negotiates the variables of the new phase in documentary in the wake of a posttraumatic consciousness: to record the testimony of a vanishing generation of witnesses of mass atrocities, to register the constraints of a present, unreliable memory, and to intervene in the present by reconstituting and revising the "past." The films discussed in Chapters 5–7 work as historiographical and aesthetic instruments to sharpen the force and actual relevance of (already known) facts.

In "Trial Stages: Rithy Panh's Parajuridical Theater" (Chapter 6), I draw a parallel between the moral and ethical investigations in the real world (judicial reenactments, court proceedings) and in art defining the shared urgency driving jurists *and artists* to introduce their respective evidences. Rithy Panh's intervention in Cambodia's accountability efforts, during the protracted process of bringing the Khmer Rouge's perpetrators to justice; his tableaus of ex–Khmer Rouge guards reenacting their routines and reciting their records of atrocity activate the dual meaning of stages in this chapter's title, the temporal processing of past trauma and the theatrical and juridical platforms to display, reflect, and adjudicate the past anew. The film's stark presentation of ambiguous states pervaded by psychic dissociation raises questions related to the appropriateness of a symptomatic, pathological interpretation of traumatic reenactment, indeed about the distinction between symptom and aesthetic as a motor of reenactment.

My closing chapter explores reenactment in relation to the problematic of transmission across generations, time, and media with an extended look at *Serras da Desordem* (*Hills of Chaos*, 2006). Made by Andrea Tonacci, a key figure in Brazilian Marginal Cinema of the 1970s and the self-ethnography movement of the 1980s, the film enacts, through a fractured intertextual surface, the ruptured sociological fabric and the fraught tangency of indigenous populations with Brazilian institutions and normative orders of racial and class belonging. I contrast *Serras*'s allegorical construct with the immediacy of other modes of documentary such as Tonacci's early video ethnography and to nonlinear narrative and long-span films that revisit the military coup aftermath through testimony and archive (Vincent Carelli's *Corumbiara*, 2007; and Eduardo Coutinho's *Twenty Years Later: A Man Marked to Die*, 1964–1984).

Serras da Desordem, the reenactment of an isolated Indian's first contact with nonindigenous Brazilians thirty years after his tribe's massacre, is a prime example of a critical challenge to progressive conceptions of time and national identity. In formal terms, the film highlights the way reenactment pushes multiple temporalities and registers to coexist in tension, in Christopher Wood and Alexander Nagel's term, anachronically.[54] Ultimately, films (or artworks) can ignore, absorb, or critically intensify reenactment's challenge to linear homogeneous time. They can reconstruct the fantasy of purity supporting the creation of an abstract and ahistorical "other" (Flaherty's timeless Inuit in Nanook), or they may, as *Serras* does, expose the inherent contingency of notions of authenticity, how origin slides according to specific historical investments, relations of dominance, and aesthetic frames.

The main question, revisited toward the book's conclusion, revolves, however, less on the authenticity of representation than on the critical possibilities presented by the protagonist's unreadable consciousness. The affectless mimicry by the ex-guards of the Khmer Rouge of their atrocities in *S21: The Khmer Rouge Killing Machine* or the psychological opacity of the Indian Carapiru as he replays a "first contact" in *Serras da Desordem* brings into play an unreliable, unreadable consciousness. These opaque performances bring an extraordinary ethical and categorical instability into the films. Invalidating the premise that reenactment leads inevitably to transmission and self-knowledge, denying in fact a self to be transformed in and through film, the contemporary films closely read in this book foreground scenarios of stasis with the real/actor as an agent of critical unease. If cinema is ontologically defined as frozen flux, reenactment is an exercise in the reverse direction, that of a critical mortification. As I grasp these and early reenactments' manner of pausing, displaying, and calling for the viewers' present reflection, I turn to cinema's stages of actualization looking for the ambiguous constancy and the permanent responsibility of acting, and reenacting, in person.

CHAPTER 1

Casting Relatives

The Spectrum of Substitution

Biographical and historical films, travelogues, ethnographic films, and activist documentaries are referential genres depicting certifiable identities and realities. They enlist surrogates—actors, relative, look-alikes, or members from a similar class or area—to recreate the past or inaccessible aspects of reality. This relative looseness in casting is an accepted convention in fictional and documentary production and, given the many possibilities, it is not self-evident that the original protagonist should herself act. For spectators of early cinema, for instance, it mattered little if an event was recreated with others or at a different time and place.[1] As Miriam Hansen and Dan Streible have pointed out, the wide acceptance of reenactment in early, sensationalistic exploitations of boxing matches and corruption scandals did not betray a naïve audience so much as one eager to watch, *in counterpart* to the news, a range of illustrative scenes regardless of their dubious authenticity.[2] According to Streible, the value of a boxing match varies according to available means for making it "visible"; "distinctions between genuine and imitation," he points out, "are not easily drawn."[3] Edward Hill Amet, who mixed "authentic footage of the Spanish-American war with re-creations he shot using miniatures," profited from "the ambiguity implied in describing a moving picture as 'reproduction,' making it unclear whether the reproduction referred to the filmed copy of an actual event or a film of a reenacted bout rather than the original one."[4]

Whether seeking to compete with news reports of battles and disasters by recreating their most spectacular features, or to extend the life of a transient but significant turning point in history, reenactment in early cinema operates as a key complement of the actual, on-the-spot recording. Used to catch up with a missed event or gesture, reenactment's retroactivity is closely allied with the ways fictional cinema harnesses the contingencies of recorded reality. In *The Emergence of Cinematic Time*, Mary Ann Doane describes the complex relation between cinema and contingency by detailing progressive transformations toward a narrative and a temporal logic autonomous from the external reality that cinema so easily records and archives. The execution film, an early subgenre of the *actualité*, crystallizes these dilemmas: the challenge of preserving the sense of actually being there, of getting rid of uneventful, "dead time." In *Execution of Czolgosz, with Panorama of Auburn Prison* (1901), the pan outside the prison links two separate realities; thereby, it assures the effect of contiguity between cameraman (and consequently the viewer) and an unfilmable, reconstructed, execution.[5]

Rather than illustrative verisimilitude, what matters is the viewer's embodied experience of a historical event. In early cinema, the issue concerns reenactment's power to make the spectator co-present with the "past." Alison Griffith considers reenactment a structuring principle of both early cinema and panoramas; the latter, she observes, compensated for the lack of movement by explicitly "foregrounding [the medium's] status as a reconstituted mode of address . . . the depicted events reassembled for the spectator were to be interpreted as if the action was happening along an immediate temporal and spatial presence and continuity."[6] Kristen Whissel has also noted the attempt to recreate a sense of "being there" in early battle reconstructions.[7] Rather "than . . . 'faking' or simulating the actuality, the actuality film aspires to achieve that which live re-enactments had already accomplished: the illusory placement of the camera-spectator as a participant observer on the scene of a historical spectacle it records/perceives."[8] Both live record and filmed reconstructions sought to recreate a vicarious participation for viewers as witnesses of history.[9]

Although *In Person: Reenactment* also investigates the performative and affective dimensions of reconstituted address, focus falls on the testimonial authority and agency of the actual protagonist; as such, the relative flexibility in substitutes characteristic of early cinema holds marginal interest. However, given this book's claim on the specificity of in-person reenactment in various postwar cinematic agendas, the recreation of habitual or group practices by social actors prevalent in social documentaries provides the most significant point of counter reference. Examining films that use *family relatives as surrogate actors*, I mean to complicate an initial division between two conceptions of casting: one that admits a greater latitude in its synthetic recreations of social type welcoming actors from the same class, geographical area, and cultural strata, and a second that insists on and magnifies an individual's irreplaceable singularity and her unique relation to an original past.

Such casting distinctions extend to differing conceptions of time, transmission, and replay, hinging, in the case of social documentaries, on habit, tradition, and other forms of embodied knowledge. Defining *performance* as "restored" or "twice-behaved" behavior, Richard Schechner points out that daily acts can have a "constancy of transmission" across many generations.[10]

Any represented behavior, those of an actor replaying his acting, an athlete her running, or a fisherman his boat skills, involves transpositions of behavior, the modeling of gestures and acts with real consequences onto sequences or "strips" of gestures that are read according to other, secondary frames.[11] The question of how to replay routine, how to convey its authentic particularity and its constancy of transmission, have practical and theoretical implications, unavoidable in dealing with reenactment.[12]

Joris Ivens's recommendations on the best way to employ people from the region to perform habitual tasks exemplify assumptions underlying social documentary reenactment in the interwar period.[13] His reflections on the authenticity of filmic representation involve considerations on casting as well as on the reconstruction of ingrained gesture. He discusses, for instance, potential casting problems in relation to a family: when preparing to make *Power and Land* (1940), he "tried to construct a synthetic farmer family, [out] of an old man alone on his farm, perhaps some neighbors and a few little kids."[14] Ultimately, when efforts "fell through," the film crew returned to the Parkinsons' farm to cast their family unit.[15] Apropos of casting nonactors, Ivens observes that a "father and son may work well separately, but badly when they are together in a scene."[16] His reflections on replaying routine activities also bear on the need to balance acting with being or doing. One should not ask a person to represent a task he does not normally perform: "the farmer takes special pride in the sharpness of his tool blades, and therefore [the documentary maker should] suggest a tool shed scene in which to make use of that fact. The key to this approach, . . . is that a real person, acting to play himself, will be more expressive if his actions are based on his real characteristics."[17] While these remarks concern a representational verisimilitude, the authorizing principle is based on a congruence between an actorly repetition and a repeated, ingrained routine. For instance, Ivens suggests anticipating "the real movements of the man, to catch the regular rhythm of his normal action," which is *"far from re-enactment."*[18]

In an original study on reenactment, Sylvie Jasen has addressed this same question of the cinematic actualization of routine. Seeking to develop a dynamic conception that "speaks to something processual and contingent, premised on a continuity between the contemporary staging of a cinematic production and the living history it engages, however distant or recent,"[19] she has coined the term "reenactment as event."[20] Discussing a contemporary intervention in ethnographic documentary, the Izuma collective's *The Journals of Knud Rasmussen* (Zacharias Kunuk and Norman Cohn, 2006),[21] Jasen sees an intent to demystify a purely mimetic and illustrative function of reenactment, to exfoliate and reveal other registers of repetition transmitted across generations, including processes of training social actors so they can replay past habits and traditions.

If Ivens's remarks on reconstructing social actors' genuine gestures for the camera provide a wealth of detail related to the cinematic translation of time and process, they seem, in their care, the reverse of Robert Flaherty's casual attitude toward the Aran islanders' present-day habits. As in *Nanook of the North* eleven years earlier, in *Man of Aran* (1933) Flaherty composed a family out of unrelated people of the same ethnic and social group (Fig. 1.1). He freely selected who would be the father, son, and mother, as well as the anecdotes and habits the film would present. For more than a half-century, Aran inhabitants had employed paraffin for lighting instead of oil obtained from shark livers. All the same, Flaherty recreated scenes of hunting basking sharks with harpoons—a practice in disuse for more than fifty years. Tiger (Colman King) was a "blacksmith by trade, but he was also a boat-builder, a fisherman and a

Figure 1.1: *Man of Aran*'s syncretic family (Joris Ivens, 1933).

bit of a farmer,"[22] and Flaherty brought a consultant to train islanders, reconstituted their harpoons and anxiously shot enormous amounts of film. Disregarding present conditions and economic relations, he produced a vision of the Aran islander mired in a romantic notion of men's struggles with the elements.[23] The marked preference for a vanished past, and the replacement of contemporary practices for anachronistic behavior, characterizes many ethnographic reconstructions; however, is especially pronounced in Flaherty's portrayal of an essential struggle between man and nature. Inasmuch as the film fastens on specific practices as the essence of the islander's lives, the family is supposed to count as archetypal, rather than (empirically) real. The family needs to be synthesized out of the social fabric—just as hours of footage are used for sequences of waves, for maximum impact.[24]

In the interwar period, questions of social physiognomy and biography (considered to be bourgeois art or, in the case of social realism, an instrument of propaganda) were highly politicized.[25] As Devin Fore notes, "for the left, social physiognomy provided a way to envisage the collective subject, while the right essentialized physiognomics into a racist pseudo science, developing a biological discourse that was eventually used to justify the eugenic policies of the National socialists."[26] He points, in particular, to August Sander's "physiognomic assault on the ideology of individualism" expressed in *Face of Our Time* (1929) and how his book's serial nature "draws attention to the networks of similitude that cut across the social strata, blending the individual faces together and integrating the unique human countenance into a portrait of the mass subject."[27] While the synthetic recreation of a family of fishermen out of islanders in *Man of Aran* combined with the anachronistic replay of practices specific to a prior generation implies a primitivist and heroic conception of island life that is far from a mass portrait, it does represent a social process and texture with a broader, and collective referential latitude.

This aspiration to timelessness is also evident in *Farrebique* (1944), Georges Rouquier's film about his family farm, even though featuring the director's actual relatives represents a singularizing step, in principle. Originally a work about the cycle of seasons, the film reflects Marshall Petain's ideology of *passéisme* "work, family and fatherland." It purposefully avoids historical and political matters (one of the brothers was a prisoner of war and after the liberation in 1944–1945 could have been part of the film but instead worked only in the crew). In contrast to films that came out after the war, *Farrebique*'s timescale is, as Dudley Andrew remarks, not that of the urgent instant but rather of the inexorable calendar year; by implication, it represents the time of the earth itself, the time that industrialization has lost track of.[28] The film distorts chronology. Slow, natural processes take place in seconds and are complemented by a narrative that mixes unique and habitual events: we see single repeated processes—making bread or gathering hay—alongside Henry's accident, the grandfather falling ill, and so on. Routine is singularized, and drama is streamlined. Both become a matter of course in a rounded cycle of the seasons (Figs 1.2 and 1.3).

Man of Aran and *Farrebique* channel notions of generational transmission into romantic, pastoral visions of life. Nonetheless, these synthetic visions contain significant elements of reenactment. First, reenactment's chronological indeterminacy is as useful for representing daily routines and longer processes such as the record of cycles and seasons. Second, both social documentary and historical fiction rely on the notion that history and geography are ingrained in gestures and physiognomies.

Figure 1.2: Chopping wood, *Farrebique* (Georges Rouquier, 1944).

Figure 1.3: Henri's accident, *Farrebique* (1944).

Someone who has lived in a particular time and space is invested with testimonial authority, whether habitual gestures or unique actions are performed. Thus, under an expansive conception of kinship, nonexistent familial ties between the actors forming the family in *Man of Aran* suggest a common point of origin, conferring the film greater historical and generational authority.

Next I reflect on the impact that casting identifiable, named social actors may have on three reenactment films: *Four Men on a Raft* (Welles, 1942–1993), *Endurance* (Leslie Woodhead, 1999), and *Sons* (Zhang Yuan, 1996). Each of these works featuring family members introduces issues that are taken up in greater depth in subsequent chapters: the representative range of in-person reenactment understood as a social issue (Chapter 2), the phenomenological dimensions of cinema (Chapter 3), and how the medium troubles transmission from an original past to an actualized present (Chapter 7).

I raise the issue of lineage in this analysis to suggest that it may not matter for particular kinds of narratives whether their cast stretches across generations who have shared a particular environment or habits, or whether the cast is restricted to closer ties. Instead, the question concerns the kind of representational grounding that blood relations and physiognomy provide, and whether measures capitalizing on artifice (a sister as a mother) and nature (an actual relative) differ significantly from effects obtained by employing actors who are not related. Does the use of relatives in family-life reconstruction have the same import as staging based on social typology and (putative) ethnographic documentation? The following examples suggest that kinship and lineage pervade cinema's representation of the transmission (of events, traits, affects) across time. In different ways—through an excess of literalness or an overemphasis on deterministic conceptions of transmission—these films transgress the principles of purely historical or biographical mimetic reconstructions.

ORSON WELLES'S *FOUR MEN IN A RAFT* (*IT'S ALL TRUE*)

Four Men in a Raft (a projected episode in Orson Welles's famously unfinished *It's All True*, 1942–1993) illustrates how the real protagonist's body serves as a conduit and extension of an event's original activist impulse. In Welles's film, four fishermen reenact the trip they undertook eight months earlier to request social benefits from the Brazilian government. The original voyage culminated with their arrival in Rio de Janeiro, where they met with President Getúlio Vargas (Fig. 1.4). The journey had received a great deal of media attention, and Welles read about it in *Time* magazine. Manoel Olimpio Meira, "Jacaré," the official spokesperson for the crew and president of the Z-1 fishing colony in Fortaleza; Jerônimo André de Souza, captain and owner of the raft "São Pedro"; and Raimundo "Tatá" Correia Lima and Manuel "Preto" Pereira da Silva traveled along the northeast coast of Brazil for several weeks, following two-thirds of the country's coast in a form of religious "promessa" (an obstacle-ridden crossing which is duly rewarded if the believer shows his faith). It was also a political mission with stops gathering support from other fishing communities on the way.

Figure 1.4: Arrival of the four raftmen after their sea journey to Rio de Janeiro.

In *It's All True: Orson Welles Pan-American Odyssey,* Catherine Benamou explains that Welles originally planned to align the film's last two episodes by moving the arrival of the *jangadeiros* in Rio from its original November date to February—to coincide with Carnival, at the center of the *Story of Samba* episode. Benamou argues that the temporal displacement of the arrival scene and its incorporation into the Carnaval sequence opened on a "deep structural level the possibility of weaving the sub-theme of the liberation of slaves, inscribed in the longtime span of the *jangadeiros*' journey as narrative, into the explicitly multi-racial mise-en-scène of Carnaval."[29] Welles's wish to create a progressive layer of the narrative, and to have it reverberate with the region's earlier history, faced challenges when the studio refused to let filming continue in color and, more consequentially, by a tragedy impacting the film's casting.[30] As Welles was preparing to shoot the first black-and-white take of the fishermen's arrival in the Guanabara Bay, the raft overturned and Jacaré, the key organizer of the fisherman's protest trip, drowned (Fig. 1.5).

In *It's All True*, Richard Wilson's 1993 documentary about the filming process, Welles claims that he owed it to the fishermen to keep shooting, even if he had to substitute Jacaré with another performer. Instead of picking a social actor from the same community, Welles chose Jacaré's brother, João, to play Jacaré in the early scenes from the voyage using a supplementary substitutive logic.

Jacaré's death prompted important narrative and casting changes. Welles's film adds a dramatic prelude: the death of a young fisherman soon after marrying

Figure 1.5: Jacaré in a still from Welles's *Four Men on a Raft* (included in *It's All True*, Orson Welles, Richard Wilson, 1942–1993).

a beautiful woman. In the fictional framework, this death is what motivates the voyage. Significantly, Sobrinho (a cousin of Jeronimo), who played the man who dies, reappears as Jacaré in some of the later footage of the voyage (Fig. 1.6).

It is tragically ironic, then—both in terms of the social aspirations of the men filmed and in terms of Welles's own designs as a filmmaker—that the death of the protagonist of *Four Men in a Raft* is revealed only in the documentary account of the uncompleted work. If the film had been made as planned and released by the studio, it would have elided Jacaré's death, thereby minimizing the significance of the fact that another fisherman was substituted for him. This would be have been in line with Hollywood's notoriously casual representation of Latin American conditions, as well as with the use of nonactors from the region in docudramas or fictions aspiring to represent a person's membership in a social group.

I discuss the implications of surrogate bodies in disguising temporal or identity discontinuities in Chapter 3. While *Torero!* (Carlos Velo, 1956) "solves" the question of mortality through a montage of composite bodies of better- and lesser-known toreros whose faces are elided (according to an editing hierarchy well documented by Anna Chisholm's study of body doubles),[31] the substitutions in *Four Men on a Raft*, while equally expedient, holds special interest in light of the film's activist framework and social documentary lineage.

Welles's first documentary approximates Eisenstein's framing style: dignifying the fishermen's physiognomies with low-angle shots as one of them delivers a speech

Figure 1.6: Three of the raftmen reenact their journey with the fourth surrogate actor hidden from view (*It's All True*, Orson Welles, Richard Wilson, 1942–1993).

about his conditions, and graphically enhancing the funeral lines stretched across the frame's diagonal. Still, Welles's casting matters in relation to the group scenes, even if it does not disturb the film's surface significantly.

Welles's decision to complete the film with a relative of the dead fisherman raises the question of whether one fisherman's image is as good as another for the purpose of example—is that mission best achieved by a person playing himself, or is a related person a better promoter of exemplarity? The film's fictive plot (motivating dramatically the request for benefits) suggests that another fellow being has or could have suffered a similar fate, but what matters is how this surrogacy appears in the film.

Clearly, reenactment does not so much demand consistent verisimilitude or authentic recreation as it calls for a deeper process of reanimation or vivification. The "ambiguity surrounding the 'fourth man' is rather joltingly resolved with the scene of the *jangadeiros* arrival when the late Jacaré appears in full view aboard the Sao Pedro in the Technicolor footage shot prior to the accident of 19 May. Welles planned to address Jacaré's sudden appearance by openly rendering him a posthumous homage in the closing narration of the film, as is indicated in the closing inter-title of the 1993 reconstruction."[32] The baffling doublings (Jacaré appearing at the end after his death, or Sobrinho emerging as Jacaré once he has "died" in a fictive sequence) attest to another logic pervading reenactment projects as they ritually establish alternate links with an original event or protagonist. As Benamou notes, the young fisherman's fictive death is "experienced and interpreted in the collective imaginary of the fishing community as a ritual of mourning for the recently departed Jacaré"[33] (Fig. 1.7).

Figure 1.7: Funeral for fisherman whose "death" motivates the journey (*It's All True*, Orson Welles, Richard Wilson, 1942–1993).

This example shows how elastic the notion of "relatives" is in anchoring the protagonist to his original. Welles's default option, to use actual family relatives of Jacaré in the film, points to an alternate paradigm—that of bloodlines—to secure a link between the surrogate body and the original protagonist. The extreme, almost literal conception of genetic continuity tying the actors to Jacaré contrasts starkly with the reenactment logic typical of 1930s social documentary, exemplified by Flaherty's *Man or Aran* from 1933 and still operative in Welles's film.

The need for a surrogate actor that arose after Jacaré's death underscores a central aspect of reenactment at stake throughout this book: the impossibility of reversing time, of catching up with an original, a limit magnified with in-person reenactment. The question the film poses—and does not resolve—is whether this rupture is consequential in expanding the reach of the example, the representativeness of this heroic event.

ENDURANCE: KINSHIP AND THE EXCEPTIONAL BODY

The parameters for plausible reenactment vary wildly. Some combination of generational logic, physical resemblance, authentic identity, and genetic relation explains why using relatives constitutes a natural extension of in-person reenactment.

An extreme example of this familial configuration is *Endurance* (Leslie Woodhead, Bud Greenspan, 1999), a biopic retracing key events in Haile Gebrselassie (the 1996 Olympics winner of long-distance running) from the age of eighteen to twenty-nine. A flashback provides the broader biographical backdrop, with members of Haile's immediate family filling in for missing ones. The credits list social actors with a shared patronym and given names: Haile's nephew is featured as a kid Haile, his sister Shawanness Gebrselassie as his mother, his first cousin Tedesse Haile as Haile's young father, and his own father Gebrselassie Bekele as himself at an older age (Fig. 1.8).

Although these familial ties are apparent only in the credits, casting actual relatives as family manifests a contortion to authenticate Haile's presence. The film commands interest in that it seeks to strike a balance between the habits and culture Haile shares with his family and his exceptionality. His presence in the film, meant to facilitate the passage between the footage of his Olympic win and material filmed expressly by Woodhead (a former ethnographic filmmaker), is the nexus of competing but complementary realist logics: the social portrayal, the individuated character, the literal performance of an expertise. At the film's center, Haile's body exposes the discrepancy between the unique recognizable star physique and all others, with the film navigating the genres of the ethnographic documentary and the celebratory biopic.

In a wonderful essay on the scale of presence of extras and bit players in Hollywood cinema, Will Straw suggests that besides backing up lead actors, extras provide a repertoire of social gestures.[34] Bit players and extras are mobilized to enact characters as well as social populations and they are hierarchically relegated to the domain of mise-en-scène.[35] They are "part of what Alex Woloch, writing on minor characters

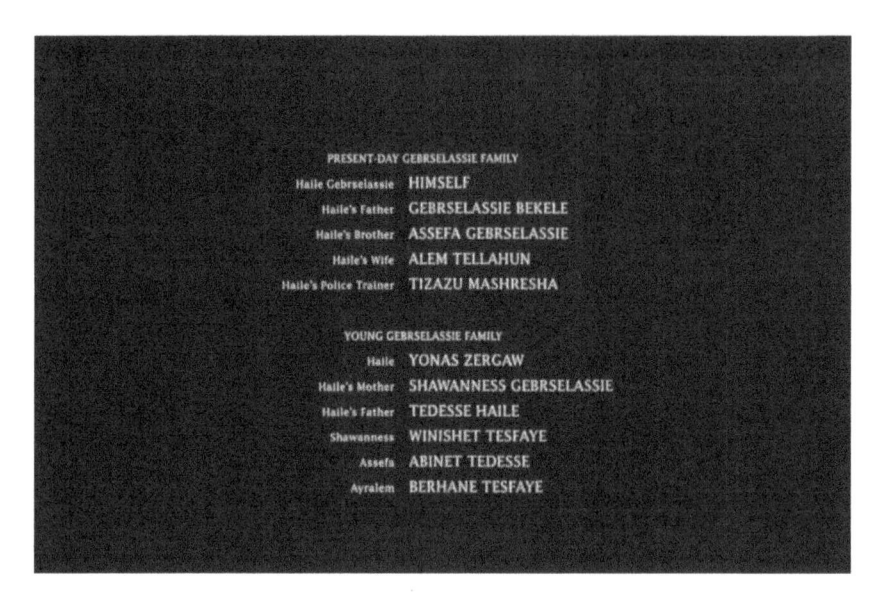

Figure 1.8: Credits for Haile Gebrselassie's present-day family in *Endurance* (Leslie Woodhead, 1998).

in literature, calls a 'distributed field of attention.'"[36] Upon this field, says Woloch, "attention may follow the dehumanized lines of graphic contiguity or direct itself, anthropocentrically, towards human faces."[37]

In *Endurance* the actual kinship and physical resemblance between Haile and his family surrogates troubles the hierarchical relation between protagonist and secondary characters described earlier. Resorting to relatives as actors the film brings into play a category of social actor midway between the social actor who populates social documentaries and the exceptional character, the protagonist himself. These secondary characters are part of the social fabric of Haile's depicted reality, extending the biopic into a socioethnographic study. But they invite into the film an infrasocial, biological link that disarms the artifice of having kin substitute for absent figures or the past. For these are indeed Gbrelessaie's relatives (see Fig. 1.9 in Color Insert, 1; Fig. 1.10).

Besides this kinship register the film introduces a phenomenological consideration of great relevance for in-person reenactment through scenes of Haile running (Fig. 1.11). Such physical actions stand out from representations of Gbrelassie's life in his native village, obscuring a clear sense of artifice and narrative, for how can we distinguish his being, his prepersonal body from his impersonation of himself when he runs, his pre-Olympic character from the later champion (Fig. 1.12)?

In sports film, the straining mutation of routine into drama needs to be articulated through visible signs—that is, bodily marks. Expertise has to be conveyed as exertion, and physical effort needs to be dramatized as an intentional drive toward pain and risk of death. Running scenes are common tropes for competitiveness, routine, and physicality. *The Greatest* (Monte Hellman and Tom Gries,

[30] *In Person*

Figure 1.10: Haile Gebrlessaie and his actual father (*Endurance*, 1998).

Figure 1.11: Haile Gebrlessaie running in *Endurance* (1998).

Figure 1.12: Archival footage of Gebrlessaie's win (*Endurance*, 1998).

1977) includes a reenacted training session. Justified as a preparation for Ali's world championship, the scene mainly channels an agonistic principle, tinged with the star's relation to finitude.

The question of why running (and walking) are privileged in conveying the inseparability between acting and being may have something to do with its exacerbation of the property of immanence Giorgio Agamben calls *pasearse*—the carrying of oneself and one's body at once. Agamben used this Spinozan expression to account for actions in which "means and end, potentiality and actuality, faculty and use enter a zone of in-distinction."[38] This in-distinction between potentiality and actuality especially matters regarding the phenomenology of sports or celebrity reenactment.

Alice Rayner's conceptualizes an act as involving intentionality (to act), materiality (to do), and performativity (to perform). While the voluntary aspect of an act "accounts for the common correlation between drama and the law in which human acts are tested or put on trial to judge the relations between agents deeds and social norms"[39] and is therefore part of an ethical accounting essential to reenactment's pedagogic and self-revising mechanism, Rayner's next two categories of an act, doing and performing, apply more straightforwardly to my discussion of celebrity reenactment biopics. She defines doing as an act severed from its intentions and reduced to material and gestural conditions—"It is the record that the arm goes up with the subtraction that I raise my arm."[40]

Sports biopics invariably replicate the performer's record of struggle and accomplishment, mainly alternating between two kinds of images: the archival record of actual competitions and images reconstituting the training and preparation that infallibly accompany the protagonist's replay of his effort. Each of these images has a special relation to the action they depict and the archival image gives evidence of a doing, capturing an untransformed moment.

For Rayner, what matters in considering the athlete's performance of his expertise is that it transcends intentionality and it is ultimately reducible to its charted physicality. Athletic performance is indicative of performance in general because it "demonstrates concretely the negotiation between the potential and capabilities of a body and the rules of the game,"[41] thus foregrounding skills as well as style. Besides such technical scrutiny, in the case of celebrity reenactment, the self-expressive element of one's professional identity, or family traits, absorbed culturally and socially, accrues the value of a signature. When one reads an autobiography, "the self-reference of the narration is complemented by the implicit self-referential value of a *particular mode of speaking*."[42] Particular abilities as well as idiosyncratic styles of acting, boxing, running, or bullfighting are very much at play in articulating the "ambiguous constancy" of the I implied by autobiographical revisitations.

Endurance's uncanny folding of actual relatives into this represented family cannot be a matter of indifference in a film finally so focused on physicality and expertise. Assuming fully the conventions of the rise to fame in the biopic genre, the film's interest lies in the multiple and contaminated valence of in-person reenactment once the star is surrounded by relatives operating as extras.

REENACTING HEREDITY: *SONS*

> I'm like your grandpa; you are like me, genetics.
>
> Li Maoje *in Sons (Zhang Yuan, 1996)*

In literature, as in social registry, names prove that someone really exists, but they also expand the diegetic world of a character by pointing to sources, a prior history in a parent or relative. Discussing the internal logic of realist fiction, Philippe Hamon states that family histories provide a special realist mooring point and potential for classification, forming a sort of "motivated" and "transparent" derivational field with the surnames playing the role of a linguistic root or stem conveying a particular piece of information: hereditary facts.

Sons (Zhang Yuan, 1996) opens up a reflection on how a family network informs the latent actuality as well as the fictional dimensions of in-person reenactment. In *Sons*, the entire Li family reenacts events leading to Li Maoje, the alcoholic father, being committed to a mental asylum. The director explains in voice-over that his young neighbors approached him with the project, and when he asked why they wanted to name the film *Sons*, Tou Zi replied, "All men are sons but not all are fathers." This remark becomes significant once we consider that hereditary behavior is the film's theme but also its structuring principle. Voiced by Tou Zi, the explanation raises the question of what it means to script a film that entertains the disturbing process of reenacting filiation.

With the father's drunkenness as a continuous, high-pitch backdrop, and his face distorted in the foreground, a parallel narrative gradually emerges suggesting there is a direct causality between the father's alcoholism and the sons' afflictions, violence and addiction.

The film is structured as a series of reproaches, mainly directed at Li Maoje by mother and sons. Several counseling scenes follow between the mother and the younger son, between the older son Tou Zi and the neighborhood counsel. In the first, most explicit sermon, the father Li Maoje talks to Tou Zi: "I failed because of drinking. I have my own reasons . . . work . . . interpersonal relations. I've told you this already many times, I'm like your grandpa. Your grandpa glutted, drunk, gambled and philandered. . . . every night someone in the family had to look for him in the night. . . . My genes are from your grandpa . . . Anyway I don't like you both drinking" (Fig. 1.13).

A compact, ironic series establishes the film's exemplary structure. As in a call-response pattern, the sons' junkie behavior follows the father's drunken scenes. When the father moves his cot into the compound's courtyard, thereby publically disgracing the family, the scene is echoed by the sons falling, vomiting, and sleeping in the streets.

"Like father like son" sums up the film's expositional tactics, defining it as a naturalist parable. The excess of admonitions and their failure in promoting any positive change become signifiers of a contemporary problematic, a confused but insistent refusal to submit to the bankrupt traditions of filial and party devotion. The insistence on heredity and addiction, traits that imply inescapable

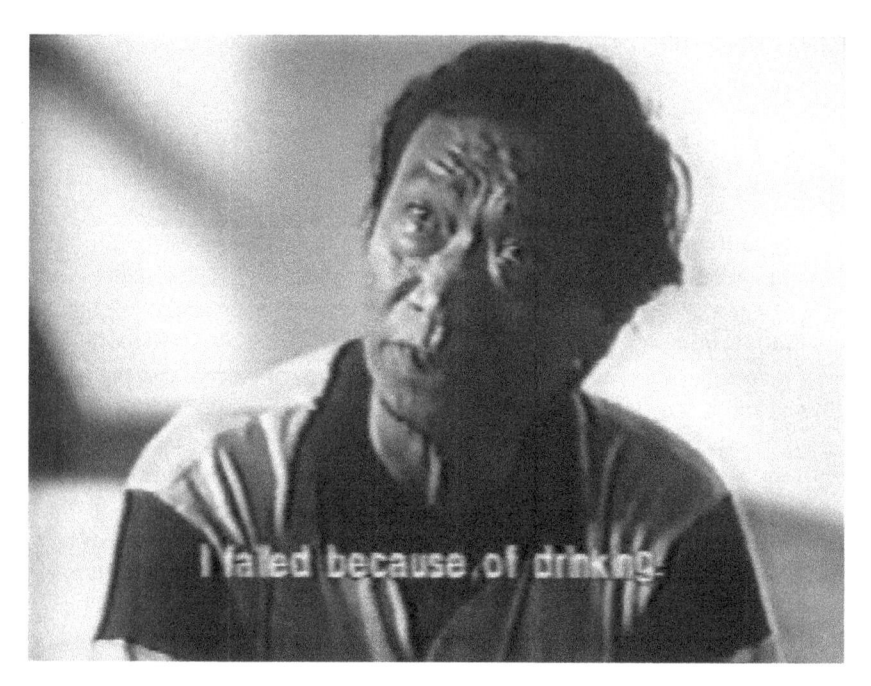

Figure 1.13: Li Maoje's genetics explanation.

cycles of repetition and ineffective intervention, is in line with Zhang's central role in the Sixth Generation of Chinese Cinema's challenge of the national taboo on representing private behavior.[43] The disaffection with the government's handling of personal affairs, evident in a series of frustrated encounters with officials, repeats Zhang's trajectory as a disaffiliated rebellious maker and prepares us for the film's critical take.[44]

Sons's single-minded focus on the ineffectiveness of handed-down models—shifts its realism from a microportrayal of urban disaffection in Beijing toward a broader comment on Chinese society. The film intervenes within a charged trope of Chinese culture: the family portrait.[45] In the late eighties and nineties, Chinese art family portraits such as family snapshots or group paintings were seen as a challenge to official imagery the same way that *Sons*'s reclamation of a "bastard spirit"[46] is in line with the filmmaker and his generation's embrace of personal stories, of rambling urban rhythms and the rejection of any collective label.

The film's paradoxical combination of crisis and paralysis, its depiction of resistance to change and its high-pitched display of irrational responses, fits the melodrama genre, whose popularity derives, as Ma Ning has argued, precisely from the significance of the family as a social unit in Chinese culture. The family has often worked as a means for the "public enactment of socially unacknowledged states."[47] The genre's erratic rhythms as well as its tendency to define its conflicts as a struggle with patriarchal authority perfectly advance *Sons*'s tracking of a collapsing parental authority and characterizes Zhang's cinema in terms of a broader generational conflict.

Violence defines the extent of exposure the filmmaker and the family are willing to reach in displaying private matters. And *Sons* especially thrives on scenes that transgress the boundary between acting and being. The father's ingestion of alcohol, the sons shooting up and having sex, and finally the chair that splits open the father's head are representations with real consequences, therefore demanding greater artifice.

After Tou Zi finds his mother in a drunk stupor sitting by the father at the foot of the bed and crashes a chair over the father's head, Li Maoje, with blood streaming down his face, declares dramatically, "I want to keep it and look at it, this is a permanent mark of a son hating his old man." At home Xiao Wei, the younger brother, tries to clean the bloodstains on the sheets with no success. An "if only" structure sums up the pathos of both melodrama and reenactment (in its belatedness). This double pathos is especially poignant in the bloodstain cultivated by the film's careful framing. For reenactment can only teach by rephrasing what seems irrevocable.

The family's excesses, reiterated continually, render reenactment's cautionary prospect vacuous. Inherited or socially acquired "bad" behavior constitutes radical indictments of a liberating mimesis and consequently of a redemptive reenactment. At the film's ending, Zhang mentions he has come in an attempt at mending the family's vicious circle. If *Sons* is a perverse version of this filial amendment, addiction may be just the visible dimension of a more disturbing senseless mimesis that places in question the reparative force of aesthetic replay.

In this film, questions of transmission, mimesis, and resemblance also play a role in the film's comments on Chinese society's malaise. The concentration on an actual father, mother, and their two sons invites the scanning of shared physiognomic traits, the detection of repeated behavior (Fig. 1.14). And the film's enhanced naturalism and the opening scene with family portraits invite precisely this scrutiny on individual traits.

Time's corrosive power, the estrangement of self apparent with in-person reenactment, is enhanced once the issue of physiognomic likeness foregrounds yet another form of replication, another odd link between origin and "copies."[48] As we begin to speculate through *Sons* about this seepage of physiognomic, biological aspects into the text, we should consider how evidence based on genetic presuppositions or repeated physical and gestural traits enters more broadly into the analysis of reenactment. What bearing does the real body of the actor have as carrier of reproducible traits once reenactment sets into action alternate forms of recursivity—theatrical, ritual, or purging? More pointedly, is the sticky present, the temporal looping of bloodlines displaced, ruptured, or reiterated in this ensemble, family reenactment? What is the role of repetitive patterns of behavior, and cyclicality in hampering the progressive stakes of reenactment? The replicating logic of genetics also applies to habit and routine, and the question becomes whether one may read the sedimentation of time in gestural patterns and voice intonation.

The striking likeness among the Li family members brings into the narrative a register of identity at odds with other operative codes of verisimilitude in cinema and reenactment. Family ties, heredity and surnames, potent signs for origin and

Figure 1.14: The Li family portrait.

succession, are in tension with reenactment's aesthetic and temporal autonomy. One is a natural and social construct based on genetic, cultural links and it presupposes continuity; the second is an arbitrary structure of narrative and fiction. My term to emphasize the tension at the heart of an aesthetics based on uprooting and differential reproduction is "a-filiation." *Sons*'s selective stress on repetition and other "natural" forms of cyclicality, added to its unredeeming narrative, perfectly instantiates a contemporary tendency in reenactment cinema we explore in the last chapter of this book.

CHAPTER 2
Neorealist Reenactment as Postwar Pedagogy

Neorealism—as I understand it—requires that everyone must be his own actor.
Cesare Zavattini[1]

In light of the practice of casting nonactors in Italian postwar cinema, a neorealist innovation,[2] Cesare Zavattini's 1953 proclamation that "everyone must be his own actor" sounded strangely embattled. *The Story of Caterina*, Zavattini and Francesco Maselli's contribution to the omnibus film *L'Amore in Città* (*Love in the City*) the same year, led the crusade to chart the future for neorealist cinema.[3] This cine-magazine followed a program: "Unknown people will play themselves, reality will be followed up close, without any fictive clothing. . . . Each event, faithfully reconstituted, embodies its own lesson, if only because it happened." Focusing on anonymous women as subjects and performers of their own experiences, the six episodes by different directors radicalize a defining feature of neorealist cinema: now, nonactors act out their own lives. The filmmakers set out to make private persons public: people whose existence is notarized in official documents. Zavattini's favorite example of an individual with a story worth sharing is Caterina Rigoglioso, a migrant from Palermo. She is seen repeating, in detail and for the camera, events in her life that have already received broad media attention: pregnant but unable to get papers or a job, she abandons her infant, faces trial for the crime, and, finally, recovers the child in an orphanage.

Acting as oneself would seem to represent a natural outgrowth of taking actors "off the streets": an intensified order of realism, whereby one *is* the character, instead of just looking the type. "Everyone" has the same populist ring as the neorealist formula evident in Zavattini's collaborations with Vittorio De Sica: chronicles of petty bourgeois or working-class characters against the backdrop of a cross-section of Italian society. But for all that, and as I will demonstrate in this chapter, this final step away from fictional roles and actors involves a new relation between experience and cinema.

I will discuss how, at a critical moment in cinematic history—and in tandem with other forms of heightened self-reference—"acting one's own role" replaces earlier conceptions of neorealist authenticity. In "Il Film Lampo," Zavattini describes his *pedinamento* poetics: "One should succeed in seeing on the screen a sort of documentary of private and public facts with the rigor and readiness of a mirror and the analytical dimension of the cinema, which reveals all the spatial and temporal dimensions of these facts."[4] *Pedinamento*, closely tracking a person's existence, emerged in response to constraints felt by the exponents of neorealist cinema from 1949 to 1953, when directors negotiated the economic and moral exigencies of filmmaking in the charged political and cultural field of the Cold War. In the early fifties, the omnipresence of American movies, mounting censorship of populist themes, and competition with star-driven features—as well as a narrow view, on the left, of what counted as realism in the first place—led to a search for credible new parameters of authenticity in cinema. Zavattini's planned redistribution of social attention in focusing on a registered individual's life and having her as actor is a reaction to the waning of social cinema and its main signifier—the nonactor, taken off the streets.

Among Italian cinemas, other breaks from the fascist model, such as rejecting the star system and using nonprofessionals, had an unequivocally democratic intent. One of the immediate impasses that postwar cinema faced involved having to "propose a portrait of the new Italian born of the war and resistance, using the framework of actors who have represented in great or small scale the Mussolini ideals of Italy."[5] As Gian Piero Brunetta suggests, the actor is "the most vulnerable point in cinema's professional crew, and . . . while the cinematographic reconstruction cannot renounce cameramen, directors, and set designers of the preceding cinema, [the new Italian cinema] declares instead the total substitutability of the actor."[6] Filmmakers advertised the casual way they discovered their actors. Lamberto Maggiorani was picked to play Antonio Ricci when he brought his two sons for an audition; Carlo Battisti, a linguist from the University of Florence, was spotted on the street after De Sica had scoured homes for the aged and organizations for retirees. This approach revealed an appreciation for a workable aesthetics tied to the common man and divorced from the established norms of fascist cinema professionalism.

Roma Città aperta (*Rome, Open City*, 1945), featuring both actors and nonactors, is exemplary in this regard. Roberto Rossellini cast Anna Magnani and Aldo Fabrizi—actors known for light comic roles—against type, "giving them serious, even tragic, roles" which "enabled them to blend with untrained actors like Marcello Pagliero [a real communist resistant] and Francesco Grandjaquet."[7] Discussing the scene where Pina dies, Magnani relates how actual locations and original protagonists infused her performance with authenticity: "during the round-up . . . I plunged back into the time when they were taking away the young people all over Rome. Kids. Because the people who were there with their backs to the wall were real people. . . . the Germans were real Germans taken from a prison camp. Suddenly I wasn't me any more . . . I was that character" (Fig. 2.1). According to the film's script assistant, "a similar round up had taken place in Via Montecuccoli a year before and the residents

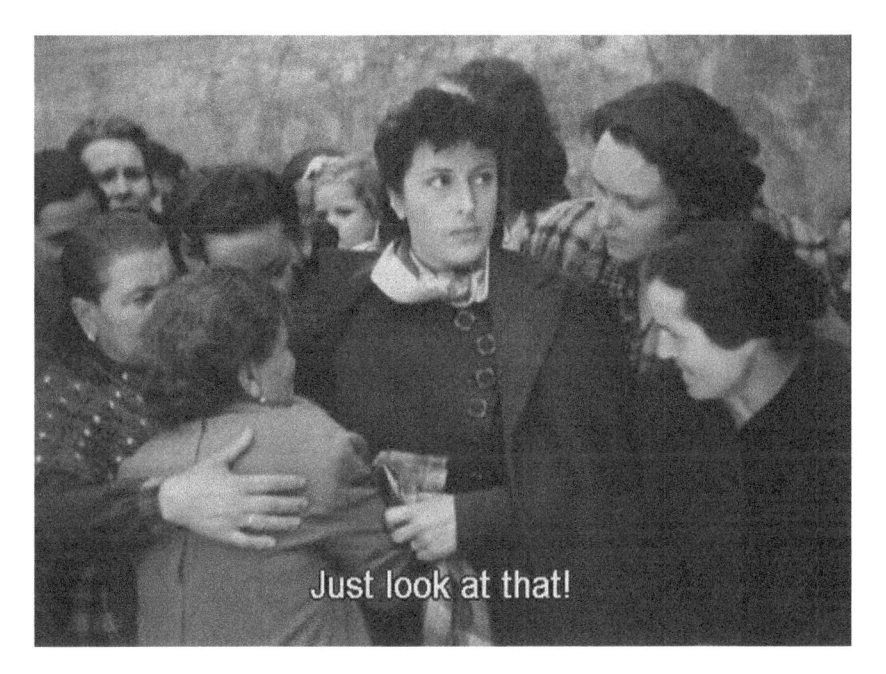

Figure 2.1: Anna Magnani with the actual inhabitants of Via Montecuccoli as extras (Rosselini, *Rome Open City*, 1945).

welcomed the production crew because, in addition to being paid as extras, 'they reckoned it was basically a film about them.'"[8]

Many of the earlier films on the war and the Resistance (*Il sole sorge ancora* [*Outcry*], Aldo Vergano, 1946; *Paisà* [*Paisan*], Rossellini, 1946; *Achtung! Banditi* [*Attention! Bandits!*], Carlo Lizzani, 1951) draw raw power from a similar synergy between different registers of authenticity; an existential link is guaranteed when social actors revisit the original event's location, thereby convincing both themselves and the audience that the characters' drama is real. Zavattini's notion of everyone acting oneself represents, in part, an attempt to claim this testimonial authority for less historically urgent realities, the nondramatic reconstitution of a common man's everyday life. Based on an individual identity, but concentrating on people who otherwise go unrecognized, reenactment becomes a method of social reparation, a way to reallocate attention: "One should remember that in the registry we all have names, and are therefore all interesting."[9] By bringing together an "everyman" and the individuality of a proper name, Zavattini takes distance from prior neorealist rhetoric and articulates the conversion principle of reenactment. In this new rhetorical economy, the hitherto anonymous individual is brought to "light" in a sort of cinematic baptism. *Having a name* equals the specific contribution that cinema's particularity and reenactment's performative act enable: the expression of previously marginalized, anonymous experience.

Two episodes from *Love in the City*, *The Story of Caterina* and Michelangelo Antonioni's *Attempted Suicides*, represent key experiments in Zavattini's integral realism. The following focuses on the meaning of stories when their real protagonists literally replay events. How and to what effect do filmmakers frame these repetitions? What form of realism results when an actual, named character performs his or her own life?

In 1953, a second omnibus film, *Siamo Donne* (*We, the Women*), also conceived by Zavattini, reworked the antispectacle credo on "enemy terrain." Now, major Italian stars portrayed common women. Individual contributions—Alfredo Guarini's *Concorso: 4 Attrici; 1 Speranza* (*Contest: 4 Actresses; 1 Hope*), Guido Franciolini's *Alida Valli*, Roberto Rossellini's *Ingrid Bergman*, Luigi Zampa's *Isa Miranda*, and Luchino Visconti's *Anna Magnani*—all revolve around the relative values of acting and being. Because a steady stream of information about their personal lives defines stars, "overturning" stardom through additional revelations is a moot point. What matters is how each film interprets the drive to elevate the common, everyday woman as the cinema's new heroine. Exploring the oxymoron of "acting oneself," Rossellini, Visconti, and Antonioni focus on the camera's inherent theatricality, as well as its ability to extract a deeper truth of social being. At stake in these early 1950s films is a modern cinema grappling with a neorealist heritage, which is itself in flux.

ZAVATTINI'S "LAST JUDGMENT" CINEMA

Zavattini's trajectory in the 1950s was marked by programmatic attempts to escape his own scriptwriting expertise. As many Italian critics have pointed out, his rejection of actors, fabulation, and spectacle calls to mind Dziga Vertov's "factory of facts": nonfiction cinema that dispenses with actors, stories, and mediation.[10] In a 1950 interview entitled "Basta con I soggetti!" ("Enough with Scripts!"), Zavattini suggests handing down the camera to young filmmakers (*kinokis*) so they can record the reality around them as directly as possible.[11]

From 1951 on, Zavattini's letters describe detailed plans for the documentary *Italia Mia*,[12] a vision of "integral neorealism" that emphasizes people's own "unmediated" voices. To De Sica, he said: "With *Umberto D* we closed a genre and with *Italia Mia*, we open another." The film "will be created by means of our ears and eyes, in direct contact with reality" and made of moments "collected as if [seen] by car."[13] After receiving no response from directors De Sica and Rossellini, he pitched his idea to publisher Giulio Einaudi. Zavattini declared that he intended to use young documentary makers since "it is the meaning, the novelty and usefulness of the project that should merit attention, not the director's name."[14] Zavattini privileges a direct record of facts, but leaves the possibility open "to provoke and stage [events]"[15]— for instance: "we see a wedding . . . [people] departing for Venezuela . . . we will stop and wait for [a woman] to give birth, recording it minutely from our point of view." The result combines direct record, staged events, and archival material: "I add the rapidity, simultaneity and the extension in time and space." Moving past a contemporary social geography, Zavattini demanded historical indicators, "glimpses of some of the more important news" to go "from the post-war to today." He called for reenactment to abridge and reconstitute past scenes: "one is launched into the past through memory, reconstruction, at times fugitive, synthetic, at other times more diffuse. . . . [W]*e will see a repetition of a scene's climax in the very place where it happened.*" Zavattini reassured De Sica that the film would advance on their prior conquests: "there will be no shadow of actors, unless . . . actors are [themselves] protagonists (aren't they part of the human panorama of Italy?)."[16]

As diaries, testimonies, and reenactment attest, the juxtaposition of authentic voices worked to absolve Zavattini the scriptwriter from his prolific imagination, his ease in telling stories.[17] For Zavattini, intellectual and artistic mediation represented a bourgeois point of view; to avoid this narrow perspective, he advocated taking a closer and closer share in the subject's life—"make a hole in the ceiling, live in the next door house, pretend to be a worker, etc."[18] After the critical success of De Sica's *Umberto D* (1952), he reiterated his belief that "the same persons who lived a story and *not the script*, must tell their story."[19] For Zavattini, as he shifted toward more improvisational modes of storytelling, focusing on the actor as author was essential, even if it meant abandoning one of his greatest strengths: crafting narrative.

From 1951 to 1953, Zavattini worked as a newspaper editor, writer, and documentary producer. His column, *L'Italia domanda* (*Italy Asks*), counted as a cornerstone of *Epoca*. He published "Diario Cinematografico" in *Cinema Nuovo*.[20] In *Love in the City*, he embraced different voices and approaches along lines modeled in *Documento mensile*, a short-lived film magazine conceived by Marco Ferreri and Riccardo Ghione as an alternative to *Settimana Incom* (the ubiquitous 1950s newsreel voicing governmental and institutional views)[21] (Fig. 2.2).

Figure 2.2: *The Spectator*, a mixed-mode cinematic magazine (*L'Amore in Città*, 1953).

Love in the City represents a film manifesto, an attempt to apply Zavattini's ideas for an unmediated cinema. Co-produced with Ferreri and Ghione, the film is a mélange of directorial sensibilities and mixed modes: investigation, analysis, and fictional reconstitution.[22] Even when *Documento mensile* (with short films by Visconti, Alberto Moravia, and Antonioni, among others) failed to be released, Zavattini optimistically numbered *Love in the City* first in a planned series.[23] *Love in the City* adopts the look of a large weekly magazine (*L'Europeo*) in presenting its six episodes (directed by Carlo Lizzani, Federico Fellini, Dino Risi, Antonioni, Zavattini and Francesco Maselli, and Alberto Lattuada). Although photos play an important role, their design, framing, and content associate them with film stills and even photo-romance. An extended credit sequence introduces the project's innovative approach: its topic is love, and the film advertises its surveillance capabilities with intimate scenes between lovers "never before seen in their actual unfolding" (Fig. 2.3). "Would you like to hear their words?" the narrator asks, enticing the public. In medium close shots, a couple on a work break talks about delaying plans for a family; a young man is asked to confirm his love again and again; yet another couple insistently discuss going out purely through expressive hand signs. A caption indicating a precise time and place frames each little scene.

Intended as part of a collection titled *The Spectator*, *Love in the City* includes scenes of buyers at a newsstand curiously leafing through a "film magazine" of the same name, showcasing its availability as mass entertainment and invoking the contemporary credentials and popularity of the weekly.[24] Each episode opens with pages

Figure 2.3: The topic of *The Spectator* is Love in the City (*L'Amore in Città*, 1953).

turning, and the credits mimic an academic journal's table of contents; thus, Carlo Lizzani's and Michelangelo Antonioni's contributions, *Love for Pay* and *Attempted Suicides*, appear under the rubric of *inchiesta* (investigation)[25] (Fig. 2.4). Alternating stills of jubilant crowds and beauty contests, as well as a series of shots zooming in on a poster of Lana Turner (*The Bad and the Beautiful*), illustrate that instead of Hollywood heroes, "we" will be inscribed within a new mass spectacle order through the surrogate of the anonymous everyday person. Thus, the eponymous spectator is invoked as both the film's addressee and its protagonist.

The documentary thrust of *Italia Mia*, initially a film and later a photographic essay with Paul Strand,[26] informs Zavattini's conception of *Love in the City*. Central to this testimonial course is the conviction that "those people"—"servants, waiters, pensioners"—had something to say.[27] The filmmakers welcomed awkward acting as evidence of the challenge their project posed to conventional spectacle: in cinema, "the whimpers [of consciousness] are not just of the person telling about herself but also of people confronting the new material—the directors and writers of cinema."[28] The public screening aimed at exposing everyday truths and embarrassing oblivious spectators is, in fact, a recurring scenario in Zavattini's discourse and the basis of his moral pedagogy.

Italia Mia's multiple scripts anticipate a larger plan for deploying reenactment as a confessional mode involving actors and audience alike. Reenacting private realities is intended to awaken the social performer to the human condition in general. As always with Zavattini, the roots of a cinema that reveals what the

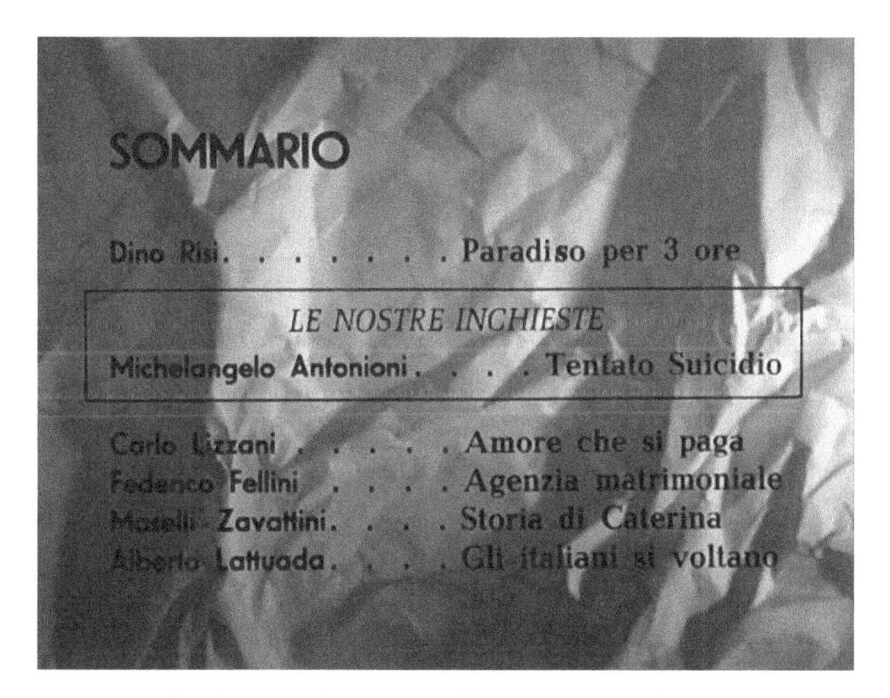

Figure 2.4: Table of contents of *The Spectator* (*L'Amore in Cittá*, 1953).

spectator does not wish to acknowledge lay in the postwar period. In his collected diaries, *Zavattini: Sequences from a Cinematic Life*, the screenwriter shares an idea he conceived 1944: going by truck (with Lattuada, Diego Fabbri, and Mario Monicelli) to a village destroyed by the war, where people were slowly resuming life among the ruins.

> We talk to them in the square; I'll say I'm guilty of this and that, at first they'll consider me a monster, but this is the only way I'll be able to act also as accuser, attribute to each his responsibilities . . . we'll be constantly dramatizing . . . some of those present try to justify themselves and they don't realize I'm offering them a chance to get it all off their chests. . . . We set a primitive screen in the center of the square and show some bits of film . . . the narrator tries to make the people in the square understand that these other men also weep, die, kill . . . the spectators get tired, they tell the moralist to go to the devil . . . Mussolini's voice appears from the rubble and we hear applause coming from that man smoking his pipe. It lasts five minutes . . . they would all like to shut up the voice from the loudspeaker but they don't know what to do.[29]

In 1949, Zavattini hoped to make a film "to be projected against the sky, visible at the same moment in every part of the earth." This "'domestic Last Judgment' . . . begun by our films just after the war cannot be interrupted."[30] This is cinema conceived as a settling of accounts, a program for political and historical catharsis. The program is also in line with the conventional view of neorealism as an antifascist front, and with a vigilant postwar consciousness for which any "evasion of reality was a betrayal."[31]

Zavattini's program for reenergizing neorealism responded to real economic and ideological constraints. From 1949 to 1953—a period when the Italian film industry had to redefine itself to survive—the social agenda and aesthetic credentials of neorealism were challenged on both the left and the right.[32] Italy's alignment with the United States during the Cold War and constant fear of electoral victories by the Communist Party led to an insidious and effective censorship of films addressing social and economic concerns. Weary of the moral capital the left had accumulated in its Resistance days, the Catholic Church and the Catholic press pushed for normalization and declared films on the war and the fascist period irrelevant for the present. In a particularly egregious instance of conservative opposition to social-leaning cinema, Giulio Andreotti wrote an open letter to De Sica (first published in *Libertas* in February 1952) complaining that *Umberto D*'s denunciation of the effects of inflation did a disservice to Italy's national image.[33] Renzo Renzi has diagnosed this tendency of the government "to feel blamed by any analysis of reality . . . leaning towards old paternalistic and fascist attitudes" as a preemptive attack on all opposition under the pretext of combating communism.[34] At the same time, however, he calls into question the oppositional quality ascribed to neorealism: "Denunciation and revelation of tragic or painful situations, often attributed to such distant responsibility, were always maintained within ideological limits . . . it was not neorealism that was revolutionary but its enemies that were fascistic."[35]

At the same time, Italian cinema faced scrutiny from the left. Embracing a socialist program that never took hold in Italian cinema, the Stalinist left condemned not only the "rosy picture" offered by neorealism but also the aesthetic experiments of directors such as Rossellini, Antonioni, and Giuseppe De Santis.[36] On a related front, Guido Aristarco, the editor of the leftist journal *Cinema Nuovo*, endorsed Lukács's conception of realism and took aim at Zavattini's neopopulist naturalism, in particular: "Chronicle, document, denunciation. All this constitutes solely the preface to true realism, which by its nature can only be critical, historical."[37] According to Lukács, immediate records of the everyday amount to a flawed, inadequate version of realism. Such an approach risks offering descriptions but little else, thereby equating minor and major events (which, in fact, was one of Zavattini's aims). In this context, Lino de Fra has argued that the challenge faced by neorealist filmmakers in moving toward a greater, deeper realism stemmed from the fact that "today the crisis is less obvious and burning, if deeper: the drama of man looked at casually seems more intimate and less 'corale' (interdependent of other social relationships and contextual factors). To authentically capture reality there is a need for a more informed sensibility, a broader narrative breadth and a sharper critical consciousness."[38] Again and again, Zavattini's projects have been faulted for bordering on naturalism, for being unable to comment on anything more than "this or that person, this or that situation."[39] *Love in the City* is deemed an extreme and failed experiment, whereas Visconti's *Senso* is supposed to exemplify true, epic realism where characters embody broader historical forces.[40]

Combating the conservative pressure for normalization and rejecting the claim that neorealism was relevant only for the immediate postwar period, Zavattini sought to explore life "in its exceptional aspects of injustice and misery."[41] Sounding an alarm about the "grave moment Italian cinema is undergoing,"[42] his address to the leftist press did "not express an isolated complaint so much as it testified to a diffuse malaise, a grave dispersion of forces and a political and operative insufficiency."[43]

The Parma Convention in December 1953, which was held to evaluate neorealism critically,[44] ultimately—and uncontroversially—equated it with a moral vocation. Adelio Ferrero, a contemporary critic, remarked that "the greatest display of verbal unanimity and voluntarism" replaced "the lack of effective unity" among the various positions.[45] Zavattini returned to a motif of immediate postwar debate, the alienated intellectual, and the need "to overcome this condition inherited from idealism [of the fascist era] through a direct contact with the popular, proletarian and urban reality."[46] His Parma address, *Il Neorealismo secondo me*, revisits his plan, already voiced in 1949, to follow a man to whom nothing happens. Now, however, "this man (one of my two or three fixed ideas) has a name and last name"; giving this man a fictional name would amount to placing "a screen between me and reality, something that delays me, and obstructs an integral contact with reality."[47]

Zavattini understood cinema as an expiatory apparatus, a morally charged stage for awakening the actors' and spectators' common humanity. Accordingly, all through 1953 he contended with those who had declared neorealism and its raison d'être dead.[48] In this ideologically constrained field, the call to "act oneself" functioned as a ritualized plea for the redemptive potential of the medium.

Zavattini saw reenactment as the way to reinstate neorealism as a social barometer, to redirect its focus on inequality in a more diffuse and complex social reality, and to reconnect with its more immediate, socially conscious postwar vocation. He launched a new, programmatic attack on morally lazy spectators, chastising the public for its desire to look away, to flee into other forms of lighter entertainment:

> In the future realism will find other forms, but for now it must become aware, *even if by cruel means*, so as to empower men to make resolutions. Let's place an unemployed person in front of a camera and then *we'll nail down the public for five minutes in front of that image projected on the screen*. This is not wanted. They cry "Montage!" so the images flow fast and the public's consciousness remains superficial and truth is not deepened.[49]

Extended duration, slow motion, and repetition are prescribed—any means of forcing a confrontation between the public and unpalatable social realities. "Someone has said that it is 'monstrous' to have Caterina Rigoglioso repeat her gesture. It is exactly this reaction, this judgment of monstrosity that betrays a fear of looking truth in the face."[50] Zavattini reiterates his intent to use cinema as an analytical tool, "to repeat that suicide gesture in slow motion" so that spectators will follow the circumstances leading a penniless mother to threaten to jump from the top of the Palace of Justice when her husband is condemned to eleven years of prison for robbery.[51] These mothers who in utter despair are ready to abandon their children are singled out to make a case for the cruelty of repetition.

The fact that Zavattini directed only for *The Story of Caterina* until he wrote, directed, and acted in *La veritàaaa* (*The Truthhhh*, 1980) says something about the stock he placed in Caterina's ritual experiment.[52] *La veritàaaa* consists of a semi-improvised rant in which Zavattini plays the part of Antonio, a raving madman who attacks everyone he meets, forcing them to tell the truth. Zavattini appears undisguised; indeed, the first draft refers to a "Z., the author who speaks with the public for sixty minutes in a row, expressing all the accumulated experience of his seventy-eight years of life, becoming *implicitly* and *explicitly* an actor."[53] The point is to collapse action and acting into one: "lacking entirely in traditional skills the actor appropriately becomes a cause of interest and *veritàaaaa*."[54]

Carlo Prandi has identified Zavattini's need to synthesize praxis and theory, artistic and intellectual experience, as the principal link to his ethical engagement and Christianity. A model needs to be lived rather than spoken:[55] "If it does not command a visible exemplary action, I don't believe in it; if its not written as a cry, it does not respect its urgency, its drama, its popularity."[56] Zavattini always relished in the figure of the fool who proclaims the truth to deaf ears; in *La veritàaaa*, he finds the perfect context for bringing this figure to life. The multiple "a"s in his title, he says, constitute a "sort of invocation, to open it to our eyes and consciousness."[57] Zavattini's chanted row of "aaas, a verbal 'happening,'" extends the promise implicit in the word's meaning into the present; making speech into act, he confirms the performative turn of his sayings, his cinema. In 1953, Zavattini had started to fulfill this demand for a fuller exemplary action in the form of dramatic, literal acting—Caterina's reenactment of her story.

THE STORY OF CATERINA

Zavattini had learned of the story of Caterina Rigoglioso through the zoom lens of journalistic sensationalism, when she was publicly tried, and then acquitted, for abandoning her two-year-old child. "Today all Italy knows what she did and why; few people have not been moved by it," remarks an announcer in the film: "After giving up her child, Rigoglioso read the newspaper headline 'Heartless Mother Abandons Her Boy,' was filled with regret, and became a nurse at the orphanage where the boy had been taken (Fig. 2.5). She then cared not only for her own child but also for the children of others." In an exemplary turn, Caterina's story concludes with social integration; it serves as a model tale of moral instruction. The care she shows for children other than her own fulfills Zavattini's prescription that reenactment allow spectators to collectively share in the difficulties of fellow human beings.

Reenactment is not Zavattini's term. Instead, he speaks of a *film-lampo*: following a given event subject in a timely, close, and immediate manner. Immediate recording and reconstructing events serve opposite purposes, which can only be reconciled by demonstrating their common stake in actuality. This performative quality is what distinguishes Zavattini's reenactment from simple illustration, that is, reconstructing scenes to fill out sensationalist news items and unrecorded events. Neorealist reenactment does not seek to recreate the phenomenal quality of events but to actualize the protagonist's experience of them, to make events relevant once

Figure 2.5: Headline about Caterina's abandonment of her son (Zavattini and Maselli, *Storia di Caterina* episode in *L'Amore in Città*, 1953).

again. As the social actor reclaims her experience, she takes an active role in her own life once more.

Zavattini explains the significance of retracing reality in this way, without intermediaries. In reliving one's experience through a "kind of ritual" and a "reconstruction with almost scientific aims," one breaks away from the "embarrassment that is always anti-collective, that is too protective of individualistic fact." One can then "acquire consciousness of the collective destiny of our acts, of its 'making public.'"[58] In terms that recall Brecht's alienation techniques, he describes the value of literal reenactment: "People understand themselves better than the social fabric and to see themselves on the screen, performing their daily actions—remembering that to see oneself gives one the sense of being unlike oneself—like hearing one's own voice on the radio—can help them to fill up a void, a lack of knowledge of reality."[59] In this sense, reenactment amounts to a "moral remake": it is "the cognitive intent of cinema that can give moral force to the anti-spectacular remake of the 'first time around.'"[60] Mauricio Grande has described this conception of cinema as a process of "knowledge in action" that "cannot therefore be limited to 'recognizing' or 'witnessing' a social and human landscape; it has to do more: it must transform it into a rite of knowledge and at the same time into a liturgical spectacle."[61]

The Story of Caterina aims for this liturgical dimension, and to this end, it fuses a penitential path with representation grounded in concrete time and space. By tracking each of her tribulations and protracting their duration, the film seeks to communicate a sense of the title character's ordeal and its dulling effects on her life. Maselli (the de facto director despite shared credits) was fascinated by the effects achieved by dollies and lighting, and he took special pride in retracing Caterina's path slowly and methodically.[62] The camera trains on each of her hardships as she adopts a stoic mask: knocking on her friend's door looking for work, trying to leave her child with the wet nurse or keeper for a little longer,[63] waiting in lines, wandering through parks and the city (Figs. 2.6–2.9). Evoking a *via crucis*, every new station in her path is punctuated by soundtrack composer Mario Nascimbene's plaintive musical refrain.[64]

Although the scenes of waiting and walking adhere to Zavattini's principle of a stalking camera, they remain in a kind of durational limbo: not long enough to evoke a sense of real time, yet longer than needed to impart information about Caterina (for instance, the time she spends navigating the city's employment system, looking for a job). Soft dissolves do not fit screen events to actual time so much as the pace of earlier examples of neorealism, such as *Umberto D* or *Bicycle Thieves*. Shapeless, the scenes convey Caterina's rundown existence. At the same time, an unintended distance results from the camera's close and relentless attachment to Rigoglioso's flat performance. The amorphous, unstructured sequences without drama correspond to moments in which literal performance and acting are meant to be indistinguishable. Even in the handful of scenes that take a closer view—Caterina and the little boy's nurse at the benefits agency, or when she feeds her son at a restaurant—the protagonist seems detached, literally beside herself. Elaborate camera movements, such as a crane shot closing in on her as she is crying, and abrupt shifts between long shots and a close-up of her looking back at her child after she has abandoned him,

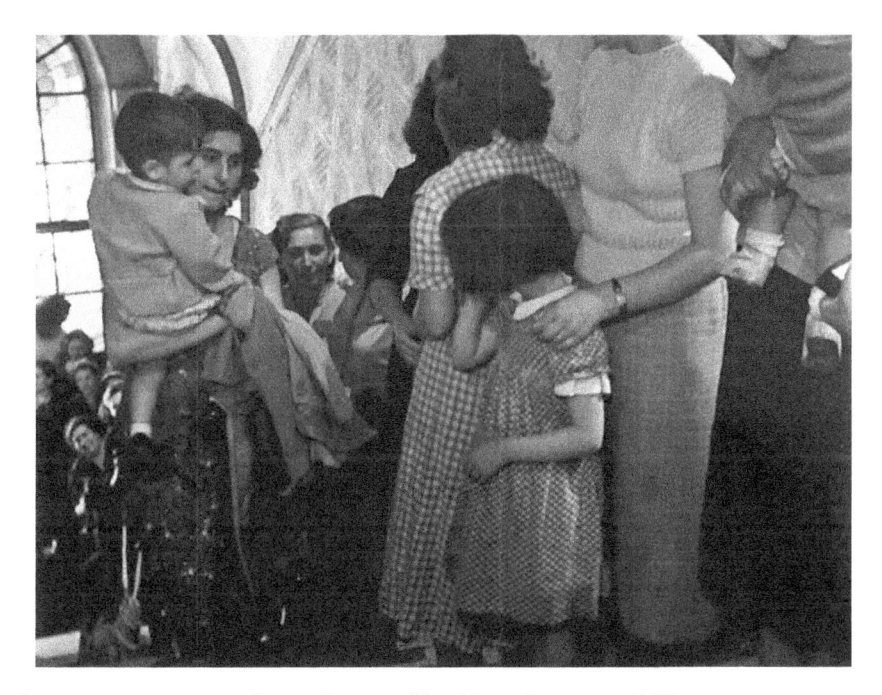

Figure 2.6: Caterina and son in line at welfare (*Storia di Caterina*, 1953).

Figure 2.7: Social portrait of Caterina's condition: women leaving children with nurses (*Storia di Caterina*, 1953).

Figure 2.8: Caterina and son walk through Rome (*Storia di Caterina*, 1953).

Figure 2.9: Tired (*Storia di Caterina*, 1953).

fail to elicit viewer identification. The film hovers, caught between two approaches to cinema: one aspiring to heighten drama by technical means (the crane), and the other loyal to the safe pace of plodding naturalism. Thereby, it veers away from Caterina, its concrete and existential core, and attends to the mechanics of narrative instead.

Despite Zavattini's intention to neutralize directorial presence, the stronger arc of storytelling overshadows reenactment's performative aspects here. As Sam Rohdie notes, Caterina's story repeats the cycle of abandonment for the sake of love that occurs in *Umberto D*.[65] As redemptive tales, both films depend on portraying material and physical ordeals: only passage through daily tribulations can connote the Christian ideals on which Zavattini's morality is founded.[66] Both films use ellipses to compensate for the long takes representing mundane events, and their representation of real time is ultimately not so different. This similarity blurs a core distinction, which should have been preserved: Caterina Rigoglioso is a real person (with a registered name and last name), whereas Umberto D, or Maria the maid, is a fictional character.

Disappointed with Caterina's performance, which proves less than true to life, Zavattini muses: "Caterina did not seem to 'take' to the cinema. But wasn't she 'Caterina?'"[67] The dramatized mise-en-scène places the fundamental dilemma of reenactment's reach for exemplarity into relief. As Caterina is asked to be what she is not—an actress—her real identity wavers. At the same time, lack of acting talent spoils any chance of verisimilitude and therefore compromises the credibility of another possible form of example, the "fictitious narrative that could nevertheless have occurred."[68]

By virtue of its compromised status, *The Story of Caterina* illustrates some of the dilemmas that result from making the social actor, with a real name and last name, exemplary. The first challenge involves adapting a real story or person to the dictates of verisimilitude (understood here both in terms of film and narrative convention, which mandates that they should appear to be true and provide examples for spectators to emulate).

"The true is not necessarily the verisimilar and it is better to serve the truth by tricking with it than to disfigure it because of a fetishism with authenticity,"[69] André Bazin remarked apropos of the breach in verisimilitude brought about by choosing Caterina to play the role. Always attuned to the vicissitudes of realism, Bazin pinpoints the contradictory requirements at the core of Zavattini's project: "if this story constitutes itself an appropriate scenario, the minute faithfulness can only undermine the dramatic construction, and also only an incredible luck could predestine the real protagonist to her employment in the film."[70] He expresses astonishment at the results: "given the parameters [this project seemed] doomed to failure. Not only the interpretation by the real heroine did not seem to me a priori to bring any supplemental guarantee, but it would seem, that this servitude would spoil the credibility, if not exposing the indecent side of this enterprise."[71] Addressing the "absurdity" of Zavattini's realism, he observes pithily: "If it is a murder, by the assassin himself, barring the victim."[72] Literal recreation represents an ontological impossibility; the rift between a verisimilar order (which the film's narrative too studiously respects) and reenactment is absolute.

Elsewhere, Bazin uses the same example to alert us to the link, implicit throughout Zavattini's rhetoric, between acting one's own story and atonement, between reenactment and culpability: "We know that the assassin doesn't look necessarily like a criminal. Necessarily we have to note that reality goes here beyond all the cautions of art. Not because the witnessing in its brutal reality renders art derisory, but on the contrary because being given this scenario (real or not) no interpretation and no mise-en-scène could better show its value."[73] The fact that this kind of story (even if fictionalized) can only be delivered by literal reenactment underscores the interdependence of the body's presence and particular kinds of model narrative.

A surrogate cannot make atonement. And yet, even while praising Zavattini and Maselli's episode above the other parts of *Love in the City*, Bazin cannot refrain from posing a final question: "would he have succeeded by taking as his hero not the victim but the seducer?"[74] The possibility of such a replacement bears on the core issue of substitutability (actor for person) that has concerned us thus far. Turning from matters of verisimilitude to morality, Bazin identifies the troubling aspect of Zavattini's notion of reenactment. When Zavattini arrogates both the roles of narrator and father confessor to himself, when he proposes his stalking camera theory with its disturbing connotations of detective work and misconduct, he fashions a scenario that justifies his intervention and the relevance of his methods: "making public" presupposes a social reality in need of redemption. And yet, when he recasts victims of society replaying their ordeals and privileges the pain of the poor as a means of promoting social awareness, he implicitly condones a sacrificial order.[75] The value of Caterina's literal performance in this ritual order attains its general applicability as an echo of Christ's martyrdom. The Christian roots of Zavattini's neorealism are evident not only in his general pronouncements of revelation through confession (adumbrated in reenactment),[76] but also in the restaging of martyrdom. Or should we say instead restaging *as* martyrdom?

For Zavattini, the importance of literal performance derives from combining dramatic performance with the kind of action that, he believes, should replace preaching or speaking to others. "Christ succeeds not because of the Gospel, but because he took on his back the problems of all." [77] As Prandi points out, Zavattini's understanding of being Christian for Zavattini has aspects of a "work in progress"; at the same time, he doubts whether immediate intervention "*during* an action would have been possible with the cinematographic medium."[78] Film reenactment forms a bridge between the immediacy of real action and cinema, for it allows Caterina to relive the "*during*" of Christian acts and of Zavattini's ethical vision. Barthélemy Amengual admires this slippage, the director acting through the performer. Noting how *The Story of Caterina* repeats gestures made by characters in other films by Zavattini, he asks: "is there a greater success than this identification, this communion with one's neighbour, than this *you* relived as *I*?"[79]

And indeed, Zavattini fits literal reenactment's narrative and formal strategy to an established tradition, the matrix of examples. *Vestigia imitando*, to follow in one's footsteps, defines the medieval exemplum, the short narrative modeled on Christ's life that was offered in sermons as a guide to proper behavior.[80] With its emphasis on humble walking without repose and echoes of redemption, *The Story of Caterina* retraces a familiar course of suffering, erring, and salvation.

We may ask why Zavattini may still need, in this circular exemplary schema, an actual individual, an existing name, for his enlightenment program. Let us take the issue of the named individual deemed so essential in this cinematic realism. The hero's name performs a key role in the rhetorical design of exemplary narratives.[81] Describing the reliance in Renaissance literature on a hero's name as a shortcut to a verb phrase summing up a number of valued deeds, Timothy Hampton is keenly aware of the selection and reduction of historical facts involved; as John Lyons notes, any example that is not frankly fictional needs to undergo "corrections" to fit proper ideological models.[82] The example must be structurally subordinated to a general principle or maxim, which it confirms or authorizes. Without serving the purpose of making a moral point, no exemplary narrative can exist. In order to install a person or story as precedent or model, one needs to assert her story's ideological credentials, its timeless serviceability both to the past that anchors it and the present it addresses. In addition, its authenticity is constantly perverted by its instrumentality—an original that has to conform to and submit to replication.

This dynamic applies to reenactment in its purposeful representation of an original event and protagonist. First, Caterina needs to assert her singularity in order to claim the mantle of a new hero of everyday life in Zavattini's discourse. Her ultimate mission, her primary role as an anonymous yet named entity, is to bolster his arguments against the illusions of fictional and mythical heroes. "Caterina Rigoglioso's name and last name" is Zavattini's shortcut phrase to promote a new social cinema that skirts the generality of fiction, founding an approach redirected to the everyday. As a rhetorical gambit, then, "Caterina" works.

On the other hand, this identity and "singularity" can only hold inasmuch as she reenacts her deeds and replays her "verbal phrase" in performance. When she does so, however, the discrepancy between original and copy, between authentic being and acting, is heightened. This visible mismatch, or representational difference, is essential, in reenactment's construction of cinematic exemplarity for it potentially makes the character generalizable.

When asked whether the story could possibly gain in social breadth if an actress had played Caterina's role, Zavattini did not answer in full. He stated that he favored any film, with actors or not, which had strong moral purpose; he found fault with those who would prefer using their old methods. He also stated that this was the last step in a natural progression giving greater authority to the neorealist actor.[83]

At least in terms of appearances, the actual person advances the agenda of the nonactor taken off the streets. Their essential distinction—that one retraces her past, the other follows a fictional script—matters only once the film is framed as reenactment. Nevertheless, the question lies in the collective import of the singularity that reenactment emphatically promotes. For Pascal Bonitzer, neorealism's main political shortcoming is its inherent incapacity to leave the realm of the individual.[84] To grasp the import of Caterina's singularity in a program that displays both generic humanism and hints of allegiance to a materialist and class-bound perspective, we have to replace our subject and protagonist with the single most frequently mentioned reference besides Caterina herself: shoes. Trailing after Zavattini's various shoe references allows us to link his shadowing aesthetics to cinema's unique footprint, retraced by Caterina herself.

FOOTPRINTS: STREETWALKERS AND MAGGIORANI'S BACK

The first segment of *Love in the City*, Carlo Lizzani's *Love for Pay*, starts with a stunningly fluid series of tracking shots from the perspective of men driving and looking for company. Mario Nascimbene's ballad-like score drives a dance of strolls and glances. For a long stretch of the road, the camera fastens on one particular woman as she gazes back. The camera dollies past her to frame another group of walkers. The narrator mentions that Yolanda has agreed to speak. A pause in the music and in the tracking shot "invites her to dance"; she responds by walking around her friends to address the camera. From afar, another woman is seen hurrying through a tunnel. The narrator states that "at times it is hard to individuate them. . . . Valli, for instance, looks just like anyone who is late from work coming home." And yet, in this script cosigned by Zavattini, Valli has a more dramatic role to play. Viewers are told that she is one of the oldest streetwalkers, known as the 'one who wanders'" (Fig. 2.10). Fulfilling the neorealist mandate to observe life at its most basic, lowly, and constitutive level, the filmmaker asks her a single, peculiar question: "How many pairs of shoes do you go through each year?" "Twenty," she says. "Of what kind, the closed type or sandals?" "Closed . . ."[85] She hears a police car approaching and hastily turns away, like a Cinderella whose magic spell has expired, to flee the night raids and the camera.

If walking expresses the characters' daily and nightly plight, shoes are a tangible measure, both material and symbolic, of this pathos. Shoes illustrate how revealing the minor and banal can be; the image combines Zavattini's dual concern with retracing the steps of his subjects and analyzing the material underpinning of their lives. In "Some Ideas on the Cinema," he expounds on his obsessive desire to close the "gap between life and what is on the screen" through a thorough analysis and breakdown of a given fact:

> A woman goes to a shop to buy a pair of shoes. The shoes cost 7,000 lire. The woman tries to bargain. The scene lasts perhaps two minutes. I must make a two-hour film . . . . I analyze the fact in its constitutive elements, in all of its "before" and its "after," its contemporaneous aspects. . . . What is her son doing at the same moment? What are people doing in India that could have some relation to this fact of the shoes? . . . . How hard did she work for [her 7,000 lire], what do they represent for her? And the bargaining shopkeeper, who is he? What interests are they defending as they bargain? The shopkeeper also has two sons who eat and speak: do you want to know what they are saying? Here they are in front of you.[86]

Figure 2.10: Valli, "the one who wanders" (Carlo Lizanni, *Love for Pay*, episode in *L'Amore in Cittá*, 1953).

Comprehensive treatment leaving no "empty spaces between things, facts and people" would tie the local to the international—the personal to the universal—since no fact, however irrelevant it may seem, exists independently. One would simply need to look at reality closely in order to excavate it.[87] Justifying his "excessive preoccupation with particulars," which risks "deforming reality," Zavattini sets out to "feel the non-hierarchy of facts": "I look at the small facts and find in them everything."[88] This same analytical, nonhierarchical attention is essential to the mise-en-scène of Caterina's or the streetwalkers' stories; indeed, Zavattini, Lizzani, and others conducted extensive research before filming.[89] Two categories of analysis are at work: first, decoupage, which aims at a synthetic reconstruction of selected gestures, inflections, places, and actions; and second, a materialist perspective on patterns of production, consumption, and exploitation (the shop owner's sons and their shoes, the shoes and their makers, sellers, etc.). We see this preoccupation in Zavattini's Marxist-inflected synecdoche of privilege: "In the novel protagonists were heroes: [his] shoes were special shoes. We instead look to find the common aspects of our characters. In my film, in your shoes, we find the same elements, the same human hard work."[90]

If spatial and temporal leaps let Zavattini imagine a broader socioeconomic picture, in practice a real difficulty arises from leaving the more pedestrian contiguity of footstep tracking. A misconceived loyalty to the concrete and its literal retracing leads the camera to fasten on the subject. Hence, the lenses of Zavattini's shadowing, candid camera poetics are mostly trained on a character's back.

Zavattini's temptation to amplify the scope of this *pedinamento* is undeniable. In his 1950 argument *Tu, Maggiorani*, a film never made about the job crisis of Lamberto Maggiorani, the actor of *Bicycle Thieves*, Zavattini cannot refrain from projecting on this iconic figure literal and fictional plots of unemployment:

> And Maggiorani walks, walks through the streets of Rome. . . . His steps shuffled and tired like those of a thousand people. On his *back* are all the characters who in the postwar invoked the help of men, the billposter Antonio, the priest of *Rome, Open City*, the children of *Shoeshine*, the boy of *Germany Year Zero* and crowds, crowds that cry in the theaters, crowds that applaud in a fraternal impulse fictive characters and do nothing for a real one.[91]

In this vision, Maggiorani's back becomes a screen for characters and spectators to commune. Zavattini embeds a warning in this condensation of cinema and life, fictional and real characters: if identification occurs, action should ensue "for the real Maggiorani." There is another practical lesson, too: the need to follow this back and magnify its significance, while, at the same time, immersing oneself to become part of this crowd, joining in with the people as they leave the soccer match en masse.

Zavattini's emphasis on literal reenactment points to a transformative dimension located in happenings, the embodied bridging of acting and act. From the outset, the spectator must understand that "in front of him" there is "a real character," which should "put him in a state of mind that changes and even revolutionizes the very idea of spectacle."[92] Participants in a film of this kind are called to "collaborate with their humble presence to the recognition of truth." Actors "are over for this kind of cinema"; instead, acting is envisioned as a routine exercise in self-knowledge.[93] Cinema is reinstalled into the social body, a means for understanding common humanity. As Maurizio Grande puts it sharply, "reenactment must produce a form of communion"—a repetition that distances but also reanimates.[94] Both the nonprofessional actor and one who relives his experience for the camera do so primarily to interpret their roles in society. The actor who replicates his own experience passes from the state of protagonist to that of "officiant."[95] This contagious notion of performance as ritual repetition allows protagonist and audience to share in a common mass of humanity.

The anonymous mass, the everyman, may be the most extreme expression of everyone acting in his or her own name. Retracing the streetwalkers' steps in Lizzani's *Love for Pay*, slowly tracking Caterina's wanderings, and intently following Lamberto Maggiorani's back as he merges into the crowd holding his son's hand, Zavattini's painstakingly descriptive, stalking cinema unfolds a poetics that links, through a series of indexical and symbolic slippages, spectator to actor and actor to human being.

ATTEMPTED SUICIDE: ANTONIONI'S SINGULARITIES

Attempted Suicides, Antonioni's contribution to *Love in the City*, starts ominously. Eerily reminiscent of a police line-up scene, a group of men and women enter and take positions against a large white screen on a bare sound stage.[96] A narrator announces that they have agreed to talk on camera about their failed suicides. A sequence of fixed shots separates them in clusters of two or three and choreographs missed connections. One of the women turns to glance at another slightly behind her, meets a harsh gaze, and turns back around. In these silent formations with empty backdrops, we recognize Antonioni's signature: static group portraits that demonstrate the loss of any sense of connection or community (Fig. 2.11). Five women are heard, one at a time, reporting what led them to attempt suicide and how they feel about it now. They reenact parts of the story. We hear two different male voices—one, the speaker's commentaries at the start and end of each vignette; the other, interrogating the women. Even before we've heard the "culprits," we know they've been indicted and their case is closed.

Given obvious limits of literal repetition, suicide is, admittedly, a curious candidate for reenactment. From the very start, the topic and cinematic approach pose acute questions about representation and repetition. An attempted suicide can be successfully repeated only because it failed. And yet in reenacting it, the person

Figure 2.11: A group of people who attempted suicide gather in sound studio (Antonioni, *Attempted Suicides* episode in *L'Amore in Città*, 1953).

confesses a desire to call attention to herself not once but twice: in reality and on camera. The immediate consequence of such exhibitionism is that, besides compromising the existential authenticity of the gesture, it may implicate the filmmaker in making these stories public. Antonioni's filmic response to this quandary is my subject here.

Attempted Suicides is often dismissed as a minor or failed experiment,[97] and the only interest it holds seems to be the way it prefigures later works by Antonioni.[98] Two of his next films portray the gesture with clinical distance, leaving motivations and consequences unresolved. In *Le Amiche* (*The Girlfriends*, 1955), the main character, Clelia, finds out that a woman she does not know has tried to kill herself in a room beside hers. As the narrative proceeds, interest in the failed suicide attempt dissipates—until, at the end, the woman tries again and succeeds. Significantly, Aldo's suicide at the end of *Il Grido* (*The Cry*, 1957) also represents an enigma. He comes back to his old town and climbs a silo; when Irma, his ex-companion, calls out for him, he looks down, wavers, and falls. The question of whether Aldo's fall is willed or a sudden fit of vertigo that fatefully decides his momentary suspension between agent and object reflects suicide's complicated status in the filmmaker's aesthetics.

The radically solitary nature of a suicide suits it ideally for Antonioni's exploration of unexplained gestures, oblique depiction of social malaise, and attention to the uncanny border between inert and live matter, object and subject. In his well-known text, "The Event and the Image," Antonioni discusses the secret of his aesthetics, describing the particular atmosphere prior, during, and around the discovery of a dead body at the beach in Nice:

> The sky is white, the sea-front deserted; the sea cold and empty, the hotels white and half-shuttered. On one of the white seats of the Promenade des Anglais the bathing attendant is seated, a [black man] in a white singlet.... The sun labors to emerge through a fine layer of mist, the same as everyday. There is nobody on the beach except a single bather floating inert a few yards from the shore.... A glance is enough to tell that the bather is dead.

"Suppose," he says, "one had constructed a bit of film based on this event and on this state of mind."

> I would . . . remove the actual event from the scene, and leave only the image described in the first four lines . . . the event here adds nothing, it is superfluous.... The dead man acted as a distraction to a state of tension. But the true emptiness, the malaise, the anxiety, the nausea, the atrophy of all normal feelings and desires, the fear, the anger—all these I felt when coming out of the Negresco. I found myself in that whiteness, in that nothingness which took shape around a black point.[99]

Noting the strict dependence of Antonioni's scenarios on this "black point," we may ask what would happen if we substitute another structuring absence—an actual suicide attempt—for the dead body. How does the filmmaker deal with the reconstruction process, as he elicits and stages the narratives on the suicides' motives and consequences?

The question of after-effects is central in Antonioni's aesthetics. Both in the narrative's progression and within a shot Antonioni veers away from the "black point," the obvious object of interest or plot, and attends to its emotional reverberations instead. Antonioni's films—"detective films in reverse," as Guido Fink puts it— revolve around a mystery (such as Anna's vanishing in *L'Avventura*, 1960), which itself disappears, leaving behind diffuse malaise.[100] The most striking moments occur when the camera simply follows an actor—when, "having just enacted an intensely dramatic scene, [the character is] left alone by himself to face the aftereffects of that particular scene and its traumatic moments."[101] In his fiction films, Antonioni inflects neutral surfaces with drama; his emphasis on documenting objects and people releases the narrative from overly rigid causality. Perceptively characterizing this trait as the "documentarism" that informs Italian neorealism, Rohdie likens the filmmaker's treatment of events to Rossellini's gradual, phenomenal apprehension of his narrative material: "The narrative 'waits' but it is not clear what for precisely until the event happens."[102] Tellingly, the sequences at issue are the suicides of Edmund in *Germany Year Zero* (Rossellini, 1948) and Aldo in *Il Grido*: no particular motivation is given; the events are "observed and then recorded but not anticipated by the narrator. The logic of the acts is clear, but only afterwards; before there had been other possibilities, only one of which was the death/suicide."[103]

Attempted Suicides poses a different challenge than either Antonioni's fiction features or his earlier short documentaries. Already in his first short, *Gente del Po* (*People of the Po Valley*, 1947), Antonioni resists the pressures and expectations of adhering to documentary filmmaking or location shooting. As Noa Steimatsky points out in her reading of Antonioni's formative documentary and modernist aesthetics, the film's searching, lyrical depiction of the Po River preserves the tension of a narrativized landscape, an objectified characterization that avoids portraying Italian regionalism and conforms neither to a conservative fascist vision nor to neorealist populism.[104]

The actual theme of *Attempted Suicides* is the after-effect of a traumatic moment. For all that, its selective representation steers clear of unpredictable, wandering vision: the discoveries held in the interstices of object and person, landscape and drama. The structural simplicity of the film's verité interviews intercut with illustrative restaging in fact proves as rigorous as a judicial inquiry. I discuss here the few but significant moments in which the rhetorical pressures of an investigative exposé and a preestablished morality are crossed by the probing inconclusiveness of Antonioni's images.

The first script draft of *Attempted Suicides*, for a film titled *Sentimental Reasons*, displays a more ambitious social exposé, with more than double (eleven) the final number of stories.[105] The film concerns, among others, Enrico Pelliccia, twenty-eight years old, who works in a fabric store and swallows liquid insecticide because his ex-wife warns his new girlfriend against him; Luciano La Porta, who poisons himself because his mother won't let him marry the girl he loves; and Maria Lucioli, who takes sleeping pills because her boyfriend did not want to see her.

The stories impart such a level of social and psychological specificity that it is clear they were clearly filmed and edited out in the final version.[106] Paolo Pacetti, who steals his mother's medications, is referred to by the narrator as a typical "postwar neurotic." His nervous tics illustrate his lack of emotional stability. The sentimental fantasies accompanying his pointless attempts to establish physical contact with women sketch an intensely troubled character. Asked if he regrets his suicide attempt, he states that it seemed inevitable at the time. "Now all is better"; he is "finally" getting married. Nella Bertuccioni's attempted suicide involves swallowing pills, coming to die at her friend's squalid hut, falling down, being robbed, losing her baby, and then marrying another man who is now in prison.

If the script presents a collective portrait of squalor, stunted hopes, and despair, the film hews to the act itself, offering a dry record of the reasons and thoughts that precede and follow the suicide attempts. Few scenes locate the characters socially. In one of the longer vignettes, the main character, Maria Nobili, exits a wool factory with a coworker. Standing at a dirt road crossing, with the housing project where she and the other characters grew up (and still live) in the background, they meet to confirm that Nobili's lover will indeed stay with his wife. The story, which could inspire a melodrama, is conveyed in a sparse and matter-of-fact way. The fraught emotional atmosphere we associate with Antonioni's films from the 1960s is rendered as a direct effect of a belated confrontation between ex-lovers replicating their official breakup in front of the wife, and the camera. Because this moment is even more difficult to represent than the suicide attempt, it gets center stage: the protagonists' paradoxical isolation when together. Reenactment's distancing effects are fully operative: the characters' stiffness actualizes the drama and awkwardness of the situation. Now, each of the three lives in a different apartment block, and Nobili still sees her ex-lover.

The main act, which is elided,[107] will guide us in understanding Antonioni's take on suicide and its aftermath. The script describes Rosana Carta's extreme destitution in detail: her job in a junkyard sorting glass and life in a house without electricity. The sequence with Rosana conveys this brutal reality with a simple pan over a few poorly built houses close to the city's barren outskirts. A neighbor opens the door to reveal her sole possession: a doll sitting on a bed. The suicide attempt itself is represented in two shots and an ellipsis: she sits on a park bench waiting. The narrator describes her state leading to the attempt. She crosses the street, stops by the curb, looks left, and then plunges off-frame. A cut coincides with the sound of a car break; after that, we see Rosanna against the white studio screen, clutching her handbag, telling about her ex-lover's jealousy and her refusal to accept the money offered by the car driver, even though she needed it badly.

In yet another sequence included in the film, Lilia Nardi, a beautiful blond, is seen leaving an apartment building by the Tiber. She leans by the parapet and then proceeds to the next riverbank. As she descends the steps, she comments in voice-over that a boy she encountered had fled when he saw her crying. As the tale's narrative and her actor move toward the climax and final location, she stops to address the camera, points to the river, and says, "That's where I did it" (Fig. 2.12). Significantly, this abrupt shift from representation to presentation, from third-person point of view to first-person direct address, coincides with the problematic repetition of her

Figure 2.12: Lilia Nardi shows where she tried to drown herself (Antonioni, *Attempted Suicides* in *L'Amore in Cittá*, 1953).

actions. She replies to the director's questions: "Did you throw yourself in?" "No, I waded in slowly, then with my foot pushed myself in and was carried away." At this point, the camera takes over the floating body's perspective. "I bumped against that column, . . . was dragged down by a current. . . . I heard voices yelling confusedly around me." For more than a minute, abstracted shots of the river's troubled waters stand for the last moments of consciousness. And yet this cannot simply be seen as an experiential, subjective representation, for the river sequence illustrates a detached, after-the-fact commentary. Its surrogate nature is manifest in its imbalanced length: the river shots stand in for an impossible representation of dying. Overly long, these shots become as opaque as the actions of Antonioni's fictional characters.

In Donatella Marrosu's story, a simple stroke dramatizes the shift from representation to direct address: a close-up intercut with the event's reenactment. Marrosu's vignette stands out for the studied ease of her performance. The narrator introduces her as a typical product of the times, living a nihilist existence. She is shown alone in a bar in the middle of the afternoon, smoking, picking music in a jukebox, flirting, dancing. Leaving a restaurant tab unpaid and donning dark glasses, she wanders the streets, trying to look like a movie star. Back in her studio flat in a "bohemian neighborhood," she stares at the mirrored door of her armoire before going through the motions of slitting her wrist in a medium shot. Then, in an ostensive gesture, the young woman turns her wrist to the camera. A close-up of her arm shows the stitch marks of the actual suicide attempt. Doubling the denotative aspect of a film shot, the close-up states: "Here is the representation of a suicide attempt." The shot encapsulates the limits of reenactment: the blade cannot trace the same path twice without literally producing a wound.

Reclining on her bed, Marrosu addresses the camera directly. A cut in the action shows her wrist still turning from its display position and holding the blade; she tells what happened next (Figs. 2.13a–g). Asked by the off-screen narrator why she

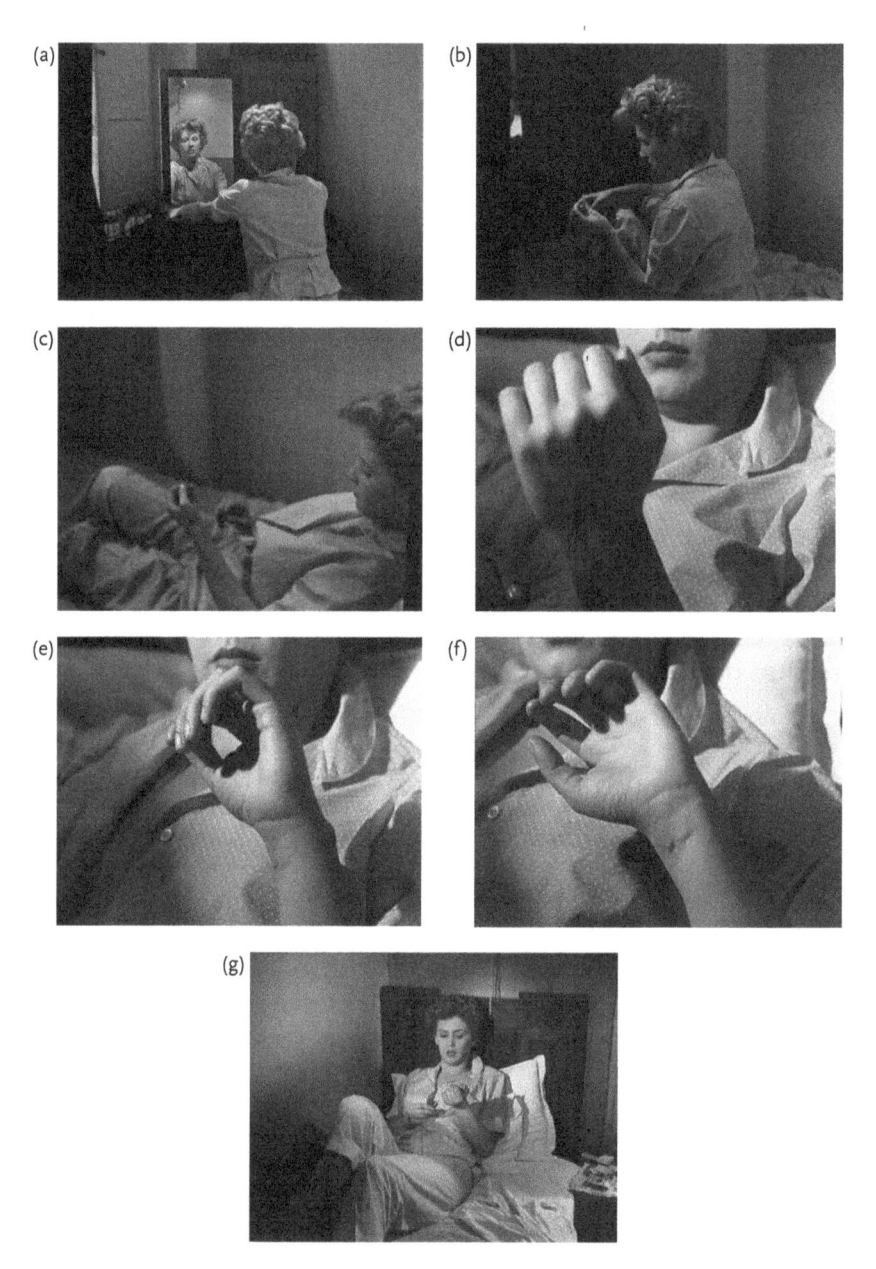

Figures 2.13a–g: Donatela Marrosu's reenacted attempted suicide sequence (Antonioni, *Attempted Suicides* in *L'Amore in Città*, 1953).

[62] *In Person*

has agreed to reenact this event, she replies: "the feeling of being more open about it . . . a second chance." Finally, Marrosu says that "it may be too late, but the one thing I want to do is to be an actress, not through a beauty contest but seriously, to study . . . to enter the academy" (Fig. 2.14).

The vertiginous slippage of representational registers in this sequence makes the film's therapeutic project explicit. The reenactment of past behavior is interrupted suddenly. Instead of a risky acting-out, the film proposes a "talking cure." Freud, in addition to Breuer, attributed a cathartic force to verbal expression, declaring that "language serves as a substitute for action . . . by its help an affect can be 'abreacted' almost as effectively . . . speaking is itself an adequate reflex, when for instance, it is a lamentation or giving utterance to a tormenting secret, e.g. a confession."[108] Substituting repetition for verbal enunciation, this scene is offered as proof of reenactment's efficacy. The foolishness of repeating such a gesture is noted and reflective talk substitutes for action. The impossibility of literal repetition leads to safe and even creative forms of representation: to tell a story or to become an actress.

This sincere avowal compromises the authenticity fund tapped by reenactment and the verité interviews. Acting constitutes the aporia of reenactment, and in this case the theatricality of feigned suicides and their replay is doubly exposed. As an exhibitionist spectacle lacking performative closure, the sole evidence of good conscience in a suicide attempt is the performer's demise. For Antonioni, attempted suicide suggests a desire for effect rather than substance, especially if framed by feminine despair. Defending the film from Guido Aristarco's charges of pretentiousness, he explains his shock at the pleasure his subjects took being in the limelight: "They were exaggerating on account of who-knows-what form of vanity or masochism.

Figure 2.14: Marrosu in Antonioni's *Attempted Suicide:* "I want to be an actress . . ."

They did not regret the action, to the point of rephrasing the wish to do it again."[109] At the risk of being "unpopular," he goes on to say that as soon as he understood such attempts as the product of an "exhibitionist complex," they no longer "distressed" him.[110] But far from accepting this relish in display, Antonioni enlists the spectator's distrust from his very first remark: "One may ask why these people have decided to come forth and make their stories public." In turn, we may ask the same of Antonioni, who seems to have multiple uses for such existential enactments. Despite—indeed, because of—their "exhibitionist complex," attempted suicides play a crucial role in the filmmaker's critique of inauthenticity afflicting modern relationships.[111]

In one of the few appreciative readings of the film, Sam Rohdie suggests that *Attempted Suicides* provides a laboratory of sorts for the many recurring failed or fake suicides that appear in Antonioni after 1953—Gianni's overdose in *The Lady Without Camelias* (1953), Rosetta in *The Girlfriends* (1955), up to Locke's switching identities with the dead Robertson in *The Passenger* (1975)—a way of killing oneself but remaining alive; the same holds for Anna's disappearance, possibly a feigned suicide, and Giuliana's suicide attempts in *Red Desert* (1964). Rohdie emphasizes the imaginative exercise involved in a feigned suicide: "to stage [one's] death, to act it out; relating the suicide turns the action into a pretext for a story, a self-representation imagining yourself as other and . . . as no longer existing."[112]

The parallels between suicide and self-performance place issues of agency and authenticity at the center of the film. As Antonioni deals with actors reliving or recounting a radical gesture of self-annihilation, it becomes urgent to precisely assign the film's moral and aesthetic agency and voice. Antonioni's efforts to elicit (and control) the unpredictability of self-representation suggests that imaginary dramas and fictional scenarios risk erupting into the real.[113]

Antonioni addressed this challenge differently on-screen and in person. Addressing Aristarco, a leftist critic whom he knows to be resistant to individual portraits, Antonioni defends his emphasis on particular, psychological causes: "Those were cases that had to do with psychology, not morality."[114] He carefully weighs these two terms, acknowledging the theme's challenge:

> I cannot bring myself to share the opinion that if someone kills himself it is to some extent everyone's fault. Suicide is such an enigmatic gesture. . . . It is true that suicide has a moral significance and that psychology cannot ignore morals, but it is also true that morality cannot ignore the teachings of psychology. Which also means that every act of suicide has its story. The commander who goes down with his ship comes to be considered a hero. We may like or dislike heroes, and yet society honors them and worships their memory. The Church itself grants its sacraments to a suicide affected by madness. This demonstrates that it is not possible to leave special causes aside and the special is the proper domain of psychology.[115]

When faced with this existential node, Antonioni is certainly not alone in trying to weigh social morality against individual motives. In his canonical study of the subject, after defining suicide as "every case of death which results directly or indirectly from a positive or negative act carried out by the victim himself, knowing that it will produce this result," Emile Durkheim became aware that his sociological perspective may be inadequate: "since suicide is an individual act which affects only the individual and would seem to depend exclusively on individual factors it must therefore belong to the field of psychology. Surely one ordinarily explains the suicide's decision in terms of his temperament, character, and biographical events?"[116]

Suicides raise in exemplary fashion the questions of causality and motivation at the center of Antonioni's radical decision to rethink social effects through symptomatic transformations in individual psychology and morality. The feigned or failed suicides recurring throughout Antonioni's films have additional impact inasmuch as they underscore the inauthentic nature of modern life through this extreme existential statement, enacted perhaps quite simply as a theatrical coup.[117] His answer to the individual or sociopolitical frame of suicides is therefore far from straightforward. Still, this is the most pressing issue in a film so obviously framed as a social investigation.

In the early 1950s, when he started making features about a morally empty bourgeoisie, Antonioni's position within an established strand of neorealist engagement stood in question.[118] He frequently had to answer for his apparent detachment from social problems[119] and justify the absence of pathos in his films, their modernist starkness. These stories refocus moral reactions, enhancing their ambiguity; in the case of accomplished suicides, they allow for contradictory readings. If the death of Rosetta in *The Girlfriends* was "certainly a suicide" and Aldo's was "an accident perhaps," "often one spoke of the first as a sacrifice or collective crime and of suicide and even execution in the second case."[120] This split reception, tending to blame no one or indict an entire social class, testifies to Antonioni's aesthetic resistance to represent direct social indictment. Citing the fact that Aldo's suicide takes place on the day of a demonstration against a NATO base, P. Adams Sitney remarks that although the filmmaker's fixation on suicides "is fundamentally existential . . . it often has political overtones. Within the repeated dissection of affluent vacuity, suicide becomes a protest against the national obsession with consumption and the futility of organized efforts at reform."[121] Such an interpretation walks a fine line in trying to contextualize and explain Antonioni's deliberately opaque representation of individual motives.

In *Love in the City*'s credits, *Attempted Suicides* is called an "inquiry." Accordingly, and because it features interviews and operates in different documentary mode than Antonioni's early lyrical shorts *Gente del Po* and *Netteza Urbana*, the film proceeds as if it stood under neorealist probation. *Attempted Suicides* film has to prove that focusing on individual voices and reasons—Antonioni has often been faulted for being overly indulgent and subjective—is centrally useful. The film also needs to stand on its own, apart from the compromised exhibitionism implicit in the stories told and reenacted by the women.

The film achieves complexity by orchestrating the truth of these stories while maintaining the authenticity and integrity of each of the women's voices. Antonioni's decision to split the narrative between subjective account, direct camera address, and third-person reenactment inserts a critical perspective in the gap between an act and its screened representation. The shifts between subjective and objective representation evident in Nardi's and Marrosu's vignettes—the ways the characters "confess" or the narrator preaches—shape how the director apportions responsibility for these radical actions.

The passage from enactment to verbal description or confession heralds Antonioni's move toward a different register for his films and realist cinema in general. Individual accounts always do more than illustrate a general condition; here, of course, the women provide reasons for their actions. Conversely, as if to compensate for its focus on "special causes," the film strains to channel the representation of one's consciousness for the public good. "They've agreed to come to our studio only because they felt that this moment of sincerity, this examination through another's gaze of the sole irreparable act in a man's life, would be useful for him and for others," remarks the narrator. The narration works as a censure, while the women's confessing performances serve as negative exempla.

Antonioni puts his subjects "on trial" precisely for coming forth with their stories. The narrator's patronizing commentary and questions underscore the futility of such drastic gestures. "Don't you think you're exaggerating?" asks Antonioni when Marrosu says it may be too late to study acting; addressing a cabaret dancer who tried to kill herself, he asks, "What about your children?" A distanced, clinical perspective is meant to buffer the obvious pathos of such stories, to qualify the relish with which they are told.[122]

By enlisting (and containing) excessively singular bodies and voices, *The Story of Caterina* and *Attempted Suicides* introduce in 1953 key issues facing realist representation, issues that become, interestingly enough, evident in cinema verité practice and in the consciousness-raising documentaries of the 1970s. In its intense focus on the private sphere, Antonioni's segment in *Love in the City* anticipates cinema verité's approach to confessionals and testimony. As Bill Nichols has suggested in "The Voice of Documentary," unframed statements can lead to a loss of context, and editorial comments often try to affirm the statements' collective resonance. The closing commentary of *Attempted Suicides* fulfills this cautionary dimension, returning one's life as a fully amended property. The segment concludes by returning to the film studio.[123] The group of men and women once physically alienated from each other wander out, chatting with each other against the white studio background; the scene represents visually the effects of "making public" through reenactment: recognizing common interests, sharing in each other's problems.

This before-and-after figuration of social alienation/integration drives home one of the film's lessons. More graphically, Marrosu's scar (and in different ways the river shot, or the elided car accident) establishes the limits of reenactment and defines the film's didactic mission. This corporeal impasse amounts to cross-checking realism with reality: reenactment cannot reverse time. The pedagogic potential of reenactment depends precisely on such irreversibility. That one cannot change the past but can merely, and barely reproduce its semblance, is the implicit drama of reenactment, as well as its explicit working morale.

Attempted Suicides stands alone in Antonioni's oeuvre inasmuch as it tidily distinguishes between correct and suspect behavior, that is, between the filmmaker's moral righteousness and his characters' reasoning.[124] This stark juxtaposition of personal motivation and accusatory interrogation reveals the costs of reconstructing real, inauthentic acts. A testimony to Antonioni's aesthetic integrity, the film's dry exposé trial is also the clearest proof of the filmmaker's conflicted implication, his investment even, in staging feigned disappearances.[125]

ANONYMOUS STARS: DONATELLA MARROSU AND ANNA MAGNANI

Donatella Marrosu, the young, pretty, unknown woman who reenacts trying to kill herself in Antonioni's *Attempted Suicides*, had appeared very briefly in two previous films: as an extra in the Italian episode of *I Vinti* (*The Vanquished*, Antonioni, 1952), and in a small part as sister Guilhemina in *La Grande Renuncia* (*The Great Renunciation*, Aldo Vergano, 1951).[126] Strikingly, her candid statement in the film that "what she would like, is to study acting, but seriously, not in one of those beauty contests, but going to the Academy," is repeated in the scene of her casting test in Alfredo Guarini's short *Contest: 4 Actresses and 1 Hope*—part of *We, the Women* (*Siamo Donne*), another Zavattini production of 1953. In Guarini's prologue, she also acts as a young woman who wishes she could become an actor (Figs. 2.15–2.17). The replication of the specific role of an aspiring actress in two films that allegedly cast nonactors playing themselves either interferes with and qualifies the films'

Figure 2.15: Donatella Marrosu in line to compete for a role in Alfredo Guarini, *Contest: 4 Actresses and 1 Hope* in omnibus film *Siamo Donne* (*We the Women*, 1953).

Figure 2.16: Marrosu, screen test 1 (Guarini, *Contest: 4 Actresses and 1 Hope*, 1953).

Figure 2.17: Marrosu screen test 2 (*Contest: 4 Actresses and 1 Hope*, 1953).

advertised quest for authenticity, or it substantiates Marrosu's vocation through her drive to get another part. In any case, her recognizable presence amounts to an ironic refrain on the issue of anonymity. As a minor star in Antonioni's film on anonymous suicide attempts who barely makes it to the second casting cut (as an extra, at that) in Guarini's narrative, Marrosu's appearance denotes the impossibility of a cinema devoid of specularization. Her acting history over these two years also changes the meaning of the scar that *Attempted Suicides* shows in close-up. A thick sign of the limits of reenactment, the scar becomes a badge of singular anonymity as well, allowing Marrosu, whom Antonioni knew as an aspiring actress, to participate in *Attempted Suicides* among other unknown women who have also tried to kill themselves. The display of her scar is therefore charged with blotting out, for the sake of this appearance, her incipiently recognizable face.

Marrosu's presence is not the sole link between *Love in the City* and *We, the Women*. Bookending the heyday of nonactors in Italian cinema, each film points to the problem of having a populist and popular cinema without stars. The need to compete with Hollywood and international co-productions pressured Italian cinema toward other models. Discussing Sophia Loren as representative of launching "new 'shapely stars' careers" (the *maggiorate*) through beauty contests, Pauline Small observes that, even though "these were not, strictly speaking, casting opportunities," the composition of the 1946 jury—including Visconti, the actress Isa Miranda, and several scriptwriters, including Zavattini—"suggests a parallel with talent scouting."[127] While casting nonprofessional actors represents common practice in postwar cinema, and "the motor of an affirmed poetic" at the start of the 1950s, the public was clearly in need, as Gian Piero Brunetta suggests, of "reference points for the 'transference of a collective imaginary.'" In the early fifties, creating a star system apart from the American one instantiated a "progressive conquest of a lost public" remaking its "social composition."[128]

Lacking in popular appeal, some of the more interesting Italian filmmakers instead started telling stories about the allure of stars; various critics have detected, between 1949 and 1953, a metacinematic reflection on the cinema world's "dream and the illusions of this dream."[129] Films such as Visconti's *Bellissima* (1951), based on an idea by Zavattini, Fellini's *Lo sceicco bianco* (*The White Sheik*, 1952), written by Antonioni, Antonioni's own *La signora senza camelie* (*The Lady Without Camelias*, 1953), Luigi Comencini's *La valigia dei sogni* (*The Suitcase of Dreams*, 1953), and Dino Risi's *Il viale della speranza* (*The Avenue of Hope*, 1953) reflect not only on cinema but also on other media spectacles: the worlds of music, variety shows, radio, and beauty contests. A need to take stock of the neorealist legacy prompted this reflexive turn internally.[130]

We, the Women presents five takes on the personal realities of being a star. Four Italian divas—Alida Valli, Ingrid Bergman, Isa Miranda, and Anna Magnani—act out private inclinations or thoughts generally deemed unbecoming for a star. The production company, Titanus Studio, initially planned to call the film *Five Confessions*, then *True*; it was meant to fund the construction of a "retirement home for the Italian cinema Artists." *Contest: 4 Actresses and 1 Hope*, as the first episode in *We, the Women*, entertains a metacinematic relation with the individuated narratives it borders. This prologue speaks the very desire that fuels a star's power, the undeniable recognition factor (Fig. 2.18). In presenting anonymous women vying for a chance at stardom, who line up only to be eliminated, the film suggests an analogy with unemployment lines; fittingly, the dialogue openly concerns the bonus of a free lunch.

Zavattini had arranged to have the actual radio broadcast contest coincide with the film's shoot.[131] Even with a host of authenticating elements—the mass of aspiring women, "direct" interviews after screen tests, scenes of the studio and the film apparatus, the title "*Siamo donne*" displayed on the studio marquis—Guarini's film comes across as scripted and contrived. Despite its putative commitment to unknown talent, the film does not escape, for instance, the convention of narrative focalization, neatly distinguishing protagonist from extras. Playing herself, the aspiring actress Anna Amendola mirrors the feelings of other women undergoing the screening process. From Amendola's point of view in a taxi, we watch the unending numbers of young women approaching the studio. After being looked over by two men who select women based on age or appearance, they are invited for a luncheon. In a coarse figuration of stardom's limelight, a floodlight scans each woman's face sitting at the long lunch table while dooming the others to obscurity. The screen tests consist of personal questions by the director while the film flirts with a casual verité mode. Needless to say, Amendola and Emma Danielli (the sole participant to also have an extended scene) are chosen; they stand up and, as the radio announcer broadcasts their names, they walk toward an empty screen.[132] The rub is obvious: while all want to become actresses and perhaps stars, at least two of the stories in *We, the Women*

Figure 2.18: Extras mobbing to be a part of *Siammo Donne: Contest: 4 Actresses and 1 Hope* (the first episode directed by Alfredo Guarini).

offer clichéd views on the costs of stars' exposed lives, their nostalgia for a normal, real-life existence. Luigi Zampa's episode in the film, *Isa Miranda*, starts by showing the title character's apartment, portraits, and awards; it then follows her as she leaves her studio and stops to help a little boy who has broken his arm. Spending time with the children whose mother is out to work, Miranda recognizes what she has missed all along—being a mother. Gianni Franciolini's *Alida Valli* presents the star, cream on her face, hair in a towel, as a "real" person. Annoyed with her promotional commitments, she promises to attend her assistant Anna's engagement party. Bored and hounded by journalists at another, fancier party, Valli leaves abruptly and heads to Anna's house, where she is tempted by the attention of the young woman's fiancé. In Anna's simple, petty bourgeois apartment, Valli's stardom becomes too visible, almost ridiculous. Dressed in white mink and a long ball gown, she never merges with the other guests. This setup, more than the verbalized quest for a bygone simpler life, establishes the contrast between the star and the nonstar. Always recognizable, Valli will never mingle or dissolve in a crowd (Fig. 2.19).

Conversely, only those who have seen Antonioni's film can spot Marrosu, the "star" of *Attempted Suicides* in *Contest: 4 Actresses and 1 Hope*. She is the woman in line right after Amendola. In her casting test—the shortest—she simply declares that she hasn't prepared anything. As we recognize her, we remember her other "screen test" in *Attempted Suicides*, where she says she would like to study acting seriously. Her appearance in these two films highlights related agendas: one promotes

Figure 2.19: Alida Valli hypervisible at her secretary's party in Gianni Franciolini's *Alida Valli* (episode in *We the Women*, 1953).

its protagonists' realness in their common anonymity; the other does the same but in close contiguity to, and in contrast with, the impassable scrim of diva recognition. Marrosu's consistent performance indicates a stabilizing tendency in acting oneself, a naturalness achieved perhaps precisely in the exercise of repetition.

Caught in a moment of transition pregnant with the possibilities of a real acting career, Marrosu's photogenic presence introduces the spectator to a new conception of modern acting, one enveloped by the documentary reality it manifests and makes literal. It is quite fitting, then, that she repeat the line, and the act, of wishing to be an actress in a sort of intrafilmic reenactment.

The modernity of this performance is especially evident in the way Rosselini and Visconti transmute the divas of *Ingrid Bergman* and *Anna Magnani*, crafting short episodes that embrace the constitutive duality of being both a star and an actress, while avoiding the hackneyed conceit of the costs of being a celebrity. Instead of changing registers from first to third person (as occurs in the other episodes), Rosselini opts for a direct camera address to frame "La Bergman's battle" with a neighbor's chicken. The chicken insistently abandons her owner, the former villa proprietor, to eat and destroy Bergman's well-tended garden of rare roses. Making no reference to cinema, this episode is ultimately, as noted by Giorgio de Vincenti, the most reflexive.[133] Camerawork is conspicuous, making scenes resemble an amateur home movie. The camera plays a curious, insistent spectator to whom Bergman tells the story, explaining her actions (Fig. 2.20). It tails Bergman's every step as she tries

Figure 2.20: Ingrid Bergman addressing the camera in Rosselini's *The Chicken* episode in *We the Women* (1953).

to find the culprit, talks with her children, wanders through the villa, and attempts to have her dog "kill and eat" the chicken. Finally, it "catches" Bergman childishly hiding the chicken in the cupboard when guests come to visit. This luminous grainy documentary register, courting contingency, is the same that radically transforms Rosselini's fictional features such as *Europa '51* (1952) and *Viaggio in Italia* (*Voyage to Italy*, 1954) into exponents of a modern cinema. As Brunetta observes, "the same period that sees Sophia Loren and others emerge as stars, sees Rosselini devoted to an experiment over Bergman that has to do with a sort of psychodrama, a destruction of the mythical aura of American cinema and the emergence of the most authentic aspects of her personality."[134] This authenticity is integral to Rosselini's modernity. Jacques Rivette praises his films of the 1950s precisely for their sketch-like incompleteness, their casual presentation of carnality and the everyday: "His films become more and more the films of an amateur. Home movies; *Joan of Arc at the Stake* [1954] is not a cinematic transposition of the celebrated oratorio, but simply a souvenir film of his wife's performance in it just as *The Human Voice* [1948] was primarily the record of a performance by Anna Magnani."[135]

Visconti's contribution, *Anna Magnani* is also singular. Like the segment directed by Rossellini, it opens a breach between the quotidian and spectacle. With subversive simplicity, it channels Magnani's polyvalence as an Italian *popolana* figure, as iconic neorealist body, the movement's diva, onto the screen. In voice-over, Magnani tells us that the story we are seeing happened ten years earlier. Already late for her act in a variety show, she stubbornly refuses to pay one lira more for her taxi ride, insisting that her dog is a lapdog and therefore should go for free. Searching for authorities to confirm her rights, she incarnates, in this long sequence, her usual persona. The "real" off-stage Magnani is the popular character we know from neorealist films, one who loudly, assertively, and successively charms three different "real" audiences: sailors who watch her arguing, military police, and finally her public in the theater (Fig. 2.21).

The film sidesteps the question of whether Magnani's spectacle lies in her "neorealistic act" or if it occurs "when she acts out the script theatrically."[136] The long scene before her stage appearance confirms cinema's imaginary of the ritualized body of the star—"warm, carnal, riveting"[137]—in an exercise, typical of Visconti, demonstrating the theatricality of social fronts. In 1949, Visconti had worked on Prosper Merimee's "La Carrozza del Sacrammento," a project that became in 1953 Renoir's *The Golden Coach*; here, Magnani had also navigated the twin realms of theater and life. In *Anna Magnani*, the final shot of the actress singing against a painted backdrop of the Pincio (the same location where we first see her in a cab)[138] recalls the ending sequence of Renoir's film: After dissolving any stability for being and acting in Renoir's baroque reflection on theatricality, Magnani appears as a distanced, overlit chrome image against the red curtain. At the same time, as Marcia Landy suggests by situating Magnani in a "real location (Quattro Fontane Theatre) and in a context in which she is acting at non-acting," Visconti recapitulates "the blurred boundaries between real and fictional situations integral to Magnani's power as performer"[139] (Figs. 2.22 and 2.23).

Figure 2.21: Anna Magnani pleading her case in Visconti's *Anna Magnani*, episode of *We the Women* (1953).

Figure 2.22: Final shot of Magnani in Visconti's *Anna Magnani*, episode of *We the Women* (1953).

Figure 2.23: Final shot of Anna Magnani in Renoir's *The Golden Coach* (1953).

In an insightful essay, Lino Miccichè sees *Anna Magnani* as a postscript to *Bellissima*, a 1951 film that already commented on Italian cinema's change in acting regimen.[140] A scene, improvised by Visconti (based on a scenario by Zavattini), offers a "lucid" and almost "cynical take on the neorealist practice of using an 'actor from the street.'"[141] Liliana Mancini, who had acted in Castellani's *Under the Sun of Rome*, appears as herself; she tells Madalena (Magnani) that she was chosen once or twice because she conformed to the needed type—then adds that "it is better not to fantasize about serious, professional acting." Tullio Manzoni and Paolo Vecchio read this entrance of another "neorealist" body as the catalyst for *Bellissima*'s central paradoxes: a real character (Iris, Mancini) speaking the truth on casting to a fictional one (Madalena-Magnani, who is a professional actress and at the same time a personage of the everyday).[142]

In March 1952, Zavattini wrote a letter to recruit a reluctant Magnani for *We, the Women*:

> I had imagined the film with you in mind and now you're not in it.... Besides other qualities you also have that of being such a true and totally human character, so direct that anything you told about yourself would magically have the right tone to become a spectacle in the best sense of the word.... Now, I don't want to annoy you with all the neorealist reasons, let's call them that, that made me think of such a film ... if only you'd give me half an hour with you. [143]

If pesky "neorealist reasons" cannot be mentioned because they will likely not appeal to the iconic star of this kind of cinema, it is also obvious that a star is needed first so she can be exposed. The paradox cleverly revealed in *Love in the City* and *We, the Women* is that cinematic theatricality proves most resilient and most salient at the edge of life and spectacle, straddling anonymity and "stardom." On the verge of a star-driven cinema, but also ahead of cinema verité's staging of authentic voices and physiognomies, neorealist reenactment, verbal or staged, hinges on the notion of an everyday heroine even if her most noticeable act lies in acting as a film extra.

CHAPTER 3

Celebrity Reenactment, Biopic, and the Mortal Body

Discussing the particular thickness of the star presence, Laura Mulvey observes that "the 'naming' that accompanies the star's first appearance on the screen is followed by a fictional baptism, her assumption of a character's identity."[1] If a star never quite disappears into a fiction, what exactly is the nature of the relationship between star, character, and actor once they fuse in the same image? What kind of personhood emerges once one's name is associated with a multiplied yet singular presence? What, in short, are the effects of such presence within a field of proliferating images that extend beyond the film text itself?

In celebrity biopics, the categorical impasse of self-reenactment is compounded by different temporal orders: the flexible order of aesthetic representation, the recurrent circuitry of star iconography, and biology, that is, the actor's aging body. Other constraints are at work, too. Long-span biographies allow the contour of an entire life. Much like any actor stretching the limits of her role, a person reenacting her own life stands both for an indefinite span and for a contracted period corresponding to the film's production date. In consequence, a chronological indeterminacy emerges, which is especially apparent and disruptive in biographical accounts spanning many years. The age of the actual celebrity/actor is purposefully undefined to facilitate broad biographical coverage. This figure's autonomous, potentially destabilizing function as well as its unmarked and purely functional temporality is what interests me here.

Sophia: Her Own Story (Mel Stuart, 1980), a made-for-TV biopic, exemplifies the quandary of representing oneself in time. In the film, Sophia Loren plays both herself and her mother, Romilda Villani. The film takes the horizon of mortality that haunts all forms of cinematic reproduction to the limit of camp. In the opening shot, Loren announces her origins as a person and star to the camera against a black backdrop, and then a cut takes us to the actress playing her mother. A composite of a mother's aspirations and her daughter's impersonation, of Loren's cheekbones and a Garbo hat, starts a relentless process of self-origination affecting distinct levels of the film's story and texture (Fig. 3.1).

The double casting subverts the common assumption that the physiognomic and physical latitude for convincing impersonation is restricted to an "appropriate" period of life—that age affects the ability to represent oneself as younger or older. Loren's dual impersonation destabilizes a genre already marked by referential fragility. In self-acted biopics, the decision to immortalize one's story and one's image simultaneously exposes the actor and the athlete to greater trouble than what André Bazin and Jean Louis Comolli discuss in the context of historical reenactment. In "Historical Fiction, a Body Too Much," Comolli notes that once an actor stands for a known historical figure, his body is ghosted by historical knowledge and by other circulating images (portraits or verbal accounts), which function as a screen and prevent "the actor and the mise-en-scène from playing on self-evidence (it can only be me) or assertion (it is me!)"[2]

The referential density and ambiguity in representing historical beings only increase when a star plays her story. The credits certify an equivalence—a person's name and surname followed by "as himself" as "herself"—but they do not ensure a transparent relation between the actual person and his or her persona. Comolli's strategic distinction between "self-evidence" and "assertion" means that the actualization of the self-involved in any embodiment of a historical figure (oneself included)

Figure 3.1: Sophia Loren as Romilda Villani as Greta Garbo in *Sophia: Her Own Story* (Mel Stuart, 1980).

depends not just on resemblance or even identity but on a performance of the self, an enacted claim.

This chapter examines how reenactment's referential malleability interferes with the teleology of the celebrity biopic, how reenactment's artificial, multidirectional temporality troubles assumptions about the linear course of a life. In the pedagogic and testimonial films examined here, the verbal commentary separates past experience from present consciousness to mitigate temporal ambiguity. While the biopic's forward thrust only enhances the celebrity's resistance to the effects of the passing of time, the celebrity biopic is invested in centering the star and confirming her in her fullest presence. As such, the self-acted star biopic provides a special lens on the representation of oneself in time that, from physical decay to irrelevance, unavoidably displays existential tinges.

Besides *Sophia: Her Own Story*, this chapter investigates another 1950s celebrity biopic defined by existential and corporeal limits. Carlo Velo's *Torero!* (1956) retraces the career of the Mexican matador Luis Procuna up to 1953 (Fig. 3.2). The film intercuts newsreel footage of the actual Procuna (as well as a host of other bullfighters) with reconstructed scenes of his awaited return to the arena (after an interruption), the present moment from which the matador recounts his life's struggles and his agonizing relation to fear and death. The obsession with mortality in *Torero!* and the uncanny casting in *Sophia* illustrate the anxious relation to finitude foregrounded in self-acted star biopics and dramatized in these films' proliferating doubles and textural hybridity.

Figure 3.2: Luis Procuna acting his own life in Carlos Velo's *Torero!* (1956).

Premised on the display of their protagonists' named recognizable bodies, the self-starred actor and sports-figures' film, common biopic subgenres, unavoidably prove self-reflexive. Films like *Sophia: Her Own Story, Torero!, The Jackie Robinson Story* (Alfred Green, 1950), and *The Greatest* (Tom Gries and Monte Hellman, 1977) provide an extended look at their subjects' talents and body images; thereby, they encourage phenomenological scrutiny bearing on aspects of performance that resist theatrical disguise: race, age, and physical changes, personal style, gestural idiosyncrasies, and tone of voice. These celebrity biopics enhance a reflexive awareness of the multiple levels of repetition threading through one's life and body. Invariably, spectators try to discern being from acting; one scans the physical body for signs of shared human condition or of embodied technique; one separates cyclical gestures and ordinary biological functions, breathing say, from movements that are part of reiterated, productive effort—acting, exercising, or sprinting to win a race.

Faced with the real person as actor, one becomes attuned to the ways an actor's physique is claimed as her own, her "personal body" (in Vivian Sobchak's useful classification), or, alternatively, channeled to dramatic effect (as in the examples given by James Naremore: De Niro's fatness in *Raging Bull* or the ravaged faces of Humphrey Bogart or Montgomery Cliff).[3] While a reading that moves between distinct registers applies to any characterization, this stroboscopic perception intensifies when a star relives her own life. In addition, much like in a writer's autobiography, the replay of an expertise—be it acting, running, boxing—qualifies as a signature: a self-expressive element of professional identity and individual style.

Jackie Robinson's presence in his own biopic is especially instructive regarding the complexity of a body image traversed by multiple orders of visibility—in particular, the discourse about race and integration of the late 1940s and early 1950s (Fig. 3.3). In her insightful analysis of *The Jackie Robinson Story*, Alessandra Raengo notes that Robinson's entrance in Major League Baseball meant continuously negotiating between promoting his visibility as an African American baseball player and the inverse need to erase his individuality and carnality by assimilating him into an all-American (and white) ideology of success.[4]

The promotion of the utopia of a colorblind America depended on shifting interest from race to performance. The press continually hinted that the greatest test of verisimilitude did not concern Robinson appearing as himself but rather the "spectacle of Robinson's performance in the field and the realization that nobody else could reproduce his distinctive playing style: 'Jackie Robinson, the only man alive who can show [such] blinding speed and smooth batting style . . . who could portray him better?'"[5]

Raengo's claim that Robinson is "a necessary signifier" because he "authorizes the integration story through his actions and not just his acting" confirms the exemplary function of in-person reenactment.[6] But another argument proves equally relevant to the relation between self-embodiment and exemplarity; it pertains to the phenomenology of acting. Not everyone agreed that Robinson should act as himself. Moreover, the individuality expressed in his unique style (and resilience) was seen by another reviewer as an actual impediment to the actor's task of translating "an individual story into a collective one."[7] Robinson's excessively embodied individuality

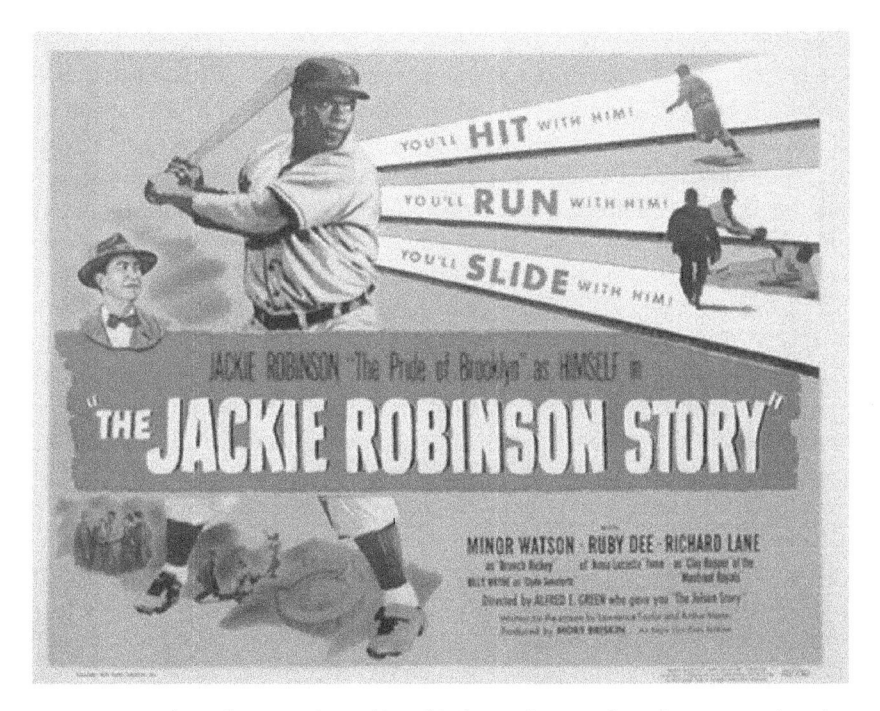

Figure 3.3: Jackie Robinson as himself in Alfred Green's *The Jackie Robinson Story* (1950).

clashes with the "suspension of disbelief required for an actor to be seen as a character" and cannot "dissipate in the glamorous immateriality, in the pure textuality, of the star image."[8] These objections, a version of Commoli's body-too-much thesis, guide Raengo's formulation of one of the main dilemmas of in-person reenactment."Too little as an actor, and too much as a body, Robinson's screen image is captive of its carnality and almost in contradiction to the iconic—exchangeable—Robinson images circulating in visual culture."[9]

A similar reading applies to Muhammed Ali and the barrage of images and quotations in *The Greatest*. Featuring a boxing star who claimed the role of a spokesperson for African Americans, advocated religious freedom, and denounced the Vietnam war, this imperfect film remains strangely moving as Ali reperforms a series of very public positions and statements. It is not age but rather a palpable distance and stiffness of performance that recasts his brilliant improvised riffs, his infamously cutting statements and invectives into a script—a series of obligingly mouthed citations. It suffices to compare documentary footage of his speeches with reenactment to see and hear the "script" at work[10]; to witness the complex tangle of role-playing and the public performance of the self.

Reenactment's retroactive narrative may be read in terms of its exemplary and redemptive mission. But celebrity biopics magnify the temporal divide once the star assumes her role. In the same way that stars often abandon their character to parade particular abilities—to dance, to sing, to mug, or to pose—celebrity reenactment films incorporate such star turns in the form of clips from the public record adding yet another image to an already crowded lineup of bodies sharing the same name. An even more conspicuous trope is the convergence of profilmic and diegetic orders through the trope of an entrance in "scene": after a number of childhood and adolescent incarnations Ali reenacts himself from the moment the footage of his fight with Liston has flashed on the screen. The historical record of the passage into celebrity is repurposed as a literal threshold for the actual protagonist to enter in scene as himself (Figs. 3.4 to 3.6). The hinge between public record and self-enactment can figure the birth of the star; however, it can also haunt the autonomy of this circulating record through reenactment, with a reminder of a corporeal, hence mortal, presence.

Temporally out of joint, the stars' presences in *Torero!* and *Sophia: Her Own Story* are my entry to discuss the existential and ontological dimensions of reenactment. Through Loren's disturbance of linearity of the biopic and *Torero!*'s composite of newsreel and reenactment, the films show reenactment to be an elastic form of representation with the capacity to problematize both cinema's temporal strictures and life narratives.

Despite their disparate genealogies, the 1950s celebrity biopics studied here can be seen in the context of two interrelated developments in 1950s cinema aesthetics and reception: (1) phenomenological and socioanthropological debates on stars initiated by André Bazin and Edgar Morin, and (2) changes in postneorealist cinema in response to postwar commodification and the emerging Italian star system, represented by Zavattini's various verité projects.

Figure 3.4: Mohammed Ali young played by an actor (Tom Gries, Monte Hellman's *The Greatest*, 1977).

Figure 3.5: Newsreel of first instance of public notoriety in *The Greatest* (Gries, Hellman, 1977).

Figure 3.6: Mohammed Ali appears as himself for the first time in *The Greatest*.

Most immediately, *Sophia: Her Own Story* commands interest because of the centrality it bestows on a highly storied presence in Italian and international cinema. This history overlaps with Zavattini's engagement as a screenwriter of major social and neorealist films. It also relates to his efforts to eliminate scripts, to find ways of "telling" the reality of the common person. As Zavattini adapted two major Loren star vehicles, De Sica's *The Gold of Naples* (De Sica, 1954) and *Two Women* (1960), he also produced two omnibus films meant, in a complementary manner, to strike a new balance between anonymity and stardom, quotidian life and spectacle. *Love in the City* (1953) articulates the exemplarity of unknown individuals; conversely, *Siamo Donne* (*We Are Women*, 1953) grants famous Italian stars a personal, intimate dimension (see Chapter 2).[11]

As a representative of neorealism, Zavattini also had an expanded international influence in Central and Latin America. Between 1955 and 1956, he collaborated with Barbachano Ponce and Carlos Velo, the team behind *Torero!*, to develop new forms of ciné-verdad in Mexico. This international dialogue and experimentation with documentary form the backdrop for self-acted biopics like *Torero!*. The new realist aesthetics of the 1950s deploys reenactment to complement archival footage in docudramas and populist biopics concerning the star's rise to fame. Significantly, however, it also extends onto a mimetic plane by demonstrating interest in common individuals' lives.

Likewise, André Bazin's relation to Velo's film is informed by an aesthetic and thematic affinity for modern experiments with realism. Bazin wrote extensively on bullfighting films and was part of the jury at the Venice Film Festival that awarded *Torero!* a special mention for "its contribution to the renewal of cinematic realism through the integration of real documents with reenactment."[12] As we will see, Bazin's trained focus on a seamless continuity between different entities or registers of the image is an extension of his attentiveness to cinema's material and documentary dimensions, awareness in great evidence in his remarks and essays on stars' and on actors' mortality.

SOPHIA: HER OWN STORY

To bring a television biopic from the 1980s into this discussion is to acknowledge Loren's convolutions to stretch her postwar persona across several decades, including greedily playing her mother in two biopics, one on her own life at forty-six years old (*Sophia: Her Own Story*, 1980), the second on her sister's life at seventy-seven (*My House Is Full of Mirrors/La Mia Casa è Piena di Specchi*, Vittorio Sindoni, 2010) (Fig. 3.7). It is also a way of recognizing the historiographical import of in-person biopic reenactment, for such an iconic actress's revisitation of the past unavoidably summons a very specific panorama of national and international cinema from the 1950s into the 1970s.

Marcia Landy has noted that Loren explicitly represents an embodiment of Italian cinema in De Sica's *Yesterday, Today and Tomorrow* (1963), a film that journeys through Italian stardom in the 1940–1960 postwar context, from the era of "neorealism"

Figure 3.7: Loren as her own mother in *My House Is Full of Mirrors* (Vittorio Sindoni, *La mia casa è piena di specchi*, 2010).

to the "economic miracle."[13] The first episode alludes to her *popolana* role in *Gold of Naples*, where "stardom is identified with the post war world on the streets."[14] The second episode starts as an extended monologue with existential undertones; on a drive through Milan, Loren is associated with the modern affluent women of Antonioni's trilogy. Written by Zavattini, the episode quickly assumes the contours of a tale on the amorality of the rich.

Given the commercial orientation of *Sophia: Her Own Story*, the film's historiographical dimension is unintentional. We see excerpts of her work from 1951 to 1953 when Carlo Ponti screens it to De Sica, but also, and with the thinnest excuse of flashbacks, a ravishing Loren pops up to illustrate a conversation with her aunt about meeting Gregory Peck, who, in the *Arabesque* insert, does a double take as he looks up distractedly and then gazes appreciatively at the star leaning by the door.

Two forms of recirculating Loren are set in motion as inserts maintain a constant iconographic backdrop for Loren's reenactment. Finally, the extraordinary decision to cast Loren as herself and her mother frames the implications of in-person reenactment. Perfectly acceptable from the standpoint of genetic descent and family resemblance, this dual casting errs in the direction of an impossible identity, a false equation between resemblance and sameness. Subverting the slim requirements of life narratives, the film betrays the tenuous constraints of linear narrative and lineage logic. Loren's embodiment of both roles challenges the succession logic of generations as well as the principle of discrete personhood—that of a single body per person. The star's defiance of a natural order is enhanced by the fact that one of these identities is her own. This violation of personhood is compounded by reenactment, a form of representation that purposefully disregards the correspondence of bodies to time: Sophia's age in both roles, matching the date of the film's production, bends the linear logic ruling the long-term biopic, that of an evolving person, of an aging physique. The film's generational scramble provokes us to think which logic—that of resemblance, genetics, social group, or age—authorizes reenactment's performance of the past.

Thematically the film's plot and production realities converge in the portrayal of Romilda living vicariously through her daughter. Almost a memorial to her mother's desires, Loren appears first as her mother winning a contest for Greta Garbo lookalikes. The association of Loren's physiognomy with Garbo's, this impersonation of one celebrity by another, complicates the fiction typical of the biopic genre: an anonymous woman's ascent from obscurity to the limelight. The film ends with Loren fulfilling her mother's desire as she becomes a star and becomes a mother in her own right, showing her newborn baby to the cameras under the credits (see Fig. 3.8 in Color Insert, 1).

This encapsulation of the arc of motherhood would seem to weirdly justify Loren's dual role, but Loren brings all this symbiosis to bear on the film's body. She replicates motherhood's problematic of reproduction and projective doubling, installing through reenactment an extracorporeal disturbance. To the fundamental uncertainty as to whether we watch Loren the actor or Loren the character, whether the body's age conforms to the depicted timeline, we may add the vexed question of "growing up" in biopics. Biographical films conventionally proceed as if the protagonist's name assured her identity across multiple actors' bodies. Whether a known actor embodies a fictional character or a celebrity acts her own story, biopics supplement a timeline with actors who impersonate earlier life stages of the protagonist. The cast in *Sophia: Her Own Story* is long: two children play the young Sophia, and Ritza Braun plays her as an adolescent and young actress (before Loren herself takes over) (see Fig. 3.9 in Color Insert, 1). These composite identities gain interest once one body takes over from the other, a relay often accompanied by a name bridge—think for instance of the ellipsis between the child and adult George/Jimmy Stewart in *It's a Wonderful Life*.[15]

And yet the discontinuity resulting from using actors as prosthetic extensions of the protagonist's life cannot compare with the more radical, perverse proposition of the same body as a placeholder for two generations. Accordingly, the scenes of Loren "becoming" herself matter in particular. One is when the fledgling actress leaves her mother's home and Sophia takes leave of her mother's role, "becoming herself" at thirty.

The relay that interests us here, however, is an earlier passage rite, the moment leading to her stardom. The awkward transfer from Loren as mother to her as daughter, from the young actress Braun to Loren herself is done by tying Sophia's life story more closely to her publicly known image. Ritza Braun (who plays Loren from age thirteen to twenty) argues with Loren/Romilda a propos of her affair with Carlo Ponti. A cut takes us to "Ponti" convincing "Vittorio de Sica" to employ the young actress in a projection booth. A series of clips of Loren's roles from 1951 to 1954 introduce us to her statuesque appearances in period films and light contemporary comedies, respectively, *Aida, Two Nights with Cleopatra*, and *A Day in Court* (Figs 3.10a–c). The shift among formats, styles, and looks of the inserts sparks the viewer's awareness of the film's materiality; the sequence intensifies the sense of Loren as a purely filmic being, part of autonomous fictional universes. As brief as this elegiac montage is, the radiant presence at its

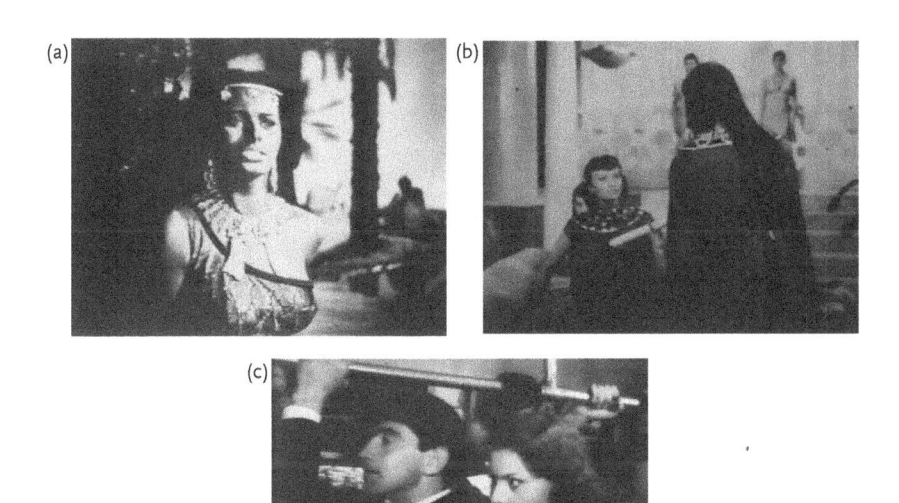

Figures 3.10: Loren projected excerpts. a) Loren in *Aida* (Clemente Fracassi, 1951). b) Loren in *Two Nights with Cleopatra* (Mario Matolli, 1954). c) Loren in *A Day in Court* (Steno, 1954).

center instantiates a losing proposition: the legendary images of Loren's excerpts contrast unfavorably with reenacted Sophia. These excerpts poignantly establish the distance between past and present Loren, as they lend to the film a broader sense of historicity than the one delineated in the banal representation of the actress's biography.

After this intense textual collage, Loren is inscribed into her own lifeline, an entrance staged as a brief backstage moment during her first major role as Dona Sofia in De Sica and Zavattini's adaptation of Giuseppe Marotta's *The Gold of Naples*. After a short exchange with the actress, De Sica moves his dolly, and we are shown a frontal long shot of Loren waiting for the tracking to start (Fig. 3.11). A much more curvaceous and full figure than Braun, Loren is easily spotted and for a moment one imagines it is as her mother that she poses for light measurements.

This moment figures reenactment's management of retroactivity across heterogeneous filmic bodies. Infallibly, the passage from relatively unknown actors to the real/actor in celebrity biopics is performed via a self-reflexive insert, a star turn, or a quotable footage of the star's first public record. This footage is strategically placed in the story, and it both represents and indexes the significant moment in which a given athlete or actor gained recognition. It marks at once the person's growth—from younger to older self but also her graduation into notoriety. In such highly mediated moments we lose the sense of the character to attend paradoxically to an image—the star can only be seen as a meld of light, celluloid, and public interest.

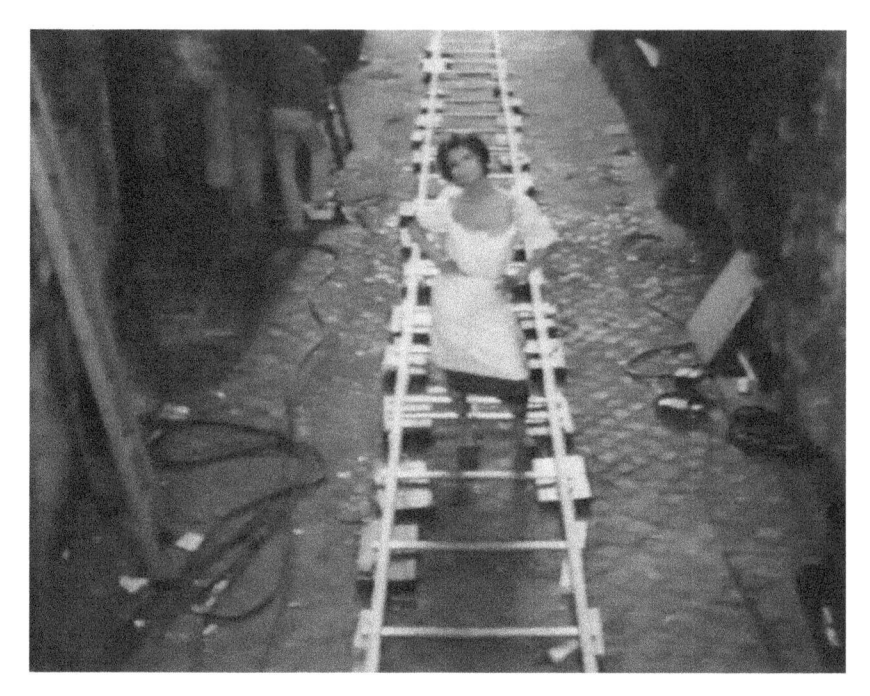

Figure 3.11: Sophia as herself for the first time in *Her Own Story* as she enters public notoriety in Vittorio de Sica's *The Gold of Naples* (1954).

The relay sequence described earlier ties the actual Sophia to her first major role twenty-six years earlier: the *pizzaiola* D. Sofia, whose riveting figure the camera follows as she triumphantly walks in the rain, while her cuckold husband limps behind (Fig. 3.12). The implication that the forty-six-year-old Sophia waiting by the camera tracks is the profilmic subject of the twenty-year-old in *The Gold of Naples* crystallizes an anxiety particular to celebrity biopics: the need to hold time, body, and narrative together. The supposedly continuous, and even indexical, relation between images with discrete replay ontologies only enhances the discrepancy. This sequence's stress on cinema's indexical materiality makes it clear that, for all its prized authenticity, reenactment's relation to time is indeterminate, neither quite in the present nor in the past. The real/actor is an efficient representational instrument, but it has no existential edge.

Mel Stuart's uncritical take on the star, in what almost amounts to a vanity project, contrasts with two distinct sets of films querying stardom—the fading star genre in Hollywood and the neorealist alternative of the anonymous or common woman. Both have distinct implications for realist aesthetics inasmuch as they invoke a carnal dimension that significantly speaks to modern's cinema demystifying thrust.

The first significant cinema concerned with stardom, which emerged in the fifties and sixties, was the subgenre of the "fading star." Here, Hollywood celebrities like Betty Davis and Joan Crawford were cast in, and even embraced, the role of the

Figure 3.12: Sophia in *The Gold of Naples* (De Sica, 1954), first success footage as transition to playing herself.

has-been. Karen Beckman argues that the "fading star genre endlessly wrestles with the ambivalence of a medium in which the body always hovers between absence and presence."[16] Reading a number of films featuring Bette Davis, who made the fading role part of her star persona, Beckman claims these films do more than demystify "the illusion that the woman on screen exists only as a fantasy of the male gaze"; they are "a forceful vision of the spectacularly vanishing woman as a figure who, though sometimes in danger of being done away with, utilizes her visibility in order to resist the very problems that arise out of that spectacular state of being."[17]

Beckman resists the notion that the fading film star "works to dispose of the mature woman,"[18] suggesting instead that stars exhibit oscillatory temporality in general. She illustrates this slippage of tenses with the commentary Addison De Witt offers at the start of *All About Eve*, a complex enunciation of the stars' structural positionality, of their temporary obfuscation as well as their persistence in another temporal scale.[19] Beckman considers that it is *All About Eve*'s "recognition of Margo's place within the temporal complexity of the star metaphor that fundamentally separates her from Norma Desmond."[20] In *Whatever Happened to Baby Jane?* the characters played by Bette Davis and Joan Crawford have always oscillated in the space between absence and presence, and since "the ambivalence of vanishing is their domain, this gives them a [greater] degree of resilience."[21]

In the star biopic, reenactment becomes another way of negotiating the staying power of a star's image. Discussing Davis and Crawford's fictional performance of aging stars, Jodi Brooks notes that "these characters and their performances offer a form of crisis in which time is loaded to breaking point—the temporality of the commodity, the temporality of stardom for women, the temporality of woman as image."[22] In particular, the self-acted biopic attests to this "refusal to leave the stage . . . [taking] the form of stretching time, of re-pacing the temporality of spectacle, display, and performance."[23]

Sophia: Her Own Story also concerns the negotiation of Loren's status as image. But instead of stretching performance time, the film deploys reenactment toward another kind of deferral. Once Sophia impersonates Sophia the actress's present appearance, the entire diegetic span of the story, the twenty years until she herself gives birth at the end of the film, needs to be recalibrated. For all that, reenactment clearly serves to stabilize Sophia's appearance for an extended block of time. The typical contraction of aging in reenactment—the fact that the actor's age does not vary as wildly as the span of the story—maintains the illusion of agelessness. The film reserves aging for her mother's character. When we see Romilda toward the film's end, in a shot, countershot conversation with Sophia, it is her impersonation as a white-haired lady that takes on the burden of measuring and relativizing time passed (Fig. 3.13).

A truism of conventional cinema is that to test her true acting abilities a star has to impersonate an older woman and a mother. Following Loren's trajectory, the film does not have to go far to reflexively comment on the age issue, for the casting for De Sica's *Two Women* provides a much more credible image of Loren as mother (Fig. 3.14) whose role was initially offered to Anna Magnani. Loren was twenty-six at the time and, as Millicent Marcus reminds us, the production of *Two Women* was conditioned on an "axiomatic insistence on [Loren]'s youth, thus requiring a prepubescent daughter to replace the voluptuous eighteen year old of the [source] novel."[24]

Such ploy to establish Loren's youth in relation to an even younger presence works in *Two Women* but backfires in *Sophia: Her Own Story*. Pushing to the fore recursivity as a key trait of reenactment, and aligning it to the ability to move, in acting, across generations, *Sophia: Her Own Story* becomes an object lesson on the frictions between ideality and contingency. The decision to cast a single actress for two characters has implications for reenactment. If one can consider reenactment simply an extension of acting, the film's convoluted handling of image and temporality registers demands a reflection on bio-rewind. Just as significantly, Loren's impersonation of mother and daughter reinforces, even as it deconstructs, the tangle of verisimilitude and authenticity intimated by taking on one's own role.

Besides the Hollywood fading star genre, another set of films querying cinema's relation to stars coincides with Zavattini's ideas on reenactment in the early 1950s. Retracing everyday lives of anonymous figures in *Love in the City* responded to a growing star culture strongly identified in Italy with shapely figures (*maggiorate fisiche*) like Loren. According to Gian Piero Brunetta, Pauline Small, and Stephen Gundle, neorealist cinema's drive for reconstruction led to a demand "for new faces

Figure 3.13: Sophia Loren as an old Romilda. Aging in *Sophia: Her Own Story*.

Figure 3.14: Sophia Loren in de Sica's *Two Women* (1960) in *Her Own Story*.

in cinema, theatre and television, that was motivated by democracy and a need for emblematic figures who stood in a general sense for Italy."[25] *Sophia: Her Own Story*'s use of the pizzaiola episode in *The Gold of Naples* as the scene in which Loren starts to impersonate herself in the biopic highlights a split in Italian cinema between a critical self-reflection or a full-fledged embrace of stardom.

Siamo Donne (*We Women*, 1953) also enlists major directors to rethink stardom in cinema. Three episodes revolve around the conceit of the celebrity yearning for relief from overvisibility. The segments directed by Rosselini and Visconti take a different direction: rather than dramatizing their character's humanity, the films flesh out the human, corporeal dimensions of actresses like Ingrid Bergman and Anna Magnani. In Rosselini and Visconti's move toward an amateur aesthetics, Brunetta identifies an experiment with authenticity meant "to [destroy] the mythical aura of American cinema"; in turn, Jacques Rivette praises all of Rosselini's 1950s films, portraits of his wife Bergman, for bearing the traits of home movies.

With their casual asides and camera address, the denuding impulse of Rosselini, Visconti, and Antonioni's episodes in *Siamo Donne* and *Love in the City* define a modern cinema invested in diminishing or problematizing the gap between being and acting. Staged as confessionals or backstage narratives, they question authenticity in a way that necessarily affects the films' form.

Compared with the fresh infusion of the documentary form in the postwar, the biopic's hybridity, its inclusion of archival materials, represents a realist aesthetic invested in a seamless verisimilitude. In these biopics the dynamic tension between contingency and ideality proper to modern cinema experiments is tamed.

And yet, even though the biopic fails to deliver more than a publicized version of known facts in a wildly circulated life story, these relatively unpolished narratives cannot prevent the reflexive dimension that arises inasmuch as the actual protagonist acts in the story of her own life. The viewer continually scans the scene for the "unstaged" aspect of the film, an added measure of authenticity, a "truer" self. And this search is operative regardless of the fact that Sophia is an actress and Procuna, the toreador, is not.

Even at its most conventional and plodding, the celebrity biopic reenactment cannot keep the viewer from focusing on the categorical, temporal gap constitutive of all representation. In the two films discussed here, the minute scans of fissures in personae or screen events, in the film's narrative and texture, point to the ultimate discontinuity rescued via cinema: death and mortality.

BAZIN'S CINE-MYTHOGRAPHIES

I want to turn to Bazin before we analyze *Torero!*'s role in the development of docudrama as well as the corporeal disturbances brought up by the film's excessive use of Procuna newsreels. For the critic's reflections on stars, on the gap between existential and cinematic destinies, on miscasting and aging celebrities is central to whether reenactment—the actual presence of the protagonist as actor—centers or scatters the "bodies-too-much" that beset the representation of existing beings.

In a series of essays, Bazin's cine-mythographies identify two incompatible horizons: the contingent life of actors, on the one hand, and the immutable fate of stars, on the other. By stressing the notion of an embodied destiny, Bazin grants his narratives on actors, historical figures, and celebrities an existential dimension. At the same time, these critical exercises replicate cinema's power to create afterlives hovering between past and present incarnations.[26] When Bazin outlines Jean Gabin's destiny, an inevitable death fulfilled in each of his characters; when he describes how even prior to his death Humphrey Bogart resembled a corpse in reprieve; when he speaks of Chaplin's aging body and his myth's parallel evolution; or in his analyses of Stalin icons in Soviet cinema, his texts resemble a macabre party where guests in various degrees of decomposition or with different and even competing claims to liveliness and uniqueness commingle.[27]

Crowded with simulacra, Bazin's articles on referential genres (on biographical or historical films) rehearse, through their emphases on duplication, the problem at the heart of his ontology: that in "embalming" a lived duration, an image indeed displays a seeming life of its own, tainting the singularity of a moment, of an identity. Each of his articles occasions thoughts on cinema's ability to create a gelled imprint of a changeable existence. Especially when writing on actual stars, whether alive, aging, or dead, he is compelled to puzzle over cinema's ontological perversion, its animistic and resurrecting function. The essays concentrate on the moment when an image, "a hallucination that is also a fact,"[28] stands freakishly side by side with a living body. This collocation traceable to Bazin's affinity for surrealism evinces as well a reluctance to tame cinema's spectrality, to reduce its multiple, coexisting, temporalities.[29]

Bazin's thoughts on cinema's power to multiply the images of stars and deadly dictators in order to endow them with a life of their own is not inconsistent with "his" ontology, his perception of the photographed object's freedom from temporal contingencies. And yet, as we compare his treatment of the Chaplin image with that of the Stalin myth, one notes a significant difference not unrelated to the films' protagonists' ethical and political positions.

Bazin associates Chaplin's cinema with existential time. Meshing flesh and celluloid, the critic has cinema partake in the fading star's finitude. His analyses of *Limelight* and *The Great Dictator* acknowledge the actor behind the character describing the "strange metamorphosis" that takes place when Charlie advances toward the proscenium and speaks: "for the first time we feel something or someone behind Charlie, a sort of terrible secret which the photographic chemistry, despite the author's will, reveals."[30] His remarks ascribe to the newly nuanced film-stock "the passage to panchromatic film stock,"[31] a decanting effect whereby the moustache floats, black and young as ever, above the pasty flesh (Fig. 3.15). At the same time, the exfoliation of the person in cinema reveals the actor's literal presence: the wrinkles are Chaplin's alone and his rigid body provides a glimpse into cinema's human dimension precisely as it meets its reproducible afterlife. The same qualifier, "rigid," gains, however, an entirely different import when applied to the erection of Stalin monuments in cinema.

In "The Stalin Myth" (1950), Bazin puzzles out the phenomenon he sees as unique to contemporary Soviet cinema, its depiction of Stalin while the statesman is still alive.[32] Even in comparison to the hero's biography, a genre in ascendance within socialist realism, Bazin feels that Stalin's statuary films are constrained by an equation of history and myth. He objects, in particular, to its complicity with a totalitarian system: "to make Stalin the determining force in the re-creation of an

Figure 3.15: Chaplin's face behind Charlie's mask (Chaplin, *The Great Dictator*, 1942).

actual historical event when he is still head of the state implicitly establishes that the meaning of his life has been definitely ascertained and that he could not subsequently make a mistake or commit treason."[33] In short, becoming, or images of becoming, are forbidden. To counter such myth-making, Bazin can only oppose the few newsreel images of Stalin at the Red Square and at the Yalta conference because "they record reality, remaining therefore fundamentally ambiguous."[34] If this phrase, representing Bazin's mandate for cinema, rings hollow in the context of Stalinist cinema, it finds a new life in his texts on death and bullfights. Conversely—and in keeping with his penchant for contingency—newsreels emerge as Bazin's paradigm for realism when dealing with historical figures: its perfect mesh with reconstructed scenes is what Bazin first remarks about *Torero!*.

As a celebrity biopic, *Torero!* occupies a privileged position in a discussion on reenactment and finitude. If the temporal and categorical relativity of the celebrity is exacerbated against the background of mortality, the telos of bullfighting films added to the contingency of newsreel record highlights the artifice of reenactment with even greater force.

CINEMA'S EXISTENTIAL ARENA

In his writings on death, Bazin repeatedly dramatizes the incompatibility between existential and cinematic temporalities. First and foremost, the subjective dimension, the "voluptuousness" of death, precludes objective representation: "[N]o one can die or make love for another," and these moments "are also indescribable since they are accomplished by the annulment of consciousness."[35] On the other hand, Bazin relies on facts to argue against cinema's potential to replicate and thereby defile the uniqueness of death: "We do not die twice" is his explanation for why the uncanniness that obsesses him—the passage from animate to inanimate, from subject to object—has to be left off screen.[36]

Bazin keeps the relation between the frozen finality of record and the changeable flow of reality in constant textual abeyance, and he recovers as ritual the threatening replay of cinema: "the representation on screen of a bull being put to death . . . magnifies the quality of the original moment through the contrast of its repetition. It confers on it an additional solemnity."[37] This supplemental solemnity, a semantic slow motion, postpones the ultimate "cut," reclaiming its sublimity for cinema and concluding that the possibility of replay has only one point of intolerable ontological contradiction: death.[38]

The temporal and corporeal limits of death as well as the rituals of abeyance related to this telos should be enough to define the inverse interest in reenactment's elastic temporality and its potential to recap on camera a stretch of one's life stalling life's forward course and figuratively delaying mortality. And yet Bazin's fascination with the human body in the cinema, suspended in a limbo between life and death, between mythical immortality, physical decay, and existential fragility, does not translate into a concurrent interest in the aporias of reenactment.

For a critic especially alert to the aesthetic potential of miscasting, his comments on reenactment are either short or pat. In his review of Zavattini and Maselli's *The Story of Caterina*, Bazin marvels at the "absurd coincidence" in casting Caterina, the actual protagonist, as actress in her own story. And when, in "The Stalin Myth," Bazin remarks briefly on boxer Marcel Cerdan who plays himself in *The Man with Clay Hands* (*l'Homme aux mains d'argile*, 1949) and *Fame and the Devil* (*Al diavolo la celebritá*), he does so in order to claim that the actual boxer's presence is entirely dispensable and that his employment in the film only highlights in extremis "the identification of the man Cerdan with his myth" (SM, 32). More to the point of this discussion on finitude and reenactment, Bazin never touched on the obvious relation of in-person reenactment to its ontological limit, death. "Toro, A Revolution in Realism," Bazin's review of *Torero!*, a reenactment and a bullfighting film, should have galvanized this reflection.

Given Bazin's insistent focus on the relationship between death and cinematic contingency, it is likely no coincidence that his review of *Torero!*, "Toro: A Revolution in Realism" appeared side by side with "Information or Necrophagy" in a page of *Radio, Cinéma, Télévision*"[39] (Fig. 3.16). In the latter piece, Bazin addresses the question, raised by a television producer, whether accidental deaths should be made public.[40] What prompts his comments is the program's feature on the discovery of a corpse inside a plane fallen at sea. "The pilot is at his post, drowned, his eyes half open."[41] Bazin's objection to the camera's chancing upon a corpse is prefaced by his own half-guilty perception of an aesthetic equality between corpses and underwater life.[42] But then, in his concluding paragraph he complicates his reservations by bracketing some deaths as existentially meaningful:"The death of a soldier, that of a lifeguard, indeed that of a torero or of a race-car driver, is an event that has

Figure 3.16: A revealing coincidence: Bazin's "Information or Necrophagy" and "*Torero!*"

some meaning, even if it's debatable."[43] Here "from the start the document (the TV program he alludes to) addresses us through the equivocal horror of our senses. But there are no exquisite corpses!"[44] With this exclamatory denegation (and its surrealist overtones), Bazin asserts simultaneously his fascination with chance and his strong need to separate intentional, risk-taking actions, accidental deaths, and the machine's reflexive record.

Bullfighting excites Bazin because of its ritual invocation of risk and the copresence between toreador, bull, *and* the audience. This constellation defines a distinct form of spectacle, one that, premised on the uniqueness of a moment and the sensations it occasions, allows the critic to magnify and contrast questions of realism and cinematic replay. However, it is only after he writes on Braunberger and Myriam's *Bullfight* in "Death Every Afternoon" (1951) that his essays on death start to correlate with his bullfight film reviews. In "Death on the Screen" (1949), Bazin makes no reference whatsoever to bullfighting; instead, he discusses public executions in Shanghai and calls attention to cinema's "scandal," its "ability to see death as a moment identical to others while it is the only one of our acts that by its very essence cannot re-start."[45] In contrast, his *corrida* film reviews stress danger, and they seem in fact to anxiously scan the screen for that instance of radical discontinuity Bazin so obsessively wants and dreads to see.

Typically these reviews establish a hierarchy based on the protagonist's exposure to risk, Bazin's measure of the real. There are compilation essay films like *Bullfight* and fiction films. Some films are played by actors and by real bullfighters as stand-ins, while others insert documentary images of actual bullfights to stand just for the perilous moments. In *Tarde de Toro* (Ladislao Vajda, 1956), three fictional toreros are played inside and outside of the arena by celebrity bullfighters: Ortega, Bienvenida, and Enrique Vera. Although Bazin discounts *Tarde de Toro* for being a scripted, staged, and choreographed fiction, he praises its mise-en-scène of integral realism, because "as soon as the camera gets close, the corrida scenes are actually interpreted by matadors that risk their lives and really kill the bull."[46]

The camera's closeness guarantees against tricks. And yet in several of Bazin's bullfight reviews it is cinema's trickery, its ability to mask the passage from one individual or animal to another, that he prizes. Bazin's passing compliment to Myriam's skill in editing *Bullfighting* is telling: "You have to pay careful attention to see that the bull that comes into view from the left is not always the one that left the screen from the right ... without us noticing the switch a 'veronica' beginning with one matador and bull ends with a different man and a different animal ... The linkage of two bulls in a single movement ... surreptitiously replaces the photo of the nonexistent bull we believe we are seeing."[47] With usual critical finesse and a few paragraphs further in the same text, Bazin turns from his admiration for the editor's creation of an illusion of a single bull out of many into the related, deeper problematic, of representing the singularity of death on film.

The same logic associating continuities and discontinuities present in Bazin's bullfight reviews structures Velo's film, and Bazin's emphasis on seamlessness alerts us to an operative displacement. Notice, for instance, what is elided or highlighted in "Toro," the review of *Torero!*. Although *Torero!* is about Procuna's fear of dying, Bazin's only mention of death occurs apropos of Manolete: "In the film on Manolete an actor played him but in the arena it was the poor bullfighter, and his death was his real death."[48] Similarly, Procuna's reenactment is barely mentioned. "Because of his initial notoriety," states Bazin, "images of Procuna were available, and the director had only to recreate some private scenes and film new bullfights with multiple cameras."[49] "Filmed in a newsreel style," he adds, "these images are indiscernible from the documentary ones."[50] As in his comments on Myriam's editing in "Death Every Afternoon," Bazin raves about *Torero!*'s seamless integration of the reconstructed and the newsreel images, precisely the move that masks the film's hybridity, its internal fissures.

Having as my two points of reference "the actor" and "real death," I will consider these filmic substitutions—one bull for another, one bullfighter for Procuna and Procuna for Procuna—as related questions of cinematic ontology and performance. The *Torero!* review's ellisions indicate actual disturbances, which are strongly interconnected in the film—Procuna's reenactment, a temporally and categorically unplaceable presence and the specter of death. I examine how *Torero!* absorbs the unstable identity of the real/actor, by looking at the film's most conspicuous quality, its hybridity and the massive proliferation of Procuna doubles.

TORERO! REPLICANTS

Torero! retraces the morning of Luis Procuna's last recorded bullfight, his time with his children, getting dressed in his "lights" costume, kissing his wife goodbye as he leaves. A sequence of flashbacks detailing his progress from a poor childhood to fame and to paralyzing fear alternates with Procuna's close-up as he rides in a cab toward the arena (Fig. 3.17). The radio announces his awaited return after a long period away from the sport, and gradually, the stakes of this afternoon are articulated in subjective voice-over: he needs to prove he is not afraid.

Like other self-acted celebrity biopics, the film features various stand-ins for Procuna as a child and young adult; it also incorporates recorded images as a captured or staged act, that is, as newsreel record or reenacted segment. Carlos Velo's background as the producer of news magazine programs and newsreels for Manuel Barbachano Ponce was a key element in the film's idea and form. What clinched the project for a biographical film on Luis Procuna was the existence of a wealth of archival material on the bullfighter in Noticiero Mexicano and the Cineteca Mexicana: signing his first contract, his wedding, meeting with stars like Dolores del Rio and the memorable return of the bullfighter to the arena in 1954 after a protracted absence. Guillermo Cabrera Infante describes the event (witnessed by the film's scriptwriter Hugo Butler)[51] that sparked the film, the dramatic afternoon when Procuna tried to recover his standing among the great matadors:

Figure 3.17: The subjective frame: Procuna reminisces on the way to the bullfight (Carlos Velo's *Torero!*, 1956).

his performance was so bad that he was fined five thousand pesos . . . With insults flying . . . Procuna offered to grant the spectators a bull as a gift. . . . When the faena with the muleta started, both bull and Procuna rivetted the public fascinated with that death match. . . . as the bull died slowly its solitary death, Procuna was lifted in glory and taken home. Now *Torero!* could start. As the winner was transformed into a living statue, the symbol of the triumph of man over beast and death, they [the producer and filmmaker] understood that they had an irritated oyster in their hand: the pearl started to take form.[52]

With the finale guaranteed, the task was to have all images indistinguishable from the existing newsreel footage. Velo followed Procuna everywhere with his reportage crew's four cameras to get extra material with which to cover the biography. He cleverly integrates disparate newsreel material as a part of the story by having the first appearance of Procuna, a young and handsome toreador, coincide with the moment he is born as a star. Over shots of him demonstrating his skills at a private ranch surrounded by the still and moving cameras of the Noticiero Mexicano, he states: "The cameramen adored me" (Fig. 3.20).

Velo "placed" Procuna into the action by matching his style to footage shot by other cameramen.[53] To recreate the scene of the audience furious at Procuna's performance, the director used the reactions to another torero who "fortunately turned his back" to the camera. Given the similar costumes and the fact that "the images were in black and white," it was easy to cut to Procuna, "shot later in a passageway surrounding the arena, where one could place the cameras without a problem."[54] To mimic a zoom, then inexistent, and convey the moment when the toro gets the bullfighter, Velo increased the number of *cogidas* (thrusts) since he had "hundreds of them in the archive, [he] just had to select those that have a torero with a similar clothing, cutting the face out in editing"[55] (Figs 3.21a–d).

These editing feats are impressive. But what deserves attention is the echo between the director's pride in a seamless texture and Bazin's astonishment at the director's ability to disguise the "switch" between a "'veronica' beginning with one matador and bull [and ending] with a different man and a different animal."[56]

Bazin's appreciation for the undetectable substitution of bodies and identities (of bulls or bullfighters) has little to do with technical virtuosity. In the critic's thinking, continuity and discontinuity are mutually determining; any mention of a seamless transitions between bodies or registers ultimately has as its reference in discontinuity, the deadly core of bullfights.

This node holds special interest when analyzing *Torero!*, an orgiastic composite of Procuna and deindividuated body parts, of bulls and matadors that function as celluloid proxies filling in the gap of actual risk for the main star. In fact, Bazin's special affinity for the film does not derive from its purported transparency so much as the manner in which the film's existentially tinged narrative—with its subjective commentary and constant announcement of fear of death—is visually and thematically tied to its manifest textural hybridity.

The film exposes its anxious relation to discontinuity and death mainly through an excess of doubles, excess with ontological and dramatic implications. The

Figure 3.18: Procuna dishonored (*Torero!*, 1956).

Figure 3.19: Procuna recovers his standing and is carried in triumph (*Torero!*, 1956).

Figure 3.20: Newsreel discovery of Procuna (*Torero!*, 1956).

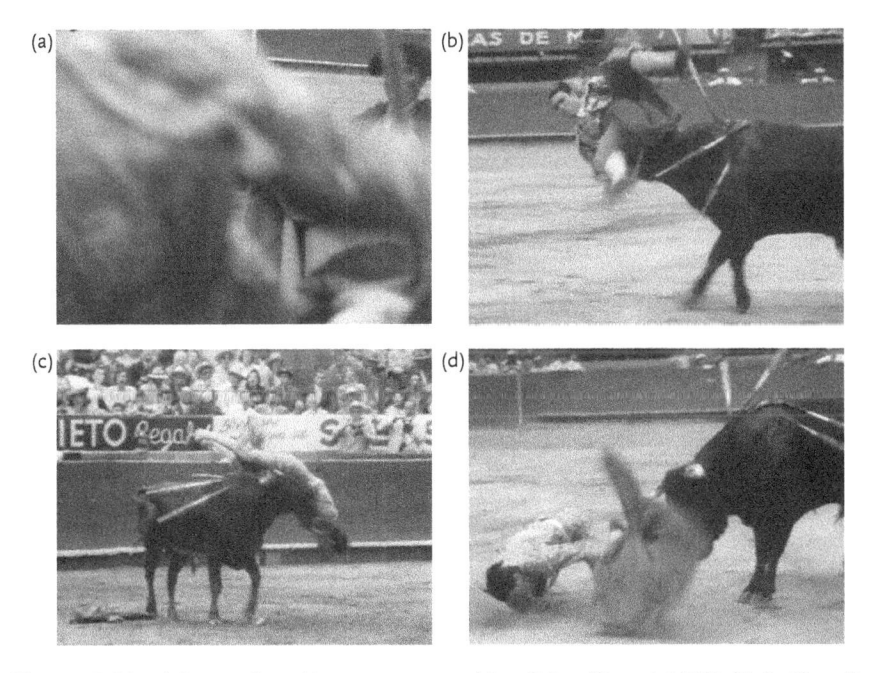

Figure 3.21: a) Procuna's accident reconstructed in editing (*Torero!*, 1956). b) Accident 2. c) and d) Accident 3.

splitting starts with Procuna, who occupies a number of categorical registers. Alongside Procuna's "prepersonal body," his biological configuration and his identifiable "personal body," the one he calls his, we are supposed to see the impersonated Procuna, a character at different points in his life.[57] Besides Procuna's doubled-up presence, there are other avatars—for instance, the invisible army of bullfighters masked by the continuity of match-in-action shots and the parade of matador celebrities framing Procuna's career. Carlos Arruza and Manolete are only two of many bullfighters who appear in the film displaying their art, risking death or dying.

These celebrities who lend the biopic historical verisimilitude introduce a compensatory economy based on visibility and erasure. The famous toreros stand apart from the anonymous bodies of toreros whose identities are effaced through the match-on-action shot. Ann Chisholm has noted that although neither body doubles or stunt men or stuntwomen are meant to be identified on the screen, the latter are better paid and are credited according to the individual talent or physical and athletic prowess they bring into the film.[58] In a scale sliding from stuntmen to body doubles and extras, "physical and sartorial likeness to stars" assures the erasure of the body doubles' identities.[59] Although these body fragments are highly particularized as indexes of a given registered bullfight, these bullfighters' identities are hijacked and obliterated along with their unseen faces.[60]

If we attend to the film's verbal dramatization of Procuna's fear, we start to see the narrative as a protracted choreography with Procuna the real/actor continually averting death while surrounded by a host of bullfighters who are either dead or about to die. The emphasis on Procuna's subjectivity, his voice-over, the recurring close-ups, reaction and point-of-view shots turn him into a safe relay for the disturbing procession of matadors displaying their art and its risks. Simultaneously, the film underscores the utter relativity of his position inside the arena or outside of it as a viewer (Figs 3.22a and 3.22b). Procuna watches Manolete in his first appearance in Mexico and then in 1946, one year before Manolete's death, Procuna shares the bill during of the inauguration of *La Mexico* the monumental new arena, with Manolete and Carlos Arruza. He follows famous matador Joselito's turn in the arena and then serves as pallbearer at his funeral (Figs 3.22c and 3.22d).

This pattern, whereby Procuna first shares the program with another bullfighter and then witnesses his wounding or death, is ironic in itself. Inasmuch as the irony is compounded several times over, the film comes to function as an identity grid through which Procuna's presence is relativized by other singular, but equally mortal, bullfighters. As colleagues are wounded or even buried, Procuna's subjective musings are supposed to tame the radical ritual co-presence of animal, torero, and audience proper to the bullfights. However, this subjectivity cannot absorb the disturbing and pervasive dissemination of matadors in the film. He is either fused via editing with other toreadors' body parts; or he watches them through binoculars mediating the spectator's perception of a matador's fate. Within the filming process he foregoes the sharpness of an individuated cornada—the goring of the flesh. Thus, the film enacts

Figure 3.22: a) Manolete seen through Procuna's binoculars (*Torero!*, 1956). b) Procuna as shocked audience (*Torero!*, 1956). c) Cornada watched by Procuna (*Torero!*, 1956). d) Procuna carrying Joselito's coffin (*Torero!*, 1956).

textually and narratively a tension between con-fusion (of bodies and doubles) and the need to stave off contagion, to safely "stay" with the living.

What is the status of Procuna's reenacted presence amid this visual and dramatic haunting? Independent of whether the bullfighter doubles are identifiable as such or serve to construct an ersatz image, the extensive use of archival footage invites a comparison between in-person reenactment and repurposed newsreel footage.

Such distinctions do matter. The two modes condition each other according to discrete forms of indexicality and authenticity—one photographic, the other performative. Reenactment's functionality—the fact that it is scripted, acted, and can therefore fill in undocumented periods of life—marks it off visually and ontologically from newsreels, which record punctual but fleeting moments in which a particular bull's horn tore through a particular torero's flesh. Conversely, the sense of contingency emanating from the arena newsreels reveals the indeterminacy of the protagonist's reenactment, its lack of existential edge.

But if these distinctions count, it is also because the film's *agon* revolves around their potential blurring. The potential contamination of dead matadors (those in the archive) and those not yet dead (Procuna), of past and present, of archive and "actual" presence, lends the film its interest. Even as Procuna accumulates a surplus of iconicity, the torero's existential anchor to the represented moment is also secondhand.

CELEBRITY REENACTMENT, BIOPIC, AND THE MORTAL BODY [103]

MEXICAN CINÉ-VERDAD, CARLOS VELO, HUGO BUTLER, AND ZAVATTINI

Torero!'s combination of actualities, reenactment, and subjective realism confounded categorization but elicited praise: the film was seen by critics as fulfilling the "ideals of modern cinema, to fuse documentary with the fictional" and as an "antecedent of European techniques of cinema verité and of free cinema."[61] It was nominated for an Oscar in the category of documentary and awarded special mention at the Venice Film Festival for "its contribution to the renewal of cinematic realism through the integration of real documents with reenactment," by a jury composed of Bazin, John Grierson, and Luchino Visconti. Writer José de la Colina referred to the film as a "new genre, a biographical essay; at once a biography of Procuna and an essay on the relation of the torero with his public, [on the] fear of the bull and fear of people."[62] La Colina's characterization of *Torero!* as a biographical essay has important consequences for the nature of in-person reenactment raising, most immediately, the question of whether Procuna's narration reflects a personal individualized experience or whether it serves instead as a platform for a more ample and generalizable reflection on finitude. The implications of the film's generic and textual hybridity in decentering the self-acted biopic start with the film's genealogy.

As a biopic, *Torero!* has a special pedigree. It was coscripted by Carlos Velo, who had made formally sharp documentaries in 1930s Spain before escaping fascism and immigrating to Mexico during the civil war,[63] and Hugo Butler, a screenwriter blacklisted in Hollywood whose screenplays included the biopic *Edison, the Man*, Renoir's *The Southerner*, and *He Ran All the Way*, among several noir films.

The film displays an early 1950s noir hybridity in its juxtaposition of dramatized events and documentary footage. The same porosity between newsreel production and fiction features evident in Louis de Rochemont's move to apply his brother's *March of Time*'s dramatized newsreel style to Hollywood feature production can be detected in the collaboration between Butler and Velo, whose extensive experience in producing newsreels was essential to *Torero!*'s aesthetic.[64] Between 1946 and 1951, Velo directed the newsreel Noticiero Mexicano de EMA (España-México-Argentina),[65] and in 1953 he started working for Manoel Barbachano Ponce, an innovative producer and major force for the budding independent Mexican cinema. In Ponce's company, Teleproducciones,[66] Velo became the director, technical advisor, and editor-in-chief of newsreel programs Tele-revista, Cine selecciones, and Camara y Cinema verdad,[67] and he was unofficially recognized as the driving force behind *Raíces* (Benito Alazraki, 1953–1954), an episode film based on short stories featuring indigenous people as actors on location. *Raíces* was unusual for focusing on a group often marginalized from the screen, and it garnered praise for its documentary authenticity. Velo's highly composed shots, reflecting his admiration for Eisenstein, set the film apart from a conventional naturalist representation.

This chorus of progressive voices includes Cesare Zavattini, who was invited by the producer Barbachano Ponce to Mexico in 1954 to help develop scripts with a strong, humanist orientation to remedy the weaknesses of Mexican cinema.[68] Zavattini had made his first Mexican contacts during a festival of neorealist films, right after his 1953 lecture "Il Neorealismo secondo me," at the Convegno de Parma; there, he called for a cinema that closely follows a person's life and has individuals play themselves.[69] In this context of rethinking realism, Zavattini's contributions to Mexican cinema illuminate the stakes of *Raíces* and *Torero!*'s use of the actual protagonist to affirm the authenticity of popular, national traits.

Among the proposed scripts, *Mexico Mio* (to be directed by Velo) proved most exciting to the intellectuals and artists who had gathered at Barbachano Ponce's house to contribute to the project of making a national documentary.[70] In these meetings, Velo explained the kinds of scenes that would fit *Mexico Mio*: "raccontini," Zavattini's term for short condensed tales based on quasi-ethnographic investigation. According to Velo, *Mexico Mio* "would have no script [and] in the style of cinema-verité [would] create [scenes] in direct contact with reality or through the detailed reconstruction of real facts."[71] The film would be structured having a day as a "man's measure," with individuals' daily lives showing "the passage from work to party, from effort to joy" across several states in Mexico.[72] The script drew heavily on a physical and a human geography with great attention to ethnographic detail and folklore; uncharacteristically for Zavattini, it called for bird's-eye views of Mexican monuments.[73] With a syncretic organization inspired by Dziga Vertov, region and class contrasts would be clustered thematically: a "birth scene in a maternity [ward] followed by the funeral of a small girl; a desperate immigration scene by the inside of a plane filled with tourists; a scene of humble ceramic workers by the same object shown in a fancy business window in Mexico City."[74] In one of the published passages we get a glimpse of the film's projected texture. It would start with the Fiesta of the Virgin, the Nation's protector, and focus on one of the penitents, Guillerma, who is on her knees by the Virgin and who follows after her husband, who has migrated to El Paso.[75]

Mexico Mio and *Cuba Mia*, a projected Cuban counterpart, were international versions of a new documentary approach whose matrix was *Italia Mia*—a film that was also never completed.[76] The "mio" of the titles signals the repossession of the nation by its anonymous citizens. When Zavattini attempted to enlist De Sica and Roberto Rosselini as directors of *Italia Mia*, his selling point was the potential for using the voices and life experiences of real people, through interviews and reenactment. The extant notes and script for *Italia Mia* and for *Mexico Mio* (officially left in Velo's hands in 1957) constitute a repertoire of original documentary formats featuring, in particular, reenacted vignettes. Addressing this aspect, Rafaella de Antonellis has suggested that Zavattini's *pedinamento* approach (closely tracking its object) is evident in how he planned filming *Mexico Mio*: a scriptwriter standing at a particular location with a notebook jots down what he sees and, after spotting individual "characters," makes them into foci of narrative interest.[77] While reenactment does not represent a programmatic aspect of *Mexico Mio*, the screenplay cuts between verité interviews and short reenacted vignettes focusing on individual characters.

Although Procuna's reenactment is not driven by the national portraiture agenda that informs *Mexico Mio*, we can speculate on the relation between these new forms of realism propped on the authentic protagonist. How does the self-reenacted biopic and the verité hybrid differently lean on and authorize the actual protagonist's voice, life, or thoughts? Does Procuna's presence as actor facilitate his claim of an individualized experience and angst as suggested in the film's adoption of a heightened subjectivity or does it promote instead the typicality of the torero's story and fate? Does the essayistic tone of the film inflect the nature of Procuna's individuality? In order to understand the status of the individualized self in *Torero!*, we need to look at the delicate balance between two narratives in the film: one, informed by the generic conventions of the biopic, promotes a national populist representativity; the other takes the hesitant existentialist tone of the noir into the more ambitious essayistic dimension of an exposé on bullfighting and finitude.

In Mexico, filming a bullfighter's rise to glory from humble origins counted as a form of social reclamation of the nation's marginalized. In a review, writer Carlos Fuentes appreciated the film's "treatment of Mexican lives—in this case of a matador—in which the viewer can recognize himself, not for particular or eccentric traits, but because of the general tone of the [film's]ambience, its vital course of personal action and reaction."[78] For Fuentes, "Procuna is interesting not as a star, but as a person."[79] Stressing the populist aspects of the film, he states that *Torero!* "draws Luis Procuna's physiognomy with accents of truth and drama, since he surrounds this personal trace with vocation elements, of a Mexican situation rarely experienced in a cinema most often made by Martians to Venusians."[80]

Analyzing the populist orientation of *Torero!*'s script, Rebecca Schreiber notes that the focus on Procuna's life exposes "aspects of the 'laborist sensibility' that Michael Denning saw in the work of cultural producers within the U.S popular front."[81] Both Velo and Butler, the film's screenwriter, had leftist leanings and their interest in the "symbolic weight of the star's origin" was exemplary of the cultural front's predilection for figures who would be "not merely a success among this sporting or artist's public, but the potential first citizen of his community or his people."[82] As Eric Hobsbawm notes, the bullfighter—like the movie star—is the "artist sprung from the unskilled poor and playing for the poor"[83]; he wins "the loyalty and allegiance of audiences through an implicit and explicit claim to represent them."[84] Such social representation comes out explicitly when audience on-screen watches the spectacle, as in a 1958 film *Los Pequenos gigantes* (1957, *The Perfect Game*), directed by Butler under the pseudonym of Hugo Mozo. Here, Cesar Faz and the famous Little League team he coaches reenact their story from the early days, overcoming discrimination abroad to claim victory over American players in the end.[85] The film painstakingly retraces the rise to stardom against the odds as an economic opportunity as well as a full entrance into citizenship—in this case the montage of Mexicans following the game in the radio and the final reception of the team by the president when they return to Mexico. Reversing *Torero!*'s ratio of archive to reenactment, this brief public acknowledgment corresponds to the sole newsreel footage in the film signaling the different coverage economy in recreating the life story of the celebrity.

While Procuna's portrayal has a clear populist dimension, the arc of his rise to fame is significantly problematized by the many matadors who appear in the film, only to die. The actualities and the obsessive reiteration of the death theme bring the biopic into the sphere, in tone and in content, of Hemingway's *Death in the Afternoon* and Michel Leiris's writings on bullfighting.

Hemingway and Leiris viewed the bullfight as a unique aesthetic ritual whose authenticity was on a par with the corrida's risk. They likened the bullfight to writing to claim for literature (and autobiography) the edginess of an actual existential confrontation. "Suppose," states Hemingway,

> a writer's books were automatically destroyed at his death and only existed in the memory of those who had read them. That is what happens in bullfighting . . . the individual, whose doing of them made them, who was the touchstone, the original, disappears and until another individual as great comes, the things, by being imitated, with the original gone, soon distort, lengthen, shorten weaken and lose all reference to the original. All art is only done by the individual.[86]

Leiris refined the stakes of this individuality by bringing into play the autobiographical dimension. As Nathan Guss puts it, Leiris saw "writing and bullfighting [as consolidating] the boundaries of the self" and the "flawless apprehension of the self" in autobiography as depending on the authenticity achieved in the instant of mortal danger.[87]

These references to literature frame a range of possible life narratives for a bullfighter. First, let's address the more direct link between *Torero!* and Hemingway's *Death in the Afternoon*. Butler, the scriptwriter was a bullfighting aficionado and had watched the famous fight in which Procuna made his comeback. He based the film on a short column titled "Biografia de Luis Procuna," but he also stated he appropriated the reflective lines on fear and death from Hemingway.[88] Butler also adopted for *Torero!*'s structure Hemingway's tragic irony in describing a celebrated torero's fate. The overly compressed sequences of Procuna sharing the arena with a toreador, followed by scenes in which his counterpart is seen gored, in the hospital, or carried in a coffin represent a cinematic version of Hemingway's ironic style—his staccato and abridged account of the death of an earlier celebrity, Joselito:

> Then comes Joselito . . . and this is Christ's truth: he was hooted . . . and had cushions thrown at him the last day he fought in Madrid the 15th may 1920 . . . while the crowd shouted "Que se vaya! Que se vaya!" Which can be translated as "May he get the hell out of here and stay." The next day, the 16th of may he was killed in Talavera de la Reina, gored though the lower abdomen so his intestines came out and he was unable to hold them in with both hands but died of traumatic shock from the force of the cornada while the doctors were working on the wound, and his face composed very peacefully in the operating table after he was dead . . . and a crowd of gypsies outside . . . and Gallo . . . outside very pitiful, afraid to go in to see his brother dead, and Alamendro the banderillero saying, "If they can kill *this man* I tell you none of us is safe! None of us!"[89]

Butler also borrows this last remark. Following a newsreel scene in which Procuna is one of the pallbearers for his friend Joselito, Procuna learns of Manolete's death by phone. Procuna then sits for a private projection of a 16mm film of Manolete's celebrated funeral in 1947. This elaborate screening is quite long, defining the significance of *another* torero's death as the site of displacement in *Torero!*. In a verbal enunciation of the film's thematics of surrogacy and identification, Procuna refers to the matadors carrying Manolete's coffin, just as he had done for Joselito: "If it could happen to someone like Manolete, then it could happen to me."

This scripted appropriation would seemingly conflict with the presumed authenticity of in-person reenactment. One of the assumptions underlying the self-acted biopic is that the I voiced by the protagonist authorizes the exclusive nature of his life events, and vice versa. Procuna's borrowed line would seem to compromise the authenticity of his experience since it shows it attached to a broader generalizable sentiment. And yet this nonexclusive, broadly applicable "thought" is a function of fiction and scripting, hence inherent to reenactment, a form of representation based on its *differance* and deferral of an original. The "me" so vehemently voiced and embodied by Procuna is largely an effect of artifice. It is intercepted by multiple proxies, including Procuna's narration voice, which, deemed too high and childish, was substituted by someone else's for fear it could expose the bullfighter to ridicule.[90]

Just as significantly, the "shareable" sense of vulnerability affect underscores the generic underpinnings of this life story. The analogy between "this man" (be it Joselito or Manolete) and "me" or "us," who are equally mortal, represents an interesting variant of the replaceability trope that typifies celebrity narratives. Here, the circularity between the unique and the replaceable is inflected by considerations on finitude and existential authenticity specific to the bullfight and inoperative in other celebrity and rise-to-fame stories.

As for Leiris, his commentary for Brauberger's *The Bullfight* (1951), specifically the film's conclusion and its play with recursivity, helps us articulate the temporal specificity of reenactment as well as the potential implication of *Torero!*'s proliferating doubles. After a montage of deadly accidents and a list of toreros who, whether "bold or prudent," cannot escape the "harsh experience," *The Bullfight* focuses on "Manolete, himself wounded as soon as the bull entered." As Manolete is being treated at a clinic, we hear: "The infirmary at Linares Square, where he met his death on 28 August 1947 was not, unfortunately, as well equipped as the clinic where he was transported this day" (Fig. 3.23). After this announcement, a short biography of Manolete is superimposed on a long bravura sequence combining two *corridas* in which he—a man who "thanks to his art . . . managed to triumph over his own mortal condition"—performed a series of hallucinating passes (Fig. 3.24).

The poetics of this conclusion relies on its subversive announcement of a death instantly belied by an image of Manolete, alive and well. This dislocated revelation promotes all images of Manolete we see from this point on as revenants. The same haunting performed by such simple cinematic play had been already used in the Hemingway/Joris Ivens collaboration, *Spanish Earth* (1937); in both cases, the casual indication of a future death before a person's present reappearance underscores cinema's unique ability to convey contingency and channel it into narrative. By overplaying the cinema's recursivity against the finality of death—as the filmmakers of *The Bullfight*, of *The Spanish Earth*, and Bazin understood so well—one can extol the utmost singularity out of cinematic repetition, proving how essential one is to the other.

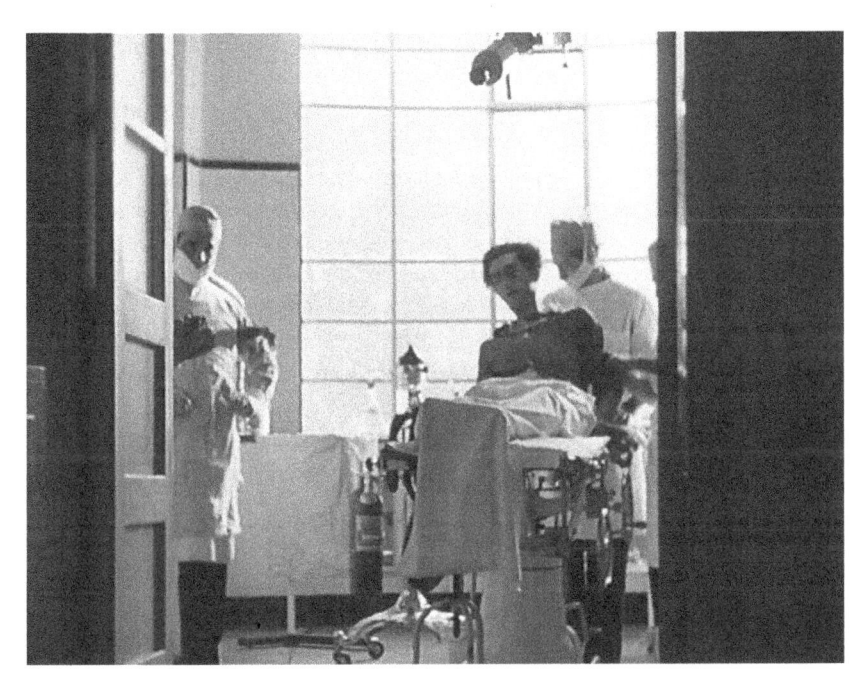

Figure 3.23: Manolete at infirmary while his death at another bullfight is mentioned in Michel Leiris's commentary (Pierre Braunberger's *The Bullfight-La Course des taureaux*, 1951).

Figure 3.24: Manolete's spectacle after his death is announced in *The Bullfight* (1951).

Leiris's words *and* their placement are central to Bazin's reflections on the ontology of the cinematic image, starting with the revised Hemingway title—Death *every* afternoon, that names Bazin's key essay on the subject. In the film, just prior to the crowds emptying the arena, the images of various matadors are faintly superimposed before fading and giving place to the bull "eternally reborn."[91] This sequence, a literal figuration of abeyance, of bodies-not-yet dead—is apposed to Leiris's strange ode to cyclicality: "No human plenitude that is not succeeded by void; no light that does not hit against the shadow's border. But when the sun comes down and another raises again, and if the day is buried by the night it only lasts until the next day . . . a new bull quick feisty . . . appears from the toril in the afternoon light. Facing this bull eternally reborn there will be always, for victory or defeat, a new torero."[92] To the eternality of this cycle Bazin responds with his brilliant reflections on cinema's recursivity: "on the screen the toreador dies every afternoon"[93]

Although *Torero!* parades many of the same figures that appear in *The Bullfight*, the suspension of Manolete's death and its fetishistic denial via the spectacular montage of triumphant passes and the faint image of superimposed matadors shares little with *Torero!*, where all retroactive movement is geared to confirm that Procuna is indeed, and in contrast to the other toreros, very much alive.

In *Torero!*, Procuna's mournful reaction to Manolete's death helps understand how the film offsets the disturbance caused by the threat of death. After watching the funeral in a private screening, Procuna visits Manolete's tomb in Spain. But here the reenacted visit is itself done by proxy, courtesy of a fellow newscaster. Procuna is filmed in Mexico at a similar cemetery while the cameraman's assistant's shadow crosses Manolete's tomb in Spain. It is this borrowed trace that, fleetingly staged, culls actuality and presence for this fiction (Figs. 3.25, 3.26 3.27a–c,).

Procuna's homage to Manolete by the grave epitomizes the complex relation of reenactment to contingency and actuality. Procuna's reenacted presence amounts to a peculiarly hollow presence lacking a precise relation to time. And yet, like the other inserts of body doubles whose identity has been effaced, the shadow lends this visit to the grave an aura of authenticity. The shadow asserts an existential link between a human being passing by Manolete's tomb at a precise moment in the afternoon, and yet this existential relation to Procuna is as fictive as the inserts of a body double whose identity has been effaced so he may complete the fictive Procuna.

The imperceptible passage from Procuna standing in a cemetery and the surrogate shadow crossing over Manolete's tomb exemplifies the fraught relation between mortality and reenactment in filmed biographies. With its own transience and indeterminacy, the shadow figures the link between the dead, the living, and the in-between. While it supposedly confers a bodily presence to the protagonist (doubles typically lack shadows), the shadow is of course hardly different from the other bodies and body traces with which it figuratively comes into contact. At a deeper level, the photographic basis equalizes all images, sounding a parallel death knell: "not only . . . are all photographs posthumous but they are ostensibly mortifying: telling of a death that was, they warn of a death coming."[94] Once Procuna turns his back while leaving through *a* cemetery (not the cemetery), he reiterates his presence as himself—not yet dead.

Figure 3.25: Manolete is dead (*Torero!*, 1956).

Figure 3.26: Procuna watches newsreels of Manolete's funeral (*Torero!*, 1956).

Figure 3.27: a) Procuna "at" Manolete's tomb (*Torero!*, 1956). b) "Procuna's" shadow crosses over Manolete's tomb (*Torero!*, 1956). c) Still alive, Procuna leaves the cemetery (*Torero!*, 1956).

CHAPTER 4
A Sort of Psychodrama

Verité Moments 58–61

Make no mistake. It is not merely a question of giving the camera the lightness of a pen ... it is a question of making an effort to see that the subjects of the film will recognize themselves in their own roles.

Edgar Morin[1]

Sociodrama deals with problems that can neither be clarified nor treated in a secret chamber. It needs all the eyes and all the ears of the community, its depth and breadth in order to operate adequately. The ideal is the drama that all can share, the amphitheater.

Jacob L. Moreno[2]

Extending Jean Rouch's insights about the cathartic potential of role-playing in *Mad Masters* (1955), sociologist Edgar Morin and Rouch envisioned *Chronicle of a Summer* (1960), their first joint venture, as a Morenian amphitheater,[3] a platform for the collective playing out of a film's "psychoanalytic truth for [an] audience who emerges from its cinematographic catalepsy and is awakened ... to [a] lucid consciousness of brotherhood."[4] In contrast to the mimetic reconstructions of neorealism, cinema verité promotes a cathartic speech that doubles as socially liberating communication and achieves, in a distinctly psychoexistential register, the Zavattinian premise that full awareness of one's acts depends upon "making them public."[5] Much like the neorealist's vision of reenactment as a public, anti-individualist lesson, cinema verité is central to the confessional-performative arc of realist cinema traced in this book.

This chapter explores the political and cultural contours of the late 1950s impetus for autocritique in France. In particular, two laboratories of self-awareness provide the focus: *The Human Pyramid* made by Jean Rouch in 1959 and *Chronicle of a Summer*. These films inaugurate a new cinematic paradigm distinct from the realist cinemas of the day. Rather than prioritizing immediacy through unobtrusive camerawork, they turn cinema into a stage for processing identity through attention to deliberating, reflective speech. Intended as a means of self-analysis, both films gather their actors for round-table discussions, intense interviews, and role-playing, modern methodologies borrowed from psychosocial studies that expose cinema's ambition to be *the* prime medium for self-revision, to test and effectively promote authentic social relations.

In 1959, as Ivory Coast was about to achieve its independence from France and the definition of a "French community" stood at issue, Rouch set out to explore exactly what such a community might be. Recognizing that relationships between Europeans and Africans were nonexistent, he made *The Human Pyramid* to spur social interactions among a group of students beyond their integrated classroom at the Cocody Lycée (a high school in Abidjan).[6] Employing improvised scenarios, he encouraged members of both groups to take on the other's perspective—including racist roles.[7] Production overlapped with the filming of *Chronicle of a Summer*, the work that lent the epithet *verité* its searching, existential quality. In *Chronicle*, the camera was meant to be a "stimulant"[8] and intervene actively: "to cut across appearances and extract from them hidden and dormant truths" so that the "action in the end is the word."[9] The verité camera and direct sound recording technology put each actor's consciousness at stake from one moment to the next, without cinema's usual masquerades, sets, or staged ceremonies.[10] By training the camera and sound recorder on an emergent subject under relentless scrutiny (like Marilou or Marceline in *Chronicle*), or boldly pushing the effects of drama into a zone of real discomfort (asking French students to act out racist roles of in *The Human Pyramid*), these films help channel fiction and imaginary projections toward a self-enlightening pedagogy.[11]

This project of self-revision aimed for a "sort of psychodrama carried out collectively among authors and characters."[12] The program coalesces in *Chronicle*'s notorious postscreening scene, when the participants heatedly analyze the artificiality or authenticity of their exchanges[13] (Fig. 4.1). In the screening room, cinema verité is blamed for promoting obscene scenes of self-exposure and contrived encounters; at the same time, however, it is commended for giving rise to moments when being proves inextricable from playing a role.[14] Acting is explicitly admitted as a welcome catalyst for authentic expression—for instance, when Jean Pierre Sergent observes that Marceline's scenes work only because she was acting (Fig. 4.2). His reference could be to her monologue in the Place de la Concorde and Les Halles or to yet another scene that could easily epitomize the complex ambition to square fiction with a deeper reality in cinema verité—a lengthy argument between Jean Pierre and Marceline that was excised from *Chronicle*.

This scene, which can be seen only in *Eté plus 50* (Florence Dauman, 2011, a documentary on the film), epitomizes the directors' wish to encompass "aspects of subjective life covered more often in fiction features,"[15] while the repeated rushes afford a peek into the film's focus on processing the self. Shot through with loaded pauses and moments of awkward self-consciousness, the scene foregrounds how cinema verité modulates screen personae. Lengthy shots and the pent-up emotion

Figure 4.1: Postscreening discussion: "You've just seen yourselves on the screen." In *Chronicle of a Summer* (Jean Rouch, Edgar Morin, 1961).

Figure 4.2: Marceline's explanation of her performance. In *Chronicle of a Summer* (Jean Rouch, Edgar Morin, 1961).

in Marceline's remarks underscore the unclear reasons for their breakup; standing on a jetty parapet with breaking waves as in the background, the couple seems appropriately alone (Fig. 4.3). Still, Jean Pierre claps his hands from time to time, marking the start of another take and exposing his contact with the off-frame crew (Fig. 4.4). The multiple takes bespeak a phenomenology of bad faith, and the synchronized sound verifies commitment to personal truth, serving as a litmus test for authenticity. Later in the same film, Marceline comments that this suffering lover resembling Monica Vitti in *L'avventura* (Michelangelo Antonioni, 1960) was only one of her many selves.

The allusion to Antonioni and to a host of selves exemplifies the existentialist roots of 1960s art and verité cinema.[16] But Marceline's casual hint to her other roles (she was active in the underground, pro-FLN Jeanson Network) points to deeper political currents of the French national and existential crisis that forms the backdrop of *Chronicle of a Summer*. As Michael Uwemedimo has noted, Morin and Rouch's interrogatory approach was in line with the "wave of opinion polls and *études psychosociales*" conducted at mid-twentieth century, as French society "anxiously questioned the . . . nature of modernization, decolonization, and ultimately Frenchness."[17] Indeed, subjecting social actors to continual self-questioning reveals a deep disenchantment with leftist and national politics. The confessional-performative impetus of *Chronicle*, its aim for total truth in interrogating its participants, expresses left-wing intellectuals' conflicted sense of allegiance in light of the French torture of Algerians, censorship of dissidence, and coercion tactics on

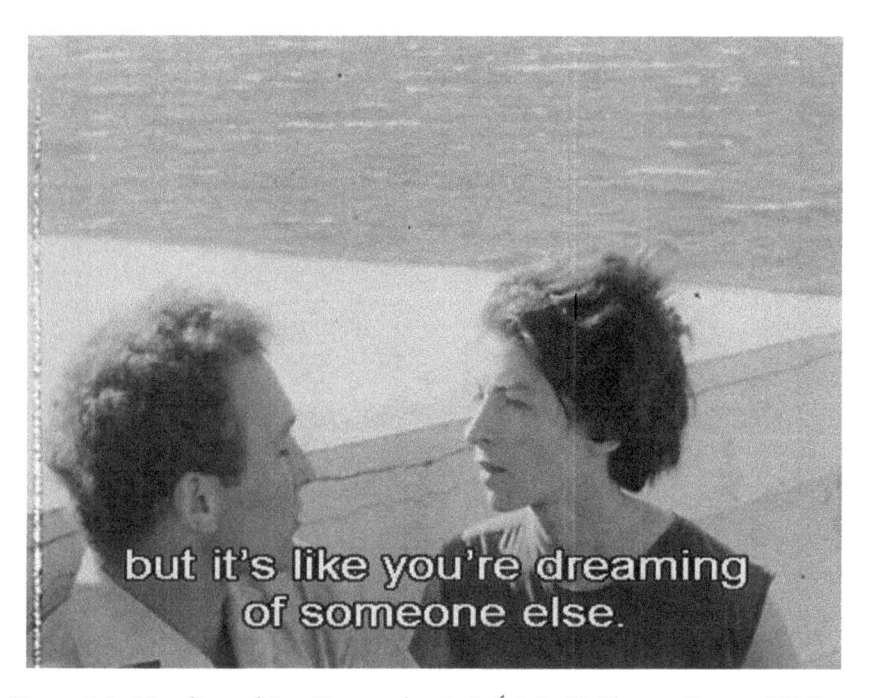

Figure 4.3: Marceline and Jean Pierre at the pier in *Été plus 50* (Florence Dauman, 2010).

Figure 4.4: Jean Pierre claps for retakes of his scene with Marceline (Dauman, *Été plus 50*, 2010).

the part of the Stalinist and French Communist Party.[18] Likewise the enactment of a new, integrated community in *The Human Pyramid* serves as a corrective to the government's empty talk about a "French Community" in its colonies. Aware that the "images of an European and African community (frequenting each other outside of the school) only took on value if they were considered a document," Rouch framed the film as a *documentary* on an experiment in sociodrama.[19] He believed that the film could only make an impact if seen as a document of a process of self-consciousness about racism.

To understand why Rouch and Morin invoke a therapeutic frame, to refract France's anxiety over its identity it is paramount to consider the French reception of psychodrama and group dynamics as part of a larger move toward self-reevaluation in the late 1950s.

Between 1954 and 1959, two experiments in applied psychology—Kurt Lewin's Research Center for Group Dynamics at the Massachusetts Institute of Technology and Jacob L. Moreno's sociometric sessions in Beacon Hill, New Jersey—had received broad attention among French social scientists.[20] Their ideas had been taught at French universities since 1947; Ann Shutzenberger credits Georges Gurvitch, who published Moreno at the *Cahiers Internationaux de Sociologie* and founded a sociometry laboratory at the Sorbonne in 1951, with the growth of the discipline in France. After the French publication of *Who Shall Survive?* in 1954, Moreno gave a lecture at the *Centre d'Etudes du Sociologie* at the CNRS (Centre National du Recherche Scientifique), where Morin was working on cinema's effects on audiences.[21] Morin's influence on Rouch at the time he was completing *The Human Pyramid* and the currency of Moreno's theories in France explain the director's invocation of "sociodrama" as his approach. Understood as a means of countering bias, both Lewin and Moreno's group therapies combined the goal of transformation at an interhuman level with democratic forms of interplay.[22] Moved by a concern with authoritarianism Lewin's work involved questioning sclerotic habits to foster the actualization of unrealized abilities, to accept and project a more flexible self in reaction to conformist, depersonalizing tendencies. Participants were evaluated in terms of dogmatism and degrees of transparency and empathy.[23] The classificatory language paralleled Moreno's sociometric methods for quantifying social nuance.[24] The aim of psychodrama, according to Moreno, was "to free the adult of cultural 'conserve'" (his term for negative, fixed patterns of behavior) and open room "for the original spontaneity that can modify the acquired structures [and] roles that block him, the conditioned responses that mechanize him."[25] The director, or "therapeutic prompter," would monitor the scene, staging and interpreting interaction, while the protagonist played out his or her experience in roles that challenged neurotic fixations.[26] Moreno saw psychodrama as a method for addressing interpersonal relations; in turn, sociodrama was conceived as a "single-stroke [exploration *and* treatment], of the conflicts that have arisen between two separate cultural orders."[27]

For Morin and Rouch, who believed in the effect of imaginary and subjective projections, psychodrama represented a unique self-critical *and* cinematic tool, giving "the subject the means to objectify his psychological world, to modify it at the same time that he dramatizes it."[28] Of course, the issue of a perverse mimesis and its potential exorcism via role-playing is central to Rouch's *Mad Masters*. Here, performances of the ritually possessed represent a symptom of, and a response to, colonialism. *The Human Pyramid*, on the other hand, mobilizes performance to counter racism and promote integration. The 1959 film sought to effect actual change, and its turn to sociodrama confirms the dialogic impact of two salient postwar discourses: forms of self and reverse ethnography as a corrective to colonialism, on the one hand, and psychology as the root of, and potentially a means of countering, racism, anti-Semitism, and authoritarianism, on the other.

During the 1950s, *Les Temps Modernes* (among other publications) provides a snapshot of these discourses' convergence as an ethos of self-questioning emerged in France. Alongside Sartre's existential psychoanalysis of Jean Genet,[29] Michel Leiris, in "The Ethnographer Confronting Colonialism," performed a trenchant analysis of ethnography's compromised position and proposed that ethnographers from colonized countries investigate their colonizers' ways of life. And, confirming the international currency of psychosocial techniques such as reverse role-playing and feedback sessions and its association with antiprejudice measures, this same issue included the second part of Moreno's "The Psychodrama of a Marriage" and Else Frenkel-Brunswik and R. Nevitt Sanford's "The Anti-Semitic Personality: Essays on Some Psychological Conditions of Anti-Semitism."[30]

After the war, addressing racism was an urgent matter. George H. Mead's classic observation—that empathy is achieved by taking on a role and objectifying oneself according to another's ideas—provided the basis for numerous programs seeking to promote more authentic exchange. Both in the United States and elsewhere, group dynamics and sociodrama counted as instruments for advancing democracy and affording antiracist pedagogy.[31] Promoted by the Commission on Community Interrelations, sociodramas were conducted with more than one thousand subjects, in order to find the optimal argument and tone for responding to bigotry. Passersby were invited to observe skits simulating public race baiting; their reactions were gauged to find the most effective "antidote."[32] Lewin's Sensitivity Training Experiment—commissioned in 1946 by the first Connecticut State Inter-Racial Commission to address grievances of the African American population—received media attention for its discovery that feedback sessions, including patients discussing their own behavior, produced marked improvements in overall attitudes.[33] In "Action Research and Minority Problems," Lewin makes a point to associate American racism with European colonialism. Significantly, regarding this nexus of therapy and antibias pedagogy, Moreno's longest example of the topical efficacy of sociodrama was reconstructing the situation leading to the Harlem riots of 1943 with an interracial audience.[34] He imagined that enacting daily situations faced in a Harlem unemployment bureau that dealt with both white and black clients would spark a cathartic momentum.[35] As each group acted out its own version of the conflict—for example, "the colored problem in the army, the colored unemployment problem"—the process would "naturally" culminate in a dramatic enactment and cathartic release of the tensions leading to the riots.[36]

To illuminate the nature of Rouch and Morin's attempts to address enduring social and political problems on a symbolic and interpersonal level, I consider in the next sections the films' interface with psychodrama, understood both in the sense of a Morenian praxis and more pervasively as *the* existentialist trope for articulating social bias through dramatic interpersonal scenarios. I structure my analysis around two discursive strands related primarily to each of these filmic experiments in self-awareness. The first regards the effectiveness of role-playing in combating bias and discrimination, a question central to *The Human Pyramid*. The second set of questions concerns the influence of group dynamic theories on *Chronicle*'s attempt to enact a nonauthoritarian form of self-baring as well as to bring the representation of labor, a key Marxist issue, into a new infrasocial configuration alongside questions of leisure and self-determination. Registered in *Chronicle*'s round-table discussions, in Marilou's faltering revelations, or in the "nascent" communication between Landry the African student and Angelo the Renault factory worker, is the desire for an authentic communication that has significant political and cultural ramifications. I analyze the cultural and political context for these confessionals as well as the impact of group dynamics on the left's attempts to retool their understanding of the working class and the everyday.

Using psychodrama as model for cinema holds ideological and aesthetic consequences. The question of how to create closure for a narrative of process and consciousness-raising is a particularly vexed issue. Accordingly, focus falls on how French verité's main tropes, its reflexive and metafictional shifts, are deeply conditioned by the impossibility of reconciling therapeutic and dramatic intent within representation.

ROLE-PLAY: THE REAL IN BALANCE

Pure scaffolding, *The Human Pyramid* is buttressed by explanatory frames at both ends to the point of excess. The film has multiple beginnings and endings; at its edges, it all but slips into a reality that is just as ephemeral. Filmed both in a classroom made of wallboards on a construction site by the Abidjan lagoon (during three consecutive school vacations) and in a mock-up of the classroom at the Gaumont studios in Paris—where Rouch substituted his own voice for those of absent teachers and used desks and blackboard as the sole props—the film operates in a space of pedagogic potentiality[37] (Fig. 4.5). The embrace of transitional states and engagement with education clarify the film's porous relation to Ivory Coast's situation on the eve of independence from France.

The Cocody Lycée had just opened in 1956, and education, a major bone of contention during colonialism, was in flux. One of West African congressional delegates' main demands—access to a French curriculum—had been achieved just the previous year; previously, policies were geared to practical and technical curricula. Once the Overseas Ministry was dissolved in 1958 and the colonies were granted independence, expanding French-style educational systems became entangled with France's need to preserve influence in Africa. The fact that the main actors are adolescents about to graduate from high school and bound for France to pursue college degrees foregrounds the complicated relation between the film's fictive platform of self-awareness and this new community in formation.

Figure 4.5: African and French students at the integrated *Cocody Lycée* in Abidjan in Jean Rouch, *The Human Pyramid* (*La Pyramide Humaine*, 1959).

At a micro-narrative level, the film stages the transition from colonialist segregation to independence and equality by alternating between scenes that feature African and French students. Rouch invites Denise, the daughter of a prominent party official (the *Rassemblement Democratique Africain*) to play Nadine's African counterpart, even though she is older than the others and does not belong to the same class. Her reasoned reflections, presented in voice-over, are meant to bolster a new African consciousness.[38] With ethnographic precision, the film depicts the worlds inhabited by European and Africans: loose images of Alain and Nadine on a motorbike against the Abidjan port and scenes at the club's swimming pool are intercut with scenes of Elola and Dominique (African students) walking through the Treichville market to meet Nathalie and going to a dance hall in the evening. The plot mirrors the rhythms of leisure and homework that govern the students' lives, punctuated by arguments on racism. A dramatized reaction by Denise when she is addressed as "*tu*" (a misplaced intimacy in French) prompts Elola's outrage. Dominique voices the film's message: by hanging out together they will create a model for change. The film oscillates between argumentation and idyllic pockets of coexistence and, unsurprisingly, such scenes hastily bypass conflict.

Typical consciousness-raising discussions convey the students' opinions, but their alternation with scenes of feigned racism complicates the viewer's sense on the social actors' actual convictions. Such ambiguity represents a key element of Rouch's use of role-play. By his own account, sociodrama provided "an extraordinary pretext, the possibility of playing a role that is oneself, but that one can disavow because it is only an image of oneself. One can then say: 'Yes, but it's not me.'"[39] Jacqueline's performance exemplifies the confusion issuing from this strategy of disavowal. A French student, she follows Rouch's directions, acting out in a racist manner and trying to generate conflict. She vehemently faults the Africans for their lack of culture and ignorance and stridently insults Nadine for going out with a black man. Jacqueline's hammy acting and crude views on Africans have an unintended distancing effect, raising doubts as to whether she is representing her own opinions or acting out racist clichés.

Embracing Rouch's reference to sociodrama, a review in *L'Express* revived "exorcism," a term associated already with Rouch, to compare *The Human Pyramid* with Moreno's method for provoking cathartic release. The reviewer argued that by "provoking an arbitrary conflict, a fixation . . . forcing the protagonists to rehash the formulas and a-priorism (the whites are vain; the blacks are big children, etc. . . .), [Rouch] was able to elicit a fictive racial confrontation, so as to effectively expose and exorcise it."[40] The review's account of the purging of racism through role-play confuses notions of acting out and negation. It grants to the "exasperation" of "rehashed formulas, "the exposure of a repressed truth (in the Freudian sense of negation). Acting out, the present reliving of unconscious wishes and fantasies, while refusing to recognize their source and repetitive character,"[41] becomes equated too simply with its outward manifestation, with a "fixation." The reverse assumption is that by activating racist views consciously and through a scripted role, students can externalize and purge these ideas.

The notion of a psychically fruitful "exasperation" of rehashed formulas underlies Moreno's favorite psychodramatic exercise. In one of his therapy sessions, Moreno showcases a woman imitating her mother-in-law in a role-reversal exercise. In his view, such mimicry represents a step toward evaluating the intensity of the patient's motivations and modulating her understanding of opposite perspectives.[42] J. B. Pontalis, one of the first thinkers to criticize Moreno's theories in France, identifies the pitfalls of scenarios involving role reversal, noting that participants retrace "known cycles of authority and dependence" replicating intersubjective structures pervaded by a sort of inertia.[43] This circularity is evident in the standstill quickly reached in the sketches between French and African students. Ultimately, what merits attention in *The Human Pyramid* is the way spontaneity (automatic, unpremeditated dialogue) reveals its dependence on existing protocols of behavior and available imaginaries.

The critical power of the caricatured positioning enacted in *The Human Pyramid* relies on a dynamic in which theatricality represents a cipher for, but also the antidote to, alienation. The existentialist principle animating Rouch and Morin's cinematic vision is that sociality, or the porosity of the self with regard to another person, can turn into an effective form of interpellation if articulated through an aesthetic artifice. Masquerade as an active response to the tyranny of social expectations is central to the basic psychodramatic thrust of early existentialist scenarios. From early 1950s writings on otherness and race to the later, psychologically inflected treatises on colonialism, one finds an affinity with the filmmaker's therapeutic and dramatic discourse.

Sartre's existential psychoanalysis of Jean Genet's life and art illustrates how social perception and individual self-construction feed off of each other: "It is always *against* the Other and the Other's intentions," Sartre explains, "that [Genet] has chosen to fight in becoming willfully and defiantly what the Other obliges him to be; yet the word 'be' assumes in his writing an active, transitive value . . . never again will he coincide with himself."[44] A similar dynamic underlies Bernard Wolfe's "Ecstasy in Black: the Negro as Dancer and Singer" (1950).[45] In this essay on black entertainers' conscious performance of black stereotypes, Wolfe rehearses the persistent existential trope at issue here: the critical reappropriation of one's reified self through exaggerated performance. There is, he suggests, a sociological constraint for the "pariah to be what he is 'really' in a caste situation—an automaton or a mask." At the same time, performing the gestures of caste on stage represents more of a conscious "maneuver than a reflex."[46] Frantz Fanon's *Black Skin, White Masks* (1952), a key point of reference in this self-analytical turn, also addresses making a reflex into a strategy.[47] Keithley Woolward detects traces of psychodramatic techniques such as "doubling, role-play, and even role reversal,"[48] in Fanon's dramatization of the objectifying impact of a white boy looking at him as a black man. Through this description, a "performance space is opened between Fanon, Fanon as persona, and his audience"[49]; thus, *Black Skin* recuperates "mask" and "play" as "the foundation of a post-colonial subjectivity [and as] paradigms for an oppositional politics praxis."[50]

If Rouch and Morin were drawn to psychodrama's promise of praxis, their program of enlightenment—to mobilize masks and role-play to expose and combat alienation and undo racism—was in perfect accord with contemporary discourses on colonialism. Frederick Cooper notes the shift in later treatises on colonialism from a sociological to a psychological and existential cast. Albert Memmi's *The Colonizer and the Colonized* (1957), which postulates that colonization can only be understood in terms of a pathological model of disease and cure, and Frantz Fanon's Manichean application of the language of mental pathology to describe the effects of colonization in *The Wretched of the Earth* (1961),[51] exemplify a pathological model based on dramatic analogies as much as existentialist discourse.

The Human Pyramid does not exhibit the solipsistic thrust and formal unity of Fanon and Sartre's literary psychodramas. Instead, the film relies on the indeterminacy of mimetic representation to achieve its pedagogic aims. The fact that the characters are real people both participating in a social experiment and acting in a film makes their agency unclear, which highlights key issues related to mimesis: we become unsure if the slurs hurled at the other students are an expression of social alienation, a theatrical framing of the racist problematic, or the result of excessive identification, a sort of mimetic saturation. To play at being racist might serve to assure one is not a racist, but it could also confirm and heighten existing bias; imitation can describe a given state or influence and model future behavior. Inviting real people to enact and experience this uncertainty, Rouch stretches mimesis into a risky but potentially critical consciousness.

Fiction offers a yardstick for assessing the efficacy of role-play for raising consciousness. Upon release, *The Human Pyramid* was often likened to John Cassavetes's *Shadows*, a film that relies on improvisation to explore interracial dynamics. In particular, comparisons addressed the impossibility of gaining consciousness in fiction. In contrast to Robinson (in *Moi un Noir*) or Nadine, who achieves heightened awareness, once "Ben Carruthers [Cassavetes's actor] ends *Shadows* he is again a theatre actor . . . after *The Human Pyramid* Denise and Jean Claude are not the same. . . . What Rouch adds is a new dimension—praxis," Jean Carta observed.[52] Still, Rouch felt that discontinuities worked against an "effective gain in lucidity." [53] He blamed interruptions in the filmmaking process, playing the role of another person, and the lack of synchronized sound recording. The first filming took place during July vacation; two extra shoots proved necessary, with students who had reached a new level of knowledge of each other and of themselves in the interim. According to Rouch, some of the students became fascinated by contemporary African problems and grew progressively more articulate: "In July they spoke like Tin Tin, at Christmas they sounded like a *Figaro* editorial, and by Easter, they felt like contributors to *l'Express*, or *France Observateur*."[54] Rouch would have preferred to shoot the film in sequence and only once[55]; dubbing seemed to compound the instability generated by role-playing. The year that separated actual scenes and the dubbing stunned even the actors, who were shocked by their previous naiveté.[56] Moreover, Rouch saw a crucial difference between replaying oneself and playing a character. In his estimation, in *The Human Pyramid* students were blocked from authentically reliving their roles in postsynchronization because they were playing someone else; in contrast, in his earlier film *Moi Un Noir* (1958), Oumarou Ganda's autobiographical performance benefited from reiteration in dubbing.[57] At the same time, Rouch never referred to the fact that he wrote Nadine and Denise's voice-over commentary—an authorial intervention that, inasmuch as it channeled characters' consciousnesses, advanced the fiction of the students' "conversion."[58] Rouch's inconsistent response—lamenting the students' articulate arguments as stilted, while remaining seemingly unconcerned by Jacqueline's stiff pretense of racism—makes it hard to assess his perspective on acting, that is, how much he expected verisimilitude, and what verisimilitude even means within the parameters of a consciousness-raising film. Instead of trying to achieve a seamlessly mutating identity, the film multiplies its breaks. Accordingly, we need to consider how this uneven, implausible theatre works in film, how its narrative structurally echoes unlikely twists in real life. The difficulty of representing a process of insight manifests itself in the film through a bold narrative displacement: a "documentary" death scene, to which we now turn.

PROVISIONAL CLOSURE: REFLEXIVITY AND DEATH IN *THE HUMAN PYRAMID*

The Human Pyramid's most engaging feature is its restless reflexivity. The brilliance of Rouch's orchestrated ruptures between the registers of fiction and documentary—being and acting—assures the film's status as a true experiment in racial relations.[59]

Let's consider Rouch's adoption of Moreno's conception of sociodrama and look at the ways cinema and therapeutic practices negotiate the passage between stage and life. As Moreno expanded his scope from individuals to collectives, and in particular, from the live psychodramatic stage to cinema, the theoretical (and practical) hurdles multiplied. To adjust the gap between process and end result, he selectively reduced real people and groups to a well-cast group of exemplary actor-patients. As he observed, the problem of "how to bring a cultural order to view by dramatic methods would be comparatively simple if (a) all the crucial roles and situations of a culture were known, (b) if a number of individual participants of this culture were on hand for the purpose of re-enactment."[60] In this light, the solution was anything but simple. What complicated Moreno's totalizing vision of sociodrama was the impossibility of guaranteeing a perfect match between social and staged worlds. Specifically, an underlying essentialism in casting vitiated all stages of his psycho- and sociodramatic theory and practice.

In "Psychodrama and Therapeutic Motion Pictures" (1944), Moreno proposed to streamline the factors central to the psychodramatic session: the action on the stage between patients and auxiliary egos, who in turn influence every member of the audience, and the effects on the film's audience whereby one "audio-ego can be therapeutic agent to every other."[61] Concerned with the apparatus effect on psychodrama's sacrosanct spontaneity, he conceded that the "psycho-technical problem at hand was to give the audience the illusion of direct communication with itself."[62] However, the identification between viewers and patients on the psychodramatic stage already hinging on a reductive conception of roles ("the German, the Negro, the Father") proves even more problematic in cinema. Since he could not exercise a mediating function here (as he did in live interactions), Moreno proposed a strictly controlled interface with a preselected audience. Selected viewers would be cast to ensure that their "syndrome (father-son conflicts, suicide conflicts)" would correspond with patients' problems.[63] He also envisioned voice-over markers of his intervention.[64]

Interested in the spread of his ideas but wary of mediation, he concluded that film should be a mere stage continuous with live therapy and a "supplement to or starter to actual therapeutic sessions."[65]

The stakes of this supplementarity lie at the heart of cinema verité's complicated reconciliation of therapy and cinematic dramaturgy. For Rouch, *The Human Pyramid* "did not illustrate a social fact but it became its own motor: as we advanced in the film, new intrigues were invented, new situations created and it was up to the students, the actors, to figure it out."[66] Rouch regretted discontinuities in the real-time record of the students' development, which he blamed on the lack of direct sound, and doubled as director and therapeutic prompter in the film, even going so far as to script the voices of consciousness for his characters. But what matters for the purposes at hand is how the film posits its ruptures as an effective and realistic representation of an incomplete, ongoing process.

Closure is particularly problematic for cinema verité. By refusing to equate the end of *Chronicle* with the project's resolution, Morin and Rouch advanced an alternate, instrumental aim for cinema. With the expression "*Nous sommes dans le bain*" (we are in the game), Morin caps his discussion with Rouch as they pace up and down the *Musée de l'Homme* corridor assessing the participants' conflicting reactions to *Chronicle*. These words express Morin's sense of the filmmakers' deep implication in the unresolved realities they have sparked. Still, it is important to examine how the dramatic, imaginative projections proposed in the films are represented as passing "into the game."

In interviews, the authors described *Chronicle*'s inconclusiveness as a "provisional response . . . to be continued" and declared that a sequel, to be made twenty years later, would account for each participant's fate.[67] Likewise, the triple ending of *The Human Pyramid* presents the film's lack of closure as an accomplishment: "What matters if a film is born or not? What really matters happens around the camera . . . this small film accomplished in its daily improvisations what years of being in the same classroom could not, namely the friendship it sparked between blacks and whites."

The very first scene of *The Human Pyramid* signals this deferred accomplishment through multiple false starts. In what stands as a summary program for interracial enlightenment, this film begins with the French and African protagonists (Nadine and Denise) strolling through Paris as the narrator declares, "a year ago they were not friends." An intertitle announces that the film has simply recorded an experiment performed with a group of adolescents. Discussing first the French and then the African students, Rouch explains that "as in a socio-drama, each participant will stick with their role, even that of stereotypical racists"; he asks whether they would agree "not [to] be [themselves] for a few weeks to discover who [they] were really at the end of the film"[68] (see Fig. 4.6 in Color Insert, 1). A sequence showing Jean Claude and Elola together illustrates the film's thesis: "Instead of mirroring reality the film created another reality. This story did not happen but the actors made up their lines and reactions during shooting. Spontaneous improvisation was the only rule."

This opening, inserted later to orient viewers to the film's fractured narrative, sets the tone for its constant, jarring reframing. The shift in tenses and the intricate interplay of narrative and illustrative scenes expose a multifaceted emphasis. First, the experiment's artifice is downplayed, then it is explicitly emphasized, and then it is denied: in a mimetic coda, a new reality of friendship is staged and recorded, passing into the film as an objective, documentary reality.

The Human Pyramid's restless reflexivity attests to its problematic ambition of ending segregation among the Abidjan students and enacting a new French African brotherhood in film. After reaching a plateau, Rouch awakens the film's potential for conflict through a long *Caprices-de-Nadine* sequence; here, his surrogate provocateur flirts with African and French friends, by turns.[69] Nadine's disregard for the consequences operates much like Christine's aimless flirtations to distract the audience from the serious matters hovering in the background of Renoir's *Rules of the Game* (1939). Nadine's serial infatuations evoke the taboo of interracial sex and marriage, with two consequences (Figs. 4.7 and 4.9).The first is a dream sequence showing Raymond and Nadine getting married, easing the edgier depiction of love between blacks and whites as a possible reality: the "marriage" takes place in the church of the Harris Cult, a syncretic religion mixing African and Christian elements. The scene invokes a textually rich, erotic, and intercultural exchange, intercutting between close ups of saints' masks and Nadine's coquettish masking of her face with her long hair. (The film was censored.)[70]

This sequence of flirtations reverberates with Paul Éluard's poem "La Pyramide Humaine," which is read in class at the moment when the loves of Nadine take flight.[71] Rouch sets his characters in magical, childlike settings—for instance, Jean Claude playing music and confiding in Nadine in an abandoned house (Fig. 4.8). Poems float over the bright blue with white images of beached cargo, which is reinvented as their favorite playground and Alain's haunt. Besides its allusion to integration, a second, significant consequence of Nadine's coquetry is the incarnation as drama of the film's actual impasse, its flirtation with making fiction reality. After Alain and Jean Claude fight over Nadine, Alain, in a show of bravado, dives into the water and is drowned.[72]

This death scene allows Rouch to reassert control of the narrative by introducing a new round of mutual recriminations. In interviews, Rouch declared that Alain's death shocked viewers only because they "forgot the repeated warnings" that "this [was] a fictional story, showing what the relations between young Africans and Europeans could be," [73] and that Alain had to be eliminated because he identified excessively with his character.[74] This statement may refer to the film's most explicit representation of French ambivalence about African interests— when the group starts a heated discussion around France and England's duty to take a position on South Africa.[75] Possibly overplaying his role as a French nationalist, Alain seeks to justify France's reluctance to take a stand against apartheid, raising the film to an uncomfortable level of discord. As Paul Henley notes, the cut to Alain projecting the film's rushes to the participants deflects the film from "'interminable' political arguments" and brings "epistemological questions" back to the fore[76] (Fig. 4.10; see Fig. 4.11 in Color Insert, 1). In the film Rouch proposes that they test the filmic experiment's limits "with a tragedy, a fiction that once filmed becomes reality, freeing those who believe too seriously in their role." Alain's "drowning" is fiction become reality, a transmutation that echoes the film's aim to serve as a catalyst for change in actuality. Up to this

Figure 4.7: Les Caprices de Nadine: Dominique (Rouch, *The Human Pyramid*, 1959).

Figure 4.8: Jean Claude (Rouch, *The Human Pyramid*, 1959).

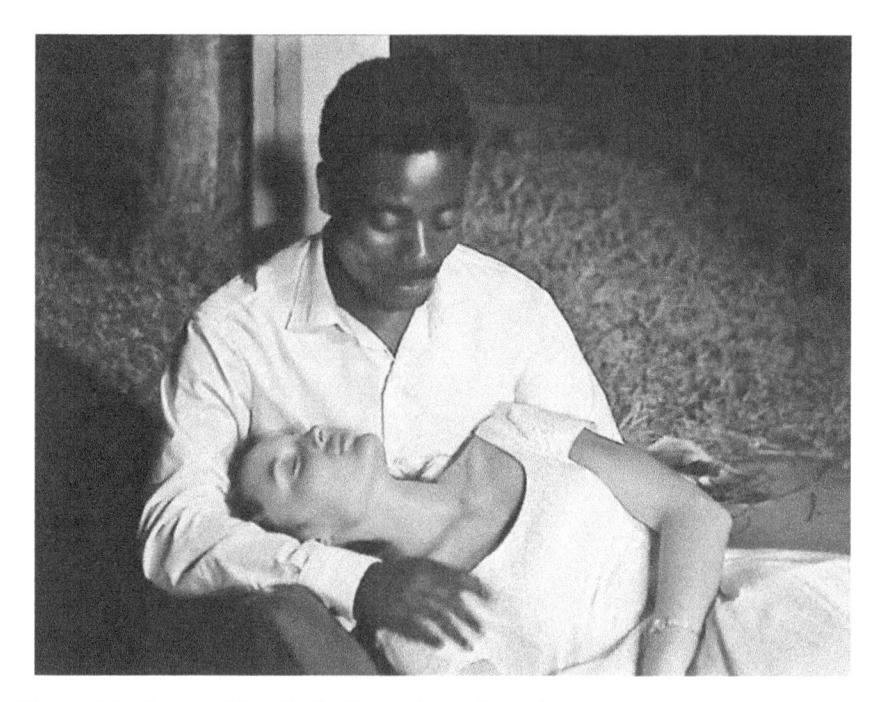

Figure 4.9: Raymond (Rouch, *The Human Pyramid*, 1959).

Figure 4.10: Discussion on apartheid and South Africa (Rouch, *The Human Pyramid*, 1959).

point, the engineered friendship between the two groups has not challenged a more insidious form of racism, nor has it contradicted the pretext of being a documentary about mutual discovery. The disturbance of the easygoing alternation between actuality and play holds obvious implications inasmuch as the film concerns the invention of possible realities.[77] Along with other metafilmic shifts, the death scene dramatizes the reluctance to operate solely in terms of what happens to occur in front of the camera. In this context, Rouch mentioned that "each passage to the other side of the camera generated greater vagueness and disconnection."[78] Considering this risk of disconnection, we follow *The Human Pyramid*'s fault lines to detect how it works through what it counts as real.

Catherine Russell's notion of narrative mortality helps place the film's startling invocation and dismissal of closure in perspective. Like other New Wave practices that moved "beyond formalist categories of open and closed endings as well as mythic categories of fate and romance," *The Human Pyramid* uses a death scene to pose the question of cinematic realism. As evident in his film *La Gare du Nord* (1965), suicide has a conceptual import in Rouch's work, introducing the real through a fictional surplus. The mechanics of Rouchian drama and its reliance on a stark break with a "life flow" is starkly evident in this fictional short. A wife (played by Nadine) nags her husband about his lack of fantasy. Her mounting complaints pressure the plot to accommodate the film's short length. This temporal constraint is formally reproduced in the film's mobile long take following Nadine into the street, and in its foreshortened dramatic arc. The resolution comes in the form of a chance encounter with a man who seems to answer to all of Nadine's fantasies, qualifying him as a dream, a suspension of reality. When Nadine refuses to follow him, he jumps onto the Gare du Nord's rails, the sole visible cut in the film. Such sudden and prophylactic injections of fiction confirm the documentarian Rouch's surrealist bent.

In *The Human Pyramid*, the arguments on apartheid and Algeria that precede the two reflexive leaps—the screening for the participants and Alain's death—equate the unresolved state of racism between French and Africans and the suspended status of reality in cinema (see Fig. 4.12 in Color Insert, 1). After these sudden veers we do not know whether the discussion is scripted or spontaneous or if it has any substantive consequence.

The new metanarrative steps guarantee an even greater ambiguity. Resolution comes in the form of a resurrection: Alain reappears for the film's final shot. Alternating by race and nationality—Alain and Denise walk arm in arm, alongside Raymond and Nadine, toward the camera. The four students are a poster image for integration (see Fig. 4.13 in Color Insert, 1). As if projected in reverse motion from a diving board, the phallic disavowal of mortality in Alain's reemergence bears a striking parallel with Manolete's appearance, erect and victorious, after his death has been announced in Pierre Braunberger's *Bullfight* (*La Course de Taureaux*, 1951).[79]

The disposal and retrieval of Alain back into the narrative parallels reenactment's elastic temporality. Coming back to fulfill a model image of interracial friendship satisfies a common reenactment plot in which the character atones for his mistakes—in this case, Alain's disruptive overidentification with his own role. Still, *The Human Pyramid* trumps any overdetermined narrative of error and redemption, blatantly enlisting fiction as a flexible instrument of disavowal and change. Inasmuch as one can assert an equivalence between "I am (not) dead" and "I am only playing a racist," the film grants fiction the power to affect reality.

The self-revision prompted by the end of colonialism finds its fullest expression expression in *The Human Pyramid*'s liminality. Whether role-play actually changed the students' views lies beyond the scope of the film, properly speaking, but the moment-to-moment shifting between activism, poetic reveries, consciousness-raising discussions, and fictive, acted conflicts stands as its own reality.[80] "Usage of the film for the film's needs: the film is constantly its own motor, its own means, it is condemned to deny itself as such," Michel Delahaye remarks in his insightful assessment of *The Human Pyramid*.[81] This mutating, formally brilliant film conveys the cinematic impasse of trying to intervene, through film and acting, in a real historical transition.

When *Chronicle* and *The Human Pyramid* were released—almost simultaneously—the filmmakers were asked to explain their vision of role-play. Morin responded *Chronicle* did not seek to experiment "with possible personas and with reactions that resemble but are not exactly theirs" so much as explore the question of "living oneself"; the film is "no longer a psychodrama but an attempt at cinema verité."[82] In what follows I contextualize this "living oneself," rethinking the political and moral imperative to subject oneself to the camera's judging scrutiny that undergirds *Chronicle*'s status as a displaced confessional and *autocritique*. Rather than being structured by fiction oscillations (as in *Human Pyramid*), *Chronicle*'s critical politics hinges on the texture and value of personal truth and authenticity.

CHRONICLE OF A SUMMER (1960–1961) AS AUTOCRITIQUE (1958)

Consider Marilou's halting disclosures in a scene from *Chronicle* that sums up cinema vérité's unique modernity, document, and drama converging in the shot's searching continuum. A long-haired woman nervously bites her lips, smokes, and hesitates in painfully long pauses. When she talks, she voices her sense of alienation (Fig. 4.14). Confirming *Chronicle of a Summer*'s confessional setup, Marilou addresses Edgar Morin: "Yes, my father." He briefly informs us she is a twenty-seven-year-old, bourgeois Italian who came to Paris three years earlier, in 1957. Overwhelmed by a bad conscience, she reveals that she initially enjoyed her lack of comfort but now is "sick of being cold in the winter, of being in the subway in the rush hour." Her sense of isolation and solipsism has reached a crisis level. "I have not even the right to kill myself, you know it would be absolutely false." A long, painful shot of Marilou silent and on the verge of tears follows.

Magnified through the close-up lens, this long take bespeaks an unflinching attention to the subject, halfway between a trial and empathetic listening. The camera's insistence contrasts with the tactful bearing of Morin, off-frame and mostly silent. Rouch spoke of "proximity" and "simultaneity" to describe his "contact camera," the intimate relation between filming and subject matter: "She was

Figure 4.14: Marilou's close-up (Rouch and Morin, *Chronicle of a Summer*, 1961).

talking so nervously I had to react. So I took those big close ups to try to get inside her."[83] The long take registers a difficult articulation, laden with tremulous pauses. As part of the director's attention to the minor as the touchstone of truth, each lingering phrase is overdetermined by a psychoanalytic hermeneutics, a symptomatic reading of reality.

This concentration on the moment when thought becomes expression is evident mostly in Marilou and Marceline's interviews. These sequences, shot in real-time shots, lead to interesting editing choices. Instead of cutting to new information, the filmmakers respect a scene's internal integrity by preserving profilmic pauses and expressive ellipses. The focus on empty time lends the film a puzzling, wavering intensity. Despite mobilizing an extensive apparatus to access truth, the film is beset by an intriguing reticence, generating, as it proceeds, the need for more statements.

The Algerian war is the main, but not the sole, basis for the film's opaqueness. The authors believed that "Summer 1960" could be "a chronicle of a capital moment in history" given recent events in Congo as well as the Melun peace negotiations.[84] One of their purposes was to broach economic, moral, and psychological problems at the end of the war. The constraints of censorship as well as the film's length—cut down from twenty-five hours of rushes—plausibly justify its significant omissions, in particular the young men's discussions of desertion.[85]

The film's peculiar combination of probing and vagueness warrants attention.[86] A number of unsettled issues emerge in Rouch and Morin's ambitious project. In a critique of the film, sociologist Lucien Goldmann noted its failure to strike a balance between abstraction and concreteness. Measuring the film's realist representation along the lines of traditional social science, he argued that particularities and generalities are present at the wrong moments and in the wrong proportions: interviews, which advance necessary details for any sociological inquiry, are too sparse and, moreover, confined to a limited sample of the population.[87] Although Goldmann acknowledges the attempt to remedy these difficulties "by replacing the characters of the habitual sociological inquiry chosen at random with people they knew more or less," this foreknowledge of characters on the filmmakers' part is not shared with the film's audience.[88] Without access to the exchange where Marilou recounts her previous involvement in leftist politics, how she learned French in a political milieu and met Morin in a debate about Poland and Stalinism, the viewer has no idea about her political allegiances. As it stands, Marilou's revelations seem to hang on pure personal angst.

Since many of the film's participants were opposed to Algerian War, if not actively fighting for the Front of National Liberation (FLN), it is understandable that there are few mentions of politics except in a long central discussion around dinner. Sam Di Iorio has insightfully linked the "inconsistencies of the film's editing and its tendency to remove some, but not all references to personal or political specifics" to Morin's phenomenological bent, his "desire to stage subjectivity as an open category which could embrace and transcend individual existence."[89] The same abstraction apparent in the discussion on politics is evident, according to Di Iorio, in the filmmakers' opting for first names to avoid generic types and individual singularities.

This abstraction is not random, and it is imperative we examine the thrust of a film that grafts a surface of political anonymity onto a politically engaged group. Instead of the general survey of Parisian mood conducted with "individuals who are quite different from each other," it interviews the directors' friends, with the cast coming close to a ciphered representation of aspects of the directors' lives (especially Morin's).[90] Conceived as "an experiment in cinematic interrogation,"[91] the film takes self-examination almost literally, then. The question of what it means to critically revisit one's own steps in 1960, a moment of intense fragility in the intellectual allegiances of the French Left, gains a special resonance in the context of this selective sharing of self-criticism.

Morin sought "to maintain, in the editing, a plurality as a way to concentrate this collective halo around the characters."[92] However, as the critical perspective extends to a younger cast of social actors, a generational transference obscures the degree to which the film works through Morin's own political disaffection. It is striking, for instance, that neither Rouch nor Morin appears as an interviewee, and that the bulk of the interviews are conducted with a group of people in their twenties. When Jean-Paul Viguier, the cameraman, poses the Algerian question to young men at risk of being sent to war, Jean Pierre reacts by stating his vision of youth is idealized. Earlier, a dejected Jean Pierre expressed his bitterness about the powerlessness of Morin's generation's politics.[93] Inasmuch as the scene was reconstructed to elide Jean Pierre's deep involvement in the pro-FLN Jeanson network—and the possibility of conscription if he failed his exam—this obfuscation (even if it occurred to protect him) can be seen as channeling a broader disillusionment, a leftist autocritique on Morin's part.

In the mid- to late 1950s, revelations of Stalinist atrocities—from concentration camps to show trials[94]—had reached a critical mass; left-wing intellectuals had to take positions. Disillusioned with the Communist Party, and following the development of nonaligned politics with the conference of Bandung, they dislocated their "matrix of interpretation and intervention from the pair proletariat/bourgeoisie to the binomy Third World/Imperialism."[95] The use of torture by the French army during the Algerian War offered a platform for intellectuals who had stifled ethical critique for years.[96] In 1955, Morin, Dionys Mascolo, Louis-René Des Forets, and Robert Antelme founded the Committee of Intellectual Action Against the War in North Africa.[97] James le Sueur noted that "embittered by the ineffectual partisan politics of the post-WWII era, the Committee initiators wanted to keep it apolitical" and make "the universalism of the French republican 'Rights of Man' the hallmark of its crusade against colonialism in North Africa and the cornerstone of its legitimacy."[98] The sustained debate between the Committee and Jacques Soustelle (an intellectual and the governor general of Algeria) bore on the identity of French intellectuals in light of the state's colonial warfare and defense of torture.[99]

Clustered around the journals *Arguments* (created in 1956 in response to Khrushchev's revelations about Stalin) and *Socialisme ou Barbarie*, Morin's group was one of the main voices of dissidence on the French Left.[100] Attacking the notion of delegated power,[101] they took aim not only at French intellectuals who claimed to speak for the Algerian independence movement, but also at communists reluctant to condemn the Soviet suppression of the Hungarian movement for independence.[102] Morin had been expelled from the Communist Party in 1951 for his perceived lack of militancy.[103] Its procedures of exclusion echoed the forced confessions of the Stalinist purges; in a perverse twist, the spontaneous revelations on the part of French intellectuals became,[104] as Mark Poster has noted, "a new genre in the pilgrim's progress from Stalinist mystification to intellectual liberation."[105] In *Autocritique* (1958), one of the most trenchant "self studies" written to exculpate partisan intellectuals at the time of the Stalinist atrocities,[106] Morin recounted his engagement—and progressive disenchantment—with the Communist Party between 1943 and 1951. Rhetorically, he asked how he could "leave the party in the middle of the Cold War . . . when it is persecuted"—then declared, "I wanted to quit because [the party] was persecutor."[107] He sought to "cleanse" himself, to render himself "transparent," so he could see clearly. Acknowledging that he often felt guilty "inside the communist party, [for] all the executions that I was the accomplice of, outside the party, all the crimes of the capitalist society," Morin decided the issue is "not to avoid culpability but . . . to say what corresponded to my feeling, to all my truth."[108]

In his cultural biography of Morin, Myron Kofman credits the sociologist's subjective approach with having "illuminated the imagery of trial at the heart of a whole generation of French Intellectuals."[109] Morin's *détournement* of the proceedings from a predetermined outcome toward a self-reflection on individual commitment points to *Autocritique*'s exceptional role in "revealing how 'existential' decisions whether to affirm or disavow communism depended on the play of identities."[110] Practicing "always saying 'one's truth,'" book and film, *Autocritique* and *Chronicle*, essay and alternative existentialist Marxism. Through solipsistic self-analyses they structure a surrogate trial that substitutes the punishing dynamics of the party with spontaneous self-exposure. As such, the film's commitment to synchronized sound must be interpreted as more than a technical means of achieving authentic realism. Morin's decision to "practice the 'self-ethic' . . . to be nothing besides a guarantor of [his] own words," comes across in *Chronicle*'s reliance on the identifiable and "self-owned" voices of its actors, as they express themselves in sync sound.[111]

Morin faced the problem of reconciling an unfettered individual and collective expression with the confessional, a mode of communication compromised by show trials and colonialist practices of torture. In this context, even modern psychosocial techniques such as sociodrama and group dynamics did not guarantee unconstrained revelation. Self-criticism was so tainted with the specter of forced confessions that even the enlistment of modern psychosocial techniques did not guarantee the truth. According to Didier Anzieu, for instance, "considered in terms of its psychological mechanics if not in terms of ideology," the American school of group dynamics training could be likened "to meetings of autocritique honored in Soviet countries."[112] Morin's push to "construct a decontaminated Marxist politics capable of dealing directly with contemporary moral issues,"[113] in *Chronicle* was purely a matter of "psychological mechanics." Self-reflection —what Morin and Rouch call psychodrama—is to be cleansed of identifiable political ideology through the objectivity of the cinematic apparatus and synchronized sound, which promote and verify the freedom and spontaneity of individuated expression. As a technological counterpart to the immediacy ideally attained by Moreno's psychodrama, cinema verité is supposed to catch social phenomena in "statu nascendi."[114]

Morin and Rouch believed in the concrete impact of imaginary and subjective projections on reality; in their eyes, cinema and psychodrama represented parallel methods for self-analysis and projective release. Karl Schoonover has observed that the status Morin accords to cinema "at the threshold of both individual consciousness ('Imagination') and engaged interaction ('Participation')," reveals it "as a socio-anthropological fact that facilitates the interpenetration of man and the world."[115] Already in his book *The Cinema, or The Imaginary Man* (1956), Morin addresses the reality of imaginary formations, describing cinema as "the product of a dialectic where the objective truth of the image and the subjective participation of the spectator confront and join each other."[116] In an interesting twist, instead of focusing on the medium's public dimension, Morin stresses its potential to protect privacy. Cinema is especially appropriate as a forum for individual liberation since it is "destined for isolated individuals in a dark theatre, invisible and anonymous but present."[117] This one-to-one communication in the darkened theater promotes identification, growth, and empathy.

As the filming of *Chronicle* was starting in June 1960, Morin wrote an essay about a key aspect of the "film/spectator dialogue." In broad terms the process of projection/identification are, first, identification, mimeticism, and exemplarity, and second, projection, catharsis, and exoneration.[118] Although this skeletal description of cinema's psychosocial dimension replicates important psychodramatic steps, Morin discusses cinema in general. After *Chronicle*, he devoted fuller attention to the interpenetration between world and image, envisioning a "provoking camera [that creates] a sort of circuit between the two protagonists and plays an operational psychoanalytic role."[119] Rejecting criticism that the film he had made with Rouch was a false psychoanalysis, he affirmed the "therapeutic idea behind [the] plan is that all communication can be liberation."[120]

This somewhat generic definition is in fact central to the filmmakers'—and in particular to Morin's—formulation of a new cinema-based forum of debate. For Morin, the appropriate strategy for promoting truth and liberating communication involves distracted sociality. Possibly inspired by a scene in Lionel Rogosin's *Come Back Africa* (1959), where leading writers and intellectuals of the South African black community are filmed sitting around a sofa in a Shebeen, drinking and discussing politics and art,[121] he recommended "commensality"[122] to encourage self-expression (Fig. 4.15).The method he proposes, having crew and actors share "excellent meals washed down with good wine," is more than a gimmick to counter the inhibiting effect of the camera; it represents a sociotherapeutic technique: this "atmosphere of camaraderie" helps to avoid "the creation of the sort of a game where each person, even if he doesn't play a role determined by someone else, still composes a character for himself."

> [Once filmed,] a simple discussion turns into an elaborate process to descend progressively and naturally into [oneself] ... Surrounded by friendly witnesses the actors at the table allow themselves to be caught up in the questions ... at which point it is pretty difficult to analyze what goes on. It is the possibility of a confessional but

Figure 4.15: Morin's "commensality" approach in *Chronicle of a Summer* (1961).

without a confessor . . . a confession to all and to no one, the possibility of being a bit of one's self.[123]

Morin's *in-vino-veritas* proposal for "being a bit of oneself" adapts the theater of confessions that haunted contemporary leftist intellectuals to his own tastes and purposes. In this wonderfully simple conception of psychodrama, the filmmaker meshes a cinematic audience of "everyone and no one" with a "friendly group of witnesses" who are unafraid of being "caught in the questions." In this way, a new, antiauthoritarian mode of self-criticism is achieved. If, in principle, Morin's view of self-expression and talking heads seems to depart from Rouch's fluid "pédovision"— walking with the camera and following one's subject closely—each approach profits from cinema verité's intimate, probing camera to fit a "sort of psychodrama" to its own intellectual and artistic needs.

A "NASCENT" REGISTER: GROUP DYNAMICS AND THE WORKER

The table of contents of *Arguments* (a journal published between 1956 and 1962) indicates, in shorthand, why *Chronicle of a Summer* became a relevant platform for self-improvement. The journal's third manifesto (1961) declares "deep dissatisfaction with all observation that is not in movement . . . all thought that does not confront its own contradictions, all philosophy that reduces itself to master-words and that does not question itself."[124] Concerned with the infrapolitical sphere of existence while embracing psychodrama and group dynamics, both film and journal strategically moved leftist discourse toward a modern approach to the politics of everyday life.[125] In the film, this focus finds expression in scenes in which Henri and Maddie state their disregard for material things and put a general stress on quality-of-life issues such as vacation and consumer aspirations, which traditional Marxists ignored.[126]

Although the journal sought to reconceptualize Marxism, it was only in 1962 that *Arguments*'s editors, in one of two issues entitled *La question politique*, linked group dynamics to the worker's interests explicitly: "the difficult search for a new politics starts from two analyses: the first a historical reconsideration of the revolutionary past (from Marx to the socialist parties, from Bolshevism to Stalinism), and the other, by confronting the paths opened by the new 'psycho-sociological' currents and the classical paths of the so called 'workers' parties.'"[127]

While this issue was published after the making of *Chronicle*, its vision agrees with Morin's wish to avoid representing "the worker problem at the level of political or union affiliations or of salary claims." For him, "conditions of industrial work should be questioned at a deeper more radical level."[128] In particular, the enactment of a factory worker's daily routine speaks volumes about the film's purposeful distance from a classical Marxist representation of labor. Harsh film lights on his face and his mother's touch wake up Angelo Borgien, a mechanic at Renault, for breakfast and his starring role in the film (Fig. 4.16). We see Angelo Borgien entering the factory, and

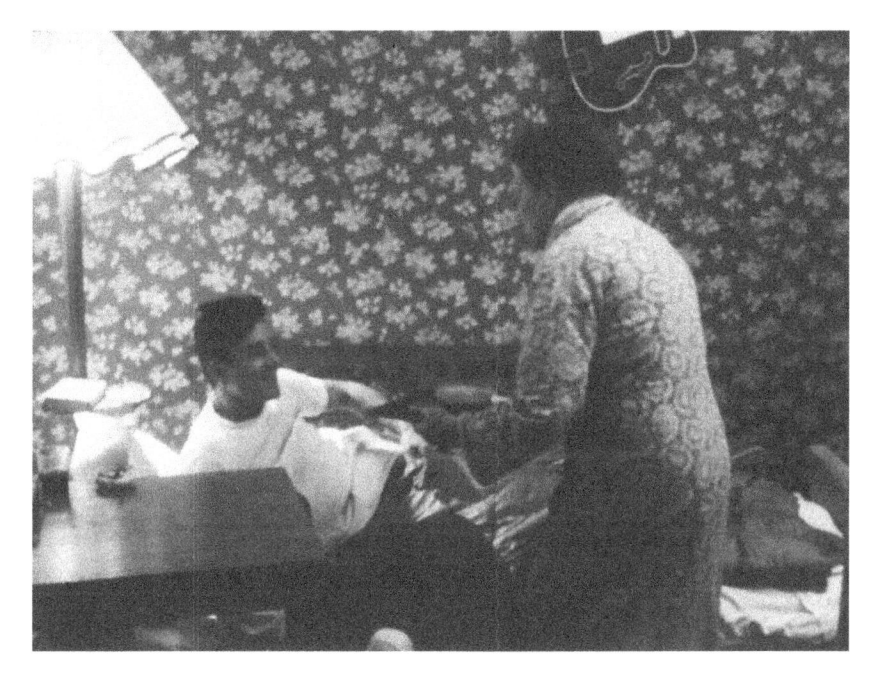

Figure 4.16: Angelo is awakened by his mother and the film lights (*Chronicle of a Summer*, 1961).

a long sequence filmed by Raoul Coutard surveys the work being done there. Angelo only reappears at the end of the day when, using a candid camera with a long lens, Michel Brault picks him up jumping into a bus and climbing the Petit-Clamart's steps to return home. He showers, changes clothes, and does some judo moves against a tree in his backyard. Then he curls up on the sofa with a book: *Danton*.

Given how opinionated Angelo is in interview scenes—and in contrast to the comparably long duration of Marceline and Marilou's memorable verbal articulation—this silent sequence is strangely tokenistic. Here, the film avoids the shared dynamic of the interview in favor of a distanced, third-person perspective. Concentrating on personal tastes and moments of leisure, this purposive focus on the individuality of a factory worker hinges on a respectful exception: the filmmakers are absent, and for the most part the camera is ignored. Angelo's portrayal is one of the longest scenes in the film; the stakes concern an alternative representation of "labor." To distance the film from vulgar Marxist and an all-too-immediate association of the worker's interests with those of unions and leftist parties, Angelo had been brought aboard the film by Jacques Gautrat (Mothé), a worker and member of the Socialisme ou Barbarie group and the author of *Journal d'un ouvrier* (*Diary of a Worker*, 1958). According to Morin, he was the only person "to describe what goes on in a factory in an illuminating way."[129] Jacques talks with the film's electrician about workers' happiness in an extended scene cut from the film, which was of such interest to Morin that he reconvened the participants to get a better record.[130] In an aside to an article assessing the group Socialisme ou Barbarie, Morin extols Georges Friedmann's examination of "the human problems and relationships inside the office" as a corrective to the perspective "that believe[s] the essential always lies in the impersonal."[131]

The critical reception of Moreno's and Lewin's ideas helps situate antiauthoritarian group dynamics at a fragile moment during the Cold War, when France was realigning with the United States. On the occasion of the publication of "Who Shall Survive?" Moreno gave a lecture at the Centre d'Etudes du Sociologie at the CNRS (National Center for Scientific Research), where Morin worked as a researcher under Friedmann. That institution's intention to open French research to American applied sociology was perceived skeptically by academics who belonged to the Communist Party. Lewin and Moreno's interventions in group-behavior modification in institutions, industries, and corporations fit well with the empirical bent of some of the CNRS's studies, as well as the view that Marxism needed to adapt to different neocapitalist realities in the postwar period.[132]

In a seeming paradox, encouraging a "more flexible self in reaction to conformist, depersonalizing tendencies"[133] was a prevalent concern in techniques of group management geared to a corporate culture context.[134] In his sharp critique of Moreno's and Lewin's theories, J. B. Pontalis identified the crux of their conservatism. He argued that Moreno's insistence on micro-sociology was merely a matter of convenience since he "never allude[d] to milieu, class, social level or education, [and recognized] racial segregation as a natural fact."[135] He voiced the same mistrust of experiments conducted in an "entirely artificial milieu" and diagnoses focused on "an amalgam of people grouped for a few hours without a task, a common past or future"[136] when discussing the theory and practice of Kurt Lewin. Perhaps aware that films such as Sidney Lumet's *Twelve Angry Men* (1957) were screened at Lewin's Institute to illustrate the democratic principles of group dynamics,[137] Pontalis characterized these group therapies as "provisional unities linking individuals for a short time" and "restricted by common tasks or danger"—in his damning assessment, a "lost patrol or twelve angry men."[138]

The fixation with the phenomenology of subjective struggle that shapes *Chronicle of a Summer* may be seen as one more example of privatization—the "decline of identities based on work and social collectivities" that Kristin Ross, following Castoriadis and Henri Lefebvre, identifies as the "dominant social movement of the period."[139] For Castoriadis,[140] "'privatization' [reflects] the impotence of men in the face of the enormous social machinery they have created and which they can now neither understand nor control."[141] Significantly, proof that "capitalism has not succeeded in destroying either class action or the positive socialization of individuals" lies in informal groups constituted by workers "fighting the atomization forced upon them by the 'external' organization of labor."[142]

Workers' councils were the subject of multiple analyses in *Arguments* as well as *Socialisme ou Barbarie*.[143] It is precisely such an informal group model that inspires the film's constitution of a micro-community. The film's pointed representation of a worker's life within the general, transformative rubric of psychodrama adapts Marxism to less alienating conditions. In *Marxisme et Dynamique de Groupe* (1962), Joseph Gabel suggests that, notwithstanding the risks of an illusory dereification achieved by apolitical means, a confrontation between Marxism and group dynamics would "[press] . . . a political ideology constantly beset by dogmatism to revise its traditional concepts and readapt to a changing reality."[144] Gabel's openness toward group dynamics in relation to Marxism reveals the intricacies of reconciling old and new forms of leftist politics. Morin and Georges Lapassade's psychosociology— a new praxis aiming "to study society while transforming it"[145]—understood experiments in group dynamics in terms of workers' interests: informal networks within corporations can escape the system's bureaucracy in a sort of "clandestine socialism."[146] Recognizing the problematic association of socioanalysis and the corporate interest in "regulating tensions," they emphasize the capacity to "reveal contradictions." Even if conflicts remain unresolved, socioanalysis's power to dereify and decrystallize old structures and create a mentality of contestation through "emotional provocation" means that group dynamics represent a viable and even scientific instrument for an alternative antiauthoritarian politics.[147]

In support of psychosociology, Morin and Lapassade reiterate Henri Lefebvre's view that no social system can disregard questions of everyday life, and no revolution can stop at property structures and state systems so long as human interrelations remain the same. The party froze into a bureaucratic state by discounting specific sciences and techniques as depoliticized: "Shouldn't a political party be like a human milieu, like a microcosm of the society it wishes to bring to life?"[148]

Morin and Rouch bring an exemplary social microcosm to life in cinema: the conversation between Angelo and Landry about workers' narrow aspirations resembles the exchange one might expect between the filmmakers and Angelo. Significantly, the meeting between the French worker and the African student, which addresses racial, class-based, and cultural differences, also represents a main object of contention in the discussions the film occasioned. The scene with the two men sitting on a staircase landing became the object of debate when participants complained that the verité-scenes were either artificial, indecent, or boring. In particular, Angelo and Landry's scene was attacked as "archi-faux" (ultra false, affected). In turn, Morin rushes to defend it as his favorite because it presents "a nascent friendship" (Fig. 4.17). The fact Morin praises it with the epithet that defines the ideals animating both cinema verité and psychodrama—the aim of capturing emerging relations in *statu nascendi*—demonstrates how much this spontaneous encounter catalyzes the film's hopes of brotherhood and communication. At the same time, Marceline's curt aside that Landry and Angelo—the black student from West Africa and the white factory worker—do not have much in common sharply undercuts this idealization.

This iconic scene of friendship in *Chronicle* echoes fraternization sequences between Africans and French students throughout *The Human Pyramid*. Even though some of the actions between Nadine and Denise, and Jean Claude and Elola seem natural while others appear staged (the final sequence of the two interracial couples striding toward the camera, for instance), what ultimately matters is their existence *on film*. The awkward naturalness of Landry and Angelo underscores the liminal state courted by cinema verité's psychodramas: whether artificial or natural, it is willed into existence and registers a process of becoming. Serge Daney's question of how to film the raising of consciousness becomes explicit as much in this scene's enforced reality as in the controversy it excites in the postscreening scene.

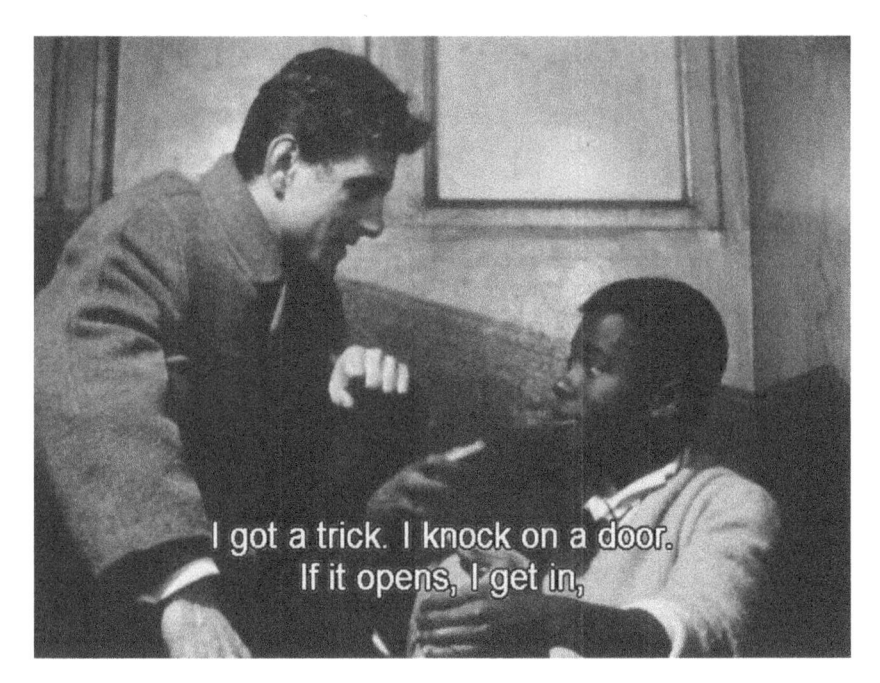

Figure 4.17: Angelo and Landry, a friendship in "statu nascendi" (*Chronicle of a Summer*, 1961).

Cinema verité's contorted efforts to adjust the performance of the self to accommodate the timeliness of an unfolding present are evident in *The Human Pyramid*'s role-play and metafilmic shifts as well as in *Chronicle*'s confessionals. However, the psychoanalytic bent of the camera in cinema verité, its (over) attention to each sinewy moment of self-actualization, cannot, by definition, be foreign to a search for a deeper historical or biographical truth.

Two canonical verité scenes, the monologues by Marceline in *Chronicle of a Summer* and Oumarou Ganda's in *Moi Un Noir*, instantiate the passage between the cathartic and self-enlightening role-playing at issue here and later, in post-Shoah testimonials. The scenes discussed in the next chapter shift the films' present-tense orientation to reenact past experiences and enter into the actual issues around which the nation kept tacit silence—French Jews sent to Nazi concentration camps and disproportionate losses suffered by West African troops in the French Army in Indochina. By honoring the testimonies of a self-identified Jewish deportee and of an itinerant black worker and ex-serviceman in Indochina through compact and self-sufficient "psychodramas," these theatrical solos establish the continuity between cinema verité's confessional thrust and the parajuridical impetus behind post-Holocaust cinema. Protracted self-revelations, unified by the singular rhythm of lengthy walking talks, Marceline and Ganda's monologues impart a particular ethical and historical stress to Rouch and Morin's ambitions for a cinema of self-revision.

CHAPTER 5

Ascetic Stages

Reenactment in Post-Holocaust Cinema

You must believe me because I am irreplaceable. When I testify, I am . . . the only one to have heard, or to have been put in the presence of this or that, at a determinate, indivisible instant.

Jacques Derrida[1]

This chapter examines how the *terrible constancy of the original site and of the original protagonist's consciousness* brings the spectral temporality of posttraumatic histories into focus. Attention falls on the aesthetic, ritual, experiential dimensions of cinema that singularize the protagonist's experience, authorizing and amplifying the scope of her testimony.

Deeply impacted by *Shoah*'s set-up of a new parajuridical relationship between truth and theater, Shoshana Felman poses a question pertinent to my inquiry on the distinct nature of in-person reenactment: If "the essence of the testimony is impersonal (to enable a decision by a . . . jury . . . about the true nature of the fact of an occurrence; to enable an objective reconstruction of what history was like, irrespective of the witness), why is it that the witness's speech is so uniquely, literally irreplaceable? What does it mean that the testimony cannot be simply reported or narrated by another in its role as testimony?"[2]

Like testimony, which "cannot be simply repeated or reported by another" without losing its performative function, in-person reenactment holds significant implications for postwar realist cinema, and it similarly admits no substitute. Until this point, the book at hand has explored the transformative value of a person reenacting her past in her own name in neorealist and verité narratives. However, post-Holocaust cinema reenactment poses a distinct set of questions about irreplaceability.[3] These accounts of death and survival foreground the basic existential and ethical links undergirding testimonial authority: "Is the witness not always a survivor?" asks Derrida in reflection on testimony's untransferable, and paradoxical, exemplarity: "This surviving speech must be as exemplarily irreplaceable as the instance of the instant from which it speaks, the instant of death as irreplaceable, as 'my death,' on the subject of which no one other than the dying person can testify."[4] More still, in a posttraumatic context, in-person reenactment has an obligation "to map the complex temporal and spatial patterns by which the absence of the real, a real absence, makes itself felt in the familiar plenitude of reality."[5]

Reenactment, a performative mode defined by a belated, supplementary relation to absence, is especially appropriate in a posttraumatic context. Given reenactment's special relation to the reality to which it refers, as well as the one it actualizes, it demonstrates, in Michael Rothberg's words, "an aesthetics of survival [which] meets its limits not so much in the impossibility of direct reference or transparent mimesis as in the dilemma of belated temporality—the impossibility of reviving the dead."[6] If, as I have argued in the preceding chapters, reenactment's belatedness is necessarily critical, post-Holocaust cinema raises the added question of how in-person reenactment frames Shoah's continual haunting as the specific "melancholia and inability to mourn."[7]

Two qualities—discrepancy and sharpness—variously used by Cathy Caruth, Gertrud Koch, Rothberg, and Ulrich Baer to describe a posttraumatic condition and aesthetics, especially illuminate the specific import of in-person reenactment in post-Holocaust cinema.[8] Caruth's work on trauma and memory has stressed the traumatized person's inability to suppress the vividness of memory as well as the unwelcome return of events relived with great intensity but entirely incongruous with the here and now of present reality. Visually and affectively, these qualities of dislocated, literal intensity shape the relations between the ascetic theatricality evident in post-Holocaust cinema and its imperatives of testimonial reenactment.

My object is a set of monologues that uniquely instantiate a posttraumatic condition through striking—visual, verbal, and gestural—delineations of absence. Marceline's monologue on her deportation and return from the camps (Jean Rouch and Edgar Morin's *Chronicle of a Summer*, 1961), Oumarou Ganda's reenacted account of his experience in Indochina (Rouch's *Moi un Noir*, 1958), and Karski's histrionic retelling of his report on the situation of the Jews in Poland to Roosevelt and Judge Frankfurter (Lanzmann's *The Karski Report*, 2010) are paradigmatic of a contemporary, post-verité testimonial sensibility that reconceives representation as a performative act of transmission, expressing as-of-yet unformulated truths.[9] Because of their testimonial quality, these monologues possess a parajuridical charge comparable to that of other contemporary documentaries modeled on pedagogic, therapeutic, and legal procedures: talking cures, role-playing, and truth and reconciliation commissions. [10]

Combining the conjuring power of theater with a stripped-down aesthetics, the scenes examined here are characterized by extended shots focused on a single figure surrounded by empty space. These performances stand at a visible remove from their referent in time and space: the Indochina War is recalled at a lagoon embankment in Abidjan, a dialogue with a Supreme Court Judge in a nondescript hotel room, Auschwitz at the Place de la Concorde. While invoking acts of mass annihilation, the compact, bracketed speeches summon absent characters and underscore their own belated nature. Through a spare theatricality, these in-person reenactments doubly summon what is not, and is, no longer there.

Filmed in natural settings, enhanced by the estrangement of a sparse theatrical mode, these solo testimonies empty out the surrounding space, transforming a definite location into a malleable stage for memory.[11] Such displacement facilitates the collapse of temporality and the dynamic repurposing of past images for present claims. At the same time, the evacuation of naturalness that allows for other forms of representation structurally parallels the most common feature of survivors' testimony: the difficulty of relaying a catastrophic experience under the condition of normality that now prevails. These ascetic stages and the concentrated monologic mode absorb and externalize the dislocations and psychic splitting of trauma and enhance the reclamation power of in-person reenactment.

Absorbing and reflecting reenactments' very attributes, its disquieting temporality and dislocation, these stark scenes pose the liminal and formal significance of "stages" in this study's title—the in-between states courted in reenactment, as an individual acts, acts out, or demonstrates her past; the steps in a process of self-reclamation as well as the theater, conceived here as a focused arena to engage the viewer in testimony's primary demand: "You must believe me because I am irreplaceable."[12] The monologues, through individuated mise-en-scène, become privileged "sites of visibility" and broadcast that underscore the problematic closure of mass catastrophe on an unprecedented scale.

Felman has theorized the nature of the impasses reached in trials that, since World War II, have increasingly been called on to resolve historical traumas.[13] Her attention falls on how trials reopen cases (e.g., Eichmann or O.J. Simpson) only to enact unresolved crises of truth on a deeper level, both societal and personal. As Caruth observes, for Felman the trial is "a *transformative* legal and testimonial *event* precisely because it creates a new language and a new legal space in which survivors become witnesses and in which traumatic memory can emerge as history for the first time."[14] The trial not only provides a legal framework for the judgment of a perpetrator's crimes but it becomes a theater of justice, "the ... actual site of visibility of a traumatic historical occurrence, which inadvertently is reenacted on the side of the law."[15]

Marceline's privileged voice as witness to the Holocaust, remarked by Rothberg and Hirsch, is discussed further in this chapter. The release of *Chronicle of a Summer* a few months after the Eichmann trial, as well as the strong parallels between Marceline's individuated claim on a survivor's past, and the trial, notable for channeling survivors' personal, traumatic stories toward a spectacle with didactic and nation-building ambitions, raises the question of how cinema, differently than a trial, creates the formal and critical conditions for a revisited scrutiny and judgment, a "site of visibility."[16]

Examining how cinema and reenactment supplement and dramatize crises of truth and of memory occasioned by the Holocaust and the colonial past,[17] this chapter shows that the "indivisibility . . . between private and collective trauma" Felman posits in major theaters of justice also inheres, in a concentrated form, in the dramaturgy of the solo testimonies and reenactment scenes discussed here.[18] The staging of singularity implicit in these monologues creates a compact scene that simultaneously conveys an irreducible individual experience and its collective, historical implications. One of the purposes of this study is to clarify how the actual person reenactment has, precisely because of its thick representational mandate, special aesthetic, memorial, and legal ramifications that are particularly germane to posttraumatic conditions. I will ask what is the unique power of a solo testimony, staged moreover so as to enhance the absent presences around its revivification of the past. And what are the qualities of cinematic theatricality that enhance the visibility and reach of this dramatized replay, and which traits ensure a suspended and continued critical effectiveness for these particular scenes.

The monologue address plays a decisive role in these testimonials' singular, performative impact. Its stark and disconcerting theatricality, its odd clarity, is particularly conducive to a broad and public self-presentation. Expression that turns both inward and outward, to the past and to the present, the monologue is simultaneously thought and revelation. Its functional association with a rhetorical address—the monologue is often heard in the courtroom, the professor's lectern, the preacher's pulpit, or the witness stand—ensures that its relay is both necessary and meaningful. And its solo theatrics also amplifies its reach. Once speech is not directed at a particular person—it claims a different sort of attention because every word counts. It is this surplus, the meaningfulness and gravitas surrounding the delivery of a public speech in the first person that circularly asserts the speaker's rights.

Marceline and Ganda replay aloud a conversation each one of them has likely had many times in their own mind. But now, amplified by the camera and Nagra, what is performed is the summoning of the world as one's witness, a trait proper to monologues. Moreover, because these scenes do not include a visible auditor, they especially command the spectator's co-presence. If, as Dori Laub has observed a propos of the testimonial dynamic, "only when the survivor knows he is being heard, will he stop to hear, and listen to himself,"[19] cinematic scenes of monologue represent a distinct form of broadcasting that embeds attention within, and across, theatrical space.

The aesthetic conditions for this demand placed on the spectator's attention are of major interest here. The films under discussion invariably display a spare, distanced mise-en-scène that compounds the instability of testimonial truth with spectatorial pressure, what André Bazin called the "unforgiving position of a witness."[20] Bazin arrived at this insight by reflecting on the interplay between theater and film, specifically the former's impact on modern postwar cinema. Discussing the ending of Jean Cocteau's *Les Parents Terribles* (1948), Bazin observes that when the camera pulls away from the scene, it is never confused with the character's subjectivity; instead, its purpose was to "see her actually looking."[21] The camera heightens this spare modern mise-en-scène, remaining within the restricted perspective of a theatrical spectator. The effect is to enforce co-presence and inescapable knowledge.

The sense of co-presence between viewer and scene is especially troubling in the case of historical sites of violent extermination. Ulrich Baer's reading of photos by Dirk Reinartz and Mikael Levin of sites of mass killings (which Levin's father encountered during WWII liberation) helps explain how spatial composition bears on belated acts of witnessing. These photos, he suggests, deploy conventions from landscape art, enlisting a romantic sensibility that leads to "a continual process of introspection and self-awareness"[22] and absorbs the viewer in a scene through an effect of co-presence.[23] At the same time, "by casting the enormity of the Holocaust within the traditional genre of landscape photography,"[24] the photos create a tension: the viewer is positioned as subject of an interiorized vision and, at the same time, confronted with a vacant terrain ("a non-distinct, empty and easily overlooked setting") that is utterly inhospitable, resistant to the experience of memory.[25] These photos "point to a link between the 'experience of place' and the enigmatic structure of traumatic memories . . . by pulling the viewer into a setting that seems inhospitable and placeless."[26] Baer points to the structural similarity between "depictions of uninhabited landscapes that refer to a viewer not to a specific spot in nature but to a heightened sense of self, and the puzzling exact encoding of spatial markers in traumatic memory that signals the presence of significant events located outside of, and yet within, an individual's mind."[27]

Baer's insights on the strange temporality associated with this unplaceable space helps frame the way post-Holocaust reenactment scenes activate the disturbing threshold between a clearly defined past and present, an original experience and its uncanny, reemerging echoes. His observation that the photos "share with traumatic memories the exactness and the unforgiving insistence on the reality of a place whose significance cannot be deduced from anything within the image"[28] pinpoints some of the elements of the ascetic aesthetic at work in post-Holocaust cinema at issue here: the melancholy sharpness and designed emptiness engulfing a lone protagonist, the disturbing sense that we, the viewers, are both implicated in, *and* excluded from, this site and this experience.

Marceline's scene in *Chronicle of a Summer* is paradigmatic of an aesthetics that beckons the world to witness. Site and speech—*Shoah*'s intended title[29]—provide the minimal prerequisites for testimonial and dramatic reenactment. Close-ups and synchronized sound signify "ownership" of one's thoughts. Marceline's speech at the start of her monologue sequence, Karski's words and silence in *The Karski Report*, and Abraham Bomba's faltering voice in *Shoah* guarantee the speech act's veracity even as they articulate a truth that defies imagination. The second key element of reenactment is revisiting (whether literally or not) the site where extreme barbarity occurred. Doubling as documentary proof and a stage, the original location gains affective force as an inert witness, a background that has "seen" the past. A vacant space that dynamically shifts its charge in relation to the present it literally marks, this backdrop addresses different histories and audiences. At the same time, it awakens other phantasms. To conceive the empty site as mimetically representing the devastation that has taken place here is to miss its rhetorical reach and efficacy. Instead, this postcatastrophic trope forms a stage where different crises of truth are enacted and different memories negotiated.

Documentaries focused on posttraumatic conditions often meet with interpretations that discern a process of "working through."[30] Such a view is problematic, however. One of the main manifestations of trauma is the inability to narratively incorporate a particular memory into the present. A sequence of events remains frozen in time, full of original vivid details but bracketed; one is unable to make sense of the past and leave it behind. From a psychoanalytic perspective, the paradox of traumatic experience is that the "literal registration of an event . . . the ability to reproduce it in exact detail . . . corresponds to its escape from full consciousness."[31] Inability to recompose a narrative about the past yields a therapeutic impasse. The conflation between the therapeutic and the aesthetic tasks of reenactment has been the default approach in innumerable studies on post-Holocaust cinema.

Although the blurry line separating acting and acting out bears on the films discussed here, it is just as important to attend to the ways they inflect reenactment's redemptive promise. Whereas Zavattini invoked reenactment's self-enlightening potential, post-Holocaust cinema enlists the same means to different ends. Thomas Elsaesser has proposed a haunting image to describe the critical mortification occasioned by Lanzmann's films: "like Dante's encounters in hell they fill the mind's eye and ear with voices and presences; they will forever speak of a history for which there is neither redemption nor exorcism."[32] Along similar lines, Janet Walker has observed that the "holocaust documentary of return" is defined by instability: "Filmed, situated testimonies delivered verbally and bodily from a significant site and in the presence of others"[33] do not assure a sense of grounding or closure. These returns "may catalyze encounters . . . seeded with past associations" (for instance, the much commented-on anti-Semitic remarks sparked by Srebnik's return to Chelmno). [34] They may also, as in mimetic reenactments, duplicate and expose the unlocatable dimension of a psychic trauma.[35] But, rather than promising some cathartic change for the protagonists, reenactment in post-Holocaust cinema succeeds only once it repeats and displays forms of traumatic impasse.

Discussing Lanzmann's foundational decision to return to sites of atrocity, Georges Didi-Huberman helps delineate how this impasse in collapsed time is vividly rendered. He states this return was "necessary, if only so that they may be able to name the site: 'Yes, this *is* the place' as Srebnik states in German. More than that it is to say, as this tense slippage reveals, that nothing has changed."[36] In the "sites of destruction [Lanzmann discovers] the power of that, which, whether destroyed or effaced, nevertheless had not changed."[37] The return to the original site gives rise to a confounding comparison boomeranging between distinct forms of absence. In *Retour à Auschwitz* (Jacques Cristobal, 1967), one of several postwar films focusing on the survivors' visitation to the original camps, Roger Abada, a survivor, mentions quizzically: "that's where they did executions, there were many. I can't imagine, it seems small now but we were 20,000 inside." Similarly, the viewer watching the stagings in the film will hold two images in mind simultaneously. The return to a site or a gestural routine—the Ner River in Srebnick's boat ride, or Abraham Bomba's cutting of hair in a borrowed barbershop in Israel—do more than facilitate the reenactment of the past. For both social actor and viewer, the vacant site operates as a stage (spatial and temporal) for negotiating the "discrepancy between what there is to see and the imagination triggered by that [which can be] seen."[38]

These words conclude Gertrud Koch's brilliant analysis of Lanzmann's cinematic articulation of the friction between present and past, indifference and horror, when representing the unimaginable. It is not by chance that this pithy formulation follows her reference to "the fictive reenacted scenarios" activated by subjective camera movements that eventually situate the protagonists—Lanzmann himself and, in turn, the viewer—in the train "that unremittingly follows the tracks into the enclosure of the [Treblinka] death camp."[39] The discrepancy "between what there is to see and the imagination triggered by that seen" is a constituent part of reenactment itself. This contrast in fact fuels reenactment's intervention: it holds the concreteness of the present and imaginative constructs about the past in tension.

Post-Holocaust cinema concertedly deploys an ascetic mise-en-scène to magnify this constitutive discrepancy. Monologues amplify the dissonance with odd dislocations: speech in a deserted area, intimacy in public, and recollections that are both imaginary and experiential. Voicing, calmly or agitatedly, an entire scene with multiple characters, the real/actor—Oumarou Ganda, Marceline Loridan, Jan Karski—serves as a filter for the multiple temporalities and dissonant realities crossing his or her consciousness. The constancy of the person's identity across past and present ensures that wherever she is, the space around her will be transformed into a theater of justice, an arena for reclamation.

In the next sections I examine discrete aspects of a stark theatricality that place the viewer in the unforgiving position of the witness—the digressive rhythms of voice over commentary and of embodied monologue and the tensioned distance in framing that locks the viewer as addressee of the scene. I ask what cinematic and psychic affects animate the imaginary scenarios that are so vividly brought into scene; what kind of mise-en-scène generates an affective circuitry between the social actor and his listener/audience; and how do cinema's profilmic and filmic rhythms intensify this critical witnessing. I also explore the ritual and critical dimensions of in-person visitation, tracking distinct modes of an insistence *of* and *on* the real, starting with how filmmakers (Resnais, Rouch, Lanzmann) gesture through camera movements toward an affective experiential revivification. To that effect I have extended the notion of reenactment from straightforward representation of a person dramatically replaying her past, or verbally testifying and reliving her own memories, to a range of performative moves deployed to conjure up the persistence of the past in the now—from the tracking shots that sweep over former extermination camps to the staccato gestures of filming and refilming in *Shoah* that quietly, or urgently, activate for the viewer the complex significance of a layered reality behind the facade of the present.

PEDOVISION: RITUAL, WANDERING WORDS

Night and Fog, by Alain Resnais, stages a bold experiment in disquieting parallels between past and present through montage that alternates between color footage of slow dollies over the vacant grounds of concentration camps and black-and-white archival images of material remains. From its earliest synopses, by researchers Olga Wormser and Henri Michel, the film assumed the form of a flashback with the deserted space charged with bringing up the past. Not only would the location serve as the path for a guided visit revealing the different functions of the camp, but it would also be the springboard "for a *digression* on each object and site encountered in the camp."[40]

Pans and tracking shots from the exterior to the interior of the camps, as well as occasional backward motion, give the film a digressive quality. Sylvie Lindeperg notes how the camera's "pensive" maneuvers—for instance, the last two shots of the opening scene, which follow the border between the camp and the world at a walking pace—place the viewer in a space "inside the camp, or rather within the floating limbo of the film's opening, between past and present, between the 'real world' and the camp." This space matches "Jean Cayrol's 1948 description of the space of 'concentration camp dreams,'" where the detainee tried to "subsist between two worlds that contradicted and deformed each other . . . so that it distorted his return to the real world," giving him "forever the feeling of 'floating,' of mental and rootless wandering."[41]

Night and Fog moves between two worlds. The images, verbal and visual, elicit the entrancing rhythm associated with wandering across this charged terrain. Cayrol's commentary and Resnais's dollies over the camp's grounds articulate confounding strata of memory; as François Niney has remarked, the film is less an "exploration than an 'imploration,'" sounding "inner space, through an interiorized vision, the route of a fatal and unpredictable memory, in which each of us takes part."[42] Confirming Resnais's intention to glide over this landscape, to convey a carpeted smoothness over a bumpy and horrific past, we have the assistant cinematographer Sacha Vierny's recollections about how impossibly difficult it was to do tracking shots in Birkenau through the piles of rubble.[43]

This same seamlessness shapes Alain Resnais's intertwined articulation of past and present in *Hiroshima mon Amour*. His smooth dollies and montage, the camera movements across shots and distinct spaces and times, create an incantatory rhythm that is conducive to evocation, to reminiscence. When Marceline mentioned she recalled Emmanuelle Riva's walk in *Hiroshima* as she wandered through the Place de la Concorde and Les Halles, she was undoubtedly influenced by Resnais's and Marguerite Duras's digressive rhythm.[44] Having Resnais as a significant precedent in linking the effects of camera movement over an empty site with an evocative "imploration," we may consider the nature of *Chronicle*'s cinematic, ritual, digressions.

In this emblematic sequence of post-Holocaust cinema, Marceline Loridan reminisces about her deportation and return from Auschwitz Birkneau walking against the Place de la Concorde in a long shot, then in a close-up. Then, as she steps under the vaults of Les Halles old market and proceeds flanked by its walls, the camera backtracks and shows the Nagra recorder's ability to send its sound signal to a camera far from its object. This parting is quite dramatic, leaving a lone female figure starkly silhouetted in an extreme long shot and surrounded by the empty spaces of the building's open structure, strongly reminiscent of a train station[45] (Figs. 5.1a–g).

More impressive than the technical feat of sync sound is the contrast between the intimate nature of Marceline's revelations and the site of address, a mostly deserted

Figures 5.1a–g: Marceline's monologue sequence in *Chronicle of a Summer* (Rouch and Morin, 1961).

public space. Against this backdrop, her words gain an almost liturgical intensity. The mise-en-scène calibrates the distance between the viewer, potential auditors, and Marceline, creating a tension between public address and undisturbed privacy. Both the Place de la Concorde and Les Halles, urban passages oblivious to Marceline's words, make it all the more imperative that we listen.

ASCETIC STAGES [149]

This minimalist scene of a personal memory turned into collective address reduces acting to its bare essentials: direct and reported speech. An ongoing testimonial present in process, the scene stands midway between personal revelation and theatre. At once insisting on the private quality of her memory and projecting it onto a cinematic arena, Marceline's monologue incorporates words spoken by the SS and her father, as well her own plaintive call, in an intensely dramatized scene:

> The Place de la Concorde is empty, empty as it was twenty, fifteen years ago, I can't remember now. "You'll see. We'll go there, work in the factories. We'll see each other on Sundays," papa said. And you used to answer me, "You're young, you'll come back. I will never return." She hums and sings. And here I am in the Place de la Concorde. I came back, you stayed. We'd been there six months before I saw you. We fell into each other's arms. Then, that dirty SS officer hit me in front of you. You said, "She is my daughter." He made to hit you. You had an onion in your hand. You put it in mine and I fainted. [Singing] When I saw you, you asked, "Mother and Michel?" You called me your little girl. I was almost happy to be deported I loved you so much. I wish you were here now.

In between these words, Marceline hums in uncanny turns of introspection. Then she starts reminiscing about her return: "When I came back it was hard. I saw them all at the station, mother, everyone. They kissed me, my heart felt like a stone. It was Michel who softened it. I said, 'Don't you know me?' He said, 'Yes, I think so, I think you're Marceline.'"

Marceline's scene, which combines a reduced theatricality and the expansiveness of actual locations, forges an image of modernity that would soon, with small variations, define other European art films: a woman wandering down city streets in a trench coat carrying a heavy tote (with the Nagra recorder) and voicing her thoughts. The monologue, a mode of communication oscillating between the private and public spheres, becomes a potent signifier of displacement and alienation. As Mark Betz and James Tweedie have observed (in reference to art cinema and the New Wave, respectively), ambling through the city gives form to a new cinematic interiority: self-reflections gain their power in contrast to the realism of actual locations.[46] Tweedie suggests that the long sequence following "Elle" through the nighttime streets of Hiroshima articulates the film's complex equation between love, annihilation, and forgetting. At the end of the sequence, he notes, "elle" refers again to the vanishing of memory, as the film's montage has absorbed each reality in its uniform flow.[47] The fact that Marceline stated that images of Monica Vitti in *L'Avventura* and Riva in *Hiroshima* crossed her mind during her monologue act suggests her reference is to wanderings primarily associated with erasure and a problematic memory.[48]

The choice of the Place de la Concorde site also betrayed a scenic ambition on Marceline's part.[49] She had suggested the location because a Hollywood film about the German occupation by Edward Dmytrik was being shot there and the place was studded with Wehrmacht direction signs and extras dressed as German soldiers. The mix of two forms of historical invocation—a perfect expression of Rouch's surreal sensibility—was upset since the film crew arrived at the location one day after the

Hollywood shoot had ended. Still, even without the borrowed grandeur of a big production, the scene is striking.

Marceline's scene condenses two main registers of modern cinema in great evidence between 1946 and 1949: the record of historical contingency and the theatricality of a monologue address (exemplified, respectively, in Roberto Rossellini's work and Jean-Pierre Melville's *The Silence of the Sea* [1947–1949]). In the late 1940s, two films by Roberto Rosselini exemplify this dual tendency. The first, *Germany Year Zero* (1947), is a rubble film marked by actual ruins and the sense of immediacy associated with postwar history. The second, *The Human Voice* (based on Jean Cocteau's play), is a frantic monologue; here, a one-sided phone conversation collapses action and reaction as the camera focuses on a single studio room and character, meant to feel as restricted as an intimate stage. Significantly, attention to a single character creates an imbalance that is especially attractive to a modern sensibility attuned to the rhythm and qualities of the text. Ultimately, the sparse mise-en-scene leads to the estrangement of the monologue form[50]—a feature that recurs in the existentialist inquiries of fifties and sixties European and French art films (*Night and Fog* and *L'Avventura*) and later, in modified form, in posttraumatic and testimonial cinemas.

For Rouch, Marceline's scene epitomizes the uniqueness of cinema verité, what he called "pedovision" (ambulatory vision). [51] This catchy name refers to adapting the practice of *cine-transe* (film-trance) from his ethnographic films to an urban setting. *Cine-transe* was a "strange state of transformation analogous to possession phenomena," whereby the cameraman director "is no longer himself, but a mechanical eye accompanied by an electronic ear."[52] In this state, he can "[lead or follow] a dancer, priest, or craftsman, [and] rather than using the zoom [take the camera] where it is most effective." [53] Walking with his camera alongside Oumarou Ganda and away from Marceline, Rouch shaped two of the most moving instances of testimony in modern cinema.[54]

Rouch was fully aware of Marceline's own trance state. He observed that her delivery proved inimitable because, influenced by the décor, she talked following the rhythm of her steps: "With post-synchronization, the best artist in the world could not obtain this inexorable rhythm, the stride of someone who speaks as she walks, and in such a place."[55]

Writing on ways of walking New York City after 9/11, Marla Carlson has discussed the dimensions of the reverie prompted by the rhythm of physical movement, as well as the trigger of particular sounds and sites. [56] The juxtaposition of real surroundings with a fictional input approximates the "normal operation of memory; that is, what is absent (the past or the fiction) filters that which is present. Naturally the fictional filters have a powerful effect upon what we perceive, what we remember and what sense we make of it. Memory threads in and out of the constant commentary that our inner voices provide and an inner eye watches memory's simultaneous show." [57]

Likewise, apropos of the pacing of Marceline's scene and its effects, Rouch observes "something that goes beyond the tragic"; these conditions represent "an intolerable mise-en-scène, like a spontaneous sacrilege [they] pushed us to do what we had never done before."[58] Rouch reconstructs the scene's uncanny dimensions, the unplanned eruption of a primal scene in the film, where the early focus of the shot was solely on an "object in motion:"

> [Les Halles] was closed, tranquil, we pushed the car ahead of her and she remained talking all by herself. At a given moment we let the car stop and Marceline came closer to the camera. We had not seen or heard anything: we had simply provoked two movements, feelings emotions memories. When we saw these images on the screen for the first time Edgar . . . suddenly said, "Yes it's the image of her return." . . . Without realizing it we had chosen a building that looked like the vaulted roof of a train station. We had fixed the camera on an object in motion and coming from the other side of horror Marceline arrived.[59]

"Ritual is a sacrilege that succeeds," stated Marcel Mauss.[60] The anthropological dictum certainly holds for Marceline's scene. An ethnologist inspired by surrealism, Rouch is keenly aware of the "unconscious" transgression effected by the camera's objective glance and he is intent on capturing the staged threshold, the passing of what is uniquely real into symbolic replay.

A short exchange between Edgar Morin and Jean Carta, critic for *Témoignage Chretien*, addresses the disturbing quality animating this symbolic replay. For Carta, Morin's demiurgic "insistence to extract remembrances [plunges] the character into the past [and prevents] her from forgetting [and thus] from regaining her moral balance"[61]—a feature he deems ethically suspect. Morin defends his performers' right to fulfill their wishes, suggesting that in Marceline's case, there is a cathartic benefit. In a pithy formulation he states: "When someone lives a vicious circle of repetition, that character who puts herself out on the screen, who is and is not herself, looking at one's double in a face-to-face [and yet] with the distance of a spectator, can get out of [her] trauma provoking a sort of transference on [her] double."[62]

The "intolerable mise-en-scène," "the spontaneous sacrilege," manifest in this scene, this "happening" refers to more than a simple breach of privacy, or, in Morin's psychoanalytic phrasing, the working-through of trauma. The possession analogy used to describe *pedovision* encompasses Marceline's digressive state but, most important, it clarifies the role of Rouch's ambulatory camera in underscoring the viewer's engagement in the witnessing experience. The estranged urban space shields Marceline, facilitating the threading in and out of her memory, while the camera immerses the viewer in this past-present space-time and imparts the conjunction between walking and talking in *Chronicle* with a broadened ritual and testimonial value.

Joshua Hirsch has situated Marceline's testimony within a modernist and posttraumatic cinematic lineage. Stylistic factors such as the "ceaseless walking, her speaking to herself rather than an interviewer or the audience, the ellipses and singing fracturing her speech as well as the extreme variations in her distance from the camera . . . [situate] the spectator inside the fragmented space of Marceline's subjectivity."[63] For Hirsch, the invisible microphone lends added realism to the scene; more important, he points to the peculiar disarticulation of address resulting from her clear speech heard at a distance. But while the viewer is affectively engaged through the digressive rhythm of Marceline's rumination and movement, two aspects of the scene qualify the shared interiority that Hirsch posits. First, the estranging theatrics of the monologue (speaking aloud in public) counters cinematic conventions of interior monologues and subjective voice-over. More still, the scene's composition—its changing frame and movement—forges mounting distance from the viewer, even while keeping him or her as a privileged point of reference. Instead of absorbing the viewer, the natural space transforms into a stage to engage the spectator in a relation of enforced but tense co-presence.

Expanding on Bazin's notion of cinematic theatricality, Barthelemy Amengual's essay "Theatre and Filmed Theater" (*Théatre et Théatre Filmé*) helps explain how Rouch creates a scenic space out of natural locations.[64] First, Amengual prescriptively emphasizes the ascesis of the décor: "On screen, the decors will be irreducibly closed, blind to the world, so as to find the constant scenic volume [and] bring back this privileged node, the space within the space, that wings install in all theaters, even in the open."[65] Besides this internal carving of a scenic space, the framing and duration of the shot are also essential. The shot should "never split the character from his actual context safeguarding the spatiotemporal continuity and contiguity of the action thanks to the depth of the field and an extreme mobility of the camera."[66]

In such "space inside a space," Amengual continues, "[n]othing can happen that does not happen from it to it."[67] This closed-off area of address where affect and meaning circulate correlates with Rouch's camera movement, which gradually comes to a halt and adopts a fixed gaze as it carves a scenic space. By the same token, it connects with the way the monologue operates in a receding perspective. When Rouch distances the camera from Marceline's silhouette at the center of Les Halles market, her voice becomes slightly detached. With its steady sound volume, the voice attains an acousmatic power functioning as if it possessed the figure inside the frame from an elsewhere. Hereby, the voice's force of interpellation is intensified and, without a visible addressee, it scans the space to find and reclaim an auditor. Shaped by this long take, the scene assumes an engaged and personified, individualized dimension designing finally an unequivocal line of address. This vector enhances the power of words that, searching for an auditor, can now be guided by particular visual clues to rest, uncomfortably, with the viewer. Rouch's strategy of "pedovision"—tracking his characters' reflective state—shapes, through camera movement, the viewer's share in his protagonists' embodied recall. Such tracking shots in *Moi un Noir*, in *Chronicle*, and in Lanzmann's *Shoah* become phenomenological correlates for the subjectivity of reenactment—reliving as close, embodied following. I return to this transference of affect to the camera when discussing *Shoah*.

MARCELINE LORIDAN, TESTIMONY WITH(OUT) AN "I"

Particularizing Marceline's story as her own—a Jewish woman's—cannot be dissociated from awareness of contemporary acts of torture and the detention centers in France's war against the Algerian independence. In *Multidirectional Memory*, Michael Rothberg contends that the French context of repression and violence toward the Algerians (leading to and including the curfew that prompted the demonstration leading to the October 1961 massacre of two hundred Algerians by the Seine) "provided triggers that stimulated remembrance of the Nazi occupation and genocide."[68] The fact that writer and Holocaust survivor Charlotte Delbo waited four years to release her camp memoirs after publishing her first book, *Les Belles Lettres*, in 1961 (a collation of letters on the Algerian question interpolated by her comments), confirms that for left-leaning intellectuals it was paramount to integrate their testimony to a broader and current political struggle.[69] Just as significant, Rothberg points out, is Marguerite Duras's article *Les Deux Ghettos* (*The Two Ghettos*), which juxtaposes an interview with two Algerian workers with an interview with a Jewish Holocaust survivor.[70] The article was published on November 1961 two weeks after the same weekly had reviewed the recently released *Chronicle*. Like *Chronicle*, it "juxtaposes the effects of colonial and genocidal policies through a comparative approach to everyday life," and even replicates the same questions.[71] The questions range from "Do you still have an easy, simple idea of happiness" to "Do you believe that your condition resembles that of anyone else?" But the questions' tense—in the present for the Algerians and in the past for the Jewish survivor—inscribes a historicizing perspective that invites answers conveying the irreducibility of each experience.[72] The most significant aspect in his detailed reading of this progressive journalistic and literary output is that rather than leading to a reductive version of an universalized Holocaust, useful to broad, humanist, and antiracist policies of the immediate postwar, the comparison between forms of ethnic, religious, and national repression leads to a multidirectional memory pliable to connect with the Holocaust without reducing either one of the sufferings alluded to in the equation.

Still, the move to match a Jewish deportee's address with a hyperindividualizing but dislocated mise-en-scène was, at that point, aesthetically and historically bold. In her memoir *Ma vie Balagan*, Marceline revealed that when she arrived from the camps, her uncle warned her not to tell anyone what she had gone through since no one would believe her.[73] While the comment might refer to unheard-of extremes of horror, her monologue raises at once the basic stakes of testimony: the sense that one "can testify only, in the strict sense of the word, from the very instant when no one can, in one's place testify to what one does," that "what one testifies to is, at that very instant one's secret; that it remains reserved for her."[74]

Hirsch observed that the association of *Chronicle*'s technical innovations and sync sound with this single, dramatic eruption of a memory of the Holocaust implied that it was not possible to "[present] a snapshot of French society in 1960 without either confronting or repressing the unresolved collective memory of deportation."[75] And, indeed, as I've discussed before, *Chronicle*'s sync sound was mobilized precisely toward an autocritique and psychodrama, manifesting, with its "snapshot of French society," a number of crises of truth in the early sixties France.[76]

In his insightful treatment of the film, Rothberg privileges Marceline's testimony as a pivotal instance in the French discourse on the Holocaust following the trial of Adolf Eichmann in Jerusalem, which defined the exceptionality of the Jewish survivor. [77] Structured around the dramatic testimony of 111 survivors, the trial brought private memories into the public for the first time, shifting the way the world perceived the Holocaust. According to Annette Wieworka, the "memory of the genocide becomes constitutive of a certain Jewish identity at the same time that it claims a presence in the public sphere." [78] The parallel between Marceline's testimony and those of survivors in the Jerusalem court is based on countering the generalized erasure of Jewish suffering in the universalizing terms of anticolonial, antiracist discourse in the immediate postwar, through a highly subjective, fragile and untransferable recall.

At the same time, however, Rothberg reads the scene preceding the testimony as evidence that it was still possible in the early 1960s to see the Holocaust as related to other histories of collective atrocity, rather than its cypher.[79] Here, Marceline casually says she could not see herself marrying a black man even though she loves dancing with them. Rouch turns to Landry and Raymond, two African students, and asks whether they know what the numbers in Marceline's arm mean; then the film cuts sharply to underline their stunned reaction and the divide between cultural perspectives[80] (Figs. 5.2a–c).

Analyzing this scene's sound archives Frédérique Berthet details Rouch's careful modulation of this scene, its "shaping in its original temporality":

> Jean Rouch, knows as an orchestra conductor, and as *connaisseur* of tempo, that he is about to create a micro-event in the experience of cinema verité. He abandons his role on camera for a behind-the-scenes voice and talks to the cameraman. Each participant knows the discussion is suspended, that the scene is being adjusted and that what is played out is no longer the present but the "after." Rouch asks the

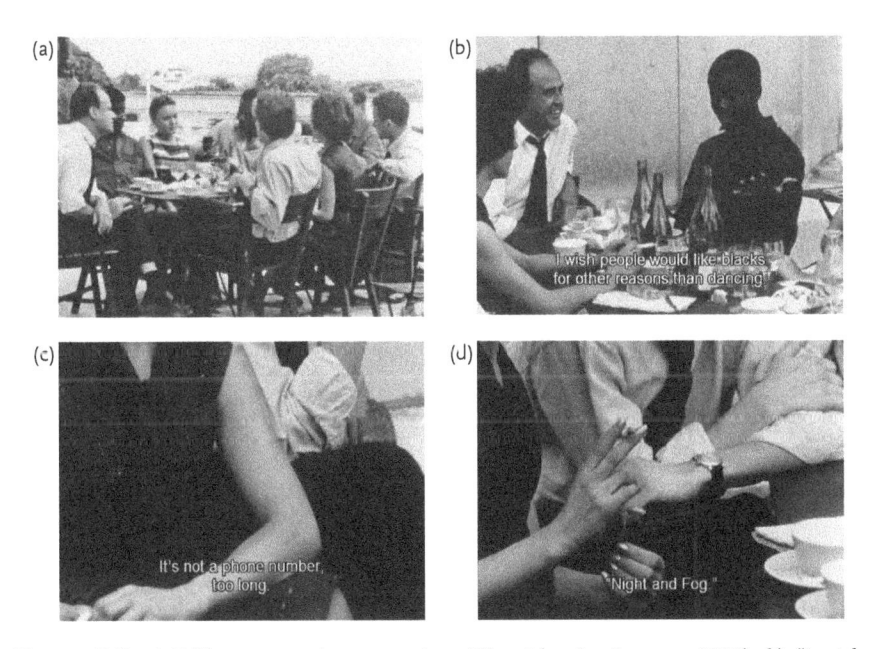

Figure 5.2: a) Table conversation on racism (*Chronicle of a Summer*, 1961). b) "I wish people would like blacks for other reasons than dancing" (*Chronicle of a Summer*, 1961). c) Rouch provokes a response to Marceline's tattooed number (*Chronicle of a Summer*, 1961). d) Raymond: I've seen a film, *Night and Fog* (*Chronicle of a Summer*, 1961).

cinematographer to go over Marceline . . . asks her to prepare herself, positioning her arm so that is "quite visible" then "answer slowly and distinctly. He thus generates during the filming a deceleration of the real that the montage will reveal culminating on . . . the freeze frame on Marceline caressing a flower with her fingers.[81]

Inasmuch as it comes right after this exchange, Marceline's monologue, which constitutes a separate scene, can be interpreted as the film's corrective and a belated requiem on France's collaboration and its fascist tendencies. In this context, Landry and Raymond's reactions form part of a chorus underlining France's history of ethnic discrimination, past and present (Fig. 5.2d). Through a cinematic montage this sequence creates a newly forged contract of "brotherhood," one of *Chronicle*'s explicit aims.[82]

As Rothberg notes, this sequence promotes solidarity on racism and anti-Semitism through the more pliable format of personal testimony.[83] Indeed, for Marceline, who identified as a Jewish, left-wing activist, public and private actions served complementary purposes. Her revelation challenged the prevalent sense that French deportees were all equally targeted.[84] At the same time, her word-act strikes a nerve with the heightened controversy about Algerian internment camps and contemporary acts of torture.[85]

To further add to the question of identity and allegiances, Marceline's involvement in the Jeanson pro-FLN network is one of many self-censored facts in *Chronicle*.[86] And although she mentioned the idea for a film on her memory of the camps dates from the moment of her testimony in *Chronicle*, she also felt France was not ready to discuss the particular plight of the Jews under Nazis in the 1960s. Instead her first film is *Algeria 62*, codirected with Jean Pierre-Sergent. [87]

Detours from the singularity of testimony may issue from particular makers' politics, but they are nonetheless unequivocally manifest in aesthetic decisions quite relevant to our discussion of reenactment voice. Already in 1955, Jean Cayrol and Alain Resnais made it clear that *Night and Fog* should not be understood "as [a] pure testimonial monument to the dead." Instead, the film sought to advance an alternate history and politics of memory: Auschwitz is allegorized as a screen memory for the current situation and violence in Algeria, and the evidence on Nazi concentrationary logic and extermination sounds the alert on the dangers of forgetting racism and discrimination closer to home.[88] The filmmakers devised a concerted aesthetic to convey the horrific everydayness of the camps' degradation and, at the same time, redirect this affect toward a contemporary reflection and activism. Key to this process of universalization are the "subjectless" tracking shots over the tabula rasa of grassy fields and the final image of the Birkenau ruins.[89]

This subjectless movement across the empty camps in *Night and Fog* is meant to induce a reflective mode in the viewer's consciousness. At the same time, and as Sylvie Lindeperg aptly observes, Cayrol's generalizing narration serves to repurpose history toward an alternative memory politics.[90] Despite Resnais's insistence that a former deportee write the words, the commentary programmatically avoids an individualized voice. Attentive precisely to this aspect, Marie-Laure Basuyaux has tracked the use of pronouns, closely reading semantic shifts in the narration. She demonstrates that "we" refers at times to "itself ('we can say nothing')," at others to present-day visitors seeing the camp ("today on the same path, it is day and sunny. We traverse it slowly, but in search of what?"), and, finally, to current and future victims of the "concentration camp scourge" ("there are those of us that gaze at these ruins with honesty and who hear nothing else than an infinite cry").[91] The sole instance of an "I" in the commentary does not refer to what the deportee has witnessed personally, "but to the [present] narrative authority of the film." Basuyaux concludes the text's paradoxical force lies in "a testimony without an I, virtually without witness but a testimony nevertheless."[92]

Released in 1961, the same year as *Chronicle of a Summer*, *The Time of the Ghetto* (Frédéric Rossif) was reviewed with continued reference to their shared approach to testimonials.[93] The film exemplifies another way of erasing the particularities of post-Holocaust testimony—in this case, through a sentimental rendition that makes both the survivor/protagonist's testimonies and the setting vague and generic.[94] The film intercuts Nazi films and stills produced under Goebbels orders (for Rossif an "objective representation" of the Ghetto) with the subjective, failing memory of forty-four survivors whose statements were recorded after they watched the footage. To minimize the glaring heterogeneity between archival images and sequences he filmed himself, Rossif subjected the documents to a special visual treatment, "lighting up some details that seemed important . . . and [drowning] the rest of the photograph in the black or white so as not to distract the spectators' eyes with the 'décor.'" Witnesses appear in front of a cyclorama of black velvet to create a photographic uniformity between past and present (Fig. 5.3) Two-hour statements

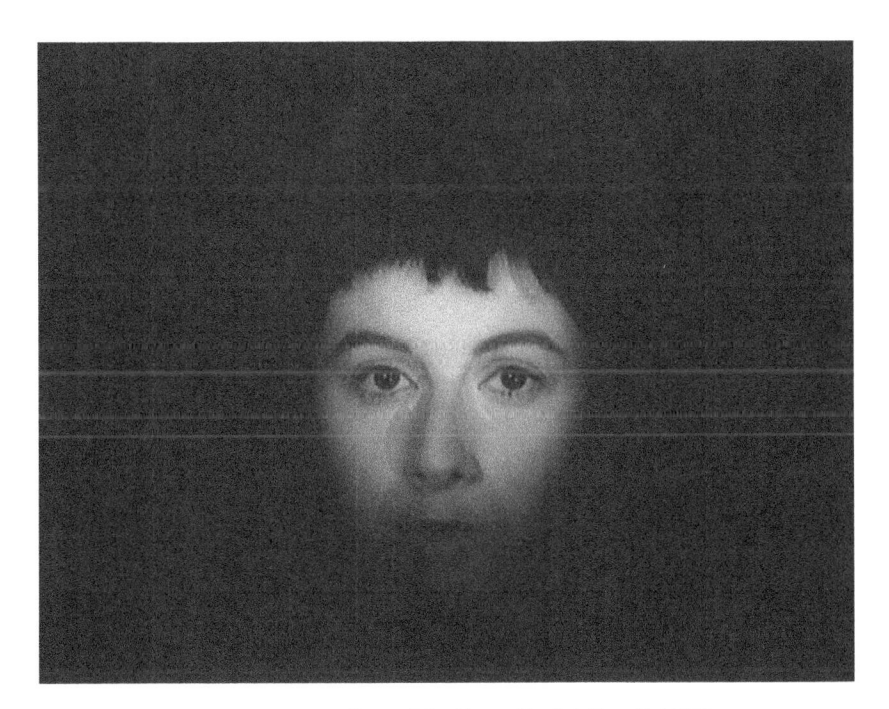

Figure 5.3: Survivor testimony in *Time of the Ghetto* (Fredric Rossif, 1961).

have been cut down to a few selected expressions. Delivered in a monotone, they were modified in the studio so they could "join . . . in an opera or oratorio."[95] This, the director felt, was the only way to achieve both the "litany-like leitmotif of suffering and memory as well as the clinical precision in the reported facts, for, if it happened that a witness lied or was mistaken on the whole, the [film's] translation of a daily memory would have great clarity."[96]

Rossif's initial instinct to display the wavering between past and present tense—the "short lapses of time in [his protagonists'] personal . . . testimony" revealing that "they relive their nightmares, they live it still, never managing to free themselves"—indeed preserved the broken quality of testimony (confirmed by later studies, such as Lawrence Langer's), survivors' struggle to situate disruptive memories riven by gaps in the context of a present, ordinary life.[97] While respecting the collapse of temporalities, the visual and aural orchestration of each speech into a unified expression blunts the sharp literalness typical of traumatic discourse. Conversely, by using the Nazi footage to signify the source of misery (e.g., one child feeding another, an old man fallen in the street), Rossif erases the doubly horrific register of this archive: the Nazis' pride in the extermination as well as the ghetto's reality (Fig. 5.4). Inasmuch as the overlit faces of the witnesses are wrested from a black void via frontal tracking shots, abstracted backdrops become the main link between testimony and ghetto images, easing access to unknowable experiences (Fig. 5.5).

Remarking that "one had to get the film (Rossif's) rid of so much art so as to render the document its unacceptable evidence," André Labarthe points to a central

Figure 5.4: Nazi footage in *Time of the Ghetto* (Rossif, 1961).

Figure 5.5: Nazi footage aestheticized in *Time of the Ghetto* (Rossif, 1961).

tenet of the ascetic realist aesthetics under discussion.[98] Part of supplying the document its "unacceptable evidence" lies in placing the film's protagonists in a present setting, specifically, in a stark spatial configuration that raises the specter of a disturbing, haunting familiarity. Marceline's scene in *Chronicle* and *Shoah* as a whole respond to this requirement both in their spatial composition and the forms of viewer embodiment and address at work.

Regarding the two major components of in-person reenactment—the actual protagonist and/or the original site—the contrast between Marceline's scene and her autobiographical film *La Petite prairie aux bouleaux* (*The Little Meadow with Birch Trees*, 2003) is illuminating.

In *Chronicle*, the testimonial reenactment is set against the light traffic of relatively empty public spaces such as the Place de la Concorde and Les Halles, whose architecture, which is reminiscent of a train station, adds an allusive charge to the scene. Rowena Santos Aquino and Hirsch, important commentators on this scene, have stressed the significance of the Place de la Concorde as a site of memory for people deported to camps in Eastern Europe. Marceline's body, situated in a "space directly connected to that past [,] presents a form of testimony starkly different from that obtained through talking head interviews."[99] The collective value of Marceline's words accrues by "referencing not only her experiences but also those of her absent father and the history of the Place de la Concorde's role in deportations."[100]

When Marceline Loridan-Ivens eventually made *La Petite prairie aux bouleaux*, the film did not reconstruct her camp experience; instead, it fictionalized her first return to Krakow in 1991.[101] The film reproduces her visit to Birkenau, which is now a museu;, however, the fact that actress Anouk Aimée plays Myriam (Marceline's Hebrew name) voids the revisitation premise. [102] Because Marceline herself is not the conduit between past and present—the first condition of reenactment—the possibility of a real interference between personal consciousness and vocalized expression, acting out and performing, vanishes.[103]

Chronicle features the enacted articulation of past and present: tentative connections that are mental, scenic, and historical. In contrast, the sole concrete element of the past to connect with the actress's dramatization in *The Little Prairie* is the museified site of Auschwitz-Birkenau. The film compensates for the lack of the original protagonist by overdoing the trope of contact, which it represents as a pilgrimage. Anouk Aimée is seen pensively walking through paths and the train track, touching her bunk in the old block (as she names the women who slept there), sticking her hand into the mud of the pit where bodies were burned and ashes thrown (Figs. 5.6 and 5.7). When Aimée/Myriam enters her former barracks and comes to the tiny bunk bed where other prisoners once lay, she touches each spot, giving them one of the other women's name, and arriving at her own spot—Myriam.

At this juncture, *La Petite Prairie* dramatizes the content of Marceline's reminiscence by reinscribing it within a different return narrative. Given that most of *La Petite prairie* consists of silent wanderings and dialogue between Marceline's former camp friends in Paris and a young German photographer she meets, what is most striking is the discrete treatment of her thoughts when she sits in her former bunk bed (Fig. 5.8). The scene starts with a dialogue between Myriam/Aimée and Marceline, the director and referent of the film: "They treated us as rats." "No, Myriam," says

Figure 5.6: Anouk Aimée as Marceline reminiscing about her companions at Birkenau (Loridan-Ivens, *La petite Prairie aux bouleaux*, 2002).

Figure 5.7: Touching the ashes at Birkenau (Loridan-Ivens *La petite Prairie aux bouleaux*, 2002).

Figure 5.8: Sitting on her former bunk, Marceline talks to herself (*La petite Prairie aux bouleaux*, 2002).

Marceline in voice off, " we weren't rats, you remember . . . told us such beautiful stories." After this peculiar double-voiced dialogue we watch Myriam lean down and rather than deploying the stream of consciousness, voice-over convention, she voices aloud the same memories Marceline recounted and dramatized in *Chronicle*. "Papa do you remember we met, it was six months we're here. You asked about Mamain and Michel, a German hit me and I fainted. When I woke up you'd disappeared. I loved you so much, how happy I was to be deported with you."

ASCETIC STAGES [161]

The dramatized replay of parts of the 1961 monologue suggests that Loridan could fulfill her desire to make an autobiographical film only by means of a form of expression related to what opened her long cinematic career and defined her identity: her monologue in Rouch and Morin's film, her creative and testimonial voice. [104] That moment of acting and testimony is now reproduced by Aimée—except that Loridan, the director, revises the original monologue by splitting its constitutive aspects into separate scenes—the wandering through the grounds of the camp/museum from the voicing of her memories in the bunk bed.

Attending to the wandering, ritual rhythm of Marceline's words in *Chronicle*, we are privy to a sense of an in-process address: the words are tentative and searching at the very moment they are listened to. As we will see in a related context, it is not the content or informative material that counts, but testimonies with an I that activate a truth possibly unknown to the speaker (and viewer), even though he knows the facts and has told the same story multiple times. This iterability is a feature of the "script" of reenactment and bespeaks its performative relation to making truth.

SPLITTING: OUMAROU GANDA'S SOLO

Toward the end of *Moi un Noir* (*I a Black Man*, MUN 1958) the protagonist Oumarou Ganda opens up to his friend Petit Jules, who listens quietly. After a fictive childhood "flashback," (footage from Niger of kids and adolescents grinning and diving in the river), Ganda abruptly abandons his nostalgia, saying: "I'm crazy, I am not in Niamey" (Fig. 5.9). Just as soon, in the now of his present moment, he starts another modality of recall, one that disallows any fictional account but the one he conjures up.

In an epic enactment of his recent past as a French Expeditionary force soldier in Indochina, Ganda begins his story, with descriptive asides, dialogue addressed to Petit Jules and playacting. Walking, parallel to the camera, with his friend over the Abidjan lagoon's elevated bank, he grabs a big stone and throws it, dives to the ground, stands up, and pretends to leap over a trench, then continues to walk while gesticulating wildly to Petit Jules (who from time to time disappears off-screen):

> I have done everything in my life, everything. You know, Petit Jules, I served in the war . . . the war in Indochina. I killed the Vietminh with a submachine gun, a knife, a hand grenade. And that's how you do it with a hand grenade, you throw it right away and you lie down flat on the ground . . . it wasn't worth it at all! Petit Jules. I did everything everything! But nothing worked for me. Listen, old friend, I just don't know, I did everything that a man should do. Everything! But nothing matters! I am still the same. See, one can stand, lie down . . . , you mustn't fear, Petit Jules, I tell you that's it. All! Kill people! Thousand, five thousand people! We hide behind the woods . . . in the bushes and we also ambushed. All, much more still. Kill people. Listen, Petit Jules: to kill a Vietminh, you raise your knife and *paf paf*, you put him on the ground. And I told my captain: I've seen the blood run, and . . . I saw

Figure 5.9: Preface to Ganda's monologue in *Moi un Noir*: "I was happy then."

friends die two meters from me. I saw friends with whom we drank coffee and after drinking coffee, die right there. And why? For nothing, for nothing my friend.¹⁰⁵ (See Fig. 5.10 a, d, e; see Fig. 5.10 b, c, f in Color Insert, 1).

Without an interlocutor, the scene, stripped down to words and a few gestures, contrasts with the natural backdrop. Its dislocated quality intensifies the psychic and testimonial dimensions of the performance. "All" (he's done) and "nothing" (death and bare, daily subsistence haunting his life) form a kind of refrain to the monologue, joining frustration and despair. Ganda directs Petit Jules to stand by his side, to "see him die . . . and, exactly as I walk with you, I die, I die . . . a grenade bursts . . . a strike of an obus. Don't be afraid, Petit Jules. I tell you only that's how it was in Indochina. I walk with you and all of a sudden I fall dead. But what's the use? It serves nothing, Petit Jules."¹⁰⁶

The stakes of Ganda's address in *MUN* can be illuminated by comparison with Rouch's earlier films, which comment as well as voice his protagonists' dialogues. The novel power of the monologue derives from its break with Rouch's authorial voice, in particular from the director's translation and channeling of his subjects' words. Discussing the contemporaneity of Rouch's films with struggles for decolonization, Teshome Gabriel maintained that the director "should have allowed Africans to have speaking parts instead of [offering] a psychological study of their reality."¹⁰⁷ And yet, even under pressure concerning his mediation of West African culture, Rouch offered aesthetic, cultural, and technical reasons for superimposing his voice over

Figures 5.10: a) Ganda's reenacted monologue of his Indochina experience (*Moi un Noir*, 1958). d). e).

unsubtitled West African actors. He also underplayed the agonistic dimension of his mediation, maintaining that it is impossible to decode "two sound sources simultaneously, as one will always be heard at the detriment of the other."[108] At the same time, he dismissed supposedly objective, "scientific exposition," which "instead of clarifying the images . . . obscures them . . . finally substitut[ing] itself completely for them."[109] Finally, he rejected synchronized sound and attempts to dub a second language as faulty approximations of commercial cinema: "far from translating, transmitting or reconciling, this type of discourse betray[s] communication."[110] Even if properly subtitled, Rouch observed, Dogon gestures could still contradict the verbal track. To the end, he defended his surrealist-inspired "cine-trance": commentary that moves between description and invocation, communion with subjects, and, in more than one sense, a form of cinematic possession.

Once Rouch started his cine-fictions, or "films in black and white," with African friends who spoke French and improvised their scenes, translation and commentary proved superfluous. Instead, another discursive transfer took place: Rouch had the actors of *Jaguar*, *Moi un Noir*, and *The Human Pyramid* comment on their actions as they face the film rushes during the dubbing process. As Colette Piault has noted, this is not a just technique to replace an absent sync sound; rather, the gap between commentary and visible action is key to the film's power. [111] "There is a splitting (or doubling) of personality" and "the action is reinforced: acted, filmed and differently replayed once words and commentary are added."[112] Much like what occurs in reenactment, the personages' postsynchronization, a feature internal to the production of Rouch's cine-fictions, inscribes a temporal *décalage* between selves—one fixed on screen, the other reanimating and actualizing his own verbal address.

Self-dubbing, voiced monologues, and feedback on one's performance are practices of splitting and self-actualization. Still, Rouch discerned a major difference between reliving one's own story and the dubbing of fictionalized accounts, and he suggested that the failure of *The Human Pyramid* to convey the characters' consciousness involved the difficulty of dubbing "assumed" personas; in contrast, Ganda dubbed the narration of his own life in *Moi un Noir*.

To grasp the import of in-person reenactment, it also matters whether the monologue in *MUN* differs from Ganda's self-presentation throughout the film and whether recreated memory differs from projected fantasy. Ganda's narration had incorporated "myriad personae registering the inseparable mixture that links real characters to their mythical doubles [and] in a second-degree doubling, fuses actor, character, function—Eddie Constantine/Lemmy Caution/Federal American agent. Or still Sugar Ray Ray Sugar Robinson."[113] Jean André-Fieschi had identified this de-centering function with the monologue mode, which splits open into a "tissue of monologues woven into a single flow made up of a sum of differences."[114]

Along the lines of the creative "fabric of monologues" woven into Ganda's self-presentation, his reenactment of his experience in Indochina has a distinct referential gravity. It takes place at the film's end, when Ganda seems unable to sustain the level of braggadocio and fantasy with which he has guided the viewer through his life in Abidjan. Coming after a dream-like flashback, Ganda's act-words function as a social gestus—"the visible result," as Brecht puts it, of "one's effort to keep one's balance on a slippery surface as soon as falling down would mean losing face." [115]

Retroactively, the scene frames the contemporary tale of migrants from Niger in the port of Abidjan as a postcolonial face-off with broader ramifications. Ganda's account indexes two major moments in the history of French decolonization on a personal register. Philippe Dewitte and Christopher Miller have argued that the inference of the African sacrifice for France was the right of citizenship, and that this moral debt became the "cornerstone of black activism in France" in the 1920s. While Ganda's words echo with the *dette de sang* incurred by the massive participation of Africans in World War I, Ganda's reenactment doesn't have to reach back to the interwar colonial history to resonate with the political awareness gained by African men who enlisted to fight in Indochina.[116]

The incongruous theatricality of the scene figures the senselessness of a West African colonial subject fighting another French imperialist war. The decolonization moment bears on the film's effort to recalibrate the voice and authority associated with ethnographic documentary. Attuned to the subjective turn opened up by Rouch's ethno-fictions, Steven Ungar, in a key essay on *MUN*, suggests that Ganda's monologue be read side by side with *Cabascabo* (1968), Ganda's first work as a director and a film that clearly adds another autobiographical turn to his scene.[117]

Like Ganda's monologue act, *Cabascabo* stages a return. The film is a fictional account of a war veteran, Cabascabo, who comes home only to lose all his pension money by overspending and lending. A flashback takes us to a scene of West African soldiers fighting for France in Indochina. We see Cabascabo questioning the war and being punished by a French official. In *MUN*, these same questions have a different reclamation valence: voiced by Ganda himself rather than a fictional character, the monologue represents the convergence of a conflicted sense of French citizenship and the potential for salvaging the possibility of autonomous critical action.

Ganda's presence as protagonist in both films ties biography to film in a kind of Möbius strip, creating a series of intra- and extratextual resonances: his own experience in Indochina and Cabascabo's thoughtless spendthrift habits parallel the precarious daily subsistence portrayed in Rouch's film. In *Cabascabo*, now visibly older, Ganda adds the status of writer and author to his former role as an actor; in a typical turn of revisionist biography and as an addendum to his bitterness in Abidjan, the character Cabascabo returns to his rural roots.

In an interview given in 1980, Ganda relays that "Treichville, the Zazouman" (the original title of *MUN*, meaning "the jaguarman," or *flâneur*) did not concern a former combatant in the Indochina war. *Cabasbaco* represents his attempt to get the "aim right, to say almost the same thing, but . . . with greater precision." His revision of the account includes the use of actual guns (as opposed to the mimed shooting that occurs in *MUN*). The surplus of realism that comes from flashbacks of war scenes and the effects of grenades—shattered bodies, dead Vietnaminh—speaks volumes about the dispossession Ganda felt as a colonial subject, or as an actor left to tell his life story in *MUN*. Read against *Cabascabo*'s plodding mimetic realism, the monologue's sparseness in *MUN* as well as the stark displacement of the action into another time and location are clearly the main motor for its representational and ritual force.[118]

We can assume that Deleuze, who appreciated Rouch's encouragement of fictional scenarios on the part of his social actors, would have ultimately included *Cabascabo* alongside the ethno-fictions of *Jaguar* and *MUN*, or the sociodrama in *THP*. That said, Deleuze held that "storytelling by a real character" is what allowed "the affirmation of fiction as a potentiality rather than a pre-established truth, a model."[119] Ganda's monologue achieves an expansive quality not just because the protagonist is the object of his own narrative, but also because in splitting from oneself, his narrative gathers some of the qualities of the epic theatre described by Fredric Jameson.

According to Jameson, the allegorical energy of Brechtian autonomization—the separation of elements standing for cause and consequence—aligns epic drama [and I would add, film reenactment] in common cause: to rescue the notion of individual action as an ethic of production, that is, the "capacity to act out our own possible and virtual actions, [using] its one-time spectacle to energize the public into a sense of multiple possibilities."[120] The strangeness and force of this mode of representation resides in the fact that the "subjective moment of decision and action itself, the 'proairesis' of the protagonist, with its wavering motives and intentions," is in evidence.

In Ganda's illustrated narration of his experience, the rational choice, the "I think" which must accompany all of one's self-representations, is paraded with its "wavering motives" and jolting rhythm. Ganda's long-winded monologue intersperses first- and third-person narrative into a rapid, manic loop, undecided as to which present or persona to stop. Split among various geographies and times and actualized in the now of vigorous falls and throws, the scene's intensity is compounded by the jump cuts necessitated by breathlessly tracking Ganda's speech through shot bursts of no longer than 25 seconds (allowed by the Bell and Howell's camera magazine). Given the lack of sync sound, these shot interruptions also led to a reconstructive montage in postproduction that "both stimulated and blocked improvisation."[121] Rouch reported that Ganda almost cried in retelling his story during a cathartic process of dubbing, one that instantiated a secondary instance of reenactment in the sound booth.[122]

Oscillating between action and reflection, Ganda's act cannot be pinned down, embodying multiple, stifled directions *in potentia*. He asserts his authority to tell his story and, even more, to choreograph its spectacle. Meanwhile, the scene's insistent reiteration of what has passed defines Ganda's testimony (and Rouch's imperative to articulate it) as entangled with the stark limits of his agency.[123]

THE KARSKI REPORT—OF A REPORT

Whether the protagonist or the filmmaker initiates a testimony or dramatic reenactment, the real/actor's agency is traversed by multiple intentions and historical or psychological exigencies. Testimony may be sparked by an internal need, but it is defined by its public, memorial mission from the start. It is singular because it cannot be reduced to mere information or description. And because testimony makes truth by attesting to an instant reserved solely to the one testifying, it cannot lie. At the same time, when one "commits [oneself] to speaking the truth, one commits oneself to repeating the same thing, an instant later, the next day and for eternity."[124]

In-person reenactment relies on the same subjective testimonial truth. If only for this reason, it is tied in principle to the iterability of a core experience. And yet "repetition carries the instant outside itself."[125] In this context, what proves relevant for us is how dramatic tropes mediate the making present of the truth, *again*.

Ganda's Indochina experience is recounted in *Moi un Noir* and fictionally dramatized in *Cabascabo*, as well as reactivated affectively during *MUN*'s dubbing session. Jan Karski's report—a reenactment of an account recounted multiple times ("I was like a machine," he said)—provides yet another facet in reenactment's complex and public refraction of the self in its compounded belatedness. Lanzmann knew of Karski's role as the Polish envoy in charge of communicating the situation in Poland, and the conditions of the Jews, to world leaders. In 1943, his testimony had tremendous urgency. He accompanied two Jewish leaders to the Warsaw ghetto and then, with the help of another member of the resistance, went into an extermination camp he erroneously believed to be the Belzec camp. He was then brought by the Polish ambassador to meet several world leaders and report on what he had seen. The first time he made his participation widely public was when, at Elie Wiesel's insistence, he participated of the Conference of Holocaust survivors in Washington, DC, in 1981 with a 35-minute-long verbal account.

The Karski Report was made into a film only in 2010. A long, two-day interview had been filmed between 1978 and 1979; 30 minutes from the first day, Karski's description of how he witnessed the Warsaw Ghetto with his own eyes, appear in *Shoah*.[126] At the start of the *Shoah* interview, Karski begins: "Now, now I go back thirty-five years." After a pause, he starts to shake his head and hand. "No, I don't go back." He starts to stand up and sits back down; after performing the same motion again, he leaves the room. He ends his testimony declaring that he "couldn't take it any more," and that he told his guides at the ghetto: "get me out." This statement about his "original reaction to witnessing the ghetto" is followed by several other negations—"Even now I don't want. I don't go back in my memory. I couldn't take any more . . . I never saw any movie . . . this was not the world." Leaving the room just as he is about to give voice to the images flooding through his memory, Karski reenacts his earlier flight.[127]

Lanzmann edited out the material on Karski's meetings with world leaders because he thought that, placed together, the different sections would weaken each other. He felt that in recounting his meeting with Roosevelt, Karski "seemed to inflate with pride . . . he became worldly, theatrical . . . and that countered the tragic [tone] that he had incarnated till then."[128] And yet, despite his misgiving regarding the scene's theatricality, Lanzmann eventually promoted the release of *The Karski Report* as evidence of the real Karski—and as a corrective to Yannick Haenel's "The Messenger," an account which, he felt, falsified the tenor of the Roosevelt-Karski encounter.[129] Lanzmann's new film, with a "form close to that of oral-history interviews with Holocaust survivors,"[130] was meant to set the record straight. This recasting of the piece in terms of oral history or documentary integrity is all the more interesting given how heavily Lanzmann edited the presentation.[131]

That this material was initially discarded and reissued fifteen years later as a standalone film—that it was deemed excessively artificial and then indisputably factual—points to its self-sufficient qualities but also its hard-to-accommodate idiosyncrasies. The scene's compounded belatedness makes it serviceable to different interpretive frames and strategic uses. On the other hand, as we will see, its core tension—belief versus knowledge—is so starkly articulated that the scene acts as a synecdoche for *Shoah*'s central thesis on the impossibility of apprehending the extreme atrocity of the Jewish Holocaust. Let us turn to the moment at stake in *The Karski Report*.

After describing his meeting with Franklyn Delano Roosevelt and the president's polite attentiveness, Karski recounts his encounter, accompanied by Cheronovski, the Polish ambassador, with Supreme Court Judge Felix Frankfurter. An extremely tall Karski mimics his interlocutor, who shrinks more and more as he listens.

"Do you know I am a Jew? Tell me about the Jews." I [Karski] became a machine. He looked smaller and smaller, listens, looks at me . . . "Now, young man, I'm no longer speaking for Frankfurter, I'm a judge of man a judge of humanity, I must be totally honest and I'm telling you I don't believe in" . . . Cheronovski breaks in: "Felix he's not lying," Karski moves to the side assuming the "role" of Frankfurter: "I did not say he's lying; I said I don't believe him because these are different things. Mr.

Ambassador, I said my mind (touches his head) my heart they are made in such a way I cannot accept." "No, No," he says, pushing with his hands. (Figs. 5.11a–g; see Fig. 5.11d in Color Insert, 1).

Karski (much like Ganda) finds words alone inadequate for what he has to say. He stands up and adopts bystanders' positions, performing the "presences" and agitated silence of those listening to him. One assumes this highly cathected energy is due to some sort of memory imprint, but we cannot discard the more technical aspect of Karski programmatically animating these exchanges. Karski is fully mobilized in his multiple conditions of testifier, informer, and dramatizer. Throughout, his most striking incarnation is that of Frankfurter's quandary, caught between knowledge and disbelief.

Figures 5.11a–g: Karski reporting his meeting with Judge Felix Frankfurter in *The Karski's Report* (Lanzmann, 2010). a) Karski as Karski. b) Karski as Frankfurter. c) Karski reenacts Frankfurter's reaction to the news about the extermination of the Jews: "No, No, No." e) "My mind." f) "My heart." g) "These are two different things."

The film's aim had never been to reproduce the factual report given to world leaders. In 1978, Lanzmann intended to have "a kind of philosophical discussion about the problem of transmission of experience: in which respect did people believe your report? Could Belzec or Treblinka have the signification they should have had for people living peacefully in Washington or New York?"[132] Cast as a general reflection on the extremity of the Holocaust, the question ultimately concerns reception. When asked about Frankfurter's sincerity, Karski justifies the judge's reaction, confirming the director's thesis that the Jewish Holocaust "was a problem without precedent, an unheard-of atrocity."[133] It "was, and remains, incomprehensible—beyond the understanding of 'sane and rational human beings.'" In the film's prologue, Lanzmann cites Raymond Aron's response when asked whether he knew what was taking place in the East. His answer: "I knew, but I didn't believe it, and because I didn't believe it, I didn't know."[134]

This same divide between knowledge and incomprehension, the same contradictory dimensions of a shocked consciousness, are evident in Karski's extratextual statements about his experience on his mission. He referred to his demeanor in these occasions as machine-like—"I was like a camera, like a recording machine," he would say, suggesting an important variant on the machinal conditions of Rouch's cine-transe.

Yet while Karski claimed he felt like a recording machine, he also said he had never spoken about his experience of the Warsaw ghetto. He distinguished clearly between the objective dimension of his reporting mission and its intimate repercussions, the personal aspects of his experience. According to Gertrude Koch, this means that he was " able to speak only with difficulty about what he had experienced—the shock he felt in the ghetto that rendered him speechless when he saw what was to be seen there."[135] That he had to revisit this difference and difficulty exemplifies Lanzmann's demand that people "re-experience situations."[136]

In front of the camera, however, Karski likely felt obliged to do more than simply tell in words what happened. His performance responds to Lanzmann's unique and complex take on transmission and theatricality. For the director, representation has to engage the viewer's present, and his protagonists must be transformed into actors. To summon what no longer exists—or to provoke an as-yet-unformulated truth—they had to do more than recount their stories; they had to act it out:[137]

> They had to give themselves over [irréalisent] to it: That's what defines imagination: it de-realizes. That's what the entire paradox of the actor is about. They have to be put into a certain state of mind but also into a certain physical disposition. Not in order to make them speak, but so that their speech can suddenly communicate, become charged with an extra dimension.[138]

Koch associates Lanzmann's conception of performance to the notion, "central to Sartrean existential psychoanalysis," that in replaying particular gestures and physical movements "everyone again becomes who he is." This "acting out" is "*Shoah*'s criterion for authenticity,"[139] and herein lies the film's continuity with cinema verité's existential lineaments and its embrace of psychodrama as a path to self-awareness.[140]

Indeed, the notion of acting out proves central to the tangle of authenticity and theatricality (or bad faith). The question, then, is how this acting out leads Karski to become who he is. In what ways does the monologue—with its agitated embodiment of multiple voices and its dissociative, layered temporality—aid the process of self-enlightenment?

Lanzmann felt *The Karski Report* perfectly accomplished his goal. Criticizing academic research on the Western response to the Holocaust as it was occurring, Lanzmann stated that "all was perfect except the proportions and the temporality, the implacable plenitude of the real, the true configuration of the impossible... they [scholars] reconstitute through a retrospective illusion, forgetful of the thickness, of the weights, the un-readability of an era."[141]

With its hard-to-place affect, Karski's communication carries the thick unreadability of an era. Lanzmann's initial misgivings about Karski's histrionics aside, the scene's theatricality trumps sincerity. Even as the belief of those involved remains historically important, what Karski's act relays in its belated and contorted excess is the ethical conundrum arising from accepting extreme atrocity as a fact. Because of its compact economy—a single person exfoliating multiple positions—the scene comes to resemble a tableau, contributing a baroque version of the unresolved tension and core aporia manifest in the apposed statements "You are not lying" and "I can't believe you."

In its exaggerated animation, Karski's reenactment allows a deeper truth, and authentic engagement, to emerge. Borrowing the persona of his incredulous listener, Karski enacts his own disbelief; inevitably, the mimicked encounter incorporates a belated melancholia. The scene's core gesture—an energetic pushing away with one's hands, a physical refusal to hear the truth—derives its power from successive, embedded relays: it passes from Frankfurter to Karski, and then from Karski/Frankfurter to the viewer—from past to present, from memory to acting and acting out. In reconstituting the "true configuration of the impossible," and in once reiterating this drama's dependence on a listener, the scene communicates an incarnated ethics where the one bearing the facts must literally, physically, share in disbelief.

FILMING AND REFILMING: PHATIC REENACTMENT

In *Shoah*, multiple variants of reenactment are at play. Take, for instance, Srebnick's literal return to Chelmno and the distinct contrast of his presence against empty sites, which admit imaginary filling in on the viewer's part. By the same token, the unlikelihood of this return is manifestly enacted once he stands flanked by a number of Poles at the end of a Sunday service. A tight-framed long take keeps Srebnick and the Poles uncomfortably close, dramatizing their incompatible claims to the same space.[142] That, in the evidence of film, Srebnik is actually there, splinters the image into a constellation of possible, and forever gone, futures (Fig. 5.12). His vacant, sad look sets off the reality of a violently shattered past, in the displayed spatial harmony of a restaging, or a posed on-camera statement.[143] Reenactment casts light on the unbridgeable gap—even as Srebnik and Chelmno's identities guarantee some sort of

Figure 5.12: Srebnik amid Poles leaving the church in Chelmno (Lanzmann's *Shoah*, 1985).

continuity—between the twelve-year-old boy made to row by the Ner River as ashes were thrown into its waters and the forty-seven-year-old man retracing his trajectory. The constancy of actor and place identity brings out the staging of the violence Didi Huberman has called the "return despite everything."[144] A signal intersection of disrupted historical trajectories, Srebnik returned becomes a charged historical index, a confronting question.[145]

But alongside these visible, returning characters I want to consider filmic returns that explicitly aim toward renewing contact with an original ground. The obsessive return to a given location related to an original event, as well as insistent figurations of contact such as stepping over a particular area or the repeated tracking of the camera over a given site, enact *and defer* a sense of a temporal or physical continuity between past and present. In this context, the term *phatic* (which refers to repeated verbal and gestural assurances of unbroken contact during a communication) emphasizes the ritual intent in reestablishing contact with the past employed in the "filming and refilming" of post-Holocaust cinema. Staccato montages pointing repeatedly to particular realities or insistent tracking shots caressing the ground are examples of cinematic actualizations meant to affectively engage the viewer.

Night and Fog's commentary and shots gliding over extermination camps and Marceline's monologue carrying the listener along as she traverses her past inwardly enlist profilmic and filmic rhythms to recruit witnesses. The digressive, entrancing nature of these wandering images and words binds the spectator to that experience and confers to it a ritual quality.

This need to preserve "the interior rhythm of the voice," to move the viewer imaginarily, is also at work in *Shoah*. Avowing he was slow in realizing the film should take place primarily on Polish ground, Lanzmann resorts to a subjective and entrancing traversal of a precise terrain to inscribe the viewer's perspective. By Lanzmann's account, it was "while shooting on the Ner River one rainy afternoon, listening to that singing child, now a forty-seven year old man (Srebnik) that [he] found the solution to the insoluble problem of how to film Chelmno, this long peasant village of low houses stretched out on either side of a single street."[146] He had the idea, he said, "of traveling through it on a horse drawn carriage a tracking shot taking in the wet road, the houses, the church, the rum of the horse its tail sweeping through space like the pendulum of a metronome the regular clatter of its hooves making it all the more terrible the words of Frau Michelson, the wife of a relocated German officer who had witnessed the ceaseless comings and goings of gas vans."[147] Information alone proved insufficient. For Frau Michelson's words to sink into the spectator's consciousness, the viewer had to share in the soothing pace of the words and the village setting. To grasp the ethical core of the scene—the indifference of witnessing, of common everyday life clashing with the "comings and goings of gas vans"— the viewer had to be placed in a pastoral setting, surrounded by a bucolic silence (Fig. 5.13). Despite our awareness that we are in a different time, the focalization effect is insidious and far from neutral.

In a different angle of approach, Lanzmann retraces Filip Muller's first encounter with the gas chambers (where he was forced to work as Sonderkommando for two years) in a strikingly overextended shot from a subjective viewpoint. Moving across

Figure 5.13: Bucolic tempo for Michelson's description (Lanzmann's *Shoah*, 1985).

the ground of the cells holding the Sonderkommando units, the camera eventually stops for a static shot of the street leading to the gas chambers; then, it starts moving again and adopts the perspective of people being gassed. It finally climbs on the chambers' flat roof, corresponding to the position of the three Nazis who address the group of Poles about to die.

Although many of *Shoah*'s tracking shots or zooms may be seen as reenacted camp arrivals, this scene has received particular attention because of its disturbing strategy of identification.[148] Rothberg suggests that this mirroring of Muller's standpoint does not violate the film's principle of nonfictionality.[149] That said, the ghostly camera is disturbing in other ways, too, especially inasmuch as it points to the director's presence. Because the "staging" (as Lanzmann calls it) occurs through editing—that is, because Muller is not transported to the original site of the camps—the filmmaker and viewers become surrogates for the experience described.

Dominick La Capra views the film's reenactment maneuvers as privileging empathy at the expense of a more analytical historical perspective and has criticized the subjective camera's surrogacy effect. In particular, he finds fault with the "secular sacralization of the Holocaust evident in Lanzmann's tendency to grant the highest, perhaps the sole legitimate status to the witness who . . . self-rendingly relives the traumatic suffering of the past—a status with which Lanzmann as a filmmaker would like to identify."[150] Indeed, as Rothberg observes (without passing judgment), this disturbing reenactment shows Lanzmann's wish to touch the real.

The number of scenes charged via words' entrancing rhythm or embodied cameras confirms the importance of "touching the real" when analyzing post-Holocaust cinema. As a mode, reenactment primarily concerns "touching time," referencing earlier events, an original real incarnated in psychic or material residues of the past. But this access can only occur as a form of theater that asserts the "principle of continuity of identity across a succession of substitutions"[151]—a process Christopher Wood and Alexander Nagel call "anachronic."[152] In contrast to securing proper origins (which is the work to which the critical term "anachronistic" refers), "anachronic" reflects "what art does" in its repetition, hesitations, and future projections. Reenactment, as art, is principally engaged in activating intertemporal dialogue.[153]

Lanzmann's attempts to reanimate the material remnants of the past gain special affective significance through repetitive, obsessive gestures. In performative terms, such insistent poking, on sites, people, and stones, amounts to a refusal to consider the past as something over and done. Such gestures form the motor of reenactment in *Shoah*, defining its ritual and rhetorical missions, through marked reiterations.[154] Indeed, nowhere is Bill Nichols's statement about reenactment truer than here: "Reenactments enhance or amplify affective engagement . . . they resurrect a sense of a previous moment that is now seen through a fold that incorporates the embodied perspective of the filmmaker and the emotional investment of the viewer."[155]

Lanzmann tried "to see through the eyes of those who were about to die," by *filming and refilming* "the slow zoom of the sign for Treblinka" by the rail tracks.[156] In order to elicit an affective reaction—to place us in the train through fictive reenacted moments—the shots frame the discrepancy between concept and experience, knowledge and shudder. Slowness and repetition are meant to dereify Treblinka and communicate to the viewer Lanzmann's original shock in acknowledging the actual existence of a town called Treblinka.

Filmic and profilmic reiterations—crossing and recrossing the tracks at the Sobibor station with the assistant postman Piwonski to survey the distance between what was or was not considered the camp—underlie the film's actualizing rhetoric. Lanzmann physically demonstrates the absurd logic of exception by taking a step over the fields while Piwonski nods in agreement. "So I am standing inside the camp perimeter, right?" "That's right. L: where I am now is fifty feet from the station and I'm already outside the camp. Yes. L: So this is the Polish part, and over there was death. Yes . . . L: Ok so here is life still. I take a single step and I'm already on the side of death"[157] (Figs. 5.14a–d). This topographical demonstration is less evidentiary than phenomenological and ethical. There is no need for an establishing shot to orient the precise location of the camp: the rhetorical stakes of the line that is traversed are related, as Richard Carter-White argues, to a more essential notion of proximity.[158] This is the absurd proximity between past and present, extreme horror and present normality, evoked as the spectator experiences the psychic or ethical reverberations of the reenacted moment, in Srebnik, or Abraham Bomba's scenes.[159] In turn, every interview, every demonstration, and every site scanned and surveyed places past and present in disquieting contact.

Unsurprisingly, Lanzmann's insistence on drawing near to the dead focuses on ruins and stones. When he describes his cinematographer falling down the steps of

Figure 5.14: a) Lanzmann and Piwonski survey the border between life and death (Lanzmann's *Shoah*, 1985). b). c) Piwonski indicates where the camp was. d) L: "Ok so here is life still."

the ruined crematoria—how he, Lanzmann, had to take over the camera to continue filming—the hand-held camera registers the emotional charge, inscribing the image with a pilgrimage affect. The tremulous camera and the extended duration of the shot simultaneously register the obstacle-ridden path and the imperative to traverse it. Reaffirming his investment in such traversals, Lanzmann claims to have filmed "[inside the camp itself] the slabs and the stones for days from every conceivable angle unable to stop turning from one to another."

> Chapuis, or Lubtchantski or Glasber would say why are you still filming stones? You've already got too much footage . . . in fact I hadn't shot enough footage and had to return to Treblinka to shoot more. I filmed them because there was nothing else to film, because I could not invent, because I would need this footage for when Bomba, when Glazar, when the farmers or indeed when Suchomel were speaking. These steles and stones became human for me, the only trace of the hundreds of thousands who died here.[160]

Although Lanzmann justified the excess footage as complement to witness accounts, the gesture cannot be reduced to an illustrative function. Its primary purpose is to reinstate singularity. In turning from one stone to another, filming in every possible season, Lanzmann's insistence on the contingent qualities of each object gets to the real, the "nothing else" there to film (Figs. 5.15a–c). This process performs a one-to-one equation of person to stone and guarantees the relation through two forms of indexicality: the cinematographic imprint and the gesture demarcating these stones'

Figure 5.15a–c Treblinka stones as singularity (Lanzmann's *Shoah*, 1985).

value now. It is this compounded indexical relation—the trace and its performed actualization—that grants ritual significance to his belated coverage.[161]

That the steles and stones Lanzmann films are from the Treblinka memorial is relevant. Discussing memorials' constitution, James Young mentions that in Madjanek and Auschwitz, the memorials that kept most of the camps' structure intact "tend to collapse the distinction between themselves and what they evoke in the rhetoric of their ruins." They do "not merely gesture toward past events but ... suggest themselves as fragments of events, inviting us to mistake the debris of history for history itself."[162] In contrast, the Treblinka memorial was designed to "suggest iconographically the greatest of all genocidal cemeteries."[163] This choice fits in with "the predominant ... figure by which Poland constructed the memory of the Shoah—fragments of Jewish tombstones."[164] As Young describes it, the visitor to that memorial steps into a huge expanse of open land enclosed by trees where a broken obelisk is surrounded by an immense graveyard of 17,000 sharp-toothed stones set in slabs of concrete. Several hundred of them bear the names of Jewish communities in Poland destroyed during the Holocaust, and only one individual's name—that of Janusz Korczac (the head of a Jewish orphanage who marched with his charge to Treblinka)—is inscribed.[165] Like sentries to the memorial area, a separate row of granite stones 2–3 meters high stands before the clearing. On each one stands the name of a country, the national homes of Jews who perished at Treblinka—Poland, France, the USSR.[166]

Lanzmann approaches these tombstones with a distinct performative aesthetics. More than the image, what matters is the procedure, the gestural obsessiveness with which he seeks to endow each shard with an erect humanity. This literalization maneuver is not surprising and hard to resist; invoking the one-to-one link between individual bodies and stones, Young writes that "between 1961 and 1964, hundreds of freight trains rolled slowly back into Treblinka, filled *not with human cargo* but with thousands of sharp granite stones."[167]

The stakes of these verbal and cinematic strategies concern recovering singularity in a context marked by annihilation. Thus, after a lengthy descriptive zoom of a forest patch, Lanzmann pans toward what looks like a mound of upturned earth to reveal a cluster of rusty spoons in close-up[168] (see Fig. 5.16 in Color Insert, 1). Just as quickly the camera draws back, returning to an image of "natural" decomposition. The view afforded by this optic closeness passes by all too fast, but in focusing on an explicit sign of human presence, it opens a gap and shudder in a film whose surface is only deceptively homogeneous.

This grouping of spoons instantly reminds one of *Night and Fog*'s depiction of material remnants. In an important contribution to debate on the ethical, moral proscription in imaging the Holocaust, Emma Wilson has argued that in summoning the material remains and object evidence of the camps concentrationary life and extermination, "Resnais seeks to bring us close to a hidden, denied dematerialized history." Significantly, she points out that these material objects and remnants are introduced as "present images of past evidence that insists, remains present, obtrudes in its very materiality."[169]

If Wilson's argument is relevant here, it is because it raises, within the realm of Holocaust film aesthetics, the question of the evidentiary image resignified as insisting presence. More important, this obtruding presence beckons to be considered as a form of human individuation thus standing as counterpoint to the digressive and contemplative tracking shots that cradle Cayrol's generalizing commentary in *Night and Fog*.

Stones, spoons: such residues of the past are made to speak via cinema. In line with *Shoah*'s combined revision of the memorial, literal, and ritual functions of the site of destruction, Didi-Huberman has identified the stone figure as the vital link between the natural ground and testimonial cinema.

> Every person in this film is constrained, by the film's categorical imperative, to deliver a speech always proffered with a similar cadence—miracle, symptom, lapse, breakdown, withdrawal—because insofar as he or she is a survivor, everyone in the film, for reasons of pain . . . remains trapped inside his or her individual story like a stone lying in a riverbed. Lanzmann thus tried to break open the stones, and the film did just that. But in order to do so, he had to come back to the sites, to their silence, in order to render this silence visible cinematically so that the site would truly speak.[170]

Through his repeated filmic "stabs" at obdurate surfaces and remnants of the past, Lanzmann revisits and complicates the line separating art and relic. His obsessive aesthetics of actualization relates to the notion of remains put forth by Rebecca Schneider in *Performing Remains*.[171] Through readings and rereadings in the "crosshatch of different temporalities," Schneider undoes the conventional separation between archive and repertoire, solid-state objects or texts fixed as original relics and their reanimation. *Remains*, in its nominal and verbal forms, signifies both a residue of the real but also its persistent call for a reader in the now: "to find the past resident in remains—material evidence, haunting trace, reiterative gesture—is to engage one time resident in another time—a logic rooted in the word 'remain.'"[172]

The viewer, carried along in fluid or forceful gesturing toward remains, confronts a troubling proximity not just between past and present, but between the living and the dead. If the Holocaust was predicated on eradicating "not only individuals and groups but ultimately also 'the concept of the human being' as such,"[173] it is precisely this concept that the brief spoon shot, in its jagged zoom, redeems. Touching the remnant and moving away so as to make it appear-disappear in the particular *fort-da* of post-Holocaust cinema reenactment.

ASCETIC STAGES, NEXT

Memorandum (Donald Brittain and John Spotton, 1965), a fluid verité documentary, records the reunion, after twenty years, of Holocaust survivors on the historic occasion of the opening of diplomatic relations between Israel and Germany and documents the Auschwitz War Crimes Trial in Frankfurt between 1963 and 1965.

At a key juncture, the film intercuts between two realities—the court and the theater. The sequence starts with the arrival of the Nazi defendants at the Frankfurt court and descriptions of their horrific feats: Wilhelm Bogen "who hit men's testicles until they died," strikes the camera with his valise; several others cover their heads or faces (Fig. 5.17). The court's interior is filmed from above as the defendants enter from a side door and immediately retreat out of sight. The narrator informs viewers that they refuse to testify in the presence of the camera on constitutional grounds (Fig. 5.18). A cut takes us to a man standing by a miniature model of the court arranging wooden dolls; the filmmakers explain that "the play *The Investigation: Oratorio in 11 Cantos* by Peter Weiss, in its final production, is about to show these [same] defendants as actors . . . and [that] the accused are seated so they are merely the extension of the audience" (Fig. 5.19).

Weiss, a German Jewish writer, attended the Auschwitz trials as a journalist. His play uses the court proceedings verbatim, condensing a twenty- month-long trial into a five-hour drama. Yet despite this documentary approach, the play does not afford unmediated access to events. On the contrary, Weiss writes that "in the presentation of the play, no attempt should be made to reconstruct the courtroom . . . Such a representation seems just as impossible to the author as a representation of the camp on stage would be."[174]

The Investigation has received extensive discussion as a paramount instance of Holocaust drama.[175] *Memorandum* highlights other questions. With its jarring edits,

Figure 5.17 A Nazi covers his face from the camera at the Auschwitz War Crimes trial in Frankfurt (*Memorandum*, Donald Brittain and John Spotton, 1965).

Figure 5.18 Nazi refuses to enter the chamber with camera present (*Memorandum*, Donald Brittain and John Spotton, 1965).

Figure 5.19 Peter Weiss prepares the model for *Investigation: Oratorio in 11 Cantos* (1965), a play on the Auschwitz Trials' proceedings. (*Memorandum, Brittain and Spotton*, 1965).

it raises the issue of individual responsibility: the camera records perpetrators at the very moment they come to testify but hide their identity. In contrast, Weiss's play allegorizes the proceedings, condensing 350 survivor testimonies into nine and assuming a Dantean canto structure. Significantly, the play's reliance on literal transcription raises the larger question of how testimony works (and should work) within frameworks and settings other than those of an actual court. A later film, *From Nuremberg to Nuremberg* (Frederic Rossif, 1989), concludes by cutting, at the very end, from archival material of the actual Nuremberg trial to Weiss's play in its opening night; it emphatically concludes with images of the audience's stunned faces as they exit the theater.

The circuitry between juridical proceedings, staged realities, and their impact on viewers informs the works discussed in the next chapter. The juxtapositions between an actual court and a wooden court model, between an international tribunal and the audience's reaction to *The Investigation*, establishes a parallel between the moral and ethical investigations in the real world and in art. Jurists and artists share a mission, but not the same kind of evidence. At this point of intersection—the revisitation of a genocide, the ongoing and often belated tribunals and assignation of responsibility, and finally the artist's imperative to intervene by proposing his own processes of adjudication—we now turn to Rithy Panh's oeuvre.

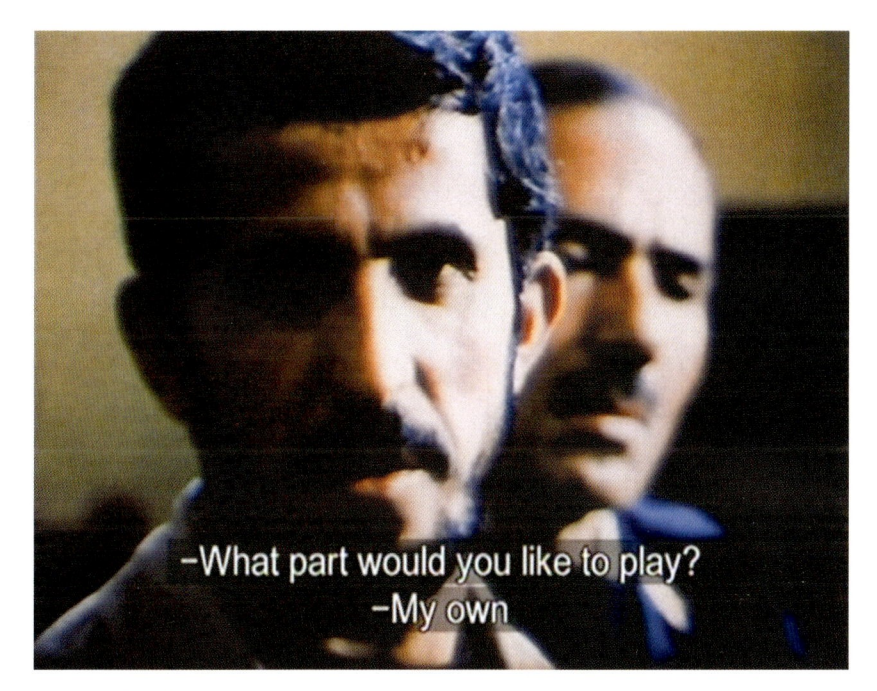

Figure 0.4: Sabzian addresses Kiarostami's 16 mm camera at the trial. (*Close-Up*, Abbas Kiarostami, 1990)

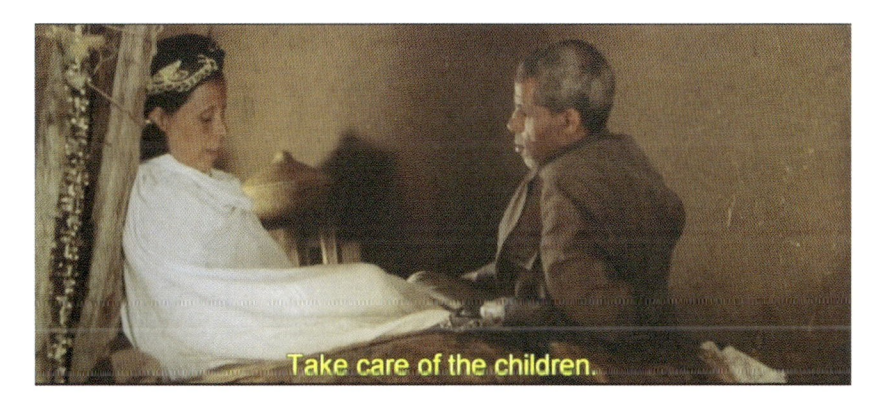

Figure 1.9: Haile's mother played by his sister, his father, and his cousin (*Endurance*, 1998).

Figure 3.8: Credits for *Sophia: Her Own Story*; Sophia as actual mother with her newborn son.

Figure 3.9: Sophia as her mother and Rizza Braun as Sophia in *Sophia: Her Own Story*.

Figure 4.6: Jean Rouch explains the idea of sociodrama to the African students (Rouch, *The Human Pyramid*, 1959).

Figure 4.11: Screening for the participants (Rouch, *The Human Pyramid*, 1959).

Figure 4.12: "Let's push the fiction one step further"—Alain jumps and "dies" (Rouch, *The Human Pyramid*, 1959).

Figure 4.13: Alain reappears into the film for the integration poster-image (Rouch, *The Human Pyramid*, 1959).

Figures 5.10: b) and c) Ganda's reenacted monologue of his Indochina experience (*Moi un Noir*, 1958). f) "I walk with you and all of a sudden I'm dead."

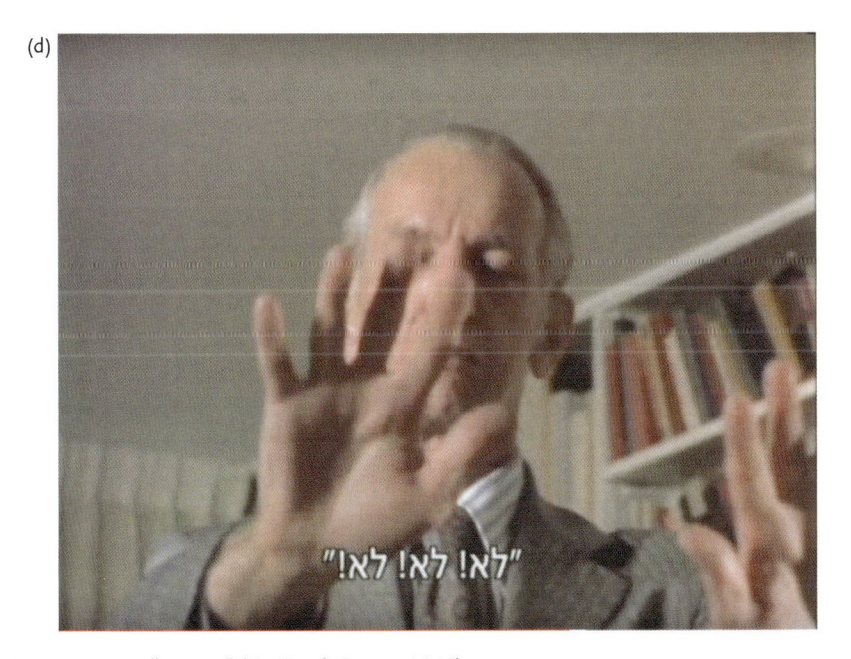

Figure 5.11: "No, No." (*The Karski Report*, 2010)

Figure 5.16 A vegetation of spoons, uncovered by the zoom (*Shoah*, 1985).

Figure 6.6 Van Nath, Houy, painting: evidentiary triangulation (*Bophana: A Cambodian Tragedy*, 1996).

Figure 6.7 Nath showing ex-staff his experience (Panh, *S21: The Khmer Rouge Killing Machine*, 2003).

Figure 6.11 Tableau of triangulation: Choung Ek painting, Duch's photo, and Nath "painting" Pol Pot (Panh, *S21: The Khmer Rouge Killing Machine*, 2003).

Figure 6.20 Duch watching *S21* outtakes of reenacted confessions (Pahn, *Duch Master of the Forges of Hell*, 2010).

CHAPTER 6

Trial Stages

Rithy Panh's Parajuridical Cinema

In one of the most haunting reenactment scenes in contemporary cinema, Poev (Kieu Ches), an ex-guard of the Khmer rouge, "unlocks," enters, exits, and "locks" the door to the former cell of the security prison S21 five times in less than four minutes. Poev "brings" a "prisoner" back from interrogation, shouting threats from the corridor window. He yanks an imaginary shackle and chain and moves a nonexistent bucket. Outside, in the corridor, stands a pile of objects, each one used at a time: a metal ammunition can as a toilet, and two smaller tin cans—one for water, the other for soup. Each "action" gets an exclusive treatment and each prisoner a specific abuse. The rote locking of the door punctuates and confirms the mechanical routine. There are "many prisoners," and each is pushed and clubbed without the respite of a summary narrative, or a bracketed clause. (Figs. 6.1a–e) In this imaginary time-space, each gesture succinctly compacts distinct orders of repetition—the hourly and daily routine, the protocol that disallows thinking, and the retracing of these acts in this ghastly theater. In a few minutes, a night routine and its various interventions are compressed, conveying to the viewer a magnified sense of the horror felt by prisoners and their exhausted guards.

The stark bareness of the room strangely enhances the imaginary scene of shackled prisoners, in filth and pain around Poev's figure. In fact, this empty space surrounding reenactors shapes an ethics of vision. In a key decision, the filmmaker chose to keep the camera either outside of the cell or, as in the second "inspection" scene, at the farthest corner of the entire area where events would have taken place. The director explained this distanced composition was born out of an instinctual aversion to entering either the guards' or the victims' point of view.[1] He felt that following gestures up close would have implied being captivated by the gestures' violence, encroaching into the victims' space and aligning himself with the guards: "If I had done [that], who would I be?"[2] At the same time the composition magnifies these scenes' hallucinatory quality.

Figures 6.1a–e: Poev reenacts his work with the prisoners in the cell (Rithy Panh, *S21: The Khmer Rouge's Killing Machine*, 2003).

The decision to remain outside the cells serves to delineate absences in *S21: The Khmer Rouge Killing Machine* (2003). Still, distance does not mean detachment. By means of fixed, extended shots or, alternatively, by correlating the camera's lateral movements (firmly outside of cells) with Poev's surveillance of "prisoners," Panh draws attention to the pulsions fueling a past that is not over. A pitiless inspection accompanies the prompted replays. In compositional terms, this *"dispositif* of visibility" resembles the deep framing of post-Holocaust monologues in its witnessing *in-position*. But, despite a similar visual disposition, with subjects "lost" amid a natural space infused with haunting absences, Poev's demonstration has nothing to do with the introspective awareness or communication effort displayed by Marceline, Karski, or Srebnick (discussed in Chapter 5). In part, because *S21* presents reenactment by perpetrators, the conjugation of a deed to an "I" is noticeably curtailed. Still, a confirmation of sorts emerges from this literal "transcription." Surrounded by the stark emptiness of the museum room, both dislocated and violently returned to an intimately known past, Poev's in-stilled, rote performance verifies his part in a larger genocidal mechanism.

This chapter explores the nature of Rithy Panh's cinematic intervention within Cambodia's process of juridical and memorial activation. Panh made *S21* and *Duch: Master of the Forges of Hell* in 2003 and 2011, respectively. Each film entertains its own dialogue with the protracted process that culminated with the creation of the Extraordinary International Chambers in the Courts of Cambodia (ECCC) in 2006 and its final implementation in 2012. The convoluted negotiations between the government of Cambodia (after the Vietnamese occupation in 1979, through the 1990s, and up to the present), the international community, and the United Nations (where the Khmer Rouge maintained representation for ten years after their fall in Cambodia) are too intricate to detail here.[3] The court, formed as an amalgam of international and national endeavors, agreed to place on trial a restricted pool of Khmer Rouge commanders, sparing a large part of the population involved "in name of a vague understanding of all Cambodians as 'victims' of the 1975–79 rupture."[4] Among many who, to this day, occupy local government positions, this group of "victims" included the S21 staff, who were recruited from rural areas as young, semiliterate adolescents in 1977. In Panh's film, a small part of this group dramatically mimics or talks about what took place thirty years earlier with Kang Kek Iew, also known as Duch, the former head of the detention center (captured in 1999, and the film's most conspicuous absence).

From *Site 2* (1989), his first film on the largest Southeast Asian refugee camp, to *The Missing Picture* (2013)—a diorama narrative on his family's plight under the Khmer Rouge—and his latest work, *Exile* (2016), a memory-scape film, Panh, who escaped to Thailand and then to Paris after his family died, has made twenty fiction and nonfiction films around the memories of victims and perpetrators. Between 1975 and 1979, 1,800,000 Cambodians were tortured and killed in extermination prisons and labor camps. Since 1995, the director has been training Cambodian crews; in 2006, he founded Bophana Audiovisual Resource Center, a multimedia center in Phnon Penh to foster the creation and maintenance of documentary archives on Cambodia to counter the catastrophic annihilation of memory exerted by the Khmer Rouge.[5]

Panh dramatizes Cambodia's ruptured history and memory by indexing actual ruin and limbo states while asserting art's regenerating power. Striking examples include the decision to use unbaked clay figures in his autobiographical *The Missing Picture* so their ephemeral quality would be a true testimony to the dead, and making a model of his own house and all other characters scaled to a figurine of himself at the age of twelve.[6] In the same vein, *The Artists of the Burnt Theatre* (2005) underscores theater's fragile hold on history through porous spaces and changeable situations. Burned in 1994 and never rebuilt, Phnom Penh's Suramet Theater and its itinerant population of squatters/artists appear in scenarios of activist resistance. Actors wonder about their future as the sounds of nearby construction of a mall announce the imminent destruction of a theater known for safeguarding Cambodian culture, its traditional dance and shadow puppeteers (Fig. 6.2). On an

Figure 6.2 Performing at the ruins of the Suramet theater in Rithy Panh's *The Artists of the Burnt Theatre* (2005).

Figure 6.3 Cyrano de Bergerac at the ruined Suramet (Panh, *The Artists of the Burnt Theatre*).

amphitheater overgrown with weeds, vignettes from a past Cyrano de Bergerac production alternate with classical Cambodian dance and scenes invoking trauma (e.g., an old woman given pink, green, and white pills for her recurring insomnia) (Fig. 6.3). The film's unique, fluid passages from French classical culture to national traditions and everyday life riddled with holes and nightmares constitute an allegorical statement on art's resilience, a high culture formulation on art and memory amid devastation.[7]

S21: The Khmer Rouge Killing Machine stands as Panh's main contribution to the nation's accountability efforts and my primary consideration on the intersection of trial and reenactment. The film starts with established conventions of postgenocide documentaries.[8] After a brief archival prologue retracing the rise to power by the Khmer Rouge in 1975, it turns to two people who survived where more than 12,380 others died: Vann Nath and Chum Mey. At first, Nath confronts ex-guards about their responsibility; gradually, however, the film turns from prosecutorial prodding to staged and distanced tableaus. Round-table discussions between perpetrators and the two survivors in the archive room and other areas of the museum give way to striking scenes in which the former prison staff either reenact their ghastly routine in solo acts or, grouped in strange formations, read aloud forced confessions obtained by torture and prepared answers admitting to counterrevolutionary crimes. With a rhetoric of reiteration, the film unfolds its own version of events; former members of the staff roam through the corridors flanking the verandas, inspect rows of wooden cells, and peer through cell windows and doors. They leaf through photos of the dead prisoners, discuss their own "biographies" written so they could pass as party faithful, or recite memos and slogans.[9]

Jacques Rancière has identified what is unique about *S21* scenarios. Much like Lanzmann in *Shoah*, Panh does not foreground discrepant witnesses' accounts (as typically occurs in confrontational documentaries); instead, he makes a film in the present about the machinery of killing. To bring out "the specificity of a killing machine whose functioning operated through a highly programmed discursive apparatus and filing system... it was... necessary," Rancière observes, "to make visible the physical reality of the machine for putting discourse into action and making bodies speak."[10] The film's entire strategy, according to Rancière, lies in "redistributing the intolerable, to play on its different representations."[11]

That the former S21 staff actually were asked to reenact the atrocities committed—as well as the fact that they were living among survivors in a transitional justice context—makes it impossible to miss the connection between *S21* replays and trials. The return to the scene of the crime[s] inevitably summons forms of inculpation or exculpation, much in the way testimony operates in reconstituting the logic of a crime in a juridical case and confession works as an indicting instrument. Panh had to assure the S21 ex-staff at the film's start that their return to the site to confront survivors was not a trial.

The director insisted he was "neither judge nor prosecutor." For Nathalie Rachlin, this claim is belied by the film's trial structure and its frame, starting with (an ex-guard) Huoy's proclamation of his innocence and ending with his confessions.[12] She identifies all basic elements of a trial in the film:

> The tribunal set in the deserted prison, the prosecutor, Vann Nath, at once the conscience of the film and the stand-in for Panh, the accused, the former employers of the prison, the witnesses for prosecution, the survivors and the evidence of guilt, the paintings, the confessions, the lists and memos, the reports detailing interrogations and executions, and finally the proof—the reconstitution of the

facts on the site of the crime, as well as the confessions by the accused. All that is missing is the verdict and the sentence.[13]

What Rancière calls *S21*'s "re-distribution of the intolerable," and Rachlin an "ex post-facto construction of an audio-visual archive of the genocide,"[14] does not fit a reparative mold and the film's force lies in its challenge to postatrocity reparation discourses. Two disturbing set of scenes—the solo reenactment of routine torture and abuse and the choral-like formations of two or more perpetrators that recirculate existing evidence, reciting it and displaying it—guide my reflection on the unique nature of replay in Panh's parajuridical scenarios.[15]

As I explore the role of reenactment in *S21*'s *else than a trial*, I indicate its alternate realm of performative efficacy by calling its scenarios *parajuridical*: actual perpetrators and victims confronting their past at the site of atrocity becomes part of an ethical/formal theater of adjudication; reenactment redefines the relation between the spectator's catharsis and critical distance.

SOLO ROUTINES: THE CRITICAL VALENCE OF ALIENATION

Panh has explained how he came up with the idea of reenactment. After three years of shooting, he noticed that Poev, one of the ex-security guards, only spoke in slogans; moreover, a gestural memory accompanied his strangely syncopated speeches.[16] Another former officer exhibited such an impossibly fragmented discourse that he only managed to finish sentences after being shown a map of the facility; even then, he "spoke" through gestures alone.[17] Alerted by the slogan-like speech, Panh could see how gestures followed ingrained orders and constituted an indissociable body-mind unit.[18]

To tap into this bodily memory, Panh took the ex-guards to the former interrogation site and recreated the past atmosphere: neon lighting and loudspeakers blasting revolutionary songs. He found a little American munitions case used as a makeshift toilet in the cell and placed it in a corner alongside other, remaining odds and ends. When Poev arrived, he rearranged the objects in the same corner where they used to stand, and then showed his meticulous order, "open[ing] up the bodily memory . . . in a chronological way." Panh explains:

> There is an order in which things are done; so before you put on or take off the handcuffs, you have the business with the (shackle) bar as well . . . When these actions were compared with the notes which had been kept by the Khmer rouge, it was exactly the way these things were done. So I imagine that nobody else apart from the guards and the victims would know exactly what happened in that camp. Because in that sequence everything is brought together and encapsulated it makes it even more violent.[19]

The experiment led to the film's logical shape. In his memoir *The Elimination*, Panh recounts how he asked the "comrade guards" to "make the gestures of the period," specifying he was "not asking them to 'act', but to 'extend their words.'" To "take the memory out of the body," it was necessary that "they start, stop, and start again ten or twenty times. Their reflexes return; I see what really happened. Or what's impossible. The method and the truth of the extermination appear."[20]

The scenes that resulted are transfixing. In a second, equally stark solo, Poev slowly walks to the middle of a large room "avoiding"—and at times "kicking"—invisible bodies. He turns to one side and "checks" a couple of prisoners' bodies, repeating aloud the orders he was to follow ("Check for a pencil, so the prisoner cannot cut his own veins," "Check for a rag so the prisoner cannot hang himself") (Fig. 6.4). Then, he turns to the other side of the room and repeats the entire routine. In a sort of mad tautology, each gesture is doubled by its literal description, a present-tense commentary. The commentary itself operates as a record of a memorized set of actions, a procedural sequence that has become second nature for the guards.

Philippe Mangeot has perceptively observed that, even though these mimicked gestures designate the victims' absence, the film does not revolve around the visible and the invisible. Instead, what proves most disturbing in these scenes is the redundancy of gesture and verbal description,[21] a redoubled literalness that merits analysis.

For Cathy Caruth, one of the paradoxes of traumatic experience is that the "literal registration of an event . . . the ability to reproduce it in exact detail . . . corresponds to its escape from full consciousness."[22] A sequence of events remains frozen in time, full of original, vivid details that defy one's ability to extract narrative sense and leave

Figure 6.4 Checking invisible prisoners (Panh, *S21: The Khmer Rouge Killing Machine*, 2003).

the past behind. That would explain the heightened role of vision in accounts of extreme atrocity; here, it functions as "the unmodified return of what happened . . . instead of being the raw material to be processed into understanding."[23] This return of the integral yet bracketed scene "corresponds to drama, since, by contrast narrative would imply some sort of mastery by the narrator, or the focalizor."[24]

Deirdre Boyle has read these acted sequences as a form of traumatic reenactment.[25] The extreme conditions of fear and violence experienced and relayed by the former guards at a young age likely resulted in posttraumatic stress disorder (as attested by Huoy's frequent migraines). Still, as Boyle and others concur, the ex-guards' passive reproduction of "tasks" also indicates the imprint of drills, the memories of military training, and the massive ideological indoctrination of Khmer Rouge forces recruited from an illiterate population.[26]

Such readings are not mutually exclusive. No single motivation accounts for either the perpetrators' gestural mimicry or the film's generalized opacity. The dissociated gestures are animated by the same compulsion to repeat that leads the person who has suffered a trauma to remember a dramatic sequence, like any "good actor . . . in its present, in its sensorial directness."[27] At the same time, however, the enhanced vividness that lets us "see" and "hear" what happened in Tuol Sleng prison does not derive simply from great acting skills or the riveting, albeit disturbing indistinction between dramatic and traumatic reenactment. The spare composition, duration, and ascetic surroundings actualize absences. In particular, the doubling of verbal and gestural information on the part of the guards forges a divide between a mandating consciousness and an obeying body, between a narrator and a dramatic actor. Independent of how this duplication is produced, it generates a specific viewer address, while making manifest a psychic or a social alienation on the part of the subjects represented.[28]

At the root of the "intolerable spectacle" of Poev's mimicked routines, Rancière identifies an implicit circular logic of iteration—"as if yesterday's torturer were ready to adopt the same role tomorrow."[29] The spouting of slogans in automaton-like fashion reveals a mechanism based on rote and uncritical learning, a system that can easily be spun through a new round of recitations even if it happens almost thirty years later and is promoted as theater.[30] Through its hellish return, the unstoppable broadcast sequence of mimicked tasks can be read as a symptom of the alienation denounced in critiques of reification; it represents the kind of unthought behavior Brecht's Marxist aesthetics was designed to undo (for instance, by splitting diegesis and mimesis and having the actor narrate his own actions).

The film configures a tableau aesthetics that encourages reflection and precludes "a crude empathy" with the characters portrayed. In Poev's solo scenes, this obstruction of the social actor's psychology occurs by enhancing his possessed state. Poev, gesticulating and reciting his protocol while beating and cursing invisible beings in a vast room, seems oblivious and utterly controlled; it is difficult to assess whether he is moved by an internal will or an externally imposed discipline. Yet the scene's hyperdefined referential clarity does not give us access to this theater's agency. The literal exactitude in reproducing a routine does not cue us as to whether it issues from unconscious uncontrollable motives or from intentional, mastered demonstrations. The two main tendencies that exemplify the difficulty of overcoming trauma—the compulsion to repeat and the compulsion to recount—seem to overlap without giving any assurance that the social actors in these tableaus are either subject to debilitating trauma or are trying to control their demons as they persist on overdetailed, literal description.[31]

The compulsiveness feeding the performance undermines any sense of personhood. Sylvie Rollet points to this testimonial void, noting that while "the camera promotes the emergence of a 'body-archive,' that keeps the obeying imprint visible . . . .[and while] repetition does not historicize the lived experience," neither Prak Khan nor Poev really exhibits a dehumanization, since "to testify" implies their constitution as subject of the testimony and that "gap . . . was and is still missing."[32]

This reflective gap is also constitutive of reenactment's confessional-performative dynamic and its ameliorative premise. In-person reenactment is based on the literal retracing of one's past, on conflating past and present in dramatic action. This verbal or mimetic replay is supposed to yield a consciousness differential, a narrative of one's implication in a past atrocity, either during the performance or after the fact, when screened.

Thinking about what authorizes autobiography, Jean Starobinski helps clarify the redemptive qualities of in-person reenactment. Since the protagonist's self-narrative is justified only if it produces a differential between past and present, this mode enhances the stakes of personal responsibility and self-reflection. "[I]f there are no implicit changes in the character's development"—that is, if no "life conversion" event has occurred—"new developments would be treated as external, historical events and a first-person narrator would hardly be necessary."[33]

In *S21*, both the notion of personhood and expectations attached to a communicative aesthetics (which relies on characters to transmit, testify, and create empathy) are frustrated by the perpetrators' stunted or opaque consciousness. This deflated personhood also raises questions about the value of in-person reenactment. Why would one need the actual protagonist's testimony if the probing of consciousness and inner (if not outward) confession constitutive of subjectivity are markedly absent?[34] I suggest, at the end of the chapter, how the film responds to this challenge through an oblique deployment of perpetrators' reaction shots in the tableau scenarios featuring groups of perpetrators.

Given the resilient opacity of *S21*'s actors' consciousness in the solo scenes, we may shift our focus from the subjects' psychology and ethics to consider the entire scene's impact—taking in the scenes' productive ambiguity in tandem with the ex-staff's benumbed performance. The question is how the film frames and magnifies the literal imprint of the past in a manner disturbingly close to the blocking-rehearsal of a theatrical scene, while, at the same time, leaving it charged with traumatic affect.

Literalness has a psychological determination, but it may also be deployed aesthetically. Discussing attempts to convey the effects of posttraumatic conditions, Ernst van Alphen mentions Tadeusz Borowski and Charlotte Delbo, who recreate obsessive interiority purely through a descriptive acuity.[35] In their work, as in *S21* and in other posttraumatic representations, acute discrepancy arises between an extremely sharp gestural display, clearly enunciated speech, a felt space, and the social actors' unfathomable psychological state.

An image combining heightened sensorial presence with a vague, unplaced, subjectivity bears relations to the perceptive conditions of psychic trauma. The spatial emptiness cradling the monologue testimonials, and, in this case, the solo demonstrations, evacuates naturalness in a way that offers structural parallels to a common trait in the testimony of survivors: the difficulty of reporting an experience of atrocity within a normal context. The gulf between the scene's descriptive sharpness and the ambiguity and opacity of this theater's social agents sustains the film's haunting irresolution.

Sylvie Rollet has noted that two framings alternate in these tableaux to establish the "film's call for a reflective audience."[36] The camera moves from extreme long shots of the rooms to close-ups of the archives or faces of the guards, "defin[ing] two regimes of spectrality—one 'centrifugal' since the field embracing the empty room opens onto what cannot be seen but which constitutes its internal off-frame: the death of thousands of prisoners . . . the other 'centripetal', closing on the face of the guards, who often look down."[37] In the latter case, she observes, "the fugue point occupies the center of the frame. . . . [T]he movement back and forth from empty to full and from the faces' opacity to deserted spaces where the ghosts of the past come to rest" creates a reflective pace and a perspective for the viewer.[38]

PAINTINGS, DESKS, FILES AND FACES: REFLEXIVE PLATFORMS

The blank surface of the table is, in the end, not nothing. It is what effects the transformation of a thing of dispute into justiciable fact.
Cornelia Visman[39]

This image exists, no one told me, I saw it.
Vann Nath, in Bophana: A Cambodian Tragedy

The tension between *S21*'s call for a reflective audience and the ex-guards' recalcitrance to testimonial closure animates the entire film's mise-en-scène. The choreographed shift between deep perspective and close-ups (of a facial expression or documents) defines different surfaces for scrutiny: paintings, blank countenances, files, and photos become equal resting points in a tableau aesthetics that troubles further any characterization of Panh's reenactment as potentially redemptive. These include internal audiences whose reactions give us no clue as to the aim or status of the scene.

Visman has suggested that the primary medium for the workings of the law is the table and the triangular division it institutes. The table creates asymmetry. Hereby, justice is "no longer a question of two conflicting sides facing off against one another (as in a tribunal). A third party [is] elevated above the two antagonistic parties deriving its authority from a different source than that of the immediate experience of injustice."[40] Thus, the table "delineates the symbolic space within which the law operates . . .[A]nd even without the laying of a weapon on the table say, the mere surface of the table indicates the thing's potential presence, which waits to be transformed into pronounceable fact."[41]

In *S21*, group scenes transform into justiciable fact an inexpressible experience of violence precisely through their fluid, triangulated mise-en-scène. A claim or proposition is made; then, it is visually or verbally related to a piece of evidence; finally, it receives confirmation either through a confession or, barring a verbal acknowledgment, pointed reaction shots.

Scenes invariably start with someone providing, describing, reading, and/or commenting on some sort of evidence—be it a photograph, a document (entries of torture or executions), confession, biography, or painting (Fig. 6.5). The individual occupies the forefront of the frame, slightly curved by the wide-angle lens, while, in the same frame or an adjacent space unveiled by a pan or a simple cut, a highly composed group of ex-guards listens. The guards are distributed in the receding perspective of one of the empty rooms at the Tuol Sleng Museum. The shot's composition and length firmly position the viewer as witness. The men, shown in a medium or long shot, either sit on the floor in a semicircle or stand by furniture brought into the room to reenact aspects of the torture and interrogation bureaucracy. Repeated with variations, this mise-en-scène configures a parajuridical theater.

The matrix of these confrontational scenarios was an unplanned encounter at the end of Panh's second film, *Bophana: A Cambodian Tragedy* (1996). Panh had carefully avoided meetings between victims and perpetrators until, one day, Vann Nath, a survivor, spotted Huoy, the former deputy head of security, at the S21 detention center. Nath places his hands on Huoy's shoulder and asks if he recognizes him; he

Figure 6.5 Handling a victim's photo (Panh, *S21: The Khmer Rouge Killing Machine*, 2003).

says he does. Nath then directs him toward the walls covered with scenes of torture commissioned and painted by Nath for the museum.[42]

As they walk through the gallery, Nath holds Huoy accountable for what happened, seeking Houy's confirmation that "this image exists" (see Fig. 6.6, in Color Insert, 1). Nath touches the painting with one hand and keeps the other on Huoy's shoulder; setting himself as the vertex of an evidentiary triangle, he links his descriptions of the horrific scenes he witnessed to their painted renditions, which Huoy in turn verifies as "real."[43]

This process of verification is repeated across the entire gallery. Nath describes what he saw, heard about, or simply overheard during the torture sessions. In front of a painting of a mother whose child is being torn from her arms by soldiers in black, Nath says: "This picture . . . it's something that I imagined . . . when I heard the cries of infants and their mothers . . . is this picture accurate?" "Yes, it is." "Did they struggle like this?" "It happened like that," I'm not forcing you to agree with me . . . If you tried to force me and if it was not true, I wouldn't say anything. It was like that, otherwise we wouldn't have killed the children of others."[44] In front of a painting of two men torturing another, he says: "This one I did not see but someone told me. I've forgotten his name, it was in 1979. Is this image exaggerated?" "No, it's correct." Nath leads Houy to another painting of a man being whipped: "This I know exists 100%.. . . . Nobody told me about it. I saw myself." Huoy: "I did not see that, but perhaps it happened." "Don't say 'perhaps'. I saw it . . . I was numb with fear . . . All these images I did not invent them, I don't want to accuse, embarrass anyone. I speak of the prisoners living here. I was among them before they took me down there to paint for them."

As conduit between his own testimony embodied in the realist-style paintings and Huoy's witnessing, Nath creates a bridge across the void and absences of the present. His actual contact with the painting and Huoy creates a physical circuitry between distinctly mediated memories— what he remembers, its iconic representation, and, at his instigation, a performative corroboration.

The "Scenes of S21" paintings are at the core of Panh's parajuridical cinema. They have a storied reality, both within *S21* and within the development of the Tuol Sleng Museum, where, alongside the mug shots identifying those killed at the security prison, they represent one of its most iconic holdings. That Nath could paint while at S21 allowed him to survive and eventually serve as proper witness. Stephanie Benzaquem notes that when Comrade Duch stood trial before the ECCC in 2009–2010, Nath became "the established 'spokesman' for many victims," and "his paintings were no longer considered crude socialist realist depictions commissioned by Vietnamese authorities to illustrate the cruelty of staff, [gaining] status as evidence used in court."[45] The paintings epitomize the filmmaker's discovery of the minimal, necessary conditions for staging his metatrial. In *Bophana*'s last scene and in *S21* they are a useful point of entry for imaging horror in an otherwise mostly empty setting. At the same time, they anchor an evidentiary formation composed of a prosecutor and a defendant. Besides their referential role, they provide a platform for an alternate adjudication in an ethical-aesthetic realm.

In another triangulated confrontation in *S21*, Nath stands in front of one of his large canvases: multiple rows of prisoners on the floor and a commandant with a whip in front of a blackboard covered with party slogans (see Fig. 6.7 in Color Insert, 1; Fig. 6.8). Repeatedly touching the depicted prisoners (including his own image), he talks about the unnecessary cruelty of the guards who did even more than was demanded of them—for instance, returning at night to kick prisoners or preventing them from surviving on bugs (Fig. 6.9). Somewhat distanced and facing the canvas, the men, five in total, stand in silence with Prak Khan and then Huoy, rigidly positioned, one slightly staggered behind the other. "What about your ability to think as a human being?" asks Nath. "If they said here is the enemy I repeated this is the enemy," states Huoy (Fig. 6.10). Prak Khan's face, occupying the foreground, grants the scene its collective repercussion, its choral reaction.

This "blackboard" scene introduces an explicit prosecutorial pedagogics: Nath's position by his painting on an easel mirrors the Khmer Rouge commandant's position by the blackboard shown on the painting. According to Rancière, one of the "redistributions of the intolerable" (in a film defined entirely by this strategy) involves "shifting positions by demoting those who have just expressed their power as torturers once again to the position of school pupils educated by their former victims."[46]

The film's very first tableau manifests this deconstruction of former orders. A wall painting of Choeng Ek, "the killing fields," with a sofa and a coffee table below it, is symmetrically framed. To the right, Nath paints with his back to the camera while a large black-and-white photo of Duch, the S21 commandant, holding his glasses, is perched on an armchair to the sofa's left (see Fig. 6.11 in Color Insert, 1). Nath

Figure 6.8 Nath's canvas of commandant with whip (Panh, *S21: The Khmer Rouge Killing Machine*, 2003).

Figure 6.9 Nath's hand on his canvas: "this one was hanging between life and death" (Panh, *S21: The Khmer Rouge Killing Machine*, 2003).

Figure 6.10 Prak Khan's and Houy's response to Nath's evidence (Panh, *S21: The Khmer Rouge Killing Machine*, 2003).

Figure 6.12 Nath's painting of his painting situation as Duch points out something (Panh, *S21: The Khmer Rouge Killing Machine*, 2003).

recalls how, as he'd paint Pol Pot, Duch would sit or stand behind him watching and talking about painters—Picasso and Van Gogh. Holding a photo of Pol Pot, Nath pretends to apply paint over a finished portrait of the Khmer Rouge leader. The painting he is "working over" depicts him standing by the Pol Pot's portrait while Duch sits on an armchair in the foreground pointing as if to explain something (Fig. 6.12).

With a number of internal frames this sequence introduces a complex field of reflexivity: the backdrop painting, the photo of Pol Pot and its painted version on a canvas representing scaled doubles for Nath and Duch, and the photo of Duch "sitting" and facing the viewer. Dislocated in time, space, scale, and depth, Duch's transformation into a cardboard figure is ironic. Simultaneously, this collage of two-dimensional imagery foregrounds the dissemination of refracting surfaces throughout the film: Duch is everywhere and nowhere.

Starting with a tableau composition, the sequence develops with Nath's soft-voiced account of how he was enlisted as painter. The delicate strokes he performs with the brush underscore the story's affect. Such reenacted gestures, the care they imply, as well as the fact they do not alter the canvas at all, capture "the temporal knotting of past and present" that Bill Nichols has described a propos of gestures that "go through the motions" of an ingrained routine; their replay awakens the duality of a "psychically real but phantasmatic linkage between now and then."[47] The fact that the gestures have no effect on the finished painting highlights the belatedness of reenactment (Fig. 6.13). At the same time, the strokes' gentleness, a necessary sign of respect toward Pol Pot, is infused with a new reference, a split temporality.

Panh's epic theater approach defines the group scenes as tableaux: rather than supporting a dramatic progression, the autonomous sequences follow an episodic structure. They are self-sufficient in their compositional impact and thematic articulation. This autonomy does not preclude internal complexity or fragmentation; often their interest lies in its arrangement of heterogeneous elements—actual bodies, documents, and objects—into a single view, a holistic composition. Before breaking down into focused views, this single, graspable picture grants the scene its initial visual and dramatic impact.

Within each tableau, gesture and voice release the layered historicity of actual people, documents, objects, and setting. The easel and paintings, but also desks and files, become props in the configuration of a new memorial-juridical arena. This selective displacement is a function of theater, transforming empty space into staged display. According to Andrew Sofer, objects function differently onstage than off. The prop is defined by its dislocated function and its signifying charge. In the film, however, theatricality consists of dialogical exchange between art and sociohistorical reality. Desks and files separate from prior functions and carry traces of the school—the legal bureaucracy of the Khmers and the museum's memorialization—into a new signifying arena.

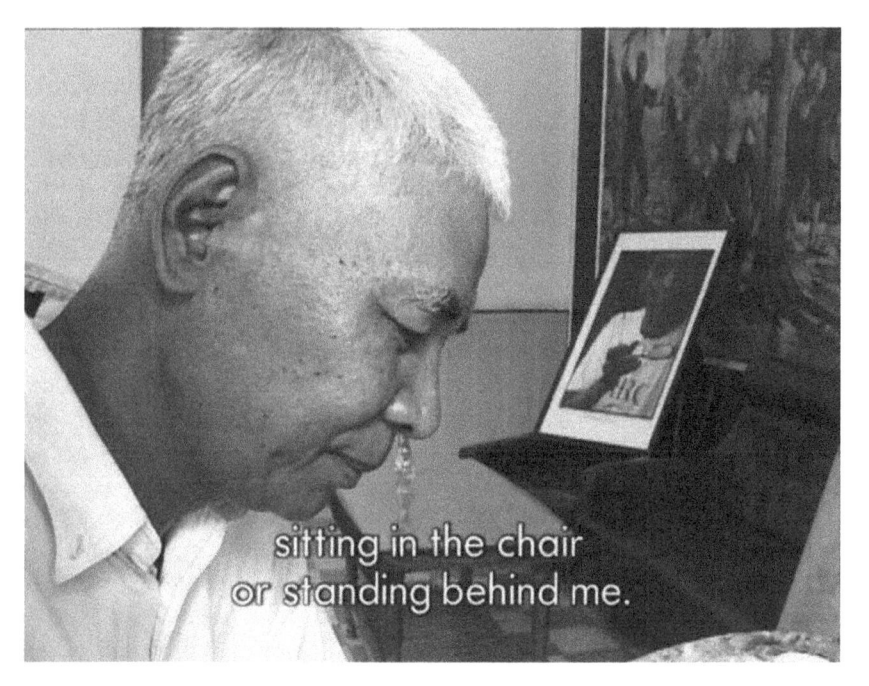

Figure 6.13 Nath "painting" Pol Pot's portrait with Duch's photo marking where he sat (Panh, *S21: The Khmer Rouge Killing Machine*, 2003).

The film's palimpsestic quality is especially conducive to Panh's conflation of reenactment and other theatrical modes.[48] Barbed wire hangs around the verandas, and rags pile up against the walls of vast rooms; it is impossible to classify (museum display? film props?). Before Panh's repossession of the space, this setting was permeated by prior histories and subsequent occupations.[49] Founded in 1960, the Tuol Sleng High School was adapted to serve as the national headquarters of the Khmer Rouge secret police S21 between 1975 and 1979. Abandoned by fleeing Khmers and discovered by the two Vietnamese photographers in January 1979, the site was almost immediately converted into the Tuol Sleng Genocide Museum, which officially opened to the public in July 1980.[50] Mai Lam, a Vietnamese officer and curator, inflected the memorialization of events with "an internationally recognized discourse on genocide—aligning the Cambodia genocide with the European holocaust."[51] Tracking the museum's changes since its founding, Stephanie Benzaquem has confirmed that the effort was "to legitimize the new authorities who had wrested the "Khmer Rouge from the fascist clique of Democratic Kampuchea (DK)."[52] Only in the 1990s and 2000s did the raw and gory aspects promoted in the 1980 museum give way to installations more appropriate to an "era of accountability and reconciliation."[53]

Deployed as props in scenes aimed at the viewer, but also as mnemonic prompts for the social actors, the files, left behind when the Khmer Rouge fled, play a unique role in the film's evidentiary project. The scope of the DK's bureaucracy is evident from the 2008 report that articulated the need to establish the Cambodia Genocide archive as part of the World Memory Archive. [54] Fourteen of the forty-six staffers assisted in documentation; the archive holds records including the confession of 4,186 detainees, 6,226 biographies of prisoners and DK members (1975–1978), lists of prisoners arriving and sent to the detention building, and statistics about those implicated in the confessions of others. Some statements go on for more than two hundred pages in a record keeping that became more systematized with typed records added to the handwritten ones in 1977. Other forms of documentation include registration files and identification photos of the prisoners upon arrival, daily logs of arrests, organizational charts, memos between Duch and Son Sen summarizing operations, accounts of torture methods, daily execution schedules, and execution orders.[55]

To procure its eligibility to the World Memory Archive the proposal from the Cambodian archive listed how it satisfied one or more of the required criteria: "a) Time—these archives represent the principal collection of documents remaining from the period of Democratic Kampuchea; b) Place—what took place within this site cannot be reconstructed from any other source with more authenticity and completeness than these archives; c) People—the essence of the security apparatus is revealed, as well as the objective condition of the prisoners and, occasionally, the spark of human dignity that resisted all possible attempts at degradation; d) Subject and theme—history, politics, and justice are shown here in their starkest form. e) Form and style—the machinery and technology of torture and death are shown in meticulous detail."[56]

The answers, generic in comparison with their incisive revival in the film, constitute one of the parameters to assess the ways *S21* dialogues with a memorial or juridical project recirculating the prison's archive. Of notice is the highly selective reference to the atrocities committed, photos of the men and women tortured and killed, or the minutely noted written confessions and records of those entered into the system and eventually killed. This material handled by the ex-staff in the present was a purposeful catalyst in promoting, according to Panh, a "broad work of memory activation." A detour through the vast context of adjudication and memorialization of the genocide undertaken contemporaneously with Panh's work helps us grasp the specificity of Panh's reanimation of files and of a repertoire of tortionary gestures.

S21'S JUDICIAL CONTEXT

In its memorialization of a machinery of killing, *S21* participates in larger global human rights initiatives seeking to provide closure to massive historical traumatic events, through narratives of atrocity and suffering aired in public fora, televised hearings, and testimonial documentary. Such undertakings include, more broadly, the International Courts' pursuits of crimes against the humanity since the early 1980s, as well as a host of parajuridical institutions such as the Truth and Reconciliation commissions of South Africa, Rwanda, and Chile.

Although no Truth commission was created for the Khmer Rouge, a number of "outreach initiatives [were] created to frame public understandings of justice and reconciliation, [using] memorial sites such as the Tuol Sleng Genocide Museum and the killing fields to help shape the Extraordinary International Chambers in the Court of Cambodia's reading of the past."[57] Peter Manning has pointed out that projects such as public education on the work of the court and on the history of the Democratic Kampuchea regime, encouraging participation in the proceedings by witnesses, complainants, or civil parties seeking reparation and providing information on mental health issues and trauma, ended up "conceptualizing DK as a problematic site of memory . . . specifically in relation to its purported remedy and amelioration through the ECCC process."[58]

Two documentaries in particular show how Panh's methods—*reenactment* and the *recirculation of evidence*—correlate with this transitional moment and its juridical proceedings even while they depart from them radically. Rémi Lainé et Jean Reynaud's *A Simple Question of Justice* (2011) follows the court's efforts to investigate Duch and also prove the guilt of four other former officials in the brutality characterizing the regime: Nuon Chea, "Brother Number Two" to Pol Pot; Khieu Samphan, President of the State Presidium; Ieng Sary, Deputy Prime Minister and Foreign Minister; and Ieng Thirith, Minister of Social Affairs. The film shows Duch being brought by the court to Tuol Sleng, the S21 site, as well as to Choeung Ek, the killing fields, in February 2008 for a judicial reconstruction in the presence of relatives of victims, Judges Marcel Lemonde (France) and You Bunleng (Cambodia), current guards, and paralegal staff.

The conjunction of the original site and the defendant's speech represents the minimal requirement for the juridical reconstitution at Choeung Ek. Asked whether children were thrown against trees that officers of the court designate, Duch confirms that they were (Fig. 6.14). Inside the Tuol Sleng Genocide Museum and former prison, as Duch is brought into different rooms, one particular reconstitution stands out. Chum Mey, one of the survivors (present also in *S21*), sits on the floor of his former cell preserved by the museum in front of the court's coinvestigative panel. He mimics how he was chained to the bed and tortured, while the guards typed his "confessions." He demands that Duch, who stands in a semicircle with other witnesses, journalists, and paralegal investigators, apologize[59] (Figs. 6.15 and 6.16).

Adrien Maben's *Camarade Duch, Bienvenu en enfer* (2012) records the same reconstitution, filmed from a side angle. The film intercuts footage covering Duch's trial, the multiple audiences (from relatives of victims to school children) brought in to watch the proceedings, and interviews with several of the witnesses (Fig. 6.17). Chum Mey's statement in court, his cross examination about his role in torture, and his crying on the stand are later shown from a screen monitor as he watches his own deposition.

Contrast is evident between the media's flurry to register the belated production of evidence as it unfolds and Panh's controlled and staged reconstruction for the film. In the later films, the legal reconstitutions at Choeung Ek and at Tuol Sleng are registered from afar or are obstructed by the many onlookers. The messy and crowded profilmic realities match an equally busy cinematic structure and texture, and the reportage's immediacy stands in marked contrast to *S21*'s programmatic visual and structural clarity. This same contrast between full/messy and empty/ordered is apparent in *Camarade Duch*'s revelation of the so-called S21 video (Fig. 6.18). The prime piece of evidence on the state of the detention center S21 at the time of the Pol Pot regime[60] exhibits deserted rooms with burned and decomposing corpses shackled to

Figure 6.14 Duch at judicial reconstitution in Choeung Ek, the Killing Fields (Remi Lainé and Jean Reynaud, *A Simple Question of Justice*, 2011).

Figure 6.15 Chum Mey's reconstitution of his torture with court note takers (*A Simple Question of Justice*, 2011).

Figure 6.16 Duch at Chum Mey's reconstitution (*A Simple Question of Justice*, 2011).

metal bed frames and pecked by birds—as well as a couple of children who have been saved. This material was shot by Ho Vann Tay, sent by Ho Chi Minh City Television to document the war against the Khmer Rouge.[61] He and his team were the first journalists to see the death camp at Tuol Sleng, abandoned in the middle of operations on January 6, 1979. While the video itself was not admitted in the court proceedings,[62] the footage is included in Maben's film; its vivid and horrific evidence of torture, and the eight remaining corpses that had not been thrown into the Cheung Ek pit, is a significant example of what is necessarily, but also programmatically, absent in Panh's work.[63]

Figure 6.17 Citizens watch court proceedings (*Camarade Duch, Bienvenu en Enfer*, Adrian Maben, 2012).

Figure 6.18 S21 video taken by Vietnam journalists when they discovered the abandoned interrogation site.

These records of the Cambodian legal process reveal a continued attention to the reaction of those watching the evidence and listening to the statements. For instance, the "S21 video" footage is not edited into Maben's film. Instead, it is shown being shown: Ho Vann Tay leads the filmmaker and the crew to a small room in the

Vietnamese archives; we watch the gruesome images as they do, through a small monitor.⁶⁴ In her analysis of the S21 archives, Michelle Caswell has noted that when the identification photos of those exterminated at S21 appear in video footage of the tribunal, documentary films, and print publications, "there is always another layer of looking . . . [In] legal testimony, interviews in documentary films and still images in the DC-Cam newsletter—mug shots are reproduced as the focal point of new images of people looking at them."⁶⁵

Within a discourse of reconciliation and acknowledgment, framing scenes as they are watched—by children at school, by relatives of the victims bused to particular sites during the trial—amounts to a choral amplification. Extending the audience of viewers is essential to achieve closure. The reflexive mode promoted in photos, films, and TV articulates that need, the same response sought at Nuremberg as Nazis are filmed watching camp footage, or Eichmann watches *Night and Fog*—or earlier on (and even more directly), when military and civilians were forced to view the camps after liberation.

Albie Sachs, a former African National Congress activist and later an architect of South Africa's postapartheid constitution, declared that "the most important part of the truth commission was not the report, it was the seeing on television of the tears, the laments, the stories, the acknowledgments. As one political scientist put it, what the truth commission did was convert knowledge into acknowledgment."⁶⁶

In actual trial films (or reenactments) reaction shots are the ultimate gauge of acknowledgment, serving as punctuation in the moral-ethical values of the process. Hereby, the most significant measure of potential closure is the perpetrators' expressions of remorse. If the juridical reconstructions by Duch—watched by legal personnel as well as some of the victims' relatives and survivors—represent a reality supplement to *S21*, the fact that Khieu Samphan, one of four indicted Khmer Rouge leaders, only admitted that the mass killings happened after watching *S21* seems to vindicate the evidentiary weight of staged reconstructions.

Finally, there is another twist to the interdependence between actual trials and testimonial cinema inasmuch as *Duch: Master of the Forges of Hell* (2011) represents a corrective to *S21*'s prosecutorial reach. For Panh, Claude Lanzmann's *Shoah*, Marcel Ophuls's *The Sorrow and the Pity*, and Fredric Rossif's *From Nuremberg to Nuremberg* (1989) offered concrete proof that film can supplement a trial. However, he felt that Duch's absence from *S21* had robbed the security prison director of a chance to respond to accusations leveled at him.⁶⁷ Panh's proposal to record Duch's upcoming trial was rejected, but the court recognized a need for memorial documentation and agreed to a film that would question him. Even as Panh produces one of the most chilling perpetrator's self-representation on film, he sensed, with great unease, that Duch used him as a coach for his defense at the trial.⁶⁸

In *Duch*, the former prison director leafs through, reads, and comments on files and documents at a table. He also watches on a laptop outtakes from *S21*: stylized tableaus featuring former guards rigidly sitting while quoting memos and files; in turn, an internal audience of ex-perpetrators listens to them (Fig. 6.19; see Fig. 6.20 in Color Insert, 1). Duch's reactions are scrutinized after each detailed account of his role in the torture and the setting of protocols. This reflective insistence has no atonement payoff in either *Duch: Master of the Forges of Hell* or in *S21*.

Figure 6.19 Panh interrogates Duch with evidence: files, photos, videos (Rithy Panh, *Duch Master of the Forges of Hell*, 2010).

PARAJURIDICAL SCENARIOS AND THE CONFESSIONAL IMPERATIVE

I use the term "parajuridical" in relation to *S21* to situate the film in relation to two kinds of operation that have reparation as an objective—one cinematic and the other institutional—which both rely on testimony and reenactment to reflect on individual or group responsibility outside of defined legal and juridical systems. The term refers, first, to a subset of legal process films that use participatory reenactment by actual defendants to construct a "kind of parallel evidentiary record,"[69] and to relitigate on film their version of events. Second, "parajuridical" refers to institutions and other pedagogic and therapeutic measures facilitating conversion and societal healing in moments of transition after a major national catastrophe.[70]

Drawing on Jennifer Mnookin and Nancy West's proposition that the entire structure of American evidence law is set up "to enable the reproduction of the ground-zero moment"[71] of the crime on trial, Kristen Fuhs has underlined the "fundamental affinity existing between reenactment, the law, and the true crime narrative." Noting that "the legal trial is already, in a sense, a conjectural reenactment of a historical event,"[72] she cites Errol Morris as an advocate for reenvisioning criminal logic: "the engine for uncovering truth is not some special lens or even the unadorned human eye," he says, "it is unadorned human reason. It wasn't cinema verité documentary that got Randall Dale Adams out of prison. It was a film that re-enacted important details of the crime."[73] Fuhs concludes that "if reenactments in juridical documentaries such as *The Thin Blue Line* (1987) allow for a re-examination of the material and contingent facts of a case, then reenactments that feature the events' original actors, or participatory reenactments facilitate a dual forensic engagement with the case on the level of history and performance."[74]

For Mnookin, films can function as "an alternative appeals process, operating in parallel to the formal (and cumbersome) legal appeals process" that addresses "the viewing public rather than appellate courts."[75] Fuhs's notion of participatory reenactment adds specificity to film's potential to reopen cases (whether symbolically or in actual fact): "the re-staging involving the actual culprit [in legal process films] conjures a particular, historically-situated self that allows a subject to reassert a sense of agency within the representation of his or her personal history."[76]

Necessarily, this activist and redemptive version of self-reclamation is absent in a posttraumatic film context. Here, the mandate is to delineate irretrievable absences rather than mitigate or "correct" bad verdicts. Films like *Shoah* and *S21* call for testimony that is unequivocally unredemptive, an ethical determination that applies even more forcefully to perpetrators' narratives of their atrocities.

Other distinctions prove relevant to the discussion of postgenocide, parajuridical films. While the legal process and juridically themed documentaries Mnookin and Fuhs mention often involve individual cases against the state,[77] *S21* engages with perpetrators whose responsibility is undeniable yet ambiguously fused with that of an autocratic, collective body. Panh's film lays bare what is always the case in postgenocide parajuridical films: the "I" is never really singular because of this conflation of individual and state.[78] Moreover, *S21* participates in a process of national justice and accounting that is already overdetermined. The film not only precedes the creation of the Extraordinary Chambers of the Court in Cambodia but also delineates a different arena of adjudication, frustrating both an obvious verdict (they are guilty) and a putative court of appeal (they may be innocent).

S21 was made in the wake of the juridical mise-en-scène and indicting impetus of post-Holocaust testimonials such as Claude Lanzmann's *Shoah*, and it preceded and influenced Joshua Oppenheimer's *The Act of Killing* (2013). In these documentaries, the pressure for victims and perpetrators to testify is accompanied by the belief that the verbal or mimetic replay of the past at the site of trauma can lead the person to a cathartic reliving and eventual coming to terms with his or her past.

Describing his views for an effective theatricality in *Shoah* (and having in mind Abraham Bomba's testimony, activated by its mise-en-scène in a barber shop), Lanzmann illuminates the confessional-performative dynamic of testimonial and reenactment film. In recounting their own story, "they have to be put in a certain state of mind, but also *into a certain physical disposition. Not in order to make them speak, but so that their speech can suddenly communicate, become charged with an extra dimension.*"[79]

This extra dimension of communication, aimed primarily at secondary witnesses, corresponds to the cathartic resolution courted in parajuridical processes conducted in public and meant to resolve cases where a sustained crisis of public authority obstructs justice. Expectations bearing on perpetrators' testimony inflect an entire discourse that extends from personal confessions in Truth and Reconciliation, and

Peace and Justice commissions to testimonial documentaries that "fail" when they cannot produce visual "proof" of repentance.[80]

Questions of cultural translation and the dramatic impact of reenactment measures involving healing narratives and practices are pertinent in grasping the complexity of perpetrator confessions—and *S21*'s difference from other films. According to Stephanie Benzaquem, the "testimonial therapy" approach adopted by the NGO Transcultural Psychosocial Organization (established in Phnom Penh in 1995) "had three objectives: to express the traumatic experience; to honor the spirits of the dead; to document human rights violations."[81] At times, the procedure shocked the therapists, as it involved survivors violently reenacting the killings. For the main, however, the method was based on the social extension of a cure into a ritual: "a survivor talked about what was his or her ordeal in the hands of the Khmer Rouge. A counselor helped turn the testimony into a written document," which was then "read aloud to other survivors and/or community members during a Buddhist ceremony."[82]

Other juridical issues such as the emphasis on individual guilt in the context of mass atrocity and trauma also have a bearing on *S21*'s sparse representation of the prison interrogations and torture. Whereas Truth commissions focus on individual confession "to avoid the spinning out of control of discords and their transformation into collective ethnic conflicts," Chris Colvin has questioned the value of extending a "therapeutic ethic" from individuals to an entire culture. This process, he observes, implies that the "memory of individual actors in the trauma is solicited in order to cure the entire society."[83] Understandably, the burden carried by the ten men forming the ex-staff of S21 and the cast of the film is an issue in defining paths for public atonement and its filmic expression.

Assessing the pervasiveness of stories of pain and suffering in postatrocity reparations, Julie Stone Peters notes: "in human rights [discourse] narrative has come to have an independent legal-political function . . . [;] it has come to be used instead of (or alongside) punishment or victim compensation—not as evidence, but as a form of redress in and of itself."[84] In this context, Nigerian author Wole Soyinka has expressed skepticism about the resolutions provided by fast-tracked narratives of disclosure, closure, and reconciliation in public commissions: "The moral element . . . remorse and repentance is too nebulous to assess . . . one can only observe that an expression of remorse has been made. Is it genuine? Impossible to tell."[85] In particular, he points to the frequently belated, and therefore "morally distorted" causality of crime, punishment, and acquittal. If we "deplore the application of *retroactive* law, that today punishes acts that were committed when such acts did not constitute crimes, (what of the morality) in a proceeding that pursues the opposite—pardons a crime through retroactive dispensation?"[86]

In 1999, Soyinka observed that, at the end of the millennium, the world seemed to be caught up in a fever of atonement. In *The Act of Killing*, Anwar Congo, one of the killers, returns to the small building terrace and demonstrates, for the camera, his garrote method of strangulation to avoid excessive blood. There, after saying "I had to do it," he starts to heave and retch over and over—but without success

Figure 6.21 Anwar Congo retching at the site of murders (*The Act of Killing*, Josh Oppenheimer, 2012).

(Fig. 6.21). Such glaring effort for what should instead be visceral stands for the pressures of the redemptive documentary genre, the wish to have a literal purge stand for an uncontrovertible catharsis and dramatic closure.[87]

The same impulse to conform to a narrative of reparation drives Panh's interpretation of what happened in the course of filming *S21*. "Strangely" Poev (the guard reenacting his gruesome routines) "had a big fever, like something came out of his body." Implying great significance to this somatic expression, he repeated "a big, big, fever.... It was very strange."[88]

Despite the director's own comments, I submit that the film resists the conversion model of testimonial documentary; that is, it does not pass a verdict or embrace a therapeutic resolution.[89] Although the film resembles a trial on the surface, with all of its elements—its setting, the accused, the evidence, and the victims— their theatrical presentation makes them highly unstable. *S21* continually voids expectations ingrained in testimonial confession by introducing an essential element of inscrutability. In particular, two issues—the visibility of remorse and the twisted causality of a belated adjudication—matter to my reading of *S21*'s retroactive presentation of the Khmer terror routines. Setting the film against a number of redemptive maneuvers and representations—from Truth and Reconciliation commissions, to testimonial therapies and participatory reenactment in legal process documentaries—allow us to probe further the performative reach of reenactment in a parajuridical context. Is reenactment's value compromised when confession is missing? Are filmed confessions in a categorical and performative continuum with those done in public at Truth commissions? What qualifies their performative efficiency as conversion mechanisms, and are they equally valuable once the social actors' acknowledgment of their acts remains, as in *S21*, unavailable? This atoning unavailability is essential to an unredemptive and critical conception of reenactment.

AN INTERNAL CHORUS: FILES AND FACES

Although actual survivors, perpetrators, documents, and sites are featured, *S21*'s theatricality—its belatedness and glaring artifice—grates against the expected testimonial authenticity underpinning the confession-conversion paradigm of human rights' narratives. Rather than bemoan this "loss" of testimonial objectivity, I would like to explore how artifice and hybridity add to the film's critical-ethical reach. The stakes involve the film's shift from a testimonial aesthetic based on individual expressions of remorse to a defamiliarizing mise-en-scène that promotes previously undisclosed evidence. The scenarios of the past that Panh activates do not reproduce what happened; instead, by presenting a fixed, illustrative version, they give rise to a proces*sing* of evidence.

In contrast to conventional documentaries, which focus on presenting information, *S21* enlists verbal or visual evidence to serve as mental prods and physical props in its parajuridical process. The process of filming took three years. Each time a witness raised a topic, he or she would work and rework it with others to incorporate multiple points of views. By Panh's account, he gave "each former worker of S21 the chance of modifying or completing his statements, but [that] confronted with the archives and testimony of the survivors, it was hard for them to hide behind a lie."[90] The process yielded a platform for reflection by juxtaposing two products of Khmer ideology: the archive and the men who handled it and generated its content.

The tableaus of men handling and reciting files relay information. However, they *do not illustrate* what took place at the security prison. The recitative quality of their speech and the emptiness permeating the space give rise to a ritual, hieratic rhythm. The scenarios lack any hint of psychological motivation or pathos; moreover, if the possessed state of the solo scenes undermines single motivations—pathology, social alienation, and aesthetic interference—this is even more so in the group scenes.

Multiple factors contribute to the men's impassive demeanor. Individuated personal speech is contaminated by indoctrination and distanced via quotation. Perpetrators obfuscate or evade placing themselves at the crime scene. Finally, a somber theatrical formation radically distances the performance, framing the authenticity of highly compromised historical actors' testimony.

In both film and court, the credibility of a given utterance depends on whether it is heard as performative statement rather than a performance. Files handled and read by the ex-staff (or, alternatively, the stiff and obviously scripted performance of social actors) undercut any possibility of personal and sincere expression. As the men read confessions they themselves wrote for the resistant prisoners, these documents' "authorship" is flagged and the stilted delivery amplifies the faulty connection between agent and speech.[91]

The film's questioning of intention, agency, and voice is oblique and derives from the mise-en-scène's resolute antinaturalism. Still, this detachment between speaker and file alerts us to the ways repetition works in the film to intervene in the present (instead of reconstructing the past). What on the surface looks like mimicry of Khmer bureaucracy in fact amounts to ostensive staging, whose demonstrative purpose is curiously scrutinized from within by a set of internal witnesses. The director's rearrangement of speakers from scene to scene constantly renews the issue of culpability and expiation. These men, standing momentarily as witnesses, create a refraction platform for the viewer; hereby, their silence signals a time/space for reflection.

Because it conjures the past in a disjointed manner, reenactment, Panh's device for promoting accountability, inevitably has a perverse dimension. When staging the men's relation to the files (they leaf through them at times crouching on the floor), Panh adds desks—an ubiquitous feature of the Khmer's judicial order.[92] In 1975, desks had migrated from their school function to take part in a bureaucracy separating victims from torturers charged with filing invented confessions. As such, they were the primary support for "courts" that perverted principles of law and justice. Accordingly, their manner of display proves significant. They serve to locate the ex-guards in a minimally referential space, blocking an area for action within the museum's vacant surrounding. Conformed by a designed void and by strangely detached recitations, these and other surfaces such as files and photos become reflexive platforms for recitations that raise questions as to which principle of justice and reconciliation art promotes.

In one striking tableau, a man sits by a desk midway into a deep empty room reading a directive that says, "Method for writing a document . . . Have them describe their treacherous lives . . . Reading will reveal the secret story, the perfectly clear cause of the espionage eating us from within according to their plan." Four men enter at the far end of the room carrying a chair rigged for torture just as he reads, "interrogation plan . . . there are two methods." As they place the chair in front of the desk, he continues, "Torture is a complementary method; comrades resort to it too easily" (Figs. 6.22a–c).

This scaled-down arrangement focuses Panh's antinaturalist juxtapositions. Like the other tableaus, this scene is a hybrid, a theatrical set-up involving real players and historical records. And yet the conjunction between the staged entrance and the statement about how easily "comrades resort to torture" is ambiguous: it can demonstrate a norm, but also, given the word choice, encourage critical examination. Apparently seamless, the scene introduces the split reading typical of reenactment: a replay of past action (infused with past routines) and its citation can possibly, but not necessarily, define a repudiation of that past.

Such simple compositions are unstable, diverting reasonable dialogue material toward alternate kinds of expression. For instance, when the three men "converse" about what the regime did to justify its arrests: "There is something I don't understand . . . if someone dug a potato to eat, they were executed but here they were not immediately killed"; "There was a tactic. They had to be interrogated to find something wrong they had done and then we killed them"; "In Angkar they wanted to govern justly and if you arrest someone you need a reason. Angkar has eyes everywhere . . . it arrests rightfully"; "If I understand when we drew a document, we made up an activity of sabotage, we invented the evidence in order to execute the prisoner. There was no court to judge him. Each man has his history, the aim was to break that memory and make from it an act of treason" (Fig. 6.23).

Figure 6.22a–c Reenacting the torture/confession sequence (Panh, *S21: The Khmer Rouge Killing Machine*, 2003). a) "In their own words." b) "Must be exercised constantly." c) "Torture is a complementary method."

Figure 6.23 "There's something I don't understand" (Panh, *S21: The Khmer Rouge Killing Machine*, 2003).

These phrases could logically shape a discussion, and the men's bearing suggests actual dialogue. But the conversation proves baffling because, whether it consists of original opinions, dry descriptions, or recited indoctrination, and whether or not the speakers understand the reasons for killing, their statements remain discrete and affectless. Even though words are subtitled in scare quotes, the voices are uniform and display no emotion. This strangely "suspended" agency produces no actual exchange. More than a dialogue, it constitutes a chorus, a host of indistinct voices with timed "entrances" unified in tone.

Another gathering mimics a meeting to assess an incident in which a prisoner got hold of a gun and shot the guard and himself. The "conversation," already stiff, slips into rigid orders: "The group meets to access their work; every day we must be attentive keeping the enemy from escaping, stealing guns, breaking keys. Be vigilant, you are not careful enough." A photo of the dead prisoner takes up the screen as support for the self-critique: "We will be vigilant and determined." In a chorus, all the guards repeat, "determined, determined, determined." Panh's montage is sharp: as the men voice their unanimous "determination," photo after photo of mangled bodies piles up in a condensed display of prisoners' fate under torture.

Inasmuch as the guards' statements pass seamlessly from descriptions to regurgitated orders and slogans, Panh may have been testing the possible emergence of a historicizing gap or narrating consciousness on their part. And yet these micro-variations accumulate in a detached, clouded agency, suggesting that the impossible distinction between ingrained orders and reflective afterthought *is* actually the point.

The monotonous delivery levels all orders of information, including the perpetrators' own reflections on their actions. Attempts to make sense of the killing machinery are reduced to one more voice in the chorus; a parallel emerges between each statement's structural role in the film and the greater bureaucracy these words helped maintain. The staging and performance strip the speakers of individuality while shaping a sense of overarching, mechanical order.

In the process, even hierarchy—which is a form of differentiation—appears as a simulacrum. In deep perspective, a desk occupies the shot's foreground while three men sit around a small table further down. On the desk, a typewriter and a pile of photos of prisoners become signifiers of the voiced statement and its memorialization: "The party forbids beating but we beat them" is repeated over a pinpointed, recognizable portrait, that of Bophana, larger than others.[93] The blocking of the scene, with a countershot of Prak Khan by the desk looking at the reader, invokes a surveyor role. But any hint of established roles unravels through the cumulative effect of tableaus, each of which presents a new arrangement of desks, chairs, files, and men (Fig. 6.24).

Even naming, the most consequential form of individuation, fails to connect person to deed. An example is a simple set-up illustrating the basic mechanism of torture and execution involving mothers and children. A group of guards sits on the floor handling photos of women; meanwhile, the music and camera pan direct us to a large painting showing children being torn from their mothers' arms (Fig. 6.25). A cut brings us back to the group of five. Four sit against a wall, while Thi sits alone at the middle of the room. At each enunciation, the camera circles back, catching the

*That way we had proof.
So we could kill the person.*

Figure 6.24 Face: Prak Khan at the end of a triangulated sequence (Panh, *S21: The Khmer Rouge Killing Machine*, 2003).

Figure 6.25 Painting of a woman trying to wrest her child from death (Panh, *S21: The Khmer Rouge Killing Machine*, 2003).

three silent witnesses in the middle, and at points the main speaker leaning on the wall identifies them: "You and Peng lied to the female prisoners; you said you were taking their children to treat them, you and Peng took those old enough to walk, Sri's group took those who were too young to walk, took them away to kill them behind the prison."

With an orchestrated shift between enunciation and reaction, the scene identifies each man's task, creating a discomfiting disjuncture: as the camera guides the viewer's attention from the reader to listeners within the scene, we are made aware that each of these gentle-looking men was involved in gruesome acts. The distanced speech and their calm disposition, as well as the camera's soothing movement, soften the brunt of personal responsibility while the content of their statements sustains the scene's disquiet.

Similar ambiguity pervades scenes featuring close-ups of documents that the perpetrators hold and comment on. The relation of the ex-guard handling the document to his agency is at once ostensive and uncertain. A finger aids in reading, and at times it even pinpoints a signature. "My name, Prak Khan," states Khan after a detailed description of levels of torture.

This particular sequence—when Prak makes an unusually candid statement, "My mind never checked my hand as I beat the prisoner"—is as close as the film gets to a personal avowal of responsibility. Evoking solo scenes in a state of "possession," his gesture marks the difficulty in separating thought and action; in the past tense, his words effectively detach then from now.

The film's impact goes beyond any single individual's conscious admission. In my discussion of the various surfaces (paintings, desks, documents) structuring Panh's scenarios, I have left for last the single most disconcerting element: an internal audience of one or more men silently listening and watching while one of them recites the documents or leafs through photos of the dead. Hereby, the face—a surface unlike any other—plays a central role. From within the scene, the guards' faces triangulate our reactions to newly generated evidence by recombining perpetrators, the archive, and the site. To borrow a phrase from Emmanuel Levinas, "the face is the evidence that makes evidence possible."

Before reflecting on the difference between the camera scanning a single perpetrator's expression for signs of remorse and the way it pauses over the group of ex-Khmers internal to each tableau, we should note that, independent of whether they recite the archive or stand guard to silence in group, the men all display a similar psychological opacity. If anything, the inner group's silence amplifies and comments on the expressive difficulties affecting all of them. What initially haunts these scenes, then, is the potential exchangeability of group members with other people. Either they are extensions of each other—which further dilutes their personal responsibility—or they hold their posts as witnesses standing for the actual emergence of an active consciousness (Fig. 6.26).

Regarding the inscrutability of perpetrators' reactions, a couple of examples establish the unique import of these groupings in *S21*. Discussing the ur-image of the perpetrator under examination—the enhanced visibility of Adolf Eichmann's

[Still from film with subtitle: "head of the interrogation group at Bureau S21."]

Figure 6.26 Internal audience: ex-guards sitting on the floor.

expression in his bulletproof glass enclosure at trial—Katherine Model remarks on how the camera "searches [to no avail] for ruptures that might betray a flicker of conscience," during "[his] unsettlingly mechanistic recitation of the horrific events he helped orchestrate."[94]

The perpetrators' opaque expression constitutes an altogether different dilemma in in-person reenactment films. First, the social actors' expressions represent a purposeful aspect of the project; they involve collaboration between the filmmaker and his subjects. More important, reenactment is meant to "pay off," that is, to facilitate a visible and transformative effect. Whether or not a plausible conversion with credible signs of atonement takes place in Oppenheimer's *The Act of Killing*, the film is a spectacular test case for the unframed display of a protagonist's perspectives; the viewer herself has to sift through layers of reality before gauging the ethics of the situation (whether now or then—during the massacres of 1964–1965). Here, theatricality complicates the fragile negotiation between performance and performativity that occurs in reenactment. Anwar's "retching" exemplifies the ambiguity haunting any acting out, as well as the ethics of perpetrators' public penance. Bill Nichols has suggested that, contrary to *The Act of Killing*, the victim's presence in *S21* balances the uncertain reception of scenes where evil deeds are confessed to but left unqualified by a stabilizing conscience. I would argue, however, that Nath's presence and the interrogatory mode he advances as a victim do not define *S21*'s ethical contours so much as the silent chorus made up of perpetrators, which opens the scene onto a reflexive operation.

In sum, the film circles around the notion of acknowledgment and responsibility with a montage of disjointed elements, favoring a sense that speaker and evidence are dissociated, that evidence is disowned. The camera, on the other hand, contravenes this dissociative quality. Its movements search for reactions, forging links and relations. Working against the lack of acknowledgment on the guards' part, the camera pans from document/photo to a face, and then to other, more distant faces. By punctuating the sequence (or the long take), it stresses "the evidence that makes the evidence possible." It pauses, just before the cut, creating pressure for continued engagement, on the viewer's part, with the perpetrator's face now.

Prak Khan's scene is exemplary in this regard. As he reads about increasing levels of pain inflicted ("mild," "hot," and "rabid" torture), the camera moves toward two other men standing with their eyes averted and heads down. The framing and the men's position around the table formally parallel Khan's; their choral silence completes the tableau, granting it ethical resonance. It is after this shot of the silent auditors that Khan declares that his head never checked his hand.

The question of how a detour through others affects the nature and weight of evidence provided complicates the narrow instrumentality of the confessional-conversion model of in-person reenactment. What can be extrapolated from the film's deliberate undermining of testimonial expression holds implications for efforts to devise a model for reenactment that is broadly critical and independent of penance—that is, a mode of replay inviting ethical and historical scrutiny rather than moralistic closure.

The chorus has a special place in this new model. It pulls the scene's focus away from single perpetrators. Thereby, it complicates the characterization of an ex-perpetrator by adding the function of witnessing. Finally, it confronts viewers with a quandary central to the Cambodian condition by calling on them to decipher an opaque surface that simultaneously represents a gear in the killing machine and a motor for a potential consciousness. The theatrical configuration of the tableau and the camera's redesigned foci impose a sense of imminent interpellation: the viewer is asked to balance all these complex factors, looking at the face, to that which is "straightway ethical."

Panh described perpetrators' difficulty in admitting their own role in the crimes as an ability to paint a precise picture except for the single blind spot, occupied by the I. His radical intervention in the testimonial conventions has to do with reminding that the I is enmeshed from the very start with the historical horrors of collective indoctrination; moreover, that it is available to aesthetic reclaiming.

In taking aim at a broader machinery of killing, Panh is able to make unique use of in-person reenactment, for it is precisely through this tool of self-reclamation and permanent responsibility that the film effects its most radical diffusion of agency. In these tableaus, in-person reenactment has the paradoxical function of alerting the viewer to the ways in which, present in scene, the ex-perpetrators absent themselves.

It is as if by bringing the ex-guards in contact once again with the evidence from the past the potential for awareness was met by an equally strong impulse for vacating the scene. Finally, and despite Panh's cloaking of the film in terms of a reparative model, his chosen tools—in-person reenactment and recitation—make the proximity between consciousness raising and consciousness dimming visible as a historically situated and impossible threshold of acknowledgment.

As witnesses to the regulated rigidity of the Kampuchea Republic script, replayed in a new historical stage and in the liminal space of a film, this silent inscrutable chorus confirms the tragic bent of contemporary reenactment films.

CHAPTER 7

Reenactment and A-filiation in *Serras da Desordem*

If legibility of a legacy were given, natural, transparent, and univocal—if it did not simultaneously call for and defy interpretation—there would be nothing to inherit. It would amount to a cause, something natural and, as it were, genetic. One always inherits a secret, which says, "Read me, will you ever be up to it?"

Jacques Derrida[1]

This chapter considers the dystopic dimension of reenactment film, attending to the figuration of return, dislocation, and what I am calling "a-filiation" in Andrea Tonacci's *Serras da Desordem* (*Hills of Chaos*, 2006). *Serras* tells the story of Carapiru,[2] a noncontacted Indian from the Awá-Guajá tribe, who reenacts events that took place twenty to thirty years earlier—including his first contact with nonindigenous Brazilians, after landowners ordered an attack that dispersed and killed members of his family group in 1977.

Over eleven years, Carapiru wandered 600 kilometers from the northeast of Maranhão to Bahia. In 1988, he met some ranchers with whom he became friendly; eventually, he stayed with a family called Aires. FUNAI (The National Foundation of Indigenous Aid) brought him to Brasilia and then back to Maranhão, where he joined remnants of his community at the Tiracambú reservation. Sydney Possuelo, the Indianist in charge of isolated Indian groups, called in an interpreter to help with the project; this young man recognized Carapiru as his long-lost father. The eventful encounter and discovery—of an as-yet-uncontacted Indian and the reunion of father and son after years of separation—made the headlines (see Fig. 7.1 in Color Insert, 2; Fig. 7.2).

Serras da Desordem freely mixes contemporary news footage and TV images with reconstructed and documentary scenes from 1988 and 2006. Both for production reasons and to signal his own conceptual distance, Tonacci alternates between digital and 35-millimeter images.[3] In addition, expeditionary films from the

Figure 7.2: TV reportage on son identifying Carapiru as his father (*Serras da Desordem*, Tonacci, 2006).

1910s and 1920s are intercut with Carapiru's reenacted present, and an extended montage of institutional newsreels and films ironically references the "Brazilian miracle" of the period. This brief synopsis of the dictatorship era "covers" Carapiru's peripatetic years (Fig.7.3f; see Figs. 7.3a, 7.3b, 7.3c, 7.3d and 7.3e in Color Insert, 2).

The film's radical deoriginating agenda includes intertextual saturation and the self-reflexive staging of a meeting between the filmmaker and Carapiru at the film's end. *Serras*'s hybrid texture, its abrupt shifts between times, black-and-white, color, and various image grains, keep its protagonist Carapiru unanchored, lost in a forest of images. The film's ostensive subject matter is a ruptured social fabric and the problematic relationship between indigenous populations and Brazilian institutions and normative orders. Within the film, Carapiru's disengaged, incongruous presence among non-Indian Brazilians, results from both a violent history of eradication and a fracturing aesthetics that involves recursive repetition and literal reenactment. This unmooring—real, enacted, and textually multiplied—is my subject here.

My term for the relevant contexts for Tonacci's deoriginating aesthetics, expressing the film's fundamental ambiguity with respect to available narratives of integration, is "a-filiation." The hyphen stresses the stakes of *Serras* uprooting aesthetics for a critical history of the nation.

Dealing as it does with Carapiru, an isolated Indian and the prime object of ethnography's salvage paradigm, Tonacci's belated reconstruction is necessarily critical. Traditionally, reenactment catches the viewer up with a missed event or gesture and is allied with cinema's fictional machinery; its narrative thrust shapes and tames the contingencies of documentary record. But when deployed to represent the Indian (an entity subjected to constant patrol, to territorializing pressure, if not outright extinction), it can, precisely because of its temporal flexibility, become complicit with allochronic discourses fixing Indian realities in a timeless past.

In fact, as a fictional actualization, reenactment offers no ethical or epistemological guarantee of rendering an original event. Rebecca Schneider has noted that

Figures 7.3 f): Newsreel of "Great Brazil" project during the dictatorship, from the "Great Brazil" montage sequence (*Serras da Desordem*, Tonacci, 2006).

because "the art or act of reenactment [involves] manipulating anachronism," the quality of temporal dislocation "can never be entirely banished from the project at hand."[4] Along similar lines, Christopher Wood and Alexander Nagel have discussed both art objects and reenactment as a form of theater that asserts the "principle of continuity of identity across a succession of substitutions,"[5] a process they have called "anachronic." Coined as an alternative to historicist readings of art charged with detecting anachronisms and surmising proper origins and contexts, the term "anachronic" is used "to say what the artwork does "qua art": "when it is late, when it repeats, when it hesitates, when it remembers, but also when it projects a future or an ideal."[6] Positing a dialogue across time illuminates the anachronic conception of art, and reenactment represents one of the main tools for activating an intertemporal dimension and sparking performative potential. Through reenactment, a film can ignore, absorb, or critically intensify its challenge to linear genealogy or temporality. It can reconstruct the fantasy of purity by forging an abstract and ahistorical "other" (e.g., Flaherty's *Nanook of the North*'s timeless Inuit), or it may expose the inherent contingency of notions of authenticity: the ways that a putative origin can shift according to specific historical investments, relations of dominance, and aesthetic frames.

"WHEN IS CARAPIRU?"

Carapiru accepts being a part of the film in order to revisit his former hosts and to travel again on a plane; however, he agrees to do so only on condition of being brought back to the reservation. That in-person reenactment involves displacement and relocation drives home the embodied, affective implications of this performance act. Deeply entangled with his personal and ethnic history as a survivor of one of the last uncontacted Tupi-Guarani tribes,[7] Carapiru's history of dislocation poses numerous problems starting with quandary of representing a *first contact* (Fig. 7.4). As Carapiru revisits the sites and people he met twenty years earlier, the question of whether multiple registers of separation and encounter are maintained emerges. Does reenactment erase or foreground these singular iterations? Who and what exactly "returns" in reenactment, and how is this return marked as such in relation to an alternate documentary conception of original emergence?

Figure 7.4: Carapiru reenacts his first contact with ranchers (*Serras da Desordem*, Tonacci, 2006).

"Where is Carapiru?" asks Ms. Aires, a member of the rancher family who took him in when he first made contact. She addresses Carapiru as if playing a game with a child, pointing to a faded photo showing him and his hosts (see Fig. 7.5 in Color Insert, 2) The scene revisits a prior stay among the Santa Luzia villagers, in 1988. However, the deeper refrain that emerges in the course of the film concerns *when* Carapiru *is*. We soon become unsure about the *when* of Carapiru's actions, as well as uncertain about how to think of him or what he himself thinks.

The narrative moves along two temporal axes. One describes the linear sequence of Carapiru's life up to his (reenacted) encounter with members of his tribe. The second demands more attention to the ways the filmmaker obfuscates linear chronology: everyday routine and repetitive behavior undo one's sense of when events take place; replaying scenes prompts the viewer to reconsider their meaning; finally, archival footage contaminates images of the present. In other words, every image is infused with the same oscillatory temporality that defines reenactment.

The film's temporal ambiguity is not restricted to the replay of unique, discrete events in Carapiru's life—for instance, his first encounter with the ranchers, or when he reluctantly separated from them and was taken away by FUNAI to Brasilia. Now, the departure scenes and goodbyes to the villagers and ranchers are replayed as theater: they convey a vague violence that is impossible to locate or to gauge (Fig. 7.6).

Carapiru's performance registers as most jarring and momentous against the backdrop of banal, regular, quotidian tasks.[8] Routine both absorbs and sets Carapiru's return, as an actor, in relief. The habitual nature of daily rituals lends itself to abbreviated forms of representation and yet, in conjunction with cinema's pointed singularity, the reference to repetitive behavior only increases the chronological confusion. Meals are prepared and eaten, as occurs every day, but when do the events on-screen actually take place? Scenes are chronologically unmarked, reminding us that cinema can serve as record of pure contingency; without narrative

Figure 7.6: Carapiru reenacts leaving the Aires ranch with Possuelo (FUNAI) (*Serras da Desordem*, Tonacci, 2006).

Figures 7.7a–c: Reenacted meal at the Aires' table (*Serras da Desordem*, Tonacci, 2006). a) At the Aires' table. b) Another meal, insert at Aires table sequence (1920). c) End of Aires meal sequence.

intervention the internal time of the image loses its links with factual, clock time. Occasionally, a simple adverb in a dialogue—"before," "then," "now"—exposes how Carapiru's figure wavers under a shaky tense. A single line—such as "I don't want him to leave, you won't leave us, will you?"—can refer to multiple departures (twice when the state tried to take Carapiru from the Aires family, and twice more in these scenes' reenactment) (Figs. 7.7a–c). The meal scenes at the Aires family home and at Sidney Possuelo's house in Brasilia normalize Carapiru's presence in the direct-time image, but a simple comment about how Carapiru does not fill his plate as much as he did when he first came splits the scene's reference in two, making it count for then and now.

A masterfully edited kitchen scene presents Carapiru as a spectral visitor. In perfect continuity, black-and-white and color shots succeed one other. We watch the rancher's wife cooking, turned to the camera (Fig. 7.8a). Suddenly a shadow fills the image: Carapiru opens a door, and the film cuts to a color shot of Robélia, the daughter, entering the same space. Another monochromatic shot shows Robélia crossing Carapiru's path as he enters the kitchen (for Figs. 7.8b to 7.8f, see Color Insert, 2) The intricate editing of different instances (and clothes) in such a simple scene foregrounds cinema along with Carapiru's very entrance into the frame to haunting effect. He is replaying for the camera what he may have done twenty years before, when he stayed with the Aires family. The slight delay between shots, the shift between color and black and white, is all that is needed to haunt the image. A simple cut or door entry suffices to register a doubt, a flash of a double take: this (scene) entrance has happened many times before, and now it is happening again.

Reenactment, cinema, and Carapiru are equated in this door entrance, a classical editing technique since D. W. Griffith. Against the backdrop of apparent normalcy, this inordinate visitor, both when he first made contact and when he returns with the film crew, becomes a marker of cinema, the very motor of its repetition and his visibility. We are left to ponder what distinguishes original happening from replay, routine from event, event from film take. Nor is Carapiru the sole revenant in the film. With remarkable economy, Tonacci replicates reenactment's strategy to have a single person (or scene) reappear in a new context eliciting a retroactive foreshadowing and releasing a set of correspondences across time.

The uncanny kinship between past and present is especially highlighted in scenes showing the circumscribed autonomy of indigenous populations. The second time the Indian community idyllically bathes by the river is shadowed by the threat of the massacre that followed the first Edenic scene in the same location. Similarly when we first see train footage in this film, it is ominously linked to annihilation: internal shots present armed men, we overhear "the Indian is another humanity," a man aims his "shooting" finger at a sign demarcating Indigenous Land. Later, the same shot of the train recurs but a brief pan extends its beginning, allowing us to identify other passengers; among them is Carapiru, chatting with his son as he is brought back from Brasilia to the reservation. Those formerly responsible for the attack (an old captain and his men) are now recognized as Indian service agents in charge of Carapiru's well-being. This second view reframes the first, partial one, as an artifice and yet they torque each other in an impossible present. Fastened by cinema's indexicality, the film and the characters split in meaning, creating a paradox: Carapiru, his son, and the old hired hand in charge of attacking the Awá-Guajá group, "victims and aggressors, inhabit a single scene."[9]

Figure 7.8: a) Ms. Aires cooking. The start of the kitchen sequence (see Color Insert, 2)

Adding to the unease imposed by shared locations, bodies, and shots, the film incorporates archival footage that replicates Tonacci's scenes in content and shape. One of the sequences consists of photos taken by the anthropologist who photographed Carapiru among the Aires family. Tonacci reproduces the content as well as composition of these photos: Carapiru skipping rope with the children and teaching them how to use the bow and arrow. In addition, the kitchen and meal scenes discussed previously are intercut with fragments of a 1920s kitchen and meal scene, featuring another family at the table (Fig. 7.7b). "What connects the dish served here and the raised spoon there," affirms Rodrigo de Oliveira, "is nothing less than the perception of a whole, the consciousness that National history is construed by having the image as an involuntary support of memory."[10] With similar frame composition and edited in perfect match-on-action continuity, these inserts institute deep rifts in historical consciousness.

In his essay "O Lugar das Imagens" ("The Place of Images"), Rocha Melo has perceptively observed that this footage, mostly taken from exploration and travel documentaries, interweaves and comments on Tonacci's own gaze.[11] The images "collaged" onto the filmed reenactment operate in different ways. Describing a simple shot of a waterfall, Rocha Melo notes that this four-second image—from a silent travelogue on the grandeur of nature in Brazil—is awkwardly perched as a subjective, dreamy point of view when Carapiru is shown sitting and looking at another waterfall. The insert, a pan from right to left, is mirrored and complemented by Tonacci's pan moving left to right. The dissolve of one to the other, the return to Carapiru as "owner" of the gaze is paradoxical: if this shot is extracted from an expeditionary film, how can it be tied to an Indian perspective?[12]

The film leaves no illusion of contact with a pristine reality standing: in short bursts, extraneous images riddle the neutral register of Carapiru's life account. For example, an archival shot of a piglet rushing through a backyard, crosses, like a fugitive shadow, a second shot of the yard where, in the present tense of *Serras*, children are running after another piglet. In another instance, the director undermines the appearance of immediacy by modeling Possuelo's first (reenacted) contact with Carapiru on institutional films promoting the state or a political-party missionary charity[13] (Fig. 7.9). Approaching Carapiru, who likes to watch kids learning in a rural school, Possuelo (an awkward actor) engages the teacher in an exchange. Despite the fact that Possuelo is a devoted Indianist known for his work with Isolated Indians—and even though he is Tonacci's friend and the first to tell him about Carapiru—the sequence evokes a past civilizing mission: a grainy image of native, uniformed children in a classroom surrounded by white-smocked men intercuts the school "attended" by Carapiru.

As if erupting from a historical unconscious, this archival commentary haunts the film's well-intentioned present.[14] Kitchen, nature, school, and backyard are visited by someone else's vision; in many cases, the perspective corresponds to that of Major Luiz Thomaz Reis, a cinematographer who accompanied Marshall Rondon's Commission on scientific explorations of the Brazilian interior. In 1910, the Commission, charged with surveying the land and laying out telegraph wiring, created the Service of Indian Protection with the mandate of integrating the Indian

Figure 7.9: Missionary school archival insert (Major Luis Thomas Reis) in Tonacci, *Serras da Desordem* (2006).

population into the national economy.[15] This mandate of integration followed a positivist premise, and scenes of Indians lined up and dressed as students appear in various moments in *Around Brazil* (*Ao redor do Brasil*, 1930), a compilation of various films shot between 1924 and 1930 and the main source for Tonacci's archival clips.[16]

Addressing the salvage paradigm in ethnographic documentary, Catherine Russell has called for an experimental ethnography that "foreground[s] 'the time machine' of anthropological representation."[17] She proposes an alternate historiographical model in which fragments of other histories bring nonlinear temporality into play. Tonacci's jarring appropriation of archival material embraces an allegorical model with a strong affinity for poetic rhymes; the formal qualities of the footage are "ostentatiously foregrounded by the very structurality that becomes immanent in them."[18] Inserted through visual rhyming but without apparent motivation, these archival sequences, gelled snippets of historicity, "become vehicles of a larger story which they carry but in which they play no [direct] part."[19] Recontextualized in a new series, scenes of expeditionary zeal reveal patterns that implicate cinema's gaze in treating paternalistically natives, children, wild landscapes, and animals. Forcing one series of images to be read through the other, the archival thread creates a noise in Tonacci's well-meaning "rescue" of Carapiru's story.

In keeping with his alignment of cinema with other forms of violence against the Indian, Tonacci matches train to film in an aural and visual trespassing of Indian land. The way the spaces between cars are filmed recalls film photograms; in between flashes of light, we can read a plaque inscribed "Federal Government. Interior Ministry. National Foundation for the Indians, Forbidden Area, Indigenous land, Banned to Strangers."[20] The railroad, built by the *Companhia do Vale do Rio Doce* to transport iron to the coast of São Luis, brought in its wake illegal invasion, disease, and development with devastating consequences for the Guajá territory and reserves. The loud music scored over the train underlines its role in scaring away game and threatening the survival of more than forty tribes in the region.[21]

Earlier in the film, soon after the reenacted massacre of Carapiru's family group, Tonacci inserts a long, jarring sequence of archival footage that sparks the film's reference to a broader national context. Once Carapiru enters the forest (to reemerge in the story "ten years later"), a series of eye-level shots of men cutting trees begins, until, shifting the scale, the film incorporates footage of deforestation, the building of the Trans Amazonian Highway, and Serra Pelada, the gigantic mining site of Carajas—projects whose dimensions can be measured only by crane or aerial shots. A light samba music dissolves into a visual series known to all who lived through the military period, the so-called Brazilian Miracle. Inane scenes of carnivalesque oblivion, bourgeois self-satisfaction, and technological prowess alternate with more punctual references to historical events (confrontations between Indians and the FUNAI and between students and the military dictatorship, and workers' strikes) (see Figs. 7.3a–e in Color Insert, 2). Collated from institutional films and newsreels—as well as well-known documentaries such as *Iracema, uma transa amazonica* (Jorge Bodanzky and Orlando Senna, 1974), *Jango* by Silvio Tendler (1984), *Linha de Montagem* (Renato Tapajos, 1982), *Fé* (Ricardo Dias, 1999), and *Jornal do Sertão* (Geraldo Sarno, 1970)—this prosthetic memory of the military era ends on a deceptively simple scene: Carapiru running down a road[22] (Fig. 7.10).

A literal notation of the actual, the shot of Carapiru conflates representation and act. Laced with metaphors of the "last man" in face of adversity, the image is one of passage, a passing image of liminality. But even here the sense of an uncontaminated indigeneity is disallowed. Flanked by barbed wire, this road is a storied landscape, and it immediately alerts us that Carapiru is crossing occupied land.

More than the synthesis of an era, or an ellipsis in Carapiru's life story, these sequences, which evince distinct referential densities, create an imbalance between a single body and its testimonial burden. Too dense to filter through Carapiru's individual story, the constellations of meaning exercise a steady allegorical pressure.

Figure 7.10: Carapiru runs emerging from eleven years of wandering (Tonacci, *Serras da Desordem*, 2006).

The overextended length of the montage sequence (itself an ironic gloss on the rhetoric of grandiosity promoted by the dictator state from 1964 to 1984) includes sensationalist images of alternate politics. It includes Kayapo Chief Raoni invading the building of FUNAI and the director of Indian services being dragged out physically, and a strike by autoworkers led by Lula, then a metallurgic labor leader, later Brazilian president. Despite opening space for a counterhistory, all these familiar tags of a "shared past" become indistinguishable in a sleek mass that overwhelms and erases Carapiru. Swallowed by this media jungle, he reappears back on the road, a naked figuration of displacement.

The disproportion between the representations of Carapiru's history and that of the country is crucial to the film's expulsion of its protagonist. Due, in part, to reenactment's wavering temporality, his awkwardness among nonindigenous Brazilians, and even within his group, constitutes the film's basso commentary on his dispossession. Such allegorical pressure is constant in *Serras*. No image is allowed to appear naked, divested of its historical and filmic envelope.

TWENTY YEARS LATER: BRAZILIAN FILMS ON "FIRST" AND RECURRENT CONTACT

A detour through two other "twenty-years-later" documentaries—Eduardo Coutinho's (*Twenty Years Later: A Man Marked to Die* [*Cabra Marcado Pra Morrer: Vinte anos depois*, 1964–1984]) and Vincent Carelli's *Corumbiara* (2009)—puts in relief the nature of Tonacci's intervention. The specificity of his option for reenactment—and its belated reconstruction—stands in contrast to films whose long-span, fractured narratives evince an activist urgency and a testimonial mission.

Structured around a filmmaker's exploration of the same subject and site over the course of decades, both *Twenty Years Later* and *Corumbiara* revisit the aftermath of the 1964 coup. The first looks at the impact of the repression of rural organizations and the remains of an idealistic alliance between the artist and the people. The second zigzags back and forth in time, tracking the decimation of Indigenous tribes caused by corporate exploitation of the Amazon since the 1970s.[23] The dialogic circuitry of past and present in Coutinho's *Twenty Years Later: A Man Marked to Die* provides a countermodel to *Serras*'s approach to its protagonist's consciousness as a filter for national history. Unlike *Serras*, which mutes Carapiru's voice and unsettles notions of origin and continuity, *Twenty Years Later* highlights its subjects' memory and consciousness; here, cinema is enlisted as a witness at a time of democratic transition.

In turn, *Corumbiara*'s inordinate first-contact scenes make us think about the status of "first contact" in the different epistemologies of ethnographic documentary and fiction.

The contrasts between these return documentaries raise the question of how much it matters if past and present are layered via dramatic reenactment, or, alternatively, if dated presents are stitched together in tension (to convey the complex historical experience and collective memory of the Peasant Leagues [*Twenty Years Later*] or to suggest the continuing mission of Indianist groups [*Corumbiara*]); whether the stress on sequential immediacy as opposed to belated reconstruction differentially impacts a film's dramatic or analytical reach.

Long-term return films illuminate an important facet of Tonacci's trajectory inasmuch as they take distance from "the seventies militant kind of Brazilian documentary and its unproblematized fusion of the maker's perspective and that of the community treated."[24] *Corumbiara*'s focus on unexpected sightings of the Kanoe and Akunsu, like *Twenty Years Later*'s uncertain testimonies of the activist-leader's widow Elizabeth and her children, privilege the present as the unquestioned domain of activist cinema. Along with the acute obsession and the obvious structural mastery typical of return documentaries, these two films display a parallel narrative in which filmmakers and their subjects textually intersect as partners in a discourse and a common memorial project. This shared biographical trajectory, the common historicity linking the aging bodies of activists—Marcelo and Possuelo, the Indianists working for the FUNAI since the 1980s, and Coutinho—to those of their subjects bears analogy to the way Carapiru's life story, reshaped through reenactment's malleable linearity, becomes a self-reflexive and historiographical tool in *Serras*. These partnership images evince the shifting dynamic of delegation in Brazilian cinema since the 1960s, creating a sort of trail of filmmaking activism in Brazil.

Twenty Years Later rescues a history doubly interrupted: that of a Peasant League activism and reenactment film (*A Man Marked to Die*) about the aftermath of the peasant leader's assassination. The film starts with Eduardo Coutinho reflecting on his involvement in the early 1960s petty-bourgeois rhetoric against imperialism and the mobilization in support of the Peasant Leagues (founded in 1955)[25]; it is accompanied by footage shot with the sponsorship of the National Union of Students and the CPC (Popular Culture Centers). Coutinho retraces the genesis of the original film, which was meant to reenact the story of Agrarian Reform struggles leading to the assassination of the Peasant League leader João Pedro Teixeira in 1962 in Paraiba, in the Northeast. This was a project typical of the solidarity between students, artists, and the people promoted by the government before 1964. *A Man Marked to Die* featured Elizabeth, the dead leader's wife, and their children, as well as people from a similar community; they were forced to film in a neighboring state because of the violence in Paraiba (Fig. 7.11). Twenty years later, in 1984, the agenda of *Twenty Years Later* was to locate those actors and to narrate the history of the Galilea region's Peasant Leagues up to 1964 through two figures, one of whom took part in the original cast of *A Man Marked to Die* (the reenactment film interrupted by the military coup). All but Elizabeth, the sole historical actor of reenacted events, gather to watch the unfinished film's rushes. Coutinho finds Elizabeth, his female protagonist, who hid from brutal military police repression under an assumed name. Before Elizabeth herself is able to meet all of her dispersed children, the film finds and leads us to eight of ten family members, restoring the family's fabric, rent since their father's death. Extended interview sessions recreate the events' chronology, illustrating the narrative with scenes from the interrupted fictional reenactment, while repeated takes of the

Figure 7.11: Elizabeth, the dead leader's widow reenacts her life in the original 1964 footafe of *A Man Marked to die* (Coutinho, *Twenty Years Later: a Man Marked to die* 1964–84)

"last shot"—a mounted-police military coup d'etat threatening Elizabeth and João Pedro (played by another man)—literalize the brutal intervention. *Twenty Years Later: A Man Marked to Die* weaves together the testimony of those who lived through the repression of peasant struggles with a history of Coutinho's interrupted reenactment project. The film's fragmentary character and its frequent repetitions assert that these bits have now been reintegrated into history, defining for Brazilian critic Jean Claude Bernadet a "victory over history's trash bin."[26]

Highlighting the stakes of returning to the 1964 past in order to "construct some form of coherence between the pre- and post-rupture moments," Bernadet points out that Rui Guerra and Nelson Xavier's 1974 *The Fall* had already flagged a historical gap by redeploying footage of *The Guns* (Guerra's cinema novo classic from 1964), showing the same actors who had played soldiers repressing hungry peasants now as migrant construction workers in Rio. Guerra and Xavier thus not only created a past for the characters but "assured [a past and a future] to that phase of cinema novo that suffered a cut in 64."[27]

Guerra and Xavier's repurposing of film footage to prosthetically expand the characters' biography, to bridge and mark the significance of national historical ruptures, bears comparison with the generative role of reenactment in Coutinho and Tonacci's hybrid projects. In each of these films, the impact of national politics on individual lives serves as a pretext for narratives with grander allegorical ambitions. Representing a more reflective stage in each of these maker's works, the films intertextually flag their intention to question cinema's role in "making" history. Weaving other archives around the protagonists of these peasant and Indigenous stories, the films intentionally force us to reconsider which history is at stake in these revisited biographies.

In the early 1960s during João Goulart's leftist government, there was a broad push to produce truly democratic culture. Inflected by a long-standing paternalistic assumption that intellectuals need to intervene on behalf of workers, the question of delegation (who stands for whom) was especially charged within Brazilian cultural history. "In such cases who was the author? Who the student?"[28] asks Roberto Schwartz, summing up this idealist interlude in Brazilian culture, which was defined by projects intent to dismantle traditional forms of knowledge transfer (Paulo Freire's pedagogy of the oppressed) and theatrical groups dramatizing information given by peasants. In these

> [times of splendid irreverence], the themes, material possibilities and the very structure of cultural production were changing together with its audience . . . . In Rio de Janeiro the CPCs (Centres for Popular Culture) would improvise political theatre at factory gates and in trades and student union meetings; and in the slums they were beginning to make films and records. The pre-revolutionary winds were decompartmentalizing the national consciousness and filling the newspapers with talk of agrarian reform, rural disturbances, the workers' movement, the nationalization of American firms, etc.[29]

In 1988, when he released *Twenty Years Later*, Coutinho distanced himself from this populist tendency, stating that the film "knows it is made from the outside in, [it] knows *it is not made by peasants*." Yet while admitting that the original film patronized and idealized the people—thereby providing a stereotypical picture of the struggle— the director claimed to value the unfinished reenactment film *A Man Marked to Die* precisely *because* of the participation of the organized rural movement.[30] Critic Jean Claude Bernadet concurred. Speculating that finishing the film "would have allowed a more critical comprehension of the trinomial conscience/consciousness-raising and action,"[31] the critic commented that the portrayal of political action by people concretely involved in agrarian reform struggles would have, for a start, dismantled the central ideological parameter justifying cultural intervention by intellectuals at the time: that only after the alienated masses' consciousness were raised would they move into action.

The idea that acting in a film opens up a determinate political path and that repetition can reignite the political intent or recover the significance of the events portrayed underlies multiple social-reenactment films. Coutinho's enduring commitment to the idea that the peasants' self-performance would somehow affect the revolutionary dynamic rests on a common conflation, invited by in-person reenactment, between auto-performance and agency. In-person reenactment tends to occlude the authorial agency in favor of an idealized vision of the peasant as actor of his actual revolution. Accordingly, both Bernadet and Coutinho are reluctant to criticize the unfinished reenactment film of 1964.

In *Twenty Years Later*, the link between the earlier project and the later one runs deep. The 1984 film radiates centripetally from the absence at the core of the interrupted film: its dead protagonist, the assassinated peasant leader João Pedro.[32] A sequence of news photos of the body in the morgue, the family, and repressed manifestations punctuates his wife's testimony. After the coup, the original project became, for all involved, equated with the very absence it tried to suture, the belated resuscitation of abortive peasant struggles.

As Julianne Burton has remarked, Coutinho's announcement that João Virginio (a peasant tortured for his politics and a character who functions in the 1984 film as a surrogate of sorts for the assassinated leader) died a few months after his interview conveys "profound skepticism about the healing potential of Brazilian redemocratization."[33] This second "decease"[34] confirms the film's belatedness, if Coutinho's return is to be seen as some form of reparation at all. Tying his project to the failures of in-person reenactment to redeem the heroic struggle of the early 1960s, Coutinho casts his reconstruction of the dispersal of former Peasant League members in a melancholic light. In turn, his inscription of filmmaking at the center of this second narrative figures the fragility of that moment of idealized alliance across class lines.

Twenty Years Later has come to epitomize the transition from sociological representativeness to individuated, subjective and contradictory testimony. One particular scene deserves discussion in relation to Tonacci's distinct take on the transmission of history. Both filmmakers implicate cinema itself in their return to past events.

The scene in question links the casualties of the military coup—the people, intellectuals, *and* Coutinho's *film*. Duda, the son of Zé Daniel (a man who led the film crew to a hiding place on the day of the coup), tells how he saved *Kaput*, a book left behind by Coutinho's film's crew in their hurried escape in 1964.[35] Although he seems to be speaking on his own behalf, we soon discover Duda's words are quoted from the preface to Curzio Malaparte's *Kaput*, describing how a peasant helped save the book's original manuscript from falling into the hands of the Gestapo. Appropriating Malaparte's words and Coutinho's legacy as his own, Duda collapses authoritarian histories (Fig. 7.12). Through an interstice of voices, Duda guarantees his role as safekeeper of Coutinho's transformative passage through their lives, establishing a front of common resistance.

Duda's expression of this legacy is compelling.[36] Soon after its release, Coutinho explained that he made the film to overcome the phantasm that the rushes of *A Man Marked to Die* would perish rotting in his apartment. If his relationship with the participants remained alive, it was "because they also had their ghosts—1964."[37] What Coutinho did not know, he said, "was the degree to which *the film's phantasm* was important for them. Suddenly a guy keeps a forgotten book, *as a negative*. And then the film and 1964 are one sole thing."[38] Coutinho characterizes the kept book as a *negative* waiting to be processed, literalizing the film's value as collective memory, a tactile, multilayered and palimpsestic surface.

Two aspects warrant notice. The first is the sustained tension holding together the extended take, Duda's uninterrupted address, and the associations of his own role

Figure 7.12: Alluding to his own role in helping Coutinho flee, Duda quotes from Curzio Malaparte's *Kaput* (Eduardo Coutinho, *Twenty Years Later: A Man Marked to Die*, 1964–1984).

in the struggle against the military with other histories. The second is Coutinho's cinematic rephrasing of the shot of Duda removing the books from the suitcase (Fig. 7.13). Reciting Duda's keep-saving gesture literally redeems it through a replay of the book's return. Installing Duda's quotation within another recursive chain, cradling textuality through a gestural denotation, Coutinho revises the alliance between intellectual and the people, trading the old tradition of delegation conveyed in his initial project—the peasants' reenactment—for the authenticating but tremulous register of verité testimony.

Made in 2006, the same year as *Serras* and covering a similar timeline and subject matter, Vincent Carelli's *Corumbiara* is instructive for flaunting what reenactment occludes—the unpredictable encounter with the real, a "first contact" with a member of a not-yet-contacted group.[39] Carelli is invited to join a group of Indianists and journalists on a mission to prove the existence of isolated Indians, as well as to confirm an attack ordered by farming interests in 1986. The film leaps to 2006 and then backtracks to incorporate the 1996–1998 and 2000 expeditions as Carelli comments on the film's convoluted timeline, acknowledging the activists' long-term efforts (parallel negotiations with the state, the judicial system, and farming conglomerates). The narrative return to contested sites and characters who have aged in the interim (e.g., the Indianists Marcelo and Possuelo, or the corporate farm lawyer) should, but does not, temper the verité temporality of sustained alertness that posits every single shot as a last chance to prop up the object existence of those represented. Over the course of the film, we witness the group making contact with two other sets of

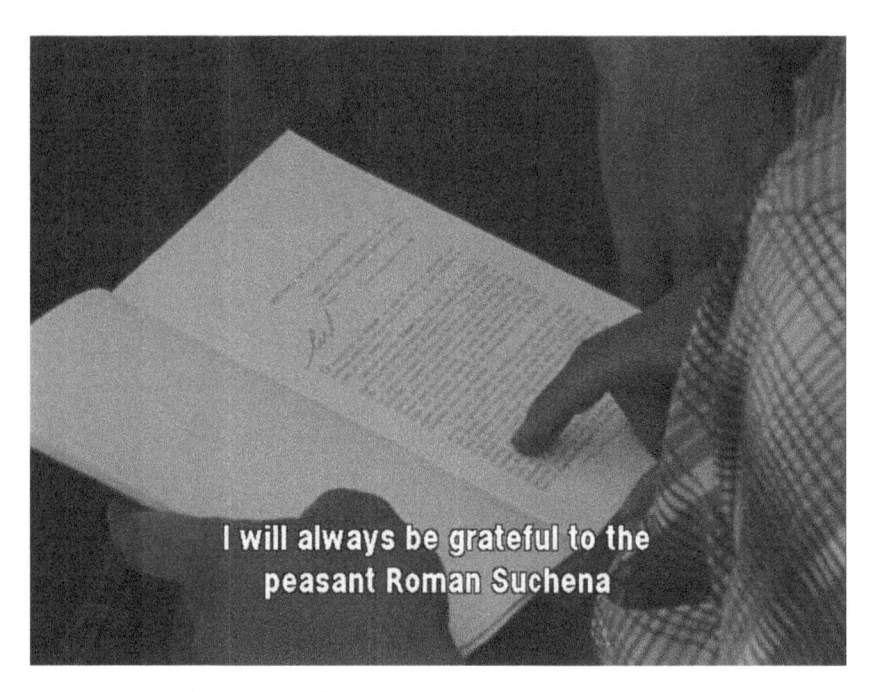

> I will always be grateful to the peasant Roman Suchena

Figure 7.13: Duda rescues the book he kept for twenty years (Eduardo Coutinho, *Twenty Years Later: A Man Marked to Die*, 1964–1984).

Isolated Indians besides the Kanoe (first a woman and her brother, then her mother and cousin): the Akunsu (five Indians of different ages) and one other elusive Indian, barely seen, who is on the move and hiding.

Winding through a thinned-out forest, the film crew suddenly stop at a clearing. Two Indians materialize at the end of the path, ghostly and silent (Fig. 7.14). The camera, aimed straight at the Kanoe couple, creates an intense effect of mirroring, reinforcing a fantasy of live, unmediated co-presence. Momentarily without a surrogate point of view, this real-time moment of frontal representation elicits anxiety: the alternating rush of projection and estrangement, the scene's uncertain epistemological yield, paradoxically confirms this first-contact with a never-before-seen Indian as an archival, *ethnographic* and *cinematic* trophy. More still, the value of this image is inseparable from its future circulation in a contested evidentiary and legal circuit involving land reclamation.

If the tactile exploration between the two groups, who hold hands and caress each other's skin and respective accessories, bolsters the thrill of this initial encounter, we should pause around this moment, which is cast as unproblematic, and rethink it in light of the reenactment mode (Fig. 7.15). We need to consider the indistinction between the reception of this image of the Canoe making contact and the performed, reenacted first contact, as seen in *Serras* when Carapiru is "first" spotted and approached by the ranchers. But we need also to briefly imagine the phenomenological experience for those involved in this encounter, especially as it is, in the case of Carapiru duplicated in acting.

[234]   *In Person*

Figure 7.14: Sighting of two noncontacted Kanoe Indians in Vincent Carelli's *Corumbiara* (2006).

Figure 7.15: The Kanoe make first contact (*Corumbiara*, 2006).

Eve Kosofsky Sedgwick notes how, more than any other sense, touch complicates "any dualistic understanding of agency and passivity."[40] The yearning to incarnate the relic, to carry an actual residue—psychic or material—of the past and simultaneously claim, *through performance*, the differing actualization of this past, defines the affective appeal of historical reenactment.[41] This gap, the syncopation between two potential functions or states, is intensified through physical encounters.

Given the freighted significance of the contact with isolated Indians and the anachronistic cast given to an uncontacted "primitive," the status of "touching the past" warrants special consideration. In order to explore the distinct qualities of the documentary method privileged by Carelli and better understand Tonacci's trajectory leading to *Serras* (he held *Corumbiara* in high esteem), the following explores the latter's approach to representing first contact in his early documentary engagement with Indians.

LEADING TO *SERRAS*

The production of *Serras da Desordem* followed a long hiatus after Tonacci's first experimental feature, *Bang Bang* (1970). In this film, the filmmaker had, as other Marginal cinema makers (Julio Bressane, Rogerio Sganzerla), turned to topics that defined an opposition to a consumerist corporate mentality: "the Indian, mythological religion, the orient and the primitive are . . . the only chance to make industrial society return to zero . . . but at the same time find an eros amidst the reigning comfort."[42] In 1977, he contacted the CTI (Center of Indigenous Work) with "Interpovos," a proposal to film intertribal video communication among indigenous communities in the Americas.[43] The only two available examples from the series, *Conversations in Maranhão* (*Conversas no Maranhão*, 1977–1980) and *The Araras* (made as a series of two episodes for TV Bandeirantes in 1980–1982, with a third episode finished later) coincide with the massive selling-off of lands around the TransAmazon Highway and the rampant capitalism that ignited attacks on nonprotected Indians such as Carapiru's group.

Tonacci believed that cultures that never touched non-Indians were fated to mutual interference in a "basic movement, almost embryonic, cellular of humanity."[44] He therefore became keen to access the Indians' perspective and to have them "participate in the creation of [their] own image."[45] While intrigued by technology as a potential means of liberation, the director wanted to determine its value for a people for whom "memory is not a form of power . . . who do not use the camera to fixate images, since their experience is that of impermanence."[46] Tonacci had imagined that *The Araras* would provide a chance "to meet the eye that does not know what an image is . . . show *what is this first interference*."[47] Although he only gained access to portable video equipment in 1982, its capacity for "instant" replay motivates the detour through the Indian's self-produced image toward an expansive sense of humanity. Film, he says, "is a form of going there to recognize oneself."[48]

Despite pioneering indigenous self-record (and influencing Carelli's "Video nas Aldeias," a long-running self-ethnography project), Tonacci's two indigenous films are most significant for contesting the boundaries of both Indian territories and documentary representativity.[49] *Conversations in Maranhão* records the Canela Apãniekrã–Timbira Orientais contesting the official demarcation of their land by governmental agency National Foundation of the Indian. They interrupt the topographers' work to "send their revindications to Brasilia" in the form of '*a letter, a film and a recording.*'"[50] *Conversations* does not try to make us comfortable with its object.[51] It simply and literally magnifies a message to the government: "the nation Canela Apãniekrã interpellates the Brazilian State," states the promotional material for the film.[52] At the end, the village elders ceremonially gather in a circle and pass the microphone to each other.

In a strategy later radicalized in *Serras*, *Conversations* calls attention to indigenous language, which separates the insiders from the outsiders who are addressed by the Canela in Portuguese. Each discussion concerns unfair land demarcation. The lengthy, redundant speeches are not valued for any new information they might contain but as an expressive imperative. The Canelas' broken Portuguese enacts all the complexities of territorial ownership and national affiliation: "T'is small, small"; "I want fix these lands; this bit, they want to pull forward, too small, it is much mistake, people mine not finding good, no vantage; how can hunt, how can walk; we want our place enlarge, the major, the lieutenant did much mistake, did not ask for us, now we are in 'agoniation,' I not know to write, not know read, but *know the line*." Because of their cropped, impoverished grammar, the words communicate both an imbalance of power and an agon. Contingently understood by those involved in the conversation, a line drawn on the sand by a Canela will be of no use in the acta of big corporate interests; instead, it forms part of the filmmaker's case: his brief is Tonacci/Canela's *letter, document, record*.

This "line" informs Tonacci's intuitive ethics of encounter, and his mise-en-scène translates into the "just" space around the Indians' communication. A zoom modulates our attention to a speaker sitting on a grassy patch, with only a silent old woman looking into the distance to hear him. He tells of a recent attack, reenacting the shouted warnings and exclamations of pain when members of the tribe are shot. Another Canela singles out each error in demarcation, naming with exactitude each patch of grass. As he points to what remains for us an indistinguishable natural continuum, the arbitrariness of the state's vision of land demarcation becomes concrete, and the Canela's rights literally memorialized.[53]

A scene from Carelli's *Corumbiara* offers further insights into the distinct stakes of Tonacci's approach. Carelli and the FUNAI discover traces of hidden utensils and excavated holes, poignant evidence of the presence of other noncontacted, cornered Indians. They explain that, for four years, they have been tracking the so-called Indian of the Hole, who refuses contact. In a sense, this refusal provides a counterpoint to the first encounter with the Canoe, who move toward the camera. Instead of an extended, real-time take, this scene condenses six hours into three minutes. Seen in a slow protruding and retreating movement, a proxy for the Indian, an arrow is detected solely through its effects, a ducking Indianist, or the blackened-out camera, a cut (Fig. 7.16). Then, fulfilling the raison d'etre of the first contact, its recording mission, the Indian's face is made visible through a zoom lens.

This sequence from *Corumbiara* highlights the interdependence between filming and event, the shared physicality of filmmaker and his subject. While this encounter aimed to produce a clear, unobstructed image of the Indian, Carelli's narrative uses the event to bolster the documentarian's ritual of publicly acknowledging an impasse. Borrowing for the camera the risk associated with the arrow, Carelli states the crew was attacked because of the camera; "ironically, it is only because [Carelli] can register the Indian's image that the Indian will legally exist." Clarice Alvarenga has cast doubt on Carelli's claim, noting that the radicality of a first encounter precedes that of a filmic encounter. The equivocation proper to any ethnographic first contact, the unconditional alterity separating the different worlds of the Indians and the whites, is mitigated through this equation of camera and arrow. Such literalism ignores thrust and direction: the camera draws near, whereas the arrow enforces distance, establishing, as Alvarenga notes, "an internal space of invisibility."[54]

Tonacci's second project, *The Araras* (1980–1982), a two-part made-for-TV series, documents the filmmaker's gradual move away from the immediacy of social activist films. Starting from a similar drive to record a first contact, *The Araras* is remarkable for ending with no images of the elusive Indians. (The third, unreleased episode starts with the Araras moving toward the camera.) The film hovers at this gradually moving borderline, while depicting extensive preparations for expeditions (mapping, reconnoitering) as well as heated arguments between the state, the Indian protection agencies, and agricultural and cattle conglomerate interests. At one point, the film interviews workers who pull down trees right by the Attraction Front Post;

Figure 7.16: Arrow as immediate risk in *Corumbiara* (2006).

it is obvious, then, why the FUNAI, charged with contacting and protecting Indian interests is, for them, indistinguishable from the farming and ranching industries that covet their land.[55]

The film enacts this con*front*ation, directly caught up in the complicated policies and interests of corporations and the state. After a surprise attack on the FUNAI agents, an arrow stuck on the front cabin is pointedly reframed (Fig. 7.17). As the Indianist relates the attack, Tonacci's camera roams; seemingly at random, it focuses on the arrows the speaker had collected and now holds in his hand. At the end of the film—after a faster sequence returning to the state's preparations for one more expedition and a scene detailing a spectacle of Indians dancing for an official event— Tonacci returns to the image of the arrow stuck at the front cabin, redesigning with his camera movement its length and its sharp point stuck in the cabin.

What interests me here is the distinction between two ways of presenting presentness, two ways of flagging the significance of the event and the filmmaker's position. The arrow shot in *Corumbiara* is attuned to the situation's volatility. It accentuates the transient interdependence between filming and scene, the co-presence of filmmaker and his subject (a fact underscored by Carelli's comments). Conversely, in *The Araras*, the arrow is presented after the fact and signified as a deeper rift.

In *The Araras* the arrow scenes announce what we are supposed to look at, and account for, underpinning the partnered nature of this communiqué shaped by the Indian's shooting and by Tonacci's shot. As in *Conversations in Maranhão*'s

Figure 7.17: The Arrow rephrased in Tonacci's *The Araras* (1981–1983).

"for-the-record" address, these subtle reframings and the not-so-subtle rephrasing of the arrow make for an emphatic proclamation.

Tonacci's decision to abandon the present tense as the heuristic ground for his exploration of isolated Indians' vision, and make *Serras* as fiction, is due in part to the bewildering effects of contact on the Araras, who were left in a state of limbo. Tonacci had imagined that *The Araras* would give him the chance "to meet the eye that does not know what an image is," but he soon noted that Indian eyes added nothing and their "unknown intentionality" remained opaque. Suddenly seeing the Indian as an object, he refused to exoticize him or exploit his pain.[56] Instead, *Serras* sets out to trouble the stability of the subject/object positions, rendering its object a fulcrum of indeterminacy.

THE ACTOR AS AGENT: CARAPIRU, PEREIO, AND TONACCI

In the "twenty-year-later" films we have been discussing, the figure of the filmmaker is calibrated to subjects' fugitive, transient, nature (isolated Indians, shifting militancy) or, alternatively, their full availability (as the Indian qua actor Carapiru). Interrogating this dynamic further, we may ask whose agency is at stake in an in-person reenactment film; where is the author (who is the actor) in the fiction Tonacci calls *Serras*? By exploring how the film, initially developed as a work of fiction, finds its character *and actor* in Carapiru, we start to grasp the filmmaker's self-figuration in this allegorical narrative. A key notion in this process of surrogation is that of *circumstantial* Indianness; and a key intertext is the actor Paulo Cesar Pereio.

When asked about the links between his Interpovos documentaries and *Serras*, Tonacci described *Conversas* as a service, an exchange, made with the Indians; *Serras*, on the other hand, was a fiction, a feature with actors (who were paid) and who were only *circumstantially indigenous*.[57] Fully assuming his authorship, he states that with *Serras*,"there is no conversation, the camera is in my [Tonacci's] hands, I am narrating the film. It is his story, but it is appropriation, with copyrights, all paid."[58]

To grasp how muting Carapiru's voice and agency contributes to the film's broader reflection on national history and loss, a slight intertextual detour proves helpful. In *Serras*, the charismatic actor Paulo Cesar Pereio appears briefly in the Great Brazil sequence (a montage of newsreels, fiction films, and documentaries from the mid-1970s on) as a man selling lumber, accompanied by a young Indian girl[59] (Fig. 7.18). Given the brevity of these shots, only those acquainted with Brazilian cinema can recognize clips of Pereio as Tião Brazil Grande, a trucker driving through unfinished portions of the Trans-Amazonian Highway in Jorge Bodansky and Orlando Senna's *Iracema: uma transa amazonica* (1974).[60]

Early in the decade, military propaganda had equated the country's natural riches with governmental economic policies, and the Trans-Amazonian Highway became a particularly powerful symbol of the country's so-called economic miracle (1967–1973). State cinema agencies commissioned bland historical epics; cinema novo directors working in the industry welcomed commissions featuring Indigenous tribes as pretexts for oblique critiques of the nation. By 1974, when *Iracema* was made, the tendency of political cinema was to stress the "tragic face of the national condition."[61]

Iracema, censored until 1980 and since then a calling card for ecological causes, has been hailed as a watershed experiment. It tells the story of an indigenous girl (played by Edna de Cassia) from the Amazon who migrates to the capital, Belém, and gradually becomes a destitute prostitute in a distant outpost by the jungle. Her fall from innocence—a clear allegory for the nation—is measured by her defiling encounters with Tião Grande.

The film's lowercase notation of a vanishing, transient reality is transgressive, an early example of documentary intervention in the real. Combining role-playing with verité interviews conducted with people he meets on the road, Pereio/Tião operates both as emissary of corporate greed (trafficking in lumber) and as the filmmakers' delegate and agent provocateur, a reporter investigating the impact of predatory practices at the frontier of the highway's construction. Lacking any empathy and with a charismatic cynicism, Pereio subjugates Iracema doubly—as a young illiterate girl but also as a nonprofessional actor from the Amazon.[62] The film shows police paid off by squatters, slave work, child prostitution, and illegal land occupation. Against the backdrop of huge forest fires, Pereio/Tião's provocative confrontations shake the paternalistic and totalizing perspective prevalent in social documentaries on workers and factory labor; at the same time, his hammy cynicism anarchically interacts with, and mimics, the chauvinist discourse on progress. With the simplest

Figure 7.18: Paulo Cesar Pereio in Bodanzky and Senna's *Iracema* (1978), quoted in *Serras da Desordem*.

mise-en-scène, an actor and a nonactress on an actual road under construction, the filmmakers transform Iracema's route into prostitution into a symbol of the nation. Unlike other Brazilian films on migration, "its unfinished road rejects any encrusted teleology," as Luis Carlos Oliveira Jr. has put it.[63]

Along similar lines, Andrea França observes: "Beyond the allegorical key of both *Iracema* and *Serras*—the relation between Iracema and the Amazon and the relation between the title of Tonacci's film and Brazil, [both films speak] of the experience of dislocation, of traces of what is about to disappear, of the tenuous limit between theatre and the world."[64] França's allusion to *Iracema* is facilitated by a common history of rampant exploitation in a region whose ecology was especially threatened during the 1970s. That said, the density of the Pereio subtext in *Serras* has mainly to do with the kind of acting and fluid agency privileged in Tonacci's aesthetics and ethics of encounter.

In *Serras*, Pereio's presence catalyzes awareness of two-way traffic between the fictive and the documental: "Even if he fulfills his function in the film for those who do not recognize him he is a live intervention as an actor within the story," stated Tonacci.[65] Given *Serras*'s unremitting heterogeneity, such a brief, self-reflexive ploy makes sense. More important, I track how Tonacci uses Pereio to ambiguate the register of identity, character, and agency in his films, a process that impacts directly on *Serras*'s casting.

For a start, Pereio is the protagonist of *Bang Bang*, Tonacci's first feature made in 1970. An underground gangster/ road movie, its "spare, anything-goes narrative," moves in spurts "with erring, autonomous characters."[66] Featuring vignettes with three characters who "act like stage props in a huge storehouse, human types awaiting rentals for a performance in a genre movie"[67] while Pereio, a disgruntled roamer, flees them. Episodic scenes succeed with no resolution—for instance, a flamenco dancer performs on a rooftop against São Paulo's cityscape, and inane pursuits are spectacularly filmed in an extended road sequence.

This seemingly unmotivated mobility has a special significance within Brazilian cinema. *Bang Bang* caps Ismail Xavier's definitive study on the subject, *Allegories of Underdevelopment*.[68] Challenging an established correspondence between the different stages of the dictatorship and the cultural political ethos, Xavier cautions against a homogeneous view of allegorical Brazilian cinema. Before the coup d'etat, cinema novo films such as Glauber Rocha's *Black God and White Devil* still projected some form of utopian telos, but especially after 1968, "migration, the central trope in Cinema Novo's visible outline of social progress" yielded to films of pure drift, devoid of "any horizon of salvation . . . of any national project."[69] Hence, throughout *Bang Bang*, this bizarre protagonist with "multiple personalities (feisty taxi passenger plus monkey-man plus idiotic hero = Paulo Cesar Pereio-personage)"[70] flows in and out of character. Director-like Pereio reduces his on-screen partner's dialogue to a script fine-tuning; he dons an apocalyptic "Planet of the Apes" mask singing a popular Lamartine Babo song while in the bathroom mirror an unmanned camera clinches this reflexive portrait. At the finale, Pereio assumes, in rapid and fluid succession, a series of stances for the camera, while his own laughter zigzags on screen as the film's optical band (Fig. 7.19).

Figure 7.19: Pereio in *Bang Bang* (Tonacci, 1970).

Against the backdrop of the disillusionment of the seventies, Pereio's role as agent of narrative disarray (in *Bang Bang*) and ideological provocation (in *Iracema*) manifests the attraction of the real/actor as a performative composite in experimental and activist projects alike. Committed to unpredictability, these borderline performances have a functional elasticity that opens room for suppler forms of cinematic critique. Pereio moves between various realities of the screen world, occupying both the margins and positions of authority.

This limbo attracts Tonacci, who has claimed both of his protagonists represent himself: "Andrea [Tonacci] is Pereio in *Bang Bang* and Carapiru here."[71] The filmmaker's identification with his unmoored characters across films made twenty-seven years apart demands attention. What does an underground film, whose matrix is the shoot-'em-up genre, have in common with a documentary reconstruction of a lost Indian's first contact and his return to his ethnic group, even as it too stretches genres (in this case, ethnographic and reportage films)? How is the author inscribed in these projects and how do the film and reenactment articulate these ambivalent, enmeshed agencies? What does Tonacci's statement mean when stating that the characters in *Serras* are "only circumstantially indigenous?"

Tonacci had stated that he conceived *Serras* when he was undergoing a difficult separation from his wife and sons and felt deep empathy with the Indian's loss of his entire family group. Carapiru's untranslated speech is a conduit for his own alienation: "I am inside a world that scares me, I do not know where it is going."[72] That the equation of Andrea Tonacci and Carapiru depends on Pereio is evident in the various casting and script stages of *Serras*. Initially, there was no plan to have Carapiru and Possuelo act their own lives. Tonacci thought Pereio "would play an actor accompanying the pre-production of a film on Carapiru to study the character of the Indian, get to know him and his village to learn how to interpret him. In the end he cannot take it takes off his clothes and goes into the forest."[73] Another early script was a fiction with Pereio playing a man lost for ten years in the city, who eventually meets his son. Later, he decided to do a classical documentary with narration. By 2002, *Serras* was no longer a typical documentary, but neither was it a scripted fiction. Finally, Tonacci settled on the script in which "Pereio is out and Carapiru is there."[74]

The multiple permutations and approximations between Indian and non-Indian, between characters and actors, signal Tonacci's reluctance to make the film from a safe outside. If his interest in Indians was based on a need to recognize himself, it is precisely this humanist pretext that stands in question here. Escaping the subject-object quandary, *Serras* poses the question of a problematic autonomy. Fiction and "circumstantial" Indianness become a way to question both the documentarian's mandate and its correlate, an objectified, Indigenous essence.

In an interview, Tonacci extends the randomness that governs his aesthetic sensibility to his characters' world view, likening Pereio and Carapiru to "little pinballs" moving at the push of a button: "One may believe one has autonomy, and indeed one may have had it once one was intertwined with a natural, more vital world, but in fact Carapiru is like the ball thrown here, expelled for ten years, thrown back to Brasilia then to the reservation. In *Bang Bang* one wants to know about Pereio, who is he? Who is he? As if giving him a name would solve the question of a man thrown around, adrift."[75] Consistent with Tonacci's conception of a threatened autonomy, both Pereio in *Bang Bang* and Carapiru in *Serras* seem teleguided.

Carapiru's dispossession is integral to his self-performance, resulting in a dislocated identity; his opacity perfectly exemplifies Tonacci's view of a corroded autonomy. As a corollary, Pereio and Carapiru's performative agency is stealthier. The performance retains a measure of unknowability for the viewer, a delay in categorical placement.[76] In order to show that Carapiru's story was not even his own—that it was "already part of a larger narrative—historicist, subjective, personal, ours"[77]— Tonacci systematically voids any prospect of an identitarian agenda. The film performs a balancing act, dispelling any hope of apprehending Carapiru as belonging to a distant, pastoral past, while simultaneously asserting his singularity and share in contemporary national time.

The plot, which features a non-Indian character and a white actor, sidesteps the register of ethnic reportage or testimony. In this sense, Pereio's relevance as potential mediator/actor in *Serras* cannot be underestimated. He is Tonacci's surrogate of choice and because of his indeterminacy as a performer, his constitutive incapacity to disappear into a character he can emerge as a mirror figure for Carapiru. In terms of performance, however, it is reenactment, the decalage from self to self, that truly clinches the film's deterritorialization. Next I discuss how Tonacci mobilizes a fissured identity to pose anew cinema's responsibility vis-à-vis a corroded national fabric.

A-FILIATION

In *Serras*, the criteria that grant coherence to a realist discourse—reference to generational cycles, inherited family traits, memory, and flashback—and the staples of a shared diegetic world or a coherent psychology are subjected to significant torques, either filtered by Carapiru's opaque subjectivity or diverted by the film's relentless recursivity. The film signposts forms of closure to Carapiru's saga—retracing his unexpected encounter with his son and his return to his reservation—while frustrating any possibility of grounding his identity. Throughout, Carapiru's passive "physical presence" remains a catalyst for questions of identity, his opacity the ricocheting surface for a continual veering and deorigination.

In its structural drive, the film continually reframes the Indian, redefining the non-Indian and "another humanity" in unforeseen ways. Here, reenactment's temporal indeterminacy does more than challenge ethnographic and documentary cinema's positivism and its predictable "findings." The film's drift across genres (fiction, documentary, and in-person reenactment) and the interplay between surrogates in casting and script (Tonacci, Pereio, and Carapiru) expand the potential of Carapiru's figure to articulate a stealthy, deterritorialized identity.

Tracking the representative field opened up by a "circumstantial indigenousness," we may ask whether reenactment accommodates any level of specificity or individuation and whether a generic Indian may not be a better catalyst to disperse surrounding stereotypes and national scripts for the Indian.

Through the question of kinship—which lineage Carapiru can claim, where he fits in, and what is the status of an isolated Indian in Brazil today—the film most clearly activates reenactment's "anachronic" quality, creating a speculative space to frame the question of Carapiru (and the Indian's) apartness.[78] To have the Indian become a piece of folklore relegated to the nation's past, or to try to define an authentic/or inauthentic Indian, bears directly on contested land rights. As we have seen, Carelli and Tonacci's indigenous films demonstrate as much. In *Corumbiara*, for instance, the Kanoes' appearance—modern shorts and plastic necklaces (as well as hats adapted from expeditionary models)—is mustered as proof of inauthenticity; the landowner's legal argument alleges that they were artificially planted by the FUNAI just to reclaim the land. Doubly dislocated, they fit neither the image of a "pure" Indian nor that of an integrated, acculturated Brazilian.

Conversely, a strict assertion of Indian authenticity may be equally detrimental politically, adversely supporting the intent to statistically count or genetically define who is Indian, thus closing, once and for all, their (legal and identitarian) case.[79] In 2006, when *Serras* was filmed, FUNAI's president Mercio Pereira Gomes stated that the judiciary system would set limits on demands for land, based on the growing number of *Caboclos* (descendants of Indians) claiming Indian ancestry. Anthropologist Eduardo Viveiros de Castro argued against state-sponsored identity policies by insisting that no third party can define what an Indian is since the Indian identity is tautegorical: "the Indian represents his own self," and this status "has nothing to do with representativeness or identity, but with singularity."[80]

Provocatively declaring that "In Brazil everyone is Indian except who isn't," Viveiros de Castro points precisely to the example of isolated Indians—"the only one[s] who can claim to be really an Indian"—to characterize the senselessness of contesting Indian identity claims in current Brazilian politics. He continues: "Let's go back to the famous categories whose intentions to define temporal stages for indigenous groups are evident: isolated, intermittent contact, permanent and integrated contact [Indians] . . . . In whose face does the gate close? An integrated Indian is no longer an Indian . . . . How frequent should the intermittency of contact be that turns an 'intermittent' into an 'integrated' [Indian]. About the 'isolated' [Indian] no one dares to say he is no longer an Indian, especially because *he is not even an Indian yet*. [Since] He *does not know* he is an Indian."[81]

Tonacci's representation of Carapiru's unawareness supports the performative identity and politics Viveiros de Castro advocates. Creating a silence buffer around Carapiru and introducing him as unaware of what or who an Indian is makes him impervious to insertion into previous, extrinsic hierarchies.

As the narrative retraces Carapiru's separation from, and return to, his group and traverses undefined presents, the film sets into play a constantly deferred scenario of integration. As soon as the prospect of anchoring Carapiru's identity emerges, it is retracted. For instance, when Carapiru encounters his son (who he thought had been killed in the massacre), the coincidence strikes us as momentous. Possuelo describes the meeting: when Txiramucú (in Portuguese, Benvindo Guajá) hears Carapiru's name, he whispers in broken Portuguese: "This is my father's name. . . . I recognizing his face. . . . He *is* my father" (Fig. 7.2). The fact that, against all odds, they are indeed father and son—that Benvindo also escaped death as a child—tinges their former separation with a tragic sense of fate. The real is *trou*matic, to use Lacan's pun. It points to an encounter almost missed, since another interpreter had been slated to come instead. A perfect melodramatic trope, this recognition scene seems to straighten out the displacements disfiguring both the reality of Carapiru's life and its textured retelling. Significantly, however, the film deflates this moment's uniqueness and, respecting the inscrutable tone of the actual original encounter, inscribes an extra level of mediation.[82] The ultimate proof, an old bullet wound that the son knows his father has on his back, is shown to us only at several removes, replayed from a 1988 TV reenactment of the original encounter.

Carapiru's body forms a screen for recurrent mediations and mis/recognitions. We see TV images of American linguists trying unsuccessfully to map Carapiru's language onto a Tupi-Guarani grid. The film also encourages our own fantasies of adoption (Carapiru's childlike passivity helps) sparked by encounters with benevolent white families: the Aires, who took Carapiru in when he first made contact in Santa Luzia, and Sidney Possuelo's family, with whom he stayed in Brasilia before rejoining the reservation. In fact, Tonacci counts on the failure of these projections to match expectations, thereby introducing a moment of doubt: "an opening to what is." Cinema, as he understands it, "passes through these gaps. What are the chances we have of seeing that the other does not correspond to our way of thinking or being?"[83]

Navigating a field of assumed genetic and tribal relatedness, Carapiru's encounters with various normative orders set his outsider position in relief. Social situations relegate him to a second exile, to an a-filiation. This a-filiation is due not only to the visible incongruity of his gestures and presence but also to his inability to socially integrate into a group (his own or another).

Typology becomes another significant foil for Carapiru. Off-the-cuff remarks about Carapiru reveal default assumptions on Indian alterity. Possuelo admits, for instance, that he initially assumed that Benvindo had recognized Carapiru not because he was his father but because they shared the same ethnicity. Having the well-meaning and experienced specialist on isolated Indians broach this possibility suggests the fragility of Carapiru's singularity as a person, raising the question whether an emphasis on ethnic origin and cultural identity betrays or reinforces Carapiru's singularity.

About the Guajá we learn nothing in the film: how they experience their immediate and ancient past, family relations, or their group/tribal identity vis-à-vis the other. The film brackets key ethnographic data. Loretta Cormier, anthropologist and Guajá scholar, points out that since the Guajá encountered in the 1970s had been shaped by an earlier colonial influence, the "acculturated-historical/traditional–a-historical schema [was] an invalid dichotomy for understanding their historical chronology."[84] As she notes, the Guajá maintained "an analogous distinction existing simultaneously in the earthly realm (where they undergo acculturation) and in a spiritual realm (where they remain 'traditional')." In these two realms, time "also took on different dimensions . . . but rather than a historical/ahistorical dichotomy it was best described as a time-quotidian/time-protean distinction. . . . In the sacred realm, the past is multiform and malleable, and Guajá agency in the multidimensional past is important in creating their cultural identity."[85] Moreover, the "iwá experience (the existence of past figures in celestial realm)" acts as a "cultural filter removing any non-Guajá elements from their past. As such they systematically decolonize their history."[86]

Cormier notes that "genealogies are neither meaningful nor appropriate for understanding the way the Guajá perceive kinship relations,"[87] an observation that significantly qualifies projections of closure incited by the dramatic father–son encounter between Carapiru and Benvindo. For one, they believe they have more than one "biological father," since "the amount of semen needed to create a child is more than one man alone would normally be able to produce"; this belief not only makes it difficult to consider their system patrilineal, but it weakens the role of paternity.[88] (Benvindo has therefore multiple fathers.) In consequence, they display genealogical and even structural amnesia, which "refers not so much to the ability to recall but to the social significance of recalling or not recalling ancestors in creating certain types of kinship systems."[89] Needless to say, this circumstance would also interfere with our notion of parenthood or filiation.

According to Guajá scholar Uirá Felipe Garcia, there is no transmission of names among the group.[90] Fathers choose names that express a relation that the child is assumed to have with an animal, plant, or object. This opens up an entirely different order of filiation. That in Guajá one calls oneself "awá," which roughly means "human," also proves significant since that is what Carapiru calls himself. Indeed, "humanity" has an expansive sense for Amazonian peoples. As Viveiros de Castro explains, the "original common condition of both humans and animals is not animality but, rather, humanity. Having been people, animals and other species continue to be people behind their everyday appearance ... the soul or spirit—the subjective aspect of being—is the universal, unconditioned given (since the souls of all non-humans are humanlike), while objective bodily nature takes on an a posteriori, particular, and conditioned quality."[91]

To foreground the Guajá and Carapiru's alternate understanding of kinship and parentage, a traditional documentary or fiction would harness, for instance, the fact that the Guajá consider monkeys—and, in particular, howler monkeys (literally, "former humans")[92]—to be kin and that, in this context, pet creation and adoption are complex forms of filiation.[93] And yet this and all the earlier considerations go unmentioned in *Serras* (even though the film exhibits monkeys as pets, as well as barbequed for food).

Rather than filling in information that would grant us the illusion of seeing the Guajá on their own terms, or becoming familiar with Carapiru, Tonacci keeps the two worlds situated in compromised and negotiated adjacency.

The film's representation of an *a-filiated* Carapiru, his presentation as an incongruous element, bears comparison to Nancy Bentley's discussion of W. E. B. Dubois's invention, in *The Fourth Dimension*, of a "counterfactual device to register an alternative space and time for those uncounted by those keeping time."[94] African American writers, she argues, could not rely "on universalist languages of intimate familism or genetic descent," because in so doing they "would erase the history most in need of representation—that of kinlessness,"[95] a state imposed on nonwhites by colonialist and slavery practices extracting "their bodies, labor, and reproductive capacities—from the sphere of the familial."[96] Rather than "bloodlines," Dubois's novel stages "the *coexistence* of a distinct zone of experience with a three dimensional world that remains oblivious to it."[97] For Bentley, these expressions of kinlessness generate a counterrealism, a "zone of imaginary history in which altered relations of power would necessarily produce alternate historical paths."[98]

Carapiru's diminished autonomy under state jurisdiction and the uprooting to which he and his tribe were subjected in the thirty years of story covered by the film parallel the effects of colonialist and slavery practices in reducing nonwhites to a state of bare genealogy, of kinlessness. Significantly, however, this is Tonacci's, and not Carapiru's, representation of a "distinct zone of experience" and "world obliviousness." The particulars of Indigenous, African, and African American loss under colonial exploitation cannot be minimized. All the same what interests me in this imperfect analogy is the awareness that an extra *discrepant* dimension is needed to express the irreducible singularity and contemporaneity of Carapiru.

Calling for an experimental ethnography to reconceive "the fate of the primitive in postmodernity," Catherine Russell has suggested that to counter the "regime of veracity of ethnographic film," one should invert "the salvage paradigm into a science fiction narrative. Science fiction's juxtaposition of modern and future push one to see dailiness and the now in tangled tension, as the film's last shot makes evident in its anachronic configuration. The film's strongest image for apposed times and regimes is a digitally inserted jet plane flying over Carapiru, who gestures to the sky while speaking in Guajá (for Figs. 7.20 and 7.21, see Color Insert, 2) The incomprehensibility of his address, the discrepancy of this tableau, caps the film's dual approach—to represent Carapiru's a-filiation but also to respect his opacity, his "other humanity." At the film's end, this tableau provokes a series of questions concerning the valence of agency and voice in a film constructed as an allegory on disrupted transmission, on eradication.

DISRUPTED TRANSMISSION

Describing Carapiru's decision to act in the film, the director revealed that even though he felt that his story concerned no one but himself, Carapiru passively complied with all the filmmaking demands, "if solely as physical presence."[99] This characterization of the social actor as an inert, available prop raises a core issue of reenactment: the degree to which the protagonist's consciousness counts in a filmed theater and what is transmitted once Carapiru's self-expression is occluded, and even blocked from viewers.

Serras challenges the social-activist film's most tempting conceit: the equation of self-performance with social agency. The film dissociates in-person reenactment from authentic relay, suspending Carapiru on multiple fronts: temporal, categorical, and expressive. We do not know present from past, real person from actor; nor do we know his thoughts. Carapiru is not introduced as an autonomous agent of his own history, and neither is cinema a transparent conduit for his voice (he is never translated) or eventual on-screen self-awareness.

At least three times the film shows Carapiru speaking at length, without a translation and strangely cut off from interlocutors. In one such scene the film frames him against Brasilia's modernist cityscape, to register the disquiet associated with this "zone of silence" surrounding him[100] (see Fig. 7.22 in Color Insert, 2). In another memorable scene, he leans by the windowsill of the Aires family's house and speaks at length in an unbroken flow of Guajá; meanwhile, the camera backtracks slowly, showing he is alone, magnifying the affect of this mimicry of transmission (for Figs. 7.23 and 7.24, see Color Insert, 2)). Even this representation of Carapiru's inaccessible self is instantly deoriginated: for it is followed by a black-and-white photo of a younger Carapiru in 1988 from the same angle, looking out the same window in a reverie (Fig. 7.24).

To further complicate this opacity, Carapiru is linked in the film to recurring images of a firebrand held by members of the group. When we first see him, we do not yet know this is Carapiru. A dreamlike sequence prefiguring the attack on the small group of Indians dissolves into images of a group of Indians on a trail choosing a place to camp. A sequence depicts convivial relationships among kin and animals. Every third shot displays a firebrand; finally, an older native woman hands it to a child (see Fig. 7.25 in Color Insert, 2). This detail gains significance later on when Wellington, one of the men in charge of the Indians' protection, tells a story that turns out to be a parable for the film as a whole. He mentions an occasion when, while helping a group of Indians escape their attackers, he asked one of them to put out his firebrand. He soon realized, however, that this act offended the man's sense of pride. In this parable, the firebrand—a simpler technology compared with a lighter or matches, but one that had been passed from generation to generation, perhaps for centuries—becomes a figure for multiple losses and ruptures.

In "The Artifices of Fire," Ismail Xavier takes stock of this metaphor, discussing how Tonacci articulates cinema's role in this break with tradition.[101] Carapiru is filmed as he leaves the reservation, taking off his shorts and donning his "Indian costume" to meet Tonacci's crew in the forest. The director then is shown indicating how he wants the scene framed, and he asks that the prop be given to Carapiru so he can, in the manner of process-oriented ethnographies, "start" a fire.

In the film's final shot, Carapiru sits on a tree stump addressing the camera in his longest untranslated speech. We hear a sound; the camera tilts up showing a digitally inserted B-52 bomber "above" Carapiru, who had just made one of his many sweeping gestures directed at the sky. Now wearing contemporary attire and posing casually, Carapiru stands eccentric to this "natural" forest. He addresses the camera as if waiting for the rest of the set to become, Méliès-like, animated. The disproportionately large, cartoonish jet plane (quite unlike any plane that is actually piloted over the Amazon) encourages allegorical interpretations. Xavier notes that the jet—an "even more inaccessible image of technology"[102] (than cinema or a lighter)—shadows Carapiru's communication; sparked by Carapiru's dreamy hand movement and cadenced speech, it refers to a twisted *iwá* (the heaven where the Awá-Guajá ancestors maintain their traditions).

Coming after a classic self-reflexive meeting between the filmmaker and his subject, this pictured simultaneity between the Indian and the plane is meant to dispel the pastoral image of the Indian. But the composite of realities and material inscriptions is too conspicuous to act ironically and it interpellates us further. A supplement, the jet sets off a set of unstable alignments of objecthood and personhood, the digital and the photographic, artifice and "nature."[103] The jet's conspicuous artifice hyperbolically rivals and qualifies that of Carapiru's presence in an unresolved oscillation (Fig. 7.20 and 7.21 in Color Insert, 2). They can be equated and flattened as objects in a scripted pose or Carapiru can be humanized in contrast to the virtual cutout seen as a stereotype of invasive power. This indistinction between artifice and nature is further compounded by the indeterminacy of in-person reenactment, split between the individual's putative autonomy in consciously redeeming an original experience and his passivity as actor. The ambiguity around the register of each element (straddling Carapiru, a named individual being, generic Indian, actor, prop) creates a steady exegetical pressure keyed to Carapiru's frontal address.

And indeed Carapiru's incomprehensible Guajá interpellates us on a humanist register. A node of obstructed communication and ostensive reflexivity, this opaque image of transmission guides this chapter's questioning of testimonial agency in literal reenactment. Can reenactment, like the firebrand, ritually animate any prospect of continuity with and transmission of the past, or should it be seen instead as a mere prop, lit up just for the film? Throughout, Carapiru's presence flickers with the promise of an uninterrupted link with an authentic past, and in-person reenactment prods us to rethink our wish for such mirages. In which ways does Carapiru's replay of his own past grant us any greater assurance of a connection with an original moment; what is transmitted across the structure of accepted substitutions that stands for identity in the guise of either theater or ritual? Once actualization is shown to be one more loop in a substitution chain, how does this tableau scene refocus, amid the film's relentless fracturing and duplication, the question of identity and testimonial voice?

Let's return to Xavier's insights on the artifices of fire. The jet plane articulates the film's running thematics of transmission and rupture, a narrative that has, at its other pole, the firebrand. Those feature insistently: at the very start of the film passing from hand to hand, commented on by the Indianists, and once again reperformed as a construct at the film's end when the filmmaker tells Carapiru to grab a firebrand and start a fire.

Firebrands evoke a history of forced flights as well as ancestral continuity. Nomadic groups such as the Awá Guajá carry their fire rather than making it. The recurring firebrands in the film underscore Carapiru's role as the carrier of another time into the present. Trying to make sense of the Guajá loss of horticultural ability and why—even in the intervals between continual displacement—they never regained the critical skill of fire-making, Cormier hypothesizes that the inability to establish new territory may have resulted from depopulation and weakness in relation to larger Amerindian groups; alternatively, the "loss of horticultural knowledge could have resulted from the enslavement of a generation of Guajá which might also explain their loss of indigenous fire-making technology."[104] This elided history and all of its ruptures are compressed in the film's final tableau and ritually memorialized in each reenacted gesture of passing the firebrand.

Performance, in Richard Schechner's felicitous phrase, is "restored" or "twice-behaved" behavior representing "constancy of transmission" across many generations.[105] In *Serras*, the firebrand and its manipulation gain temporal and referential amplitude through association with dailiness, the "staying power" of "a fleshy kind of 'document' of its own recurrence."[106] The film inserts this "twice-behaved" dailiness in a centuries-long sequence of recurring gestures, and projecting backward and forward it recalls, in cinema, a common humanity.

Analyzing Filipino supernatural and ghost films, Bliss Cua Lim sees the fantastic "as a mistranslation of heterogeneous temporalities into the universalizing code of homogeneous time." The "violence of this translation" evinces parallels between the temporal management of the fantastic and that of the Indian in ethnographic film, their common need to institute a separate realm of "the primitive." "Competing epistemological frameworks—secular and enchanted worlds—for example, have in the fantastic become objects of representation, *concretized in the mise en scène*."[107] The presence of immiscible, supernatural beings within the modern world configures a temporal critique of the linearity of modernity's forward-driven time.[108]

Carapiru displays a similar intractability, a resistance to meshing into a background. The analogy with the supernatural sheds light on the tableaus of temporal discrepancy that shape *Serras*. The film's intertextual recursivity—reverberations between images, phrases, or persons—summons other times, creating a fantasmatic force field. Historical indexes in search of the new now of their legibility—images from TV, newspapers, and expeditionary documents—swirl around Carapiru's figure. Carapiru's costumed nakedness, a presence despoiled of essence, closes the film on a suspended note. The multiple, material densities of reenactment and documentary images, archival and verité, still and moving, become the foil to a single, ongoing disturbance, Carapiru's categorically undefined reference and temporality. That Carapiru is actually here but strangely absent, that his presence is at odds with the present it refers to is both a result of Tonacci's targeted mobilization of reenactment's hesitant temporality and an allegory for an intractable alterity, for another humanity. Reenactment and the film's splintered surface frame "the Indian" as irrevocably uprooted, an agent of bereavement and kinlessness.

CONCLUSION
Senseless Mimesis

Serras da Desordem's flirtation with flashes of recognition and return instantiates the perverse attraction for questions of mimesis in contemporary reenactment cinema. In Claude Lanzmann's *Shoah* (1984), Rithy Panh's *S21: The Khmer Rouge Killing Machine* (2003), Abbas Kiarostami's *Close-Up* (1990), and Zhang Yuan's *Sons* (1996), reenactment regurgitates the real in the form of repetitions that are unconscious, accidental, and compulsive. These films' ascetic mise-en-scène—the duration and hyperacuity of their realism—magnifies the haunting of the real. A host of troubling duplications—uncanny coincidences, abiding prejudices, strange similarities, and hereditary vices—traverse the films and complicate our reading of these images role and rhetoric.

Another common trait of these works is the extreme degree to which the protagonist, relocated to the site of personal ordeals, experiences and communicates the shock of being out of place or dislocated. Throughout the book, I've tried to isolate the specific ways each film sharpens this disjointed quality and, at the same time, enhances the protagonist's dual and temporally split condition.

In particular, the status of the present impacts the critique the films perform. In my analysis of twenty-years-later films, I compared various modes of revisiting the past in structural terms, highlighting the distinction between the testimonial, the verbal construction that assumes a retrospective view; and reenactment, the mimetic restaging or psychic reliving of past events, as if events were unfolding in the present at hand.

In contrast, this conclusion turns to another way of nuancing and complicating the notion of the present in reenactment. How does the explicit retracing of singular, past events affect other forms of temporal continuity and repetition defined by longer time spans such as tradition and routine? Given that the reenactor is supposed to intervene—to correct a particular narrative or bring about a critical consciousness in his actualization of the past—what is his role once he mimetically enacts and therefore participates in existing scenarios of stasis (e.g., the cycle of addiction in *Sons* or the traumas of the Holocaust and Cambodian genocide)? In short, how does the transformative or didactic impetus of reenactment work within situations marked by immutability, permanence, or repetition? A seemingly minor sequence in *Serras*, which appears to offer unconstructed reality, opens a perspective on this convergence between realism, mimesis, and reenactment.

For the ten minutes leading up to the spectacular ending—where Carapiru takes off his clothes, dons his Indian costume, and heads to the forest to meet the filmmaker and address us under a digitally inserted jet—we witness what may be construed as Carapiru's current condition: an apparently inane sequence that maps a repetitive indigenous experience. This scene opens a clearing in the film's dense surface, suggesting that other, more straightforward modes of representation may be as effective in critically framing Carapiru's bare, temporally dislocated present.

Throughout the film, Tonacci has consistently rephrased Carapiru's dispossession by framing him alone or apart from others. But his isolation is most striking when he joins his group. During the shooting, he was suffering from tuberculosis—a disease historically responsible for the decimation of entire Indigenous groups, which still disproportionately affects them as underprivileged members of Brazilian society. He was kept during meals in a semiquarantine—eating and standing apart from the others in social occasions (Fig. 8.1). For the viewer, this implausible apartness—he is, after all, back with his group—completes a picture of a-filiation that is congruent: Carapiru's personal trajectory replicates a multicentury Indigenous trauma.

Awá Guajá scholar Uirá Felipe Garcia points out that although Carapiru's case was the most documented and emblematic, such cases were not rare in local and national news. Other Indians made even greater treks, and others died: "What they lived through in the last 40 years were various massacres leading to rampant flights" that "displayed an Awá form of reaction to invasion and territorial loss given they are foragers and hunters."[1] Garcia also mentions that Carapiru was different after his return in 1988. When he came to the forest of Pindaré, 500 kilometers away from

Figure 8.1: Carapiru stands apart in social gatherings.

his original area in the Porto Franco woods, he was treated as a "savage," a quasi-human—he did not hunt with the others and forgot how to sing. He stated he had "died a little," having spent many years of privation, solitude, and sadness (a notion fundamental to the conception of person for the Awá)[2] (Fig. 8.2).

Like much that informs the film, we never learn about Carapiru's disease or any immediate reason for his apartness. Cinematically rephrased to denote a more metaphysical isolation, these images are tangled with his past sadness: his illness signals from within his share in his group's endemic dislocation. This fusion of the actual and the historical, of Carapiru's biographical trajectory and that of other Indians and Indigenous groups, secretes a noxious, critical current that spreads throughout the scene.

At the Caru reservation, minimal metonymical reframings depict a reduced horizon of expectation. We watch the Guajás' convivial relation with animals as well as their preparation of monkeys to barbeque (see Fig. 8.3 in Color Insert, 2; Fig. 8.4). A pile of monkey bodies appears in a long individual take, and then again in a closer shot (see Fig. 8.5 in Color Insert, 2; Fig. 8.6). Gradually a series of shots of young children playing with sharp knives, pointy tools, sticks, and broken mirrors and aiming their bows in mock battle accumulate an undercurrent of violence and misery, and we vaguely wish this reality were an effect of stylization.[3]

Disquieting as they are, these images correspond to the realities at the Caru and Tiracambú reservations. Triggered by the film's pattern of recurrences, we intuitively compare these Indians at the reservation with the same social actors in edenic scenes at the start of the film (Fig. 8.7) with animals, humans, and children equally cared for and coddled,[4] and we barely recognize them. Instead of flowing pans that evoke a pastoral life by linking Indians of all ages and animals, this sequence is built of dry cuts conveying a world of little variation and suffocating stasis. Images of senseless mimesis—recurrent images of poorly dressed children in oversized hand-me-down T-shirts emblazoned with corporate logos, repeatedly hitting and learning to hit, defending food and possessions—constitute a definite intervention both for its

Figure 8.2: Carapiru isolated.

Figure 8.4: Playing, cooking monkeys.

Figure 8.6: Rephrased barbequed monkeys.

Figure 8.7: Early Edenic Awá Guajá life.

theme and for its form: this peculiar focus on cyclical return is enveloped in a bland realism, a homogeneous texture that cuts into the film's hybrid surface (Figs. 8.9 and 8.11: see Figs. 8.8 and 8.10 in Color Insert, 2).

The reservation sequence proves shocking because it abandons the earlier textual layering for a stark presentation devoid of any obvious aesthetic gesture, ethnographic explanation, or redemptive rhetoric. Instead of inviting an exegesis of the film's allusions and correspondences—instead of pushing us to read Carapiru's disaffiliation in relation to the national fabric—this sequence of images confronts us with bare reality. And if we grant even a measure of authenticity to the early pastoral portrayal of Indian nomadic life, we do so because we forget the degree to which the latter sequence, presenting a degraded reality through a seeming transparent naturalism, is just as constructed.

Serras's stress on artifices of transmission (e.g., the firebrand and drawing attention to modes of cinematic mediation) has been read in contrast to Robert Flaherty's

Figure 8.9: Kid with pointy object.

Figure 8.11: Kid with bow and arrow.

CONCLUSION [257]

essentialism, his reconstitution of mythical daily life among the Inuit or Aran islanders' immutable traditions. However, Jean Rouch's and Luis Bunuel's ethnographic surrealism sheds fuller light on the underside of Tonacci's meditation on the harsh contemporary realities faced by the Guajá.

Jean-André Fieschi suggests that the fantastical clarity of Rouch's *Mad Masters* provokes disturbance because of the "illusion of an absence of any manipulation in the filmed material":

> Bound up with the "elsewhere" made manifest, the quizzical otherness, so close and yet so far, there is the strangeness of what we see, defined as such solely by cultural differences; and there is the narrative method, unimpeachable in its logical sequence, introducing the fantastic along with an unfamiliar causality. Enhancing these powers, as is right and proper, there is every semblance of innocence, of simply stated fact: *you see how it is*."[5]

In Rouch's film, the voice-over commentary and scenes of Gold Coast laborers in their daily work in construction sites, which abruptly interrupt the Hauka possession rituals, constitute examples of a "surrealist moment in ethnography." Hereby, "the possibility of comparison exists in unmediated tension with sheer incongruity": a surreal moment otherwise, as James Clifford contends, "smoothed over in the process of ethnographic comprehension."[6] Fieschi suggests that to make sure that incongruity will not be explained away, a key strategy is paradoxically to hyperbolize the "inanity of any exotic vision of the other."[7] To achieve critical efficacy, cinema needs to match the inanity of its pro-filmic object, "declaring and making visible its impotence,"[8] and, more still, "to preclude compassion, an aesthetically and politically anachronistic response, in order to achieve any form of effectiveness."[9] This prescription of "cinema's cold technical eye" corresponds to Tonacci's unsentimental depiction of the Guajás' present life: "by showing it frontally and from the outside, the film refuses to see more than anachronism and inadequacy."[10]

Indirectly illuminating Tonacci's radical starkness, Charles Tesson suggests how Bunuel presents us with a world of uncertain links and difficult ruptures by means of tautology: "there, a human being is a human being, an animal an animal, and a thing a thing" fast becomes "there where the human being is less a human being than the improbable residue of what is neither an animal nor a thing." The resulting astonishment, a natural tendency of Bunuel and Tonacci's cinema, poses the question: "in which way the human being is not also an animal and a thing?"[11]

Framed standing by a door, Carapiru kicks a dog passing by, initiating another roaming movement of the camera that stops, once again, to register minor territorial disputes (Figs. 8.12 and 8.13). A pet animal, a coati tied to a pole, is shown twice circling around and around (see Fig. 8.14, in Color Insert, 2; Fig. 8.15). This miniature captivity exposes a disturbing limbo, a banal yet unplaced sign of alterity. As we watch, we enter a circuit of shared (creaturely) existence, linked to the Guajá as they are to the monkeys they believe to be their kin. Tonacci implicates us in a shared sense of loss and in "another humanity." The phrase—"the Indian is another humanity"—is mentioned twice in the film, once with the negative connotation

Figure 8.12: Carapiru apart.

Figure 8.13: Carapiru kicks dog who guides the camera's roaming movement.

Figure 8.15: Rephrased circling in close-up.

of those intent on destroying indigenous groups, the second positive. A senseless mimesis underscores this stark scene and the fluid process of becoming to which Tonacci subjects the notion of "another humanity." Much like "Giorgio Agamben's concept of 'whatever being,' such existence is not 'being, it does not matter which,' but rather 'being such that it always matters.'"[12] After Tonacci's signature rephrasing shots, we come to the film's last tableau shot and are able to understand Carapiru's awkward, bare presence as essential for a critical historiography and the "accounting" of national histories of exclusion.

Relying on recursive accumulation, bringing Carapiru (and other images) back through one more representational loop, one more cycle of dispossession, Tonacci transforms Carapiru's apparition; thereby, he reiterates the propensity of contemporary reenactment to display present and past blurred in an indistinct stasis. Shot in a "straight documentary" manner, deliberately presented from an outsider's perspective, the scattered signs of a different culture and way of life are shown in the form of a ruin. This corroded fabric, presented through a pseudo-direct, objective detachment, clinches Tonacci's allegorical vision.

One may ask why, at this stable point in the narrative, when Carapiru has been relocated, once again Tonacci deploys this cold documentary eye, this programmatic indifference? How does this distanced look, this strategic reframing delineate an approach different than that of denunciation films?[13] Just as important, what is the relationship between this scene's sticky present to the rest of the film's regimen of duplication and temporal and categorical uncertainty? How, in short, is reenactment's critical edge effective when the gap between present and past seems inexistent—when the protagonist's agency serves to reiterate a former order instead of commenting on it?

Alice Rayner defines, with Aristotle, an act as intentional. It is aligned with narrative and subject to retrospective views and repeatability. The voluntary aspect of an act "accounts for the common correlation between drama and the law in which human acts are tested or put on trial to judge the relations between agents, deeds and social norms."[14] As she pointedly observes: "the mimetic is not something inherent in the act ... nor is it simply a mirror of some absent or other reality; it is instead the place at which the perception of acts adheres to prior assumptions about the relation of agents and acts and the proportions between voluntary and involuntary."[15]

This notion of mimesis as an "ethical accounting [and] not simply a reflection or imitation" lies at the core of reenactment's pedagogic and self-revising mechanism. If acts engage practical, juridical, and signifying constructs, then filmed reenactment corresponds to a public reframing of an act's significance so that "the perception of acts," in the present, may adhere to "prior assumptions about the agents and acts."

The possibility of making representation usable, or exemplary, is lacking in films that starkly reiterate unredeemable realities. In part, this has to do with the different aesthetic regimen of the films analyzed here, which pushes the viewers to the point of discomfort, a sense of co-presence. Thus, the reservation sequence in *Serras* radically questions the ethnographic construct of allochrony—the notion that the Indian exists in another time. Magnifying the co-presence between that reality and the viewer, this deceptively neutral representation proves puzzling. It solicits, at the deepest level, decoding of both cinematic and social mimesis. Are we witnessing actual processes of learning with children's play as the motor of a transmissible order, or instead the filmmaker's emphasis? The insistent representation of children holding sharp objects folds risk, danger, and aggression into a routine theater, and the film leaves it to us to disentangle one from the other.

Discussing the mimetic imperative—the notion that imitation corresponds to "the natural order of things"— Christopher Prendergast has observed that the "logical matrix of mimesis is formed from the combination and confusion of three (heterogeneous) kinds of sentences: a descriptive (how things are), a prescriptive (you must accept things as they are), and a normative 'there is an authority validating the previous sentences.'"[16] The disentanglement of these three orders drives the various modernist impulses to defamiliarize and expose the arbitrariness of realist and naturalist constructs.

Serras's "you see how it is" sequence "gather(s) in itself notions of norm and transgression, conservation and subversion"; this juxtaposition, according to Prendergast, dramatizes the productive ambiguities of two paradigms of mimesis—Barthes's *nausea* and Plato's *poison*. For Plato, mimesis occasions a poisonous break in the proper classification and division of images, causing an out-of-control proliferation. Barthes, in turn, construes mimesis as "an essentially conservative and conserving force—confirming order with a nauseously bland security."[17] The sequence at the reservation in *Serras* proves disturbing inasmuch as it secretes the same temporal referential uncertainty (reenactment's poison) that pervades each filmed and repeated gesture and echoed image.

Given the instrumental purpose of reenactment films—their ritual, juridical, memorial, or pedagogic functions—the import of an unredemptive reenactment is difficult to define. Reenactment in Tonacci, Lanzmann, Panh, and Zhang Yuan is far from a neutral strategy. If nothing else, I hope to have traced, through this admittedly limited selection of cinematic works, an alternate form of realist representation, an aesthetics of pressured co-presence, with the power to spark continued questioning.

Figure 7.1: TV coverage on finding Carapiru, an isolated Awá Guajá Indian (*Serras da Desordem*, Tonacci, 2006).

Figures 7.3: A few images from the "Great Brazil" montage sequence (*Serras da Desordem*, Tonacci, 2006). a) Newsreel promoting "Great Brazil" during the dictatorship. b) *Iracema* (Bodanzky and Senna, 1976) quoted in "Great Brazil" sequence. c) Transamazonica Highway. d) Funeral of Tancredo Neves. e) Raoni (Indian movement chief) visits Brazilian sites..

Figure 7.5: Identifying himself in photo from 1988: Where is Carapiru? (*Serras da Desordem*, Tonacci, 2006).

Figure 7.8: b) Ms. Aires cooking. c) Carapiru enter the kitchen. d) Robelia enters the kitchen. e) Robelia and Carapiru cross in black and white. f) Kitchen routine.

Figure 7.20: Carapiru's last "communication" (Tonacci, *Serras da Desordem*, 2006).

Figure 7.21: Digitally inserted plane in Carapiru's last tableau (Tonacci, *Serras da Desordem*, 2006).

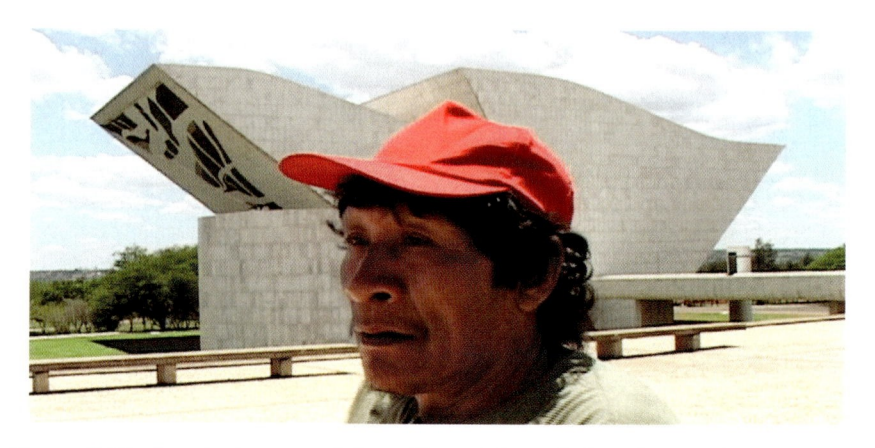

Figure 7.22: Carapiru in a zone of silence (Tonacci, *Serras da Desordem*, 2006).

Figure 7.23: Carapiru talks untranslated (Tonacci, *Serras da Desordem*, 2006).

Figure 7.24: Carapiru by window in 1988 photo (Tonacci, *Serras da Desordem*, 2006).

Figure 7.25: Firebrand passed on from woman to child (Tonacci, *Serras da Desordem*, 2006).

Figure 8.3: Monkeys as pets.

Figure 8.5: Barbequed monkeys.

Figure 8.8: Kids at the reservation.

Figure 8.10: Kids at reservation.

Figure 8.14: Pet coati circling.

SELECT BIBLIOGRAPHY

Note: To avoid redundancy, this bibliography is restricted to writing relevant to the notion of reenactment, its temporal and categorical dislocations, and its relations to trauma, theatricality, and evidence. Valuable references on insights by filmmakers as well as secondary sources on the particular histories surrounding these makers' concerns—neorealism, cinema verité, psychodrama, post-Holocaust cinema, and so on—are available in the endnotes.

Agamben, Giorgio. *Potentialities: Collected Essays in Philosophy*. Edited and translated by D. Heller-Roazen. Stanford, CA: Stanford University Press, 1999.

Agnew, Vanessa. "History's Affective Turn: Historical Reenactment and Its Work in the Present." *Rethinking History: the Journal of Theory an Practice* Volume 11, Issue 3 Reenactment (2007): 299–312.

Agnew, Vanessa. "Introduction: What Is Reenactment?" *Criticism* 46, no. 3 (2004): 327–339.

Amengual, Bathelemy. *"Théatre et Théatre Filmé."* In *Cinéma et Théatralité*, edited by Christine Hamon-Sirejols, Jacques Gerstenkorn, and André Gardies, 30–42. Cahiers du Gritec, Institut de la Communication et des Arts de la Representation, Université Lumière-Lyon 2. Lyon: Aleás, 1994.

Antonioni, Michelangelo. "The Event and the Image," *"Attempted Suicide*: Suicides in the City." In *The Architecture of Vision: Writings and Interviews on Cinema*, edited by Carlo di Carlo and Giorgio Tinazzi, 51–53, 71–73. New York: Marsilio Publishers, 1996.

Antonioni, Michelangelo. "Prima Stesura dell'Episodio 'Ragioni Sentimentali' [Tentato suicidi]." In *Il Primo Antonioni,* edited by Carlo di Carlo, 247–274. Bologna: Capelli, 1973.

Arns, Inke. "History Will Repeat Itself." In *Strategies of Re-enactment in Contemporary (Media) Art and Performance*, edited by Inke Arns and Gaby Horn for Hartware MedienKunstVerein and KW Institute for Contemporary Art, 37–63. Frankfurt am Main: Revolver—Archiv für 1 aktuelle Kunst, 2007.

Baer, Ulrich. "To Give Memory a Place: Holocaust Photography and the Landscape Tradition." *Representations* 69 (Winter 2000): 38–62.

Bal, Mieke, Jonathan Crewe, and Leo Spitzer (Eds.). *Acts of Memory: Cultural Recall in the Present*. Hanover, NH: Dartmouth, 1999.

Bangma, Anke, Steve Rushton, and Florian Wust (Eds.). *Experience, Memory, Reenactment*. Revolver and Piet Zwart Institute, 2005.

Bazin, André. "Death Every Afternoon." In *Rites of Realism: Essays on Corporeal Cinema*, translated by Mark Cohen and edited by Ivone Margulies, 27–31. Durham, NC: Duke University Press, 2003.

Bazin, André. *"Information or Necrophagy."* In *Andre Bazin's New Media*, edited and translated by Dudley Andrew, 124–125. Los Angeles: California University Press, 2014.

Bazin, André. *Toro: une révolution dans le realism*; "Information ou nécrophagie." *Radio, Cinéma, Télévision* 408 (November 10, 1957).
Bazin, André. "Après-midi de Taureaux: 90 minutes de verité." *Parisien liberé* 3780 (November 5, 1956).
Bazin, André. "L'amour à la ville." *Observateur* 354 (February 22, 1957).
Bazin, André. "Le Neorealisme se Retourne." *Cahiers du Cinéma* 69 (March 1957).
Beckman (Redrobe), Karen. *The Vanishing Woman: Magic, Film and Feminism*. Durham, NC: Duke University Press, 2003.
Beckman (Redrobe), Karen. "Gender, Power, and Pedagogy in Coco Fusco's *Bare Life Study #1* (2005), *A Room of One's Own*, and *Operation Atropos* (2006)." *Framework* 50, no. 1 (2007): 125–138.
Benamou, Catherine L. *It's All True: Orson Welles's Pan-American Odyssey*. Los Angeles: University of California Press, 2007.
Bentley, Nancy. "The Fourth Dimension: *Kinlessness* and African American Narrative." *Critical Inquiry* 35 (2009): 270–292.
Blanchot, Maurice, and Jacques Derrida. *The Instant of My Death /Demeure: Fiction and Testimony*. Stanford, CA: Stanford University Press, 2000.
Boyle, Deirdre. "Shattering Silence: Traumatic Memory and Reenactment in Rithy Panh's S-21: The Khmer Rouge Killing Machine. *Framework: The Journal of Cinema and Media* 50, no. 1/2 (2009): 95–106.
Brooks, Jodi. "Performing Aging/Performance Crisis (for Norma Desmond, Baby Jane, Margo Channing, Sister George and Myrtle)." *Senses of Cinema* 16 (September 2001). sensesofcinema.com/2001/john-cassavetes/cassavetes_aging
Burns, Elizabeth. *Theatricality: A Study of Convention in the Theatre and in Social Life*. New York: Harper, 1972.
Caruth, Cathy. *Trauma: Explorations in Memory*. Baltimore: Johns Hopkins University Press, 1995.
Charraga Pineda, Tarcisio Gustavo, and Elvira Vera Soriano. *Cesare Zavattini en México. Un documento para la historia del cine nacional*. Tesis de licenciatura. ENEP-Acatlán, UNAM, 1985.
Chisholm, Ann. "Missing Persons and Bodies of Evidence." *Camera Obscura* 43, no. 15 (2000): 123–161.
Commoli, Jean Louis. "A Historical Fiction: A Body Too Much." *Screen* 19, no. 2 (1978): 41–54.
Coutu, Walter. "Role-playing and Role-taking, a Clarification."*American Sociological Review* 16, no. 2 (April 1951): 180–187.
Cua Lim, Bliss. *Translating Time: Cinema, the Fantastic and Temporal Critique*. Durham, NC: Duke University Press, 2009.
Derrida, Jacques. *Specters of Marx: The State of the Debt, the Work of Mourning and the New International*. Translated by Peggy Kamuf. New York, NY: Routledge, 1994.
Doane, Mary Ann. *The Emergence of Cinematic Time: Modernity, Contingency, the Archive*. Cambridge, MA: Harvard University Press, 2002.
Epstein, Jean. "Nos Lions." In *Écrits sur le Cinéma* 1 (1921–1947), 193–196. Paris: Seghers, 1974.
Erickson, Ruth. "The Real Movie: Reenactment, Spectacle, and Recovery in Pierre Huyghe's *The Third Memory*." *Framework* 50, no. 1 (2009): 107–124.
Felman, Shoshana. *The Juridical Unconscious: Trials and Traumas in the Twentieth Century*. Cambridge, MA: Harvard University Press, 2002.
Felman, Shoshana, and Dori Laub. *Testimony: Crises of Witnessing in Literature, Psychoanalysis and History*. New York: Routledge, 1992.
Fernández, Miguel Anxo. *Las Imágenes de Carlos Velo*. Promociones Culturais Galegas, S.A. Edicion gallega, 2002.
Fortichiari, Valentina, and Mino Argentieri (Eds.). *Cesare Zavattini: Opere, Diario cinematografico; Neorealismo ecc*. Preface by Gian Piero Brunetta. Milano: Classici Bompiani, 2002.

Freeman, Elizabeth. *Time Binds: Queer Temporalities, Queer Histories*. Durham, NC: Duke University Press, 2010.
Fuhs, Kristin. "Re-imagining the Nonfiction Criminal Narrative: Documentary Reenactment as Political Agency." *Concentric: Literary and Cultural Studies* 38, no. 1 (March 2012): 51–78.
Fuhs, Kristin. "The Whole Truth and Nothing but the Truth: Documentary Film and the Socio-politics of Justice." Ph.D. dissertation, USC, 2011.
Gelley, Alexander (Ed.). *Unruly Examples: On the Rhetoric of Exemplarity*. Stanford, CA: Stanford University Press, 1995.
Goffman, Erving. *Frame Analysis: An Essay on the Organization of Experience*. Boston: Northeastern University Press, 1986.
Grayson, Richard. "History Will Repeat Itself: Strategies of Reenactment in Contemporary Media Art and Performance." *Art Monthly* 313 (February 2008). https://www.questia.com/magazine/1G1-174599895/history-will-repeat-itself-strategies-of-re-enactment
Griffiths, Alison. "'Shivers Down Your Spine': Panoramas and the Origins of the Cinematic Reenactment." *Screen* 44, no. 1 (March 2003): 1–37.
Hampton, Timothy. *Writing from History: The Rhetoric of Exemplarity in Renaissance Literature*. Ithaca, NY: Cornell University Press, 1990.
Hansen, Miriam B. *Babel and Babylon: Spectatorship in American Silent Film*. Cambridge, MA: Harvard University Press, 1991.
Hirsch, Joshua. *Afterimage: Film Trauma and the Holocaust*. Philadelphia: Temple University Press, 2004.
Horsman, Yasco. *Theaters of Justice: Judging, Staging, and Working Through in Arendt, Brecht and Delbo*. Stanford, CA: Stanford University Press, 2011.
Ivens, Joris. *The Camera and I*. New York: International Publishers, 1969.
Ivens, Joris. "Collaboration in Documentary." *Films* 1, no. 2 (Spring 1940): 30–42.
Jasen, Sylvie. "Reenactment as Event in Contemporary Cinema." PhD dissertation, Carleton University, Ottawa, 2011.
Kahana, Jonathan. "What Now? Presenting Reenactment." Dossier on Documentary Teenactment. *Framework* 50, nos. 1 and 2 (Spring and Fall 2009): 46–60.
Kitamura, Katie. "'Recreating Chaos': Jeremy Deller's *The Battle of Orgraeve*." In *Historical Reenactment: From Realism to the Affective Turn*, edited by Ian McCalman and Paul Pickering, 39–49. New York: Palgrave McMillan, 2010.
Lambert-Beatty, Carrie. "Make Believe: Parafiction and Plausibility." *October* 129 (2009): 51–84.
Loridan-Ivens, Marceline. *Ma vie balagan*. Paris: Robert Laffont, 2008.
Lutticken, Sven. Ed. *Life, Once More: Forms of Reenactment in Contemporary Art*. Rotterdam: Witte de With Institute, 2005.
Lyons, John. *Exemplum: The Rhetoric of Example in Early Modern France and Italy*. Princeton, NJ: Princeton University Press, 1989.
Margulies, Ivone. "Actor/Real: Re-enactuación y transmisión en S21 y Serras da Desordem." In *La Escena y La Pantala: Cine Contemporaneo Y el Retorno de lo Real*, 138–158. Buenos Aires: Ediciones Colihue S.R.L., 2013.
Margulies, Ivone. "Bazin's Exquisite Corpses." In *Opening Bazin: Postwar Film Theory and Its Afterlife*, edited by Dudley Andrew and Hervé Laurencin, 186–199. New York: Oxford University Press, 2011.
Margulies, Ivone. "Bodies Too Much" and "Exemplary Bodies: Reenactment in Loves in the City, Sons and Close Up." In *Rites of Realism: Essays on Corporeal Cinema*, 1–23 and 217–244. Durham, NC: Duke University Press, 2003.
Margulies, Ivone. "Re-enactment and A-filiation in Andrea Tonacci's Serras da Desordem." *Cinephile* 7, no. 2 (Winter 2011): 5–14.
Margulies, Ivone. "A Sort of Psychodrama: Cinema Verité and France's Self-Analysis." *South Central Review* 33, no. 1 (Summer 2016): 68–79.
McCalman, Ian, and Paul Pickering (Eds.). *Historical Reenactment: From Realism to the Affective Turn*. New York: Palgrave McMillan, 2010.

Mnookin, Jennifer. "Reproducing a Trial: Evidence and Its Assessment in *Paradise Lost*." In *Law on Screen*, edited by Austin Sarat, Lawrence Douglas, and Martha Merril Umphrey, 153–200. Stanford, CA: Stanford University Press, 2005.

Mnookin, Jennifer, and Nancy West. "Theaters of Proof: Visual Evidence and the Law in *Call Northside 777*." *Yale Journal of Law and the Humanities* 13, no. 2 (2001). http://digitalcommons.law.yale.edu/yjlh/vol13/iss2/1

Moreno, J. L."Psychodrama and Therapeutic Motion Pictures." *Sociometry* 7, no. 2 (May 1, 1944): 238, doi:10.2307/2785414

Moreno, J. L."The Concept of Sociodrama: A New Approach to the Problem of Intercultural Relations." *Sociometry* 6, no. 4 (November 1943).

Nagel, Alexander, and Christopher Wood. *Anachronic Renaissance*. Cambridge, MA: MIT Press, 2010.

Naremore, James. *Acting in Cinema*. Los Angeles: University of California Press, 1988.

Nichols, Bill. "Documentary Re-enactments: A Paradoxical Temporality That Is Not One." In *Given World and Time: Temporalities in Context*, edited by Tyrus Miller, 171-192. New York: Central European University Press, 2008.

Pavsek, Christopher. "The Black Holes of History: Raoul Peck's Two Lumumbas." *Framework* 50, no. 1 (2007): 82–94.

Raengo, Alessandra. "A Necessary Signifier: The Adaptation of Robinson's Body-Image in 'The Jackie Robinson Story.'" *Adaptation* 1, no. 2. doi: 10.1093/adaptation/apn019 http://adaptation.oxfordjournals.org/

Rayner, Alice. *To Act, to Do, to Perform: Drama and the Phenomenology of Acting*. Ann Arbor: University of Michigan Press, 1994.

Rothberg, Michael. *Traumatic Realism and the Demands of Holocaust Representation*. Minneapolis: University of Minnesota Press, 2000.

Rothberg, Michael. *Multidirectional Memory: Remembering the Holocaust in the Age of Decolonization*. Stanford, CA: Stanford University Press, 2009.

Rothberg, Michael. "The Work of Testimony in the Age of Decolonization: *Chronicle of a Summer*, Cinema Verité, and the Emergence of the Holocaust Survivor." *PMLA* 119, no. 5 (2004): 1231–1246.

Russell, Catherine. *Experimental Ethnography: The Work on Film in the Age of Video*. Durham, NC: Duke University Press, 1999.

Santos Aquino, Rowena. "Necessary F(r)ictions: Reenactment, Embodied Historiography and Testimony." PhD Dissertation, UCLA, 2011.

Schechner, Richard. *Between Theater and Anthropology*. Philadelphia: University of Pennsylvania Press, 1985.

Schneider, Rebecca. *Performing Remains: Art and War in Times of Theatrical Reenactment*. New York: Routledge, 2011.

Schwartz, Hillel. *The Culture of Copy: Striking Likenesss, Unreasonable Facsimiles*. Cambridge, MA: MIT Press, 1998.

Schwartz, Louis George, *Mechanical Witness: A History of Motion Picture Evidence in U.S. Courts*. New York: Oxford University Press, 2009.

Shimakawa, Karen. "The Things We Share: Ethnic Performativity and 'Whatever Being.'" *Journal of Speculative Philosophy* 18, no. 2 (2004): 149–160.

Skoller, Jeffrey. *Shadows, Specters and Shards: Making History in Avant Garde Film*. Minneapolis: University of Minnesota Press, 2005.

Sobchak, Vivian. "Being on the Screen: A Phenomenology of Cinematic Flesh or the Actor's Four Bodies." In *Acting and Performance in Moving Image Culture: Bodies, Screens, Renderings*, edited by Jorg Sternagel, Deborah Levitt, and Dieter Mersch, 429–443. New Brunswick, NJ: Transaction Publishers, 2012.

Starobinski, Jean. *The Style of Autobiography*. In *Autobiography: Essays Theoretical and Critical*, edited by James Olney, 73–83. Princeton, NJ: Princeton University Press, 1980.

Steimatsky, Noa. *Italian Locations: Reinhabiting the Past in Postwar Cinema*. Minneapolis: University of Minnesota Press, 2008.

Straw, Will. "Scales of Presence: Bess Flowers and The Hollywood Extra." *Screen* 52, no. 1 (Spring 2011).
Streible, Dan. *Fight Pictures: A History of Boxing and Early Cinema.* Los Angeles: University of California Press, 2009.
Taylor, Diana. *The Archive and the Repertoire: Performing Cultural Memory in the Americas.* Durham, NC: Duke University Press, 2003.
Thompson, John O. "Screen Acting and the Commutation Test." In *Movie Acting: A Reader*, edited by Pamela Robertson Wojcik, 37–48. New York: Routledge, 2004.
Viveiros de Castro, Eduardo. "No Brasil todo mundo é indio exceto quem não é." In *Encontros*, edited by Renato Sztutman, xxx-xxx. Rio de Janeiro: Editora Azougue, 2007.
Walker, Janet. "Documentaries of Return: 'Unhomed Geographies' and the Moving Image." In *Just Images: Ethics and the Cinematic*, edited by Boaz Hagin, Sandra Meiri, Raz Yosef, and Anat Zanger, 114–129. Newcastle upon Tyne, UK: Cambridge Scholars Publishing, 2011.
Walker, Janet. *Trauma Cinema: Documenting Incest and the Holocaust.* Los Angeles: University of California Press, 2005.
Whissel, Kristen. *Picturing American Modernity: Traffic, Technology and the Silent cinema.* Durham, NC: Duke University Press, 2008.
Williams, Linda. "Mirrors Without Memories: Truth, History, and the New Documentary." *Film Quarterly* 46, no. 3 (Spring 1993): 9–21.
Wojcik, Pamela Robertson. "General Introduction." "Typecasting." In *Movie Acting: A Reader*, edited by Ed Wojcik, 1–14, 165–168. New York: Routledge, 2004.
Woloch, Alex. *The One vs the Many: Minor Characters and the Space of the Protagonist in the Novel.* Princeton, NJ: Princeton University Press, 2003.
Wood, Christopher. *Forgery, Replica, Fiction:Temporalities of German Renaissance Art.* Chicago: University of Chicago Press, 2008.
Zavattini, Cesare. "Il Film Lampo, Svillupo del Neorealismo." In Neo- realismo ecc, edited by Mino Argentieri, 89–91. Milan: Bompiani, 1979.
Zavattini, Cesare. "La Veritàaaa: Primo abbozzo per la versione "film da camera" del soggetto La Veritàaaa." In *Cesare Zavattini: Opere 1931–1986*, edited by Silvana Cirillo. Milano: Bompiani, 1991.
Zavattini, Cesare. "Some Ideas on the Cinema." In *Film: A Montage of Theories*, edited by Richard Dyer MacCann, 216-228. New York: E.P. Dutton, 1966.

NOTES

INTRODUCTION
1. Cesare Zavattini, "Some Ideas on the Cinema," in *Film: A Montage of Theories*, ed. Richard Dyer MacCann (New York: E.P. Dutton, 1966), 222.
2. Jean Epstein, *"Photogenie de L'imponderable"* in *Écrits* (Paris: Éditions Seghers, 1975) 1: 128.
3. Jonathan Flatley clarifies that "to be similar to something is precisely to not be the same as it. Neither incommensurate nor identical—related, but distinct—similarity is a third term aside the same-different binary." Flatley, "From Like: Collecting and Collectivity," *October* (Spring 2010), 74.
4. Ibid.
5. See Jennifer Mnookin, "Reproducing a Trial: Evidence and Its Assessment in *Paradise Lost*," in *Law on Screen*, eds. Austin Sarat, Lawrence Douglas, Martha Merril Umphrey (Stanford, CA: Stanford University Press, 2005), and Kristin Fuhs, "Re-imagining the Nonfiction Criminal Narrative: Documentary Reenactment as Political Agency," *Concentric: Literary and Cultural Studies* 38, no. 1 (March 2012), 53. Fuhs's felicitous notion of "participatory reenactment" is similar to what I've identified as the activist, exemplary potential of in-person reenactment. For an excellent analysis of how this form of self-representation in juridical contexts fits within the broader panorama of personal voice in documentary, see also Fuhs, "The Whole Truth and Nothing but the Truth: Documentary Film and the Socio-politics of Justice," PhD dissertation, USC, 2011.
6. Bill Nichols, "Documentary Re-enactments: A Paradoxical Temporality That Is Not One," in *Given World and Time: Temporalities in Context*, ed. Tyrus Miller (New York: Central European University Press, 2008), 172.
7. Vanessa Andrew talks of historical reenactment as involving forms of conversion: "testimonials by reenactors attest to profound experiences that are markers on the hard road to knowledge: they begin as novices, undergo trials, acquire skills and experience and are finally inducted into a community of dedicated reenactors." The marks on body and psyche left by the trials of hunger, claustrophobia, seasickness, or whatever other tribulation during the process of reenacting attests doubly to the testimonial conversion structure—that the knowledge results from experience and that it is perceived to be true. Vanessa Andrew, "What Is Reenactment?" *Criticism* 46, no, 3, 330. The entire issue edited by Andrew constitutes essential reading on the limits of reenactment as a form of knowledge.
8. Jean Starobinski, *The Style of Autobiography*, in *Autobiography: Essays Theoretical and Critical*, ed. James Olney (Princeton, NJ: Princeton University Press, 1980), 73–83.
9. Ibid., 78.
10. Ibid.
11. Ibid., 79.
12. Ibid.
13. Ibid.

14. See Jonathan Kahana's introduction to his edited dossier "Reenactment in Contemporary Documentary Film, Video and Performance" for a compact and smart overview of the field of reenactment in cinema. Kahana, "What Now? Presenting Reenactment," *Framework* 50, no. 1 and 2 (Spring and Fall 2009): 46–60. On contemporary art's interest on fictive biographies and archives, see Carrie Lambert-Beatty, "Make Believe: Parafiction and Plausibility," *October* 129 (2009): 51–84.
15. The most extensive writing on reenactment has been in art catalogue essays, owing to the interest in marrying forms of replay with a historical critical revision (*Life, Once More: Forms of Reenactment in Contemporary Art*, ed. Sven Lutticken, at Witte de With [2005]; *Experience, Memory, Reenactment* at the Piet Zwart Institute [2004]; *Now Again the Past: Rewind, Replay, Resound* at Carnegie Art Center [2006]; *History Will Repeat Itself, Strategies of Reenactment in Contemporary Media Art and Performance*, at the Institute of Contemporary Art in Berlin [2007–2008]; and *Realisms—The Cinema Effect*, at the Hirshhorn Museum in Washington). More recently, Claire Bishop, in *Artificial Hells: Participatory Art and the Politics of Spectatorship* (New York: Verson, 2012), has broached a topic of related interest to in-person reenactment: the practice of delegated performance, where nonprofessionals are paid to represent an artist by performing an aspect of their socioeconomic identities (Santiago Serra, Maurizio Cattelan, Jeremy Deller). Questions related to the politics of surrogacy are of course relevant to understanding the ways in which casting the actual protagonist differently matters. With the exception of Rebecca Schneider's *Performing Remains: Reenactment in Theatre and War* (New York: Routledge, 2011), a spectacular theorization of reenactment in live performance and civil war reconstructions, writings on reenactment have approached it as sociological phenomena or as a historical interpretive tool. Civil war reenactments and British and German television series that reconstruct the daily life of past centuries have, for instance, been characterized as history's affective turn, that is, representations typified by conjectural interpretations of the past, the collapsing of temporalities and an emphasis on affect, individual experience and the everyday. That the valorization of affect and embodiment comes at the expense of a more analytical historiographical perspective is widely discussed in Vanessa Agnew's "History's Affective Turn: Historical Reenactment and Its Work in the Present," as well as in the essays collected in Ian McCalman and Paul Pickering (eds.), *Historical Reenactment: from Realism to the Affective Turn*. See also Vanessa Agnew, "Introduction: What Is Reenactment?" *Criticism* 46, no. 3 (2004): 327–339.
16. Omer Fast's *Spielberg's List* (2003) interviews people who had worked as extras in the making of *Schindler's List*, at a site close to the Plaszow concentration camp in a recreated complex that still stands. Some of the older interviewees get the events of the film entangled with their memories of the 1940s. Rather than expressing an abstract dismay at this conflation, the work instead seems to wonder at these intersections and lets them suggest ways that cinema might operate as a site and agent of memory. Richard Grayson, "*History Will Repeat Itself, Strategies of Reenactment in Contemporary Media Art and Performance*," Art Monthly 313 (February 2008), np.
17. On Elizabeth Subrin's *Shulie* see Elizabeth Freeman, "Packing History, Counter(ing) Generations," in *Time Binds: Queer Temporalities, Queer Histories* (Durham, NC: Duke University Press, 2010), 65–85.
18. See John D. Lyons, *Exemplum* (Princeton, NJ: Princeton University Press, 1989). See also Alexander Gelley, ed., *Unruly Examples: On the Rhetoric of Exemplarity* (Stanford, CA: Stanford University Press, 1995).
19. According to Aristotle, "there are two kinds of examples: namely one which consists in relating things that have happened before, and another in inventing them oneself." Aristotle, Rhetoric 2.20.1393 a-b. Both are relevant in the context of reenactment exemplarity.
20. Often associated with medieval literature, the term *exemplum* denotes any narration in an oratorical or preaching situation.
21. Timothy Hampton notes that "the aim [is] to move readers to various types of moral and political behavior" by seeking to "provide the reader with a variety of options

for possible action in the world" and "educate the faculty of judgment and seek to influence behavior within a specific social sphere." Hampton, *Writing from History: The Rhetoric of Exemplarity in Renaissance Literature* (Ithaca, NY: Cornell University Press, 1990), 4.

22. "An example from the past will most probably contain a pattern that will be pertinent to the situation under deliberation." And it is its "potential for further occurrence or replicability that allows [its] rhetorical use." Lyons, *Exemplum*, 8. See also Gelley, *Unruly Examples*, 3.

23. Gelley, *Unruly Examples*, 3.

24. Hampton, *Writing from History*, 3. Hampton explains that the "imitation of exemplars as models of comportment is one form of hermeneutic application, a technique whereby the Renaissance seeks to reactivate the past," an "application of a text to action in the world," that is central to the neorealist conception of in person reenactment. Indeed, as Gadamer suggests, when we understand a text from the past, we have already applied it to the present insofar as we understand what we need, taking from the past event's particularity whatever is required to our context and situation.

25. Michel de Certeau, *The Practice of Everyday Life* (Los Angeles: University of California Press, 1984), 149.

26. April Alliston, "Female Sexuality and the Referent of Enlightenment Realisms," in *Spectacles of Realism: Gender, Body, Genre*, ed. Margaret Cohen and Christopher Prendergast (Minneapolis: University of Minnesota Press, 1995), 13–14.

27. Ibid., 14.

28. Brecht cited in Ben Brewster, "The Fundamental Reproach (Brecht)," *Cine*TRacts 1, no. 2 (Summer 1977): 52.

29. Ibid.

30. Bertold Brecht. "The Street Scene," in *Brecht on Theatre*, trans. John Willett (New York: Hill and Wang, 1964), 121.

31. Ibid., 122.

32. Ibid.

33. Ibid.

34. Bill Nichols, "Documentary Re-enactments," 180. See also his description of Brechtian distanciation as a particular category of reenactment, 184.

35. Ibid., 181. The same shift between first- and third-person demonstration is central to Pierre Huyghe's *The Third Memory*. See Ruth Erickson, "The Real Movie: Reenactment, Spectacle, and Recovery in Pierre Huyghe's *The Third Memory*," *Framework* 50, no. 1, 107–124.

36. Sylvie Jasen, "Reenactment as Event in Contemporary Cinema," PhD dissertation. Carleton University, Ottawa, 2011. Jasen mentions Joris Ivens's remarks on the "generative potential of reenactment in a discussion of his 1933 film *Borinage*, in which a reenactment of a miners' protest that took place several weeks prior transformed into an actual protest. . . . the scene which had been especially repeated just for the film, developed into a real scene, a real demonstration, because of the pre-existing tense political situation in *Borinage*." Jasen, "Reenactment as Event," 18.

37. Ibid., 43, 45.

38. Kahana, "What Now?," 52–53. This elaboration on the OED is one of the many smart insights in Kahana's essential introduction to reenactment understood in a more general sense.

39. Diana Taylor, *The Archive and the Repertoire: Performing Cultural Memory in the Americas* (Durham, NC: Duke University Press, 2003), 28. Rebecca Schneider's contemporaneous article, expanded into a chapter in her book *Performing Remains: Art and War in Times of Theatrical Reenactment* (New York: Routledge, 2011) also explores this tension; see 90–101.

40. Taylor, *The Archive and the Repertoire*, 28.

41. Ibid.

42. Ibid., 28–29.

43. Ibid.
44. Ibid.
45. Zhang Zhen mentions that Wu Wenguang's on-location aesthetic represents a cinematic operation in the "present tense by virtue of being present on the scene." This poetics of "on the scene" shooting is exemplified by Jia Zhangke's *Pickpocket*, among others, and it "goes hand in hand with a new politics represented by amateur cinema," which attempts returning to ordinary people the right to participate in the production of filmic images about themselves. "Small wonder that so many in the urban generation films, fictional or documentary or docu-dramatic, often engage nonprofessional actors to play themselves. . . . The urgency of this temporality of the here and the now is fueled by the relentless pace of urbanization but also the urge to intervene in a process that is rapidly erasing urban memory and producing a collective amnesia." Zhang, *The Urban Generation: Chinese Cinema and Society at the Turn of the Twenty-first Century* (Durham, NC: Duke University Press, 2007) 20, 21.
46. Anna Grimshaw, *The Ethnographer's Eye: Ways of Seeing in Anthropology* (London: Cambridge, 2001), 80. Despite the historical grouping of neorealism cinema verité, direct cinema in the United States and Canada as realist aesthetics of visual immediacy, Rouch's fifties and sixties work is best understood in terms of the transformative agenda for reenactment discussed in Chapter 4.
47. Think, for instance, of the difference between the start of *Love in the City* (1953), presented in a series of vignettes candid camera shots of couples mixed in with scripted scenes and compare it with the questions addressed to passersby in *Chronicle*. While both beginnings gesture toward the objectivity of a random sampling, the key difference lies in the credit given in cinema verité to a person's voice and experience.
48. See Hirsch, *Afterimage: Film Trauma and the Holocaust* (Philadelphia: Temple University Press, 2004), 65–68; Rowena Santos Aquino, "Necessary F(r)ictions: Reenactment, Embodied Historiography and Testimony," PhD dissertation, UCLA, 201: 85–86; Skoller, *Shadows, Specters and Shards: Making History in Avant Garde Film* (Minneapolis: University of Minnesota Press, 2005); Michael Rothberg, *Multidirectional Memory: Remembering the Holocaust in the Age of Decolonization* (Stanford, CA: Stanford University Press, 2009).
49. See Janet Walker's "Documentaries of Return: 'Unhomed Geographies' and the Moving Image," in *Just Images: Ethics and the Cinematic*, eds. Boaz Hagin, Sandra Meiri, Raz Yosef, and Anat Zanger (Newcastle upon Tyne, UK: Cambridge Scholars Publishing, 2011), 114–129.
50. Shoshana Felman, "The Return of the Voice," in Felman and Dori Laub, *Testimony: Crises of Witnessing in Literature, Psychoanalysis and History* (New York: Routledge, 1992), 258–268; Linda Williams, "Mirrors Without Memories: Truth, History, and the New Documentary," *Film Quarterly* 46, no. 3 (Spring 1993), 9–21. I discuss this problematic in more detail in Chapter 5.
51. Louis George Schwartz, *Mechanical Witness: A History of Motion Picture Evidence in U.S. Courts* (New York: Oxford University Press, 2009).
52. Ibid.
53. Janet Walker, *Trauma Cinema: Documenting Incest and the Holocaust* (Los Angeles: University of California Press, 2005), 110.
54. See Alexander Nagel and Christopher Wood, *Anachronic Renaissance* (Cambridge, MA: MIT Press, 2010), 14.

CHAPTER 1

1. The excellent scholarship on the role of reenactment in the temporal and affective logics of early cinema actualities justifies this detour before moving on to my discussion on conceptions of surrogacy and casting in postwar cinema. In the 1930s *March of Times* Newsreels, a wildly heterogeneous collage of stock footage, impersonations and literal vignette reenactments of signatures or speechmaking were the norm. When Albert Smith and Stuart Blackton, founders of the Vitagraph

Company, missed the Battle of Santiago Bay during the Spanish American War, incipient special effects were improvised, and news made accessible. They used ship miniatures, smoke from a cigar to represent shotgun fire, and the film was lauded as a feat of on-the-spot pictures of a historical event. The same was true of Siegmund Lubin recreating *Fighting Near Santiago*, in Philadelphia, The Battle of Manilla Bay constructed on a Manhattan roof by Vitagraph, and many others. See Hillel Schwartz's dizzying account of reenactments and filmed recreations—of battles and boxing matches in *The Culture of Copy: Striking Likenesss, Unreasonable Facsimiles* (Cambridge, MA: MIT Press, 1998), 280–291. In "Taking the Camera to War," A. Smith, a film producer, recounts the adventures of reconstructing battles. Kevin Macdonald and Mark Cousins, *Imagining Reality: The Faber Book of Documentary* (London: Faber and Faber, 1996), 14–16.
2. Miriam B. Hansen, *Babel and Babylon: Spectatorship in American Silent Film* (Cambridge, MA: Harvard University Press, 1991), 31. Dan Streible, *Fight Pictures: A History of Boxing and Early Cinema* (Los Angeles: University of California Press, 2009). Streible's book is a spectacular account of the convergence of cinematic and boxing spectacles as well as the flexibility in accepting copies in the rushed market of early entertainment.
3. Streible, *Fight Pictures*, 126. According to Streible, "fake fight films met with a mixed reaction because they derived from conflicting practices, accepted forms of re-presentation that predated motion pictures, and misrepresentations contrived to deceive" (Ibid., 128). He situates the extremely fluid reception of films of reenacted fights in a fast-moving ground of marketing spurred by the wish to "see" the actual fight in its sequential development but also to verify the new technological advancements in reproducing movement itself.
4. Streible, *Fight Pictures*, 67.
5. Mary Ann Doane, *The Emergence of Cinematic Time: Modernity, Contingency, the Archive* (Cambridge, MA: Harvard University Press, 2002), 145–147.
6. Alison Griffith defines the "panorama effect as one of re-visitation, of witnessing again, in modified form, that which has occurred in a different time and place." Griffith, "Shivers Down Your Spine," 2 7 Screen 44 (Spring 2003).
7. Kristen Whissel, *Picturing American Modernity: Traffic, Technology and the Silent Cinema*. (Durham, NC: Duke University Press, 2008).
8. Whissel mentions Richard Abel's contention that prior to 1908 the difference between recording a current public event as it was happening and reconstructing a past or even present historical event in a studio was relatively insignificant. What mattered according to Abel "was that a representation of the 'historical' differed from a representation of the purely fictive or imaginary—which meant that referential differences mattered more than differences in modes of representation . . . in other words the 'historical scene' was bound to the actualité within an unbroken continuum uniting historical past and present." This allowed French filmmakers such as Pathé and Meliès to "exploit the shared 'family resemblance' between historical reconstructions and actualites." Whissel, *Picturing American Modernity*, 72.
9. Whissel, 98. Whissel's larger argument is that the battle reenactment's placement of the spectator on the "scene" of historical trauma and its mode of repetition provided a cultural form for revealing and mastering the shock of warfare experienced by the soldier on the new frontier and, by extension, the nation as it became an overseas empire. Ibid., 100.
10. Richard Schechner, *Between Theater and Anthropology* (Philadelphia: University of Pennsylvania Press, 1985), 36.
11. Erving Goffman elaborated on Bateson's study of animal play to account for the ways an actual act is transposed onto another representational level. He will call primary the frame for behavior that has actual consequences—for instance, competing in an actual race, and secondary frame, the preparatory movements modeled on but not driven by the primary activity's purpose. In the transposition of a "strip" of competitive

running for one of *training for competitive running*, there may be a significant change in sequencing with the expansion or contraction of particular moments of the sequence. See Erving Goffman, *Frame Analysis: An Essay on the Organization of Experience* (Boston: Northeastern University Press, 1986), 44–54.

12. The book considers the exfoliation of ingrained routines, the layering of sequences of "transposed behavior" in their phenomenological and evidentiary dimensions. The questions of routine, traditional practices, or indoctrination are taken up again in Chapter 6 when we examine the significance of the ex-guards of the Khmer Rouge's mimicry of their indoctrination as part of a machinery of killing and in Chapter 7 when we discuss *Serras* perverse senseless mimesis—its disturbing presentation of an Indian reservation.

13. Joris Ivens, *The Camera and I* (New York: International Publishers, 1969), 187–194. Joris Ivens warns though that the force of documentary, its "convincingness" lies in that it is "always taken on the spot," and that "too much emphasis on reenactment can be dangerous." "There will always be, he states, certain themes that are best carried out in a purely documentary style, but there are others that demand considerable reenactment, and by reenactment I mean the reconstruction of an emotional situation, not merely the redoing of a familiar act." Ivens, "Collaboration in Documentary," *Films* 1, no. 2 (Spring 1940), 35. Jean Epstein also becomes interested in working with nonactors. After finishing *The Fall of the House of Usher*, an experimental studio-made film, Jean Epstein moves to Brittany to film seaweed gatherers and fishermen of the islands of Ouessant, Bannec, and Balanec. The filming of *Finis Terrae* leads to an epiphany on the true destiny of cinema and he converts to this sort of docudrama, acted with Indigenous people: "no professional could have rendered this same type of men and women with the same degree of truth. Because in this frame, and this authentic atmosphere, all 'act' would have destroyed the very spirit conceived for the film." Epstein, *"Nos Lions,"* in *Écrits sur le Cinéma* 1 (1921–1947) (Paris: Seghers, 1974), 196. Such a film with "natural interpretation" should not constitute "an exception," but in representing "all countries, all social classes all professions . . . one should use natural settings, actual stories and authentic atmospheres" (Ibid.). Other remarks reveal how Epstein's version of authentic behavior and natural cinema impinges on and corrects the behavior of his "natural interpreters." He mentions that they only had to "learn" not to look at the camera. They also had to "unlearn" their "bad habit" of singing "a number of songs while making stereotyped gestures." "We had," says Epstein, "to force them to renounce this bad actor's habit." Fixing the social actors' role-playing so it looks more natural, conforming to some notion of fisherman. "Like every Breton that comes back from service he knew a number of songs which he sang along with half a dozen stereotypical gestures. It was necessary also to have him give up this bad actorly habit." Ibid., 195.

14. Ivens, *The Camera and I*, 189.
15. Ibid.
16. Ibid., 191.
17. Ibid. As interesting is Ivens's grasp of the interrelation between the camera and repetitions happening in the real world and in the profilmic reality.
18. Ibid.
19. Jasen, "Reenactment as Event in Contemporary Cinema," 25.
20. Ibid. Jasen makes use of Diana Taylor's theorization of the distinction between archival materials and performance practices, a discussion especially pertinent in the cases of indoctrination or traditional gestural and work routines and their physical and mental imprint. I discuss this aspect further in Chapters 6 and 7.
21. In her excellent dissertation, Sylvie Jasen mentions that "*Journals*, a feature that recounts the Danish explorer's meeting with an Igloolik shaman while on an expedition in the Arctic during a period of transition in Inuit communities from Shamanism to Christianity . . . was made in Igloolik, Nunavut, with the participation of local Inuit residents as actors and crew, for whom the project of reenacting a traditional way of

life in and for the film served a pedagogical function." Jasen, "Reenactment as Event in Contemporary Cinema," 139.
22. Paul Rotha, *Robert Flaherty, a Biography*, ed. Jay Ruby (Philadelphia: University of Pennsylvania Press, 1983), p. 114.
23. J. C. Messenger, Jr., "Flaherty, Man of Aran Revisited: An Anthropological Critique," *Visual Anthropology* 20, no. 5 (May 2010), 363. http://dx.doi.org/10.1080/ 08949468.2001.9966840. The article corrects the misconceptions concerning the islanders' practices in *Man of Aran*.
24. Bill Nichols refers to these kinds of reenactments as "typifications," noting their predominance in 1930s and early forties documentary. He associates this modality of representation (citing Flaherty specifically) as devoid of concrete temporal specificity, a "single entity," taken as exemplary of an entire class, to the typical particular. See Bill Nichols, "Documentary Re-enactments: A Paradoxical Temporality That Is Not One," in *Given World and Time: Temporalities in Context*, ed. Tyrus Miller (New York: Central European University Press, 2008), 184.
25. See Devin Fore, "The Secret Always on Display: Caricature and Physiognomy in the Work of John Heartfeld," in Fore, *Realism After Modernism: The Rehumanization of Art and Literature* (Cambridge, MA: MIT Press, 2012), 243–304. On social realist novel and its uses of biography, see Katerina Clark's "The Stalinist Myth of the 'Great Family,'" in *The Soviet Novel: History as Ritual* (Chicago: University of Chicago Press, 1985), 114–135.
26. Devin Fore suggests that "in both cases (left and right), however, it is clear that the human face that returns in the interwar art is now a serialized structure, no longer an inviolable locus of individuality but an assemblage of coded elements that undermines all claims to uniqueness." Fore, "The Secret Always on Display," 274.
27. Ibid.
28. Dudley Andrew, "A Film Aesthetic to Discover," on *érudit* (site); 24–26. *Cinémas* 17, no. 2–3 (Spring 2007): 47–71.
29. Catherine L. Benamou, *It's All True: Orson Welles's Pan-American Odyssey* (Los Angeles: University of California Press, 2007), 88. Welles was aware, she adds, that "it was a *jangadeiro* Francisco Jose de Nascimento aka the "Dragon of the Sea," who brought an end to slavery in Ceará (the northeast) in 1884 by staging a work stoppage of jangadeiros charged with shuttling slaves to Fortaleza from ships anchored offshore," a fact that circulated still in early forties oral narratives. Ibid.
30. Ibid., esp. 50–55 and 88–100. Welles even filmed the arrival in Technicolor, with the raft lifted from the water, and converted into a "Carnaval" float in the next episode.
31. Ann Chisholm, " Missing Persons and Bodies of Evidence," *Camera Obscura* 43, 15, no. 1 (2000), 139.
32. Benamou, *It's All True*, 50–55.
33. Ibid., 54. Interestingly these are all films on fishermen communities that trade off individualized recreation for a collective portrait.
34. Will Straw, "Scales of Presence: Bess Flowers and The Hollywood Extra," *Screen* 52, no. 1 (Spring 2011), 125.
35. Ibid.
36. Ibid. See also Alex Woloch, *The One vs the Many: Minor Characters and the Space of the Protagonist in the Novel* (Princeton, NJ: Princeton University Press, 2003), 17.
37. Ibid.
38. Giorgio Agamben, *Potentialities: Collected Essays in Philosophy*, ed. and trans. D. Heller-Roazen (Stanford, CA: Stanford University Press, 1999), 235.
39. Alice Rayner, *To Act, to Do, to Perform: Drama and the Phenomenology of Acting* (Ann Arbor: University of Michigan Press, 1994), 13.
40. See Rayner, *To Act, to Do, to Perform*, 26.
41. See Rayner, 136, fn. 32. "When athletes are performing their skills what becomes perceptible is skill or style . . . . Style actualizes the game but the perceptible is not the game but qualities of play . . . The performance fills the space between capacities

and rules or situational demands. And it fills that space with qualities more than substance. Indeed the conventional division between style and substance accounts for the persistent belief that performance is merely show, hence pretense, hence false consciousness or bad faith. The show rather is identical to actuality." Ibid.

42. Starobinski, "The Style of Autobiography," in *Autobiography: Theoretical and Critical Essays*, ed. James Olney (Princeton, NJ: Princeton University Press, 1980), 74.

43. Zhang Zhen writes about the subject populating the new urban Chinese cinema, a "motley crew of plebeian but nonetheless troubled people on the margins of the age of transformation—ranging from aimless bohemians petty thieves, KTV bar hostesses, prostitutes and postmen to neighborhood police officers, taxi drivers alcoholics homosexuals the disabled migrant worker and others." Moreover, as she emphasizes "these characters, often played by non-professional actors, share the same contemporary social space as the filmmakers as well as the viewers. This cinema thus constructs a specific temporality that is constantly unfolding in the present, as both a symbiotic partner and a form of critique of the social to which it tries to give shape and meaning." Ed Zhang Zhen, *The Urban Generation: Chinese Cinema and Society at the Turn of the Twenty-first Century* (Durham, NC: Duke University Press, 2007), 3.

44. Zhang Yuan is part of the Sixth Generation Chinese filmmakers. His films often tap onto marginalized topics and they are produced independently from government funding. Zhang's choice of themes—the mentally retarded in *Mama* (1990), gay life in *East West Palace* (1998), the everyday and the routine of control in Tiananmen *The Square* (1994), and his record of rock star Cui Jian in *Beijing Bastards* (1993)—is in line with other critical attempts to record an expanded rebellious consciousness. Zhen Zhang mentions that, in the most difficult years of 1994 to 1996, some of the most daring films by the new generation were made almost simultaneously to *The Square*, *East West Palace*, Wang Xiaoshuai (*Frozen, So Close to Paradise*) and that Zhang Yuan was part of a small group of independent filmmakers who in 1993 and 1994, respectively, submitted their work to the Tokyo and Rotterdam Film Festivals without the official state seal of approval. They were thus issued a ban by China's film bureau, sent to sixteen state-owned studios, processing labs, and equipment rental services so as to effectively forestall any further independent moves on the part of these filmmakers. Zhang, *The Urban Generation*, 11.

45. Family portraits also emerge as a generational and historical bridge. Nicole Huang notes that "contemporary Chinese artists have used family portraits from the 1960s and 1970s . . . to reinvent the very idea of the camera, the album and the familial gaze as vehicles of longing, remembering and contesting." She gives the example of Zhang Xiaogang, whose *Bloodline: The Big Family* (1993–2000) outlines "the myriad faces of conformity" and comments "directly on the place of family portraits in personal and collective memories." The common thread running through these experiments is "their expression of a relationship with a reconstructed past," and "the family portrait becomes an important cultural genre, in dynamic contrast to photographic propaganda of the same period." Nicole Huang, "Locating Family Portraits: Everyday Images from 1970s China," *Positions* 18, no. 3 (2010), 671.

46. See Berenice Reynaud, "Zhang Yuan's Imaginary Cities: The Theatricalization of the Chinese 'Bastards,'" in Zhen Zhang, *The Urban Generation*, 264–294.

47. Ma Ning, "Symbolic Representation and Symbolic Violence: Chinese Family Melodrama of the Early 80s," *East West* 4, no. 1 (December 1989), 79–83.

48. Foucault suggests that resemblance "predicates itself upon a model it must return to and reveal" while "the similar develops in series that have neither beginning nor end that can be followed in one direction as easily as another, that obey no hierarchy but propagate themselves from small differences among small differences." Foucault, *This Is Not a Pipe*, translated and edited by James Harkness (Berkeley: University of California Press, 1982), 44.

CHAPTER 2

1. Cesare Zavattini, "Some Ideas on the Cinema," *Sight and Sound* 23, number 2 (October December 1953): 64-69 reprinted in *Vittorio de Sica: Contemporary Perspectives,* eds. Howard Curle and Stephen Snyder (Toronto: Toronto University Press, 2000), 59.
2. Karl Schoonover asserts that Neorealism asks us to recognize certain bodies as evidence of the performer's status as an amateur . . . that the non professionalism of certain performances must be detectable, visibly obvious to the spectator through a comparison to other types of acting—often within the same film. We might say then that the question of labor haunts any contemplation of these films." Schoonover, *Brutal Vision: The Neorealist Body in Postwar Italian Cinema* (Minneapolis: University of Minnesota Press, 2012), 70.
3. Besides *The Story of Caterina* (or *Love of a Mother*), *Love in the City* is composed of Carlo Lizzani's *Love for Pay*, Dino Risi's *Paradise for Three Hours*, Federico Fellini's *Arranged Marriage*, Alberto Lattuada's *Italians Turn to Look*, and Michelangelo Antonioni's *Attempted Suicides*. The first mention of Caterina is in *Diario Cinematografico*, translated in *Sequences of a Cinematic Life*. For more on the genesis of *Il Spetattore*, see Luciano de Giusti's "Vita breve de *Documento Mensile*," an insert in Augusto Sainati's "La Cronaca Filmata," in *Storia del Cinema Italiano, Vol. VIII, 1949-1953*, ed. Luciano de Giusti (Venice: Marsilio Edizione, 2003), 98-99.
4. Zavattini's theory of *"pedinamento"* is described in "Il film Lampo." See Zavattini's *Film-Lampo: Sviluppo del neorealismo* (1952) and *Che cos'é il film lampo* (1953), in Opere, Cinema: Diario Cinematografico: Neorealismo ecc., ed. Valentina Fortichiari and Mino argentieri (Milan: Bompiani, 2002), 711-713 and 708-710.
5. Gian Piero Brunetta, *Storia del Cinema Italiano*, Vol. III: *dal Neorealismo al milagro economico, 1945-1959* (Roma: Editori Riuniti, 1998-2001), 250.
6. Ibid., 248-249. Brunetta noted that neorealism "hypothesizes a kind of 'turn over,' in which the old crews can still be used in genre films, or interpretations that demand a repetitive or automatic staging, while duties of greater responsibility and creative were assigned to characters just assumed without any prior experience." Ibid., 252.
7. See David Forgács, *Rome Open City* (London: BFI, 2000-2007), 27, 24.
8. Ibid., 54.
9. Cited in Saverio Vollaro, "Zavattini e il Neorealismo," in *Rivista del Cinema Italiano* 7 (July 1954): 36.
10. See Giorgio De Vincenti, "Sperimentalismo," in *Lessico Zavattiniano: Parole e idée su cinema e dintorni*, ed. Guglielmo Monetti (Venice: Marsilio, 1992), 253-260; Giulia Fanara, *Pensare il Neorealismo: Percorsi attraverso il Noerealismo Cinematografico Italiano* (Rome: Lithos, 2000), 328-239; Stefana Parigi, "Il Pensiero de Zavattini," in *Storia del Cinema Italiano Vol. VIII, 1949-1953*, 508. A comprehensive analysis of Zavattini's work can be found in Stefania Parigi's *Fisiologia dell'Immagine: Il Pensiero di Cesare Zavattini* (Torino: Lindau, 2006).
11. The prologue and some of the episodes in *Love in the City* mark the beginning of Zavattini's interest in documentary filmmaking. The collective filmmaking spirit is most pronounced in *Le Italiane e l'Amore* (1961) and *I misteri di Roma* (1963). A cinema of multiple camera eyes is developed in *Cinegiornale della pace* (1963) and especially in the *Cinegiornali liberi and Cinegiornale del proletariato* (1968-1973).
12. Cesare Zavattini, *Una, Cento, Mille Lettere*, ed. Silvana Cirillo (Milan: Bompiani, 1988), 387-392, 397-405.
13. Ibid., 390.
14. Ibid., 405.
15. Ibid., 387-388.
16. Ibid., 390-391.
17. About Zavattini's "struggle" with his imagination, see *Una, Cento, Mille Lettere*, 178. This is also the period of his rift with De Sica, around the director's claim to have willfully transformed *Umberto D* from Zavattini's initial "usher from humble

conditions" to an "ex-statale" (a bourgeois character), see 168–173; see also Francesco Bolzoni's "*De Sica e Zavattini sul Tandem*" in *De Sica: Autore, regista, Attore*, ed. Lino Miccichè (Milan: Marsilio Editori, 1992), 134–135.

18. Sandro Petraglia, "Cesare Zavattini, Teorico del neorealismo," in *Il Neorealismo Cinematografico Italiano*, ed. Lino Miccichè (Venice: Marsilio, 1999), 219. See also "Attore," in *Lessico Zavattiniano: Parole e idée su cinema e dintorni*, ed. Guglielmo Monetti (Venice: Marsilio, 1992), 36.
19. Cesare Zavattini, "*Il Neorealismo Continua*," in *Cesare Zavattini: Opere, Diario cinematografico; Neorealismo ecc.*, ed. Valentina Fortichiari and Mino Argentieri, 715–716.
20. See Argentieri, "Giornalismo," in *Lessico Zavattiniano*, 98–101.
21. See Luciano de Giusti, "Vita breve de Documento Mensile," in *Storia del Cinema Italiano Vol VIII, 1949–1953*, 98–99.
22. Zavattini's ecumenical vision, his desire to embrace, under a broad neorealist umbrella, any "product of moral and social interests that is alive and contemporary," is evident in the variety of approaches that comprise *Love in the City,* from Dino Risi's direct cinema reconstruction of three hours in a working-class dance hall, to Alberto Lattuada's candid camera extravaganza on Italian men turning to look at women (some of whom were planted starlets). Fellini's *Arranged Marriage*, the sole episode in the film to employ actors, tells the story of a man looking for a prospective wife for his very rich friend who suffers from a strange disease, turning nightly into a wolf-man. The film's drawn-out beginning attests to the continuing power of neorealist iconography. As he searches for a matrimonial agency, the young man traverses long corridors in a dilapidated tenement building, glimpsing scenes of hardship through open doors. Lost in this figurative maze offering glimpses of typical neorealist scenes of daily strife, he finally gets to the agency and the marriage proposal, which is surprisingly accepted by a poor young woman. Fellini's "road beyond neorealism" is here a corridor walk, so long that the camera assumes a subjective perspective identified with a character who, much like Fellini himself, is about to take leave of certain neorealist formulas—vide the narrator's cynical and then guilty approach to his own hoax.
23. De Giusti, "Vita breve de *Documento Mensile*," 98–99.
24. Italian cultural studies book on popularity of the fotoromanzo and photo weeklie à la *Life* magazine.
25. As Noa Steimatsky notes, this may be the origin of a term that becomes central to the investigative films of the sixties—Francesco Rosi's *Salvatore Giuliano*, for instance.
26. With Paul Strand's collaboration, *Italia Mia* eventually turns into a project for a book in 1955 collecting common people's testimonies. Cesare Zavattini and Paul Strand, *Un Paese* (Torino: Einaudi, 1955). Zavattini, *Comme non ho fatto "Italia mia," Rassegna del film* 12 (March 1953): 26.
27. Zavattini, "Il Neorealismo secondo me," in *Cesare Zavattini: Diario cinematografico; Neorealismo ecc.*, 762.
28. Ibid., 762–763.
29. Cesare Zavattini, *Zavattini: Sequences from a Cinematic Life*, trans. William Weaver (New Jersey: Prentice-Hall, 1970), 10–11.
30. Ibid., 26.
31. Zavattini cited in Vollaro, "Zavattini e il Neorealismo," 25.
32. See Gian Piero Brunetta, *Storia del Cinema Italiano dal 1945 agli anni ottanta* (Rome: Editori Riuniti, 1982), 147–152. For an excellent overview of some of the debates and new cinematic strategies informing the "crisis of neorealism," see the "Transitions" section in Millicent Marcus, *Italian Film in the Light of Neorealism* (Princeton, NJ: Princeton University Press, 1986), 121–208.
33. See P. Adams Sitney's *Vital Crises in Italian Cinema* (New York: Oxford University Press, 1995),107.
34. Renzo Renzi, "Laici e cattolici," in *La Bella Stagione: Scontri e incontri negli anni d'oro del cinema italiano* (Roma: Bulzoni Editore, 2001), 111.

35. Ibid., 112.
36. See the "Censorship" chapter of Gian Piero Brunetta, *Storia del cinema Italiano: dal neorealismo al miracolo economico 1945-1959* (Roma: Editori Riuniti, 2001), 73-96.
37. Guido Aristarco, *Neorealismo e Nuova Critica Cinematografica, Cinematografia e Vita Nazionale: tra Rottura e Tradizioni* (Firenze: Nuova Guaraldi, 1980), 82.
38. Lino del Fra, "Il film storico e il neorealismo," in *Rivista del Cinema Italiano* 5-6 (May-June 1954): 69-70.
39. Armando Bonelli, "L'idee di Zavattini," in *Rivista del Cinema Italiano* 11-12 (November-December 1954): 75.
40. See Aristarco, *Il Mestiere del critico/Quando il cinema era nuovo, Recensioni degli anni cinquanta,* ed. Lorenzo Pelizzari (Edizione Falsopiano, 2007), 85-87, 90-98. For Zavattini's sense of betrayal by Visconti's *Senso*, see "Una grossa botta in testa al neorealismo," in *Antologia di Cinema Nuovo, 1952-1958,* ed. Guido Aristarco (Florence: Guaraldo, 1975), 888-892.
41. Zavattini, "Tesi sul Neorealismo," in *Cesare Zavattini Cinema*, 741.
42. Zavattini, "Si presentano vestiti in tutu e decretano che il neorealismo e morto," in *Cesare Zavattini Cinema*, 737-740.
43. Gian Piero Brunetta, *Il Cinema Neorealista Italiano: Storia Economica, Politica e Culturale* (Roma, Gius Laterza & Filgi Spa Digital Edition 2015). My translation. https://books.google.com.br/books?id=5G6ODAAAQBAJ&pg=PT126&lpg=PT126&dq=insufficie nza+politiche+Brunetta+cinema&source=bl&ots=4KnlKJNk9i&sig=4ygtpQzV0k1x gZoYS6_2TIRSGr8&hl=en&sa=X&ved=0ahUKEwjn94793b_bAhUEHJAKHQwdA_ YQ6AEIJzAA#v=onepage&q=insufficienza%20politiche%20Brunetta%20 cinema&f=false.
44. Ibid., 761.The scope of the convention (attended by, among others, Pietro Germi, Sergio Amidei, Federico Fellini, Vittorio de Sica, Carlo Lizzani, Renzo Rezi, Francesco Maselli, and Mario Gromo, and convened by Zavattini) was to reaffirm the existence of and possibility to develop neorealism in Italy. At its conclusion a document affirmed the positive value of neorealism, the need to critically study and diffuse its value, and a vote was cast that the Parliament and State organs should take in account the value of Italian culture as freely intended. Editor's note in *Cesare Zavattini: Diario cinematografico; Neorealismo ecc.*, 768.
45. Adelio Ferrero, "La 'Conscienza di Se': Ideologia e Verita Del Neorealismo," in *Il Neorealismo Cinematografico Italiano; Atti del Convegno della X Mostra Internazionale del Nuovo Cinema*, ed. Lino Micciche (Venice: Marsilio Editori, 1975), 244.
46. Brunetta, *Storia del Cinema Italiano*, 137. Renzi believes that given the bland ideological position of neorealist films and the constraints of a contaminated ideological debate, Zavattini's abstract formulations are inevitable. Renzi, "Laici e cattolici," 113.
47. Zavattini, "Il Neorealismo Secondo me," in *Cesare Zavattini Cinema*, 759.
48. See in particular Zavattini,"Si presentano vestiti in tutu e decretano che il neorealismo e morto," "Tesi sul Neorealismo," "Il Neorealismo secondo me," and "Il Neorealismo Continua," in *Cesare Zavattini Cinema*, 737-740, 741-751, 752-769.
49. Zavattini, "Tesi sul Neorealismo," in *Cesare Zavattini Cinema*, 750.
50. Ibid., 749.
51. Zavattini, "To Antonio Baldini," *Una Cento Mille Lettere*, 177.
52. He first offers the project to Renzo Rosselini, but he ends up directing it with Francesco Maselli, a young director.
53. Zavattini, "La Veritàaaa: Primo abbozzo per la versione "film da camera" del sogetto La Veritàaaa," in *Cesare Zavattini: Opere 1931-1986*, ed. Silvana Cirillo (Milano: Bompiani, 1991), 1492.
54. Ibid. See also Stefania Parigi in *Fisiologia dell'Immagine: il Pensiero de Cesare Zavattini*, 92-93, where she develops a Christian model for Zavattini's emphasis on immediacy and on the necessary conjunction of reflection and praxis.
55. Carlo Prandi, "Zavattini: Cristo, il cristianesimo, I cristiani," in *Diviso en Due, Cesare Zavattini: Cinema e Cultura Populare* (Roma: Edizione Pierluigi Eride, 1999), 82.

56. Zavattini, *Polemica col mio tempo* (Milano: Bompiani, 1997), 52–54, cited in Prandi, Zavattini: Cristo, il cristianesimo, I cristiani," 82.
57. Ibid., 1491.
58. Zavattini, "Il Film Lampo, Svillupo del Neorealismo," in *Cesare Zavattini Cinema*, 712.
59. Zavattini, "Some Ideas on the Cinema," in *Film: A Montage of Theories*, 222.
60. Maurizio Grande, "Personaggio," in *Lessico Zavattiniano*, 194.
61. Grande, "Attore," in *Lessico Zavattiniano*, 31.
62. See Francesco Maselli's commentary on the DVD of *L'amore in Città: Film a Episodi*. Minerva Classic, La Memoria del Cinema Italiano.
63. Peasant women who live half a mile from Ferentino, making seven thousand lire boarding the children of maidservants in Rome.
64. The DVD of *L'Amore in Città* has a detailed interview with film critic Luca Bandirali on Mario Nascimbene's score for *Love in the City* and *The Story of Caterina*, in particular.
65. Sam Rohdie, *Antonioni* (London: BFI, 1990), 106.
66. See Saverio Vollaro's extended analysis of Zavattini's apostolic vision in Vollaro, "Zavattini e il Neorealismo," 38–39. See also P. Adams Sitney's analysis of De Sica's and Zavattini's films in *Vital Crises of Italian Cinema: Iconography, Stylistics, Politics* (Austin: University of Texas Press, 1995), 96.
67. Zavattini, "Some Ideas on the Cinema," in *Film: A Montage of Theories*, 227.
68. Both Aristotle and Cicero suggest three basic forms of examples: the historical "account of actual occurrences remote from the recollection of our own age"; the argument, "a fictitious narrative which nevertheless could have occurred"; and the fable, a "narrative in which the events are not true and have no verisimilitude." Cited in John Lyons, *Exemplum: The Rhetoric of Example in Early Modern France and Italy* (Princeton, NJ: Princeton University Press, 1989), 8.
69. André Bazin, "L'amour à la ville," *Observateur* 354 (February 22, 1957): 19.
70. Bazin, "Le Neorealisme se Retourne," in *Cahiers du Cinéma* 69 (March 1957): 46.
71. Bazin, "L'amour à la ville," *Observateur*, 19.
72. Bazin, "L'amour à la ville," in *Écran nouveau* (February 28, 1957): 25.
73. Bazin, "*Le Neorealisme se Retourne*," 46.
74. Bazin, "L'amour à la ville," *Observateur*, 19.
75. P. Adams Sitney perceptively analyzes this same problematic responsibility as he rethinks De Sica's notion that all his films are about egoism. "Are we to read the protagonists of each of the four films as egoists or as the victims of egoists, or perhaps as both? Ultimately what does he mean by egoism?" The lack of solidarity implicit in a selfish individuated response is indeed an interesting trait in the films complicating an easy indictment of social ills. Sitney, *Vital Crises*, 79–81.
76. Many have remarked on the Christian roots of Zavattini's narratives, despite his clear anticlericalism. For a sharp reading of *Bicycle Thieves* that incorporates Franco Fortini's own understanding of these aspects of the work, see Sitney, *Vital Crises*, 95–96. See also Renzi, "Laici e cattolici," 215: Neorealism has "on a popular plane that process of conscience and self-judgment which are active virtues of individuals with a Christian education." If we add the confessional process implicit in cinematic reenactment, we can clearly see how Zavattini reimagines and stages his guilt-inducing cinema.
77. See Zavattini, *Incontro con Cesare Zavattini, scrittore*, primavera 1972–estate 1974, in *Voci d'oggi sul Vangelo*, prefazione di I. Mancini, ed. C. Ciattaglia (Rome: Cinque Lune, 1974), 451–463. Cited in Prandi, *Zavattini: Cristo, il cristianesimo, I cristiani*, 45.
78. Zavattini, *Neorealismo ecc.* (Milano: Bompiani, 1979), 157.
79. Bathélemy Amengual, "Amore in Città," in *études Cinematographiques* 32–35 (Summer 1964): 172.
80. Ibid., 9.
81. Timothy Hampton, *Writing from History: The Rhetoric of Exemplarity in Renaissance Literature* (Ithaca, NY: Cornell University Press, 1990), 25.
82. Lyons, *Exemplum*, 8–14.

83. Zavattini, "Il Neorealismo Fatto Morale," in *Cesare Zavattini Cinema*, 786–787.
84. See Pascal Bonitzer's analysis of the failure of neorealism to constitute itself as a revolutionary cinema. Bonitzer, "Neorealismo: Quale Realismo?" in *Il Neorealismo Cinematografico Italiano*, 224–225.
85. Such purposefully banal questions are precisely the ones criticized by Guido Aristarco in his review of *Love in the City*. See *Il Mestiere del Critico quando il cinema era nuovo: recensioni dagli anni cinquanta*, ed. Lorenzo Pellizzani (Roma: Edizioni Falsopiano, 2007), 83.
86. Zavattini, "Some Ideas on the Cinema," in *Film: A Montage of Theories*, 224.
87. Ibid., 217–219.
88. Zavattini, *Neorealismo ecc*, 118–119.
89. Zavattini describes in detail the research for Lizanni's films, in *Sequence of a Cinematic Life*, 33–36.
90. Zavattini, *"Tesi sul neorealismo,"* in *Cesare Zavattini Cinema*, 744.
91. Zavattini, "Tu, Maggiorani," in *Uomo, vieni fuori! Soggetti per il cinema editi e inediti*, ed. Orio Caldiron (Rome: Bulzoni, 2006), 144.
92. Zavattini, "Il Neorealismo Fatto Morale," in *Cesare Zavattini Cinema*, 788. Many have written on Zavattini's *cinegiornali* projects, his reportage films made in the sixties and early seventies. In these films Zavattini accomplishes his idea of a lighter, nonnarrative cinema. See Parigi, *Fisiologia dell'imagine: il pensiero di Cesare Zavattini* (Turin, Linadu, 2006), 290–291.
93. Zavattini, cited in Grande, "Attore," in *Lessico Zavattiniano*, 36.
94. Grande, "Personaggio," in *Lessico Zavattiniano*, 194.
95. Grande, "Attore," in *Lessico Zavattiniano*, 32. In Italian *officiante* with its liturgical implications.
96. Giorgio de Vincenti refers to the white background or voided area typical of all of Antonioni's work—the fog in *Il Grido*, the latensification in *Blow Up*, the suspended landscapes in *L'Avventura*—as a sign of a phenomenological cinema aware of itself: the screen on which to "write" something which is not only "reality," not only "artifice," but the problematic encounter between the two. De Vincenti, "I Film sul Cinema," in *Storia del Cinema*, 312.
97. See Guido Aristarco's criticism of the formalist calligraphic approach in the film in Aristarco, "Amore in Città," in *Cinema Nuovo* III, no. 27 (January 15, 1954): 27–28. Giorgio Tinnazi deems the film a failure, stating that the planes of reality and reconstruction remain so separate they expose the prevalence of specularization and make the testimonies look as if they have been mechanically inserted. For an appreciative and smart reading of the film, see Sam Rohdie, *Antonioni*, 106–113.
98. Lino Micciche claims exactly that in a short dismissal of the work, "Antonioni dans les années cinquante," in *L'oeuvre de Michelangelo Antonioni Vol. I, 1942–1965*, ed. Carlo di Carlo (Rome, Ente autonomo di Gestioni per il Cinema, 1987–1988), 283.
99. Antonioni, "The Event and the Image," in *The Architecture of Vision: Writings and Interviews on Cinema*, ed. Carlo di Carlo and Giorgio Tinazzi (New York: Marsilio Publishers, 1996), 52–53.
100. I translate here the title of Guido Fink, "Antonioni et le film policier `a l'envers," in *L'oeuvre de Michelangelo Antonioni* (Rome, Cinecittà International 1992).
101. Antonioni, "A Talk with Michelangelo Antonioni on his Work," in *The Architecture of Vision*, 24–25.
102. Rohdie, *Antonioni*, 149. On the question of temporal delay and its imprint on the character's phenomenology, see Marie-Claire Ropars Wuillermier, "L'espace et le temps dans l'univers d' Antonioni," in *Études cinematographiques* 36–37 (1964): pp. 17–33. See also Millicent Marcus on the continuity of Antonioni's work with a neorealist tradition constantly revising the relation between observer and the phenomenal world, 206.
103. Rohdie, *Antonioni*, 149.
104. Steimatsky's chapter "Aerial: Antonioni's Modernism," in her book *Italian Locations: Reinhabiting the Past in Postwar Cinema*, p. 32, brilliantly accounts for the

genealogy of Antonioni's modernist aesthetics through a close reading of his first documentary film and its initial announcement in a photo-essay. This is the first work to rigorously analyze the nuances of the filmmaker's early documentary work within the fascist modernist aesthetic context. See Steimatsky, *Italian Locations: Reinhabiting the Past in Postwar Cinema* (Minneapolis: University of Minnesota Press, 2008), 1–39. Referring to this same documentary production, Renzo Renzi defends Antonioni's suspended aesthetics as a "form of protest, of responsibility," cogently linking the filmmaker's "detachment" and his "apparent drift from naturalism" to an engagement with "the thrill of a choice, maybe of a reality to change, for sure a reality to refute." Renzo Renzi, "Cronache Dell'Angoscia in Michelangelo Antonioni," in *La Bella Stagione: Scontri e incontri negli anni d'oro del cinema italiano* (Roma: Bulzoni Editore, 2001), 193.

105. See Antonioni, "Prima Stesura dell'Episodio 'Ragioni Sentimentali' [Tentato suicidi]," in *Il Primo Antonioni,* ed. Carlo di Carlo (Bologna: Capelli, 1973), 247–274.
106. Ibid.
107. Interestingly, the elided suicides are most apparent in the cases that are not by self-poisoning.
108. Sigmund Freud, *Studies on Hysteria* (1895d), S E, II, 8.
109. Antonioni, "*Attempted Suicide*: Suicides in the City," in *Architecture of Vision,* 73. "Suicidi in Città" was published in *Cinema Nuovo* 31 (February 1954).
110. Antonioni, "*Attempted Suicide*: Suicides in the City," in *Architecture of Vision,* 72.
111. Appreciating the Rouchian aspects of Antonioni's film, Amengual states that labeling the film exhibitionist may mask its greatest feat, facing the difficult psychology involved in suicides. The film results, he says, in "the most complete confession by a suicide and the surprising verification, of *the Human Condition*'s insight that '*one only kills himself in order to exist*.'" Amengual, *Études cinematographiques* 36–37 (1964): 172.
112. Rohdie, *Antonioni,* 108–109.
113. Ibid. On the same topic see David Gianetti, *Invito al cinema di Michelangelo Antonioni*, in *Michelangelo Antonioni: I Film e la Critica 1943–1995,* ed. Maria Orsini (Roma: Bulzoni Editore, 2002), 101–102.
114. Ibid.
115. Ibid.
116. Emile Durkheim, "Suicide" in *Readings from Emile Durkheim,* ed. Kenneth Thompson (New York: Routledge, 2004), 68.
117. See Antonioni, "A Talk with Michelangelo Antonioni on His Work," in *The Architecture of Vision,* 23. For a smart reading of the significance and prevalence of feigned suicides in Antonioni's work, see, Rohdie, *Antonioni,* 106–111.
118. He does not submit easily to pigeonholing, insisting on having a pioneering role in the neorealist movement with his documentary *Gente del Po* (along with Visconti whose *Ossessione* was also made in Ferrara that same year). He maintained that the bulk of the film (now only nine minutes long) presented socially explicit sequences on the squalor of the communities along the river, footage destroyed when the negatives were transferred to Salo in 1943.
119. Micciché, "Antonioni dans les années cinquante," 280.
120. Guido Fink, "Antonioni et le film policier `a l'envers, 185.
121. P. Adams Sitney, *Vital Crises,* 104. See also Lino Micciché, "*Antonioni dans les annés cinquante*," 284.
122. Guido Fink states that "the moralism in a Antonioni film folds over itself: in his films reality seems static and the characters are condemned from the start, totally alienated and with no chance of escape. The sentence has not been delivered but the process is finished before even starting." Fink, 185.
123. Francesco Bolzoni sees *Attempted Suicides* as the extreme conclusion of Antonioni's discourse: "A chronicle studied not by a cynic but by an implacable flogger. It is with an extreme moral hardness that the author drives his character to sin, to perdition to put them down. What was at first an attempt to understand becomes judgment. It is not solely people that have failed but people that sin and betray, before all, her own

dignity. The values of the morale seem by themselves to mean nothing, but even so the condemnation persists." Bolzoni, "Un ritratto di Antonioni," *Rivista del Cinema Italiano* 10 (October 1954): 61.
124. *Vanquished*, a film commissioned by a Catholic group in 1952, dramatizes with actors three real-news pointless murders committed by young people in Italy, France, and England. The most explicitly political of the episodes, showing a MSI (Italian Socialist movement) terrorist killing himself in "deluded act of political courage," was censored, while the remaining stories align the senselessness of these acts with an oblivious bourgeois class. The Italian story is about a rich young student involved in smuggling cigarettes. As he tries to escape the police, he ends up killing someone and eventually dies at home in front of his shocked parents. The English story about a man who kills so he can sell his story to newspapers brings out the second bind in making documentaries on sensationalist subjects, the problematic interface between the media's (and Antonioni's) publicizing interests and the singular, private nature of individual life-and-death decisions.
125. Antonioni, "A Conversation on His Work," in *The Architecture of Vision*, 117. Seven years later in an interview for the *Cahiers du Cinéma*, when Antonioni was asked whether he sees his episode as exemplary of neorealism, he asserted an ideal of total and complex depiction: "the true neorealist film Zavattini talks so much of would have included both the characters' pride in what they had done and their happiness (almost against their will) that they were still alive. I should have put all that on film there right away."
126. Credits for Donatella Marrusu films.
127. Pauline Small, *Sophia Loren, the Moulding of a Star* (Chicago: University of Chicago Press, 2009), 17.
128. Antonioni, "A Conversation," 249.
129. Brunetta explains this metacinematic trend as a profound mark left on the Italian cinematic system by the conversion from the professional model to this neorealist overturning of the professional. Brunetta, *Storia del Cinema Italiano*, 253–254.
130. De Vincenti, "I Film sul Cinema," 307.
131. Ibid., 314, ff.3.
132. Both Amendola and Danieli had short film careers, with the former acting in Jean Renoir's *French Can Can* (1954) and the latter becoming a known television hostess.
133. De Vincenti, "I Film sul Cinema," 315.
134. Brunetta, *Storia del Cinema Italiano*, 260.
135. Jacques Rivette, "Letter to Rossellini," in *Cahiers du Cinéma: The 1950s. Neo-Realism, Hollywood, New Wave*, ed. Jim Hillier (Cambridge, MA: Harvard Film Studies, 1985), 196.
136. Lino Micciché, "Luchino Visconti: Congedo dal neorealismo," in *Storia del Cinema*, 453.
137. De Vincenti, "I Film sul Cinema," 316.
138. Micciché, "Luchino Visconti," in *Storia del Cinema*, 453.
139. Marcia Landy, *Stardom, Italian Style: Screen Performance and Personality in Italian Cinema* (Bloomington: Indiana University Press, 2008), 107.
140. Ibid.
141. Tullio Masoni and Paolo Vecchi, "Zavattini or Visconti? 'Belissima' col senno di poi," in *Zavattini Cinema*, ed. Tullio Masoni and Paolo Vecchi, 132n3.
142. Ibid., 124.
143. Cesare Zavattini, *Una, Cento, Mille Lettere*, ed. Silvana Cirillo (Milan: Bompiani, 1988), 174–175.

CHAPTER 3

1. Laura Mulvey, *Death 24 X a Second: Stillness and the Moving Image* (London: Reaktion books, 2006), 175.
2. Jean Louis Commoli. "A Historical Fiction: a Body too Much" *Screen* 19, no. 2 (1978), 47.

3. See Vivian Sobchak, "Being on the Screen: A Phenomenology of Cinematic Flesh or the Actor's Four Bodies," in *Acting and Performance in Moving Image Culture: Bodies, Screens, Renderings*, edited by Jorg Sternagel, Deborah Levitt, and Dieter Mersch (New Brunswick: Transaction Publishers 2012), 429–443; and James Naremore's *Acting in Cinema* (Los Angeles: University of California Press, 1988), 20. Naremore's book and in particular his analysis of three distinct notions of the performance frame—Chaplin's *Kids Auto Races*; Godard's *Breathless*, and Wenders's and Nick Ray's *Lightning over Water* remains one of the clearest and most valuable analysis of modern cinema sensibility in relation to performance. See Naremore, *Acting in Cinema*, 9–21.
4. Alessandra Raengo, "A Necessary Signifier: The Adaptation of Robinson's Body-Image in 'The Jackie Robinson Story'" *Adaptation* 1, no. 2, doi: 10.1093/adaptation/apn019 http://adaptation.oxfordjournals.org/ at New York University on January 1, 2015.
5. See Raengo, "A Necessary Signifier," 88–91.
6. Ibid., 101.
7. The *Chicago Defender* reviewer also brings up a version of the Paradox of the actor, suggesting that Robinson cannot/should not be expected to reexperience it: "We'd like to see a real story, told with all the tears, joy and heartbreak as the Jackie Robinson story was honestly lived . . . and we just can't see Jackie able to relive his life 'effectively' for millions of movie goers to grasp its meaning. They will be so busy criticizing . . . his *acting*, which all could be eliminated if a *real* actor played the part" (March 4, 1950) [emphasis added]. Ibid., 99.
8. Ibid., 100.
9. Ibid.
10. Given the public nature of Ali's politics, it is not exactly clear what gets rephrased in these diluted citations. While reenactment's belatedness always implies a mission, one possible reference for Ali's "catching up" may be his interrupted career when he refused to serve in the Army in 1967. Reenactment's retroactive rephrasing grants this forced gap in Ali's ability to represent America in boxing arenas (as well as to his politics) an added significance.
11. See Chapter 2, in this book in particular pages 67–76.
12. According to Miguel Anxo Fernandez, in the XVII *Mostra Internazionale D'Arte Cinematografica di Venezia*, there was wide recognition of *Torero!* with a note on the part of one of the jurors to the film's contribution to realism. Fernández, *Las Imágenes de Carlos Velo* (Promociones Culturais Galegas, S.A. Edicion gallega, 2002), 135. Most relevant information on Velo comes from Fernandez's comprehensive study of the author's career.
13. Marcia Landy, *Stardom, Italian Style* (Bloomington: Indiana University Press, 2008), 125.
14. Ibid.
15. See Susan Smith's wonderful analysis of this relay between two bodies in "There's More Than One George Bailey! The Sharing of Character Between Child Actor and Adult Star in *It's a Wonderful Life*," *Screen* 53, no. 4 (Winter 2012): 440–446. doi:10.1093/screen/hjs048
16. Karen Beckman, *The Vanishing Woman: Magic, Film and Feminism* (Durham, NC: Duke University Press, 2003), 156.
17. Ibid.
18. Ibid., 169.
19. Ibid. Beckman refers to Eduardo Cadava's consideration of the connection between stars and photography, a discussion (via Walter Benjamin's work) that usefully sheds light on the ontological and representational crises that stars can provoke: "This [star] light which in a flash travels across thousands of light-years, figures an illumination in which the present beats within it the most distant past and where the distant past suddenly traverses the present moment. This emergence of the past within the present, of what is most distant and closest at hand, suggests that, like the flash of similarity, starlight appears only in its withdrawal . . . like the photography that presents what

is no longer there, starlight names the trace of the celestial body that has long since vanished. The star is always a kind of ruin." See Cadava, *Words of Light: Theses on the Photography of History* (Princeton, NJ: Princeton University Press, 1997), 29–30.
20. Beckman, *The Vanishing Woman*, 170.
21. Ibid., 185.
22. Jodi Brooks, "Performing Aging/Performance Crisis (for Norma Desmond, Baby Jane, Margo Channing, Sister George and Myrtle)," *Senses of Cinema* 16 (September 2001), np, sensesofcinema.com/2001/john-cassavetes/cassavetes_aging/
23. Ibid.
24. Millicent Marcus, *Filmmaking by the Book: Italian Cinema and Literary Adaptation* (Baltimore: Johns Hopkins University Press, 1993), 77.
25. Stephen Gundle 1999: 378, cited in Pauline Small, *Sophia Loren: Moulding the Star* (Chicago: Intellect, 2009), 16.
26. For a more extended reflection on Bazin and mortality, see Margulies, "Bazin's Exquisite Corpses," in *Opening Bazin: Postwar Film Theory and Its Afterlife*, ed. Dudley Andrew and Hervé Laurencin (New York: Oxford University Press, 2011), 186–199. I want to thank Dudley Andrew for his comments on that piece, which I integrate in part here.
27. André Bazin, "The Destiny of Jean Gabin," in *What Is Cinema?* Vol 2. Essays selected and translated by Hugh Gray. Foreword by François Truffaut, new foreword Dudley Andrew (Berkeley: University of California Press, [1950] 2005), 176–178; "Mort d'Humphrey Bogart," in *Qu'est que ce le cinéma?* Vol III *Cinéma et Sociologie* (Paris: Ed. Cerf, 1960), 83–88.
28. André Bazin, "The Ontology of the Photographic Image" in *What Is Cinema?* Vol 1. Essays selected and translated by Hugh Gray. Foreword by François Truffaut, new foreword Dudley Andrew (Berkeley: University of California Press, 2005), 16.
29. See Adam Lowenstein, "The Surrealism of the Photographic Bazin, Barthes, and the Digital *Sweet Hereafter*," *Cinema Journal* 46, no. 3 (2007): 54–82.
30. Bazin, "Landru—Verdoux—Charlot," *Education* Populaire, Doc 48, 6 np.
31. Bazin, "The Myth of Verdoux" in *What Is Cinema?* Vol. 2, 120.
32. André Bazin, "The Stalin Myth in the Soviet Cinema," in *Bazin at Work*, ed. Bert Cardulo, 23–40 (New York: Routledge, 1997). See also Dudley Andrew, *André Bazin* (New York: Columbia University Press,1990), 137–144; and Antoine de Baecque, "Georges Sadoul, *Les Lettres françaises* et le cinéma Stalinien en France," in *La Cinéphilie, invention d'un regard: histoire d'une culture 1944–1968* (Paris: Fayard, 2003), 84–88.
33. Bazin, "The Stalin Myth," 37.
34. Ibid., 31.
35. Bazin, *La mort à L'Écran*, *Ésprit* 159 (September 1949): 442.
36. Bazin, "Death Every Afternoon," 30.
37. Ibid., 31.
38. Ibid., 30–31.
39. Bazin, "The Stalin Myth," 32.
40. Bazin, "*Toro: une révolution dans le réalisme*." The article is published side by side with "*Information ou nécrophagie*," in *Radio, Cinéma, Télévision* 408 (November, 10, 1957). I make this point in "Bazin's Exquisite Corpses."
41. Bazin, "*Information or Necrophagy*," in *Andre Bazin's New Media*, edited and translated by Dudley Andrew (Los Angeles: California University Press, 2014), 124–125.
42. Ibid.,125.
43. Bazin states "this unforgettable image came back to [him] when [he] ran into its more hallucinatory supplement in color during a newsreel playing at the cinema," one that reminded him of an underwater ride in the style of *Le monde de silence*. Ibid., 124.
44. Ibid., 125.
45. Ibid.
46. Bazin, "La mort à L'écran," *Esprit* 159 (September 1949), 442–443.
47. Bazin, "Après-midi de Taureaux: 90 minutes de verité," *Parisien liberé* 3780 (November 5, 1956).

48. Bazin, "Death Every Afternoon," trans. Mark Cohen. Ed. Ivone Margulies, *Rites of Realism: Essays on Corporeal Cinema*, 27–28. "Mort tous les après-midi," *Cahiers du Cinéma* 7 (December, 1951) in In this quote I combine "Death Every Afternoon," with "La mort à l'écran," published in *Esprit* 159 (September 1949).
49. Bazin, "Toro: une révolution dans le réalisme."
50. Ibid.
51. Ibid.
52. In her book on Hollywood refugees, Jean Rouverol, wife of Hugo Butler, suggests the idea for the film was his. She describes his interest in bullfighting, and in particular the bullfighting season of 1953–1954 when Procuna gained back his standing. She tells how Hugo came home to report on the afternoon excitement and to telephone George Pepper with an idea for another project. Rouverol, *Refugees from Hollywood: A Journal of the Blacklist Years* (Albuquerque: University of New Mexico Press, 2000), 77.
53. Guillermo Cabrera Infante recreates the film's genesis in *Un Oficio des siglo xx*. G.Cain, Cited in Anxo Fernandez, *Las Imágenes de Carlos* Velo, 138.
54. Fernandez mentions that this detailed account was directed to an audience of cineclub and cinephiles from Portugal and Spain when the filmmaker discussed the film after a screening in 1985. See Anxo Fernandez, *Las Imágenes de Carlos Velo*, 139.
55. Ibid., 144. Velo points out that the sole false touch relates to the direction of the shot since that particular camera placement would not have been possible during an actual bullfight.
56. Ibid., 143.
57. André Bazin, "Death Every Afternoon," 27–28.
58. For an important categorization of bodies on screen, see Vivian Sobchak, "Being on the Screen: A Phenomenology of Cinematic Flesh or the Actor's Four Bodies," 429–443.
59. Ann Chisholm, "Missing Persons and Bodies of Evidence," *Camera Obscura* 43, Volume 15, no. 1 (2000), 139.
60. Ibid.
61. John O. Thompson makes a similar point in "Screen Acting and the Commutation Test," in *Movie Acting: A Reader*, edited by Pamela Robertson Wojcik, 39 (New York: Routledge, 2004).
62. Jorge Ayala Blanco, *La aventura del cine Mejicano* (Mexico: ERA, 1968), 262–266. Cited in Anxo Fernández's *Las imagenes*, 135.
63. Charraga Pineda, Tarcisio Gustavo, and Elvira Vera Soriano, *Cesare Zavattini en México. Un documento para la historia del cine nacional*. Tesis de licenciatura. ENEP-Acatlán, UNAM (1985), 39–40.
64. Velo had an impressive career early on dividing his time between biology and filmmaking. In Spain he made important documentaries. A cinephile, he admired Flaherty's *Man of Aran*, as exemplary of the best cinema, one in "which it is a question of an anonymous hero." Anxo Fernandez, *Las Imagenes*, 29.
65. Butler was a known screenwriter who moved to Mexico City in 1947 to flee McCarthyism. In Mexico he collaborated with Luis Buñuel, scripting *The Young One* (1960) and *The Adventures of Robinson Crusoe* (1954). Among the noirs Hugo Butler scripted under his name or under cover in the United States are *From This day Forward*, 1946; *World of Ransom*, 1954, *The Big Night* (Losey, 1951), *He Ran All the Way* (John Berry, 1951), *The Prowler* (Losey, 1950), and *Eye Witness* (Robert Montgomery, 1949).
66. A newsreel series generated by General Azcarate, an important figure in the Mexican government.
67. *Retrato de un pintor, Toreros mexicanos, La pintura mural mexicana, Corazón de la ciudad* y *Arte público* are some of the short film titles produced by Ponce's *Teleproducciones*.
68. His collaborators were José Miguel García Ascot, Luis Buñuel, Manuel Michel, and Rubén Gámez and writers Carlos Fuentes and Juan García Ponce.
69. Barbachano Ponce invites Zavattini in June–July 1955 for a scriptwriting workshop with a detailed schedule foreseeing the completion of the projects and they define their projects—(Oil, *El Petroleo*,) *El anillo* (on a magical ring suggestive of *Miracle in Milan*),

and *Mexico Mio* initially called *Carretera Panamericana* (the PanAmerican road). In 1957 he travels with Fernando Gamboa. Gamboa was a curator involved in promoting political Mexican art first in Republican Spain and later across multiple biennials. He was an important link in bringing Spanish exiles from the civil war to Mexico. During the 1940s, he created a number of exhibitions at the Museum of Anthropology and the National History Museum and directed many of these institutions. Between 1954 and 1956 he got involved in filmmaking to support his curatorial projects through one of Barbachano's series Teleproducciones, directing the documentary Mexican mural painting and Carbaval at Huejotzingo. See Raffaella de Antonellis, "*México mio:* il film non realizzato di Za" from Inform-n.239 21 December 2007 *Stampa italiano all'estero Dalla rivista italo brasiliana Forum Democratico.* This short article is a concise account of the project *Mexico Mio*.www.forumdemocratico.org.br /Inform and Anxo Fernandez, *Las Imágenes de Carlos Velo,*123.
70. de Antonellis, "*México mio*," np.
71. According to de Antonellis, 25 percent of the screenplay is published in Charraga Pineda, Tarcisio Gustavo, and Vera Soriano, Elvira. Ibid. The first treatment is from December 1955 and after intense debates in 1954–1955 and a trip through Mexico by Zavattini and Fernando Gamboa when they shot some material, Zavattini writes a letter in February 1959 officially abandoning the project. By December 1958 the project seemed to be about to start with Zavattini enthusiastically stating that Barbachano and Velo as well as their collaborators have been "notating minute by minute the life of their countrymen in the course of a day, in Tehuantepec, in Ciudad Juarez, or in Oaxaca; to them and to me it is pressing to give reports on Mexico in a way that one can feel the crossing with the essential problems of the modern world." Cited in "Mexico Mio," Cesare Zavattini, *Uomo, Vieni Fuori! Arguments for the cinema published and unpublished,* ed. Orio Caldiron. (Roma: Bulzoni Editore, 2006), 363. An ample correspondence between Velo and Zavattini is available at the Zavattini Archive and according to Fernandez, hundreds of files on Mexico as well as records of the conversations around the project are in Velo's archive. See Anxo Fernandez, *Las Imágenes de Carlos Velo,* 244.
72. Carlos Velo, "*Cronica breve del cine documental en Mexico . . .*" Mexico, 1985, unpublished. Cited by Anxo Fernandez, *Las Imágenes de Carlos Velo,* 244.
73. He states: "Mexico February 17th would be perfect, but it would be too risky. The idea of the day is liberating. One can move depending of the director's will from one place to the next with cuts." Charraga Pineda et alt. *Cesare Zavattini en México*.163–164.
74. During one year a crew of thirty collaborators among them ethnographic and literary consultants, biologists, economists, and folklore and music specialists "had scanned the country's regions collecting 40,000 meters of film, which would not be used except the material which Velo edited into a 6 hours reel." The idea was to interview people of all social classes, and to include testimony on important Mexican personalities— they cite for instance Dr.Atl, a painter who battled for public art promoting the mural movement in Mexican art. De Antonellis, "*México mio*: il film non realizzato di Za" from Inform-n.239 21 December 2007 *Stampa italiano all'estero Dalla rivista italo brasiliana Forum Democratico.* .
75. Ibid.
76. "Mexico Mio", Cesare Zavattini, *Uomo, Vieni Fuori!* 357–361.
77. That Dziga Vertov's contrapuntal, day-in-the-life organization is a noticeable influence for *Mexico Mio*'s conception is explained by the fact that Umberto Barbaro, Guido Aristarco, Zavattini worked as a "cultural agents of translation among Soviet, Italian, and Cuban [and Latin American] models of film cultures in their critical, institutional, and artistic forms." As Masha Salzkina argues, these figures represented a particular development of Italian cinematic culture that went beyond a mere adoption of the visual or narrative tropes of neorealist cinema. Salazkina, "Moscow-Rome-Havana: A Film-Theory Road Map," *October* 139 (Winter 2012), 110.

78. The alternate title of *Mexico Mio, The Panamerican Road* indicates the film's survey ambitions. And even as he participated in a lively debate with a prominent group of writers and intellectuals about the appropriate themes for a public vision of Mexico, Velo's concerns revolved around the shaping of disparate materials, in particular the fluid linkage of the *raccontini* and the different regions of the country into a unified whole.
79. Information collected by Emilio Garcia Riera, *Revista de la Universidad de Mexico* (1956), 243. Cited in Anxo Fernandez, *Las Imágenes de Carlos Velo* xxx, 145. Carlos Fuentes would later collaborate in the script adaptation of Juan Rulfo's *Pedro Paramo* made into a film directed by Velo and produced by Barbachano Ponce.
80. Ibid.
81. Rebecca Schreiber, *Cold War Exiles in Mexico: U.S. Dissidents and the Culture of Critical Resistance* (Minneapolis: University of Minnesota Press, 2008), 117.
82. Michael Denning, *The Cultural Front: The Laboring of American Culture in the Twentieth Century* (London: Verso, 1997), 154.
83. Eric Hobsbawm, *The Jazz Scene* (New York: Faber and Faber, 2014). ebook (np).
84. Ibid.
85. See Schreiber, *Cold War Exiles in Mexico*, 41.
86. Hemingway, *Death in the Afternoon* (New York: Scribner, 1932; First e-book edition 2002), 83.
87. Nathan Guss, "Danger and Literature: Michel Leiris and the Corrida," MLN 124, no. 4 (September 2009), 952.
88. The short column was published in the Mexican popular magazine called *Cancionero Picot*. On the use of Hemingway, see Emilio Garcia Riera, in *Historia documental del cine Mexicano*, from the newspaper *Novedades*, 2 June 1957. Anxo Fernandez, 137, ft 4.
89. Hemingway, *Death in the Afternoon*, 191.
90. In a reenacted serenade scene we can actually hear Procuna's high-pitched voice.
91. Leiris commentary for *The Bullfight* (Brauberger and Myriam 1951).
92. This is Leiris French commentary for *The Bullfight* (1951): "*aucune plenitude humaine a quoi ne succeed le vide; aucune lumiere qui ne se heurte a la limite d'ombre. Mais quand le soleil s'est couche un autre soleil revient et, si le jour est enterre par la nuit, cela ne dure que jusqu'a l'eclosion d'un nouveau jour. Un taureau neuf, rapide, vigoreux, batailleur et portant la tête haute—debouche du toril dans la lumière de fin d'apres midi. En face de ce taureau eternellement renaissant il y aura toujous, pour le triumphe ou por la chute, un nouveau torero.*"
93. Bazin, "Death Every Afternoon," 31.
94. This observation by Garret Stewart (25) is cited in Lucy Fisher's excellent analysis of *Marlene*, Maximilian Schell's deconstructed biopic of Marlene Dietrich. See Garret Stewart, *Between Film and Screen: Modernism's Photosynthesis* (Chicago: University of Chicago Press, 1999), 52.

CHAPTER 4

1. Edgar Morin, "Chronicle of a Film," in *Ciné-Ethnography*, ed. and trans. Steven Feld (Minneapolis: University of Minnesota Press, 2003), 231–32.
2. J. L. Moreno, "The Concept of Sociodrama: A New Approach to the Problem of Intercultural Relations," *Sociometry* 6, no. 4 (November 1943): 446–447.
3. For a comprehensive account of the origin and thrust of Moreno's psychodrama and its relation to theatrical forms, see David Kent and Cathy Carter, "The Origin and Development of Psychodrama and its Relationship to Radical Theatre," *Group Psychotherapy and Psychodrama* 27, nos. 1–4 (1974): 71–82.
4. Morin, "Chronicle of a Film," 233–234.
5. Cesare Zavattini, "Il Film Lampo, Sviluppo del Neorealismo," in *Cesare Zavattini Cinema*, 712.
6. Colin Young and Martin Zweiback, "Going out to the Subject," *Film Quarterly* 13, no. 2 (Winter 1959): 41.

7. Rouch paraphrased in *"La Pyramide Humaine"* in *L'Express* (April, 20, 1961). The issue compares *Shadows* and *The Human Pyramid* in exhibition the same week in Paris.
8. Jean Rouch, interview with G. Roy Levin, *Documentary Explorations: 15 Interviews with Film-Makers* (New York: Doubleday, 1971), 136.
9. Morin, "Chronicle of a Film," 252. These same ideas are expressed in "Jean Rouch and Edgar Morin: La decouverte du cinema verité," interview with Louis Marcorelles and André Labarthe, *France Observateur* 555 (December 22, 1960): 27.
10. Morin, "Chronicle," 230.
11. See Walter Coutu, "Role-playing and Role-taking, a Clarification,"*American Sociological Review* 16, no. 2 (April 1951), 180. Elizabeth Burns stresses, with reference to George H. Mead's notion of taking a role, that the intention of the performance is paramount and that playing a role (taking the attitudes of another) is exclusively affective and "can be switched to another realm of social reality or turned off," while "the performance of an occupational role (role-playing) is intended to be at the same time affective and effective." Elizabeth Burns, *Theatricality: A Study of Convention in the Theatre and in Social Life* (New York: Harper, 1972), 133.
12. Ibid., 233.
13. In another description of this scene he states that he had dreamed of "a sort of confrontation . . . with multiple cameras and microphones recording not only the reactions to the film, but also the conversations that would start up spontaneously . . . a big final scene where the scales would fall from our eyes and conscience would be awakened, where we would take a new Tennis Court Oath in order to build a new life." Morin, "Chronicle," 233–234. Cited in Sam Di Iorio, "Total Cinema: *Chronicle of a Summer* and the End of Bazinian Film Theory," *Screen* 48, no. 1 (2007): 39. Di Iorio mentions that the scene was added later after a weaker discussion had been shot.
14. When in this postscreening discussion Jean Pierre Sergeant provocatively mentions that Marceline's scenes worked only because she was acting, he could be referring to her reenactment monologue in the Place de la Concorde and Les Halles or to a lengthy lover's argument between the two that was excised from *Chronicle*.
15. Morin, "Chronicle," 252.
16. Sam Rohdie, *Antonioni* (London: BFI, 1990), 108. Rohdie likens the feigned and actual suicide scenes that appear in Antonioni's fiction films to imaginative acts that stage death in order to envision one "as other."
17. Michael Uwemedimo, "Inventing the Interview: The Interrogatory Poetics of Jean Rouch," in *Building Bridges: The Cinema of Jean Rouch*, ed. Joram Ten Brink (London: Wallflower, 2007), 251–252.
18. Margulies, "*Chronicle of a Summer* (1960) as *Autocritique* (1959): A Transition in the French Left," *Quarterly Review of Film and Video* 21, no. 3 (2004):173–185; Michael Rothberg, "The Work of Testimony in the Age of Decolonization: *Chronicle of a Summer,* Cinema Verité, and the Emergence of the Holocaust Survivor," *PMLA* 119, no. 5 (2004): 1231–1246; DiIorio, "Total Cinema," Graham Jones, "A Diplomacy of Dreams: Jean Rouch and Decolonization," *American Anthropologist* 107, no. 1 (March 2005) are some texts addressing these films' relation to the period's politics.
19. See Margulies, "*Chronicle of a Summer* (1960) as *Autocritique* (1959): 173–185.
20. See Dimitri Voutsinas, *Dix Années de Psychologie Française 47–56: Recueil des articles de psychologie parus dans les revues françaises.*
21. Further in the chapter I discuss the specificity of Morin's appropriation of psychodrama in *Chronicle*.
22. See Frances Cherry and Catherine Borshuk, "Social Action Research and the Commission on Community Interrelations (Experts in the Service of Social Reform: SPSSI, Psychology, and Society, 1936–1996)," *Journal of Social Issues* (Spring 1998). See also Alfred. J. Marrow, *The Practical Theorist: the Life and Work of Kurt Lewin* (New York: Basic Books, 1969), 214–215. On the Black-Jewish Alliance and sociopsychologists's work in the Commission on Community Interrelations under Kurt

Lewin's leadership see Murray Friedman, *What Went Wrong?: The Creation & Collapse of the Black-Jewish Alliance* (New York: Simon and Schuster, 1995), 137.

23. Gerald Bernard Mailhiot, *Dynamique et genese des groupes: actualités des decouvertes de Kurt Lewin* (Paris: Editions L'Epi, 1968), 137, 147.

24. Ibid. Since the psychological engagement needed for authentic exchange is not an innate gift and depends on learning "to open oneself to another and objectify oneself according to this other view" he suggests a series of training group sessions following non-autocratic guidelines. The two responsible professionals "should refuse to play traditional roles to discourage dependence . . . [or] to intervene with theoretical considerations . . . Instead they should assume the role of catalyst for their attitudes in relation to the other, respect to rhythms and psychological moments of each, opening and welcoming of any self expression . . . as the participants try to communicate with each other." Interestingly Lewin discusses the problems encountered once the agents, supposed to be models of interpersonal authenticity "have to adopts other roles besides the permissive and the safety ones.

25. Jean-Bertrand Pontalis, "Pour un nouveau guérisseur: J. L. Moreno," *Les Temps Modernes* 108 (1954): 932.

26. "The proof of reality which in other therapies is only a word here is verified in scene." J. L. Moreno, *Psychotherapie de Groupe et psychodrame* (Paris: PUF, 1959), 160.

27. J. L. Moreno, "The Concept of Sociodrama," 439.

28. Pontalis, "Pour un," 936.

29. Jean Paul Sartre, "Jean Genet, ou le Bal des Voleurs" (Jean Genet, or the Thieves Ball) was a series of six articles published in successive issues of 1950 *Les Temps Modernes* 57 (July) 12–47; 58 (August) 193–233 (and assuming at this point the title of Jean Genet, fragments); 59 (September) 402–443; 60(October) 668–703; 61 (November) 848–895. These were later rewritten as *Saint Genet, Actor and Martyr*, trans. Bernard Frechtman (New York: New American Library, 1964).

30. Leiris, "L'ethnographe," *Les Temps Modernes* 58 (August, 1950.) Sanford and Frenkel-Brunswick article LTM 60 (October) is from *The Authoritarian Personality* coedited with T.W. Adorno and Daniel J. Levinson (New York: Harper & Brothers, 1950); Le psychodrame et la psychotherapie des groupes; Introduction au psychodrame: Psychodrame d'un mariage, Anne et Frank. Temps Modernes *LTM* 59 and 60, in *Who Shall Survive: A New Approach to the Problem of Human Interrelations* (Washington, DC: Nervous and Mental Disease Publishing Co., 1934). On the American history of this postwar moment see Murray Friedman, *What Went Wrong?: The Creation & Collapse of the Black-Jewish Alliance* (New York: Simon and Schuster, 1995).

31. In 1954 Pontalis noted that the technique of sociodrama channeled "an entire orientation of American sociology interested in [catching] racism at its birth, before it crystallizes in institutions." "Pour un nouveau," 944.

32. See Frances Cherry and Catherine Borshuk, "Social Action Research and the Commission on Community Interrelations," *Journal of Social Issues* (Spring 1998). On the CCI under Kurt Lewin see Friedman, *What Went Wrong?* 137. Moreno's prime example of sociodrama's efficacy was tellingly the reconstruction for an interracial audience of the situation leading to the Harlem riots of 1943. "The Concept of Sociodrama," 444–446.

33. On The Inter-Racial Commission see Alfred J. Marrow, *The Practical Theorist: The Life and Work of Kurt Lewin* (New York: Basic Books, 1969), 212–213.

34. Ibid., 444–446.

35. Ibid., 444.

36. Ibid.

37. The school setting was quite relevant given the importance of education in West Africa. One measure of equality was the adoption of a French curriculum, as opposed to the former practice of teaching Africans the minimum necessary for technical jobs.

38. Nadine Ballot, "La Pyramide humaine: Nadine Ballot," interview with Joram ten Brink, in *Building Bridges: The Cinema of Jean Rouch*, ed. Joram ten Brink (London: Wallflower, 2007), 135–144.
39. 7 Blue, 1967, 85.
40. *L'Express* (April 20, 1961), 1.
41. Jean Laplanche and J. B.Pontalis, *The Language of Psychoanalysis* (London: Karnac Press, 2004) 4, 262–263.
42. This filmed session is not an instance of a therapeutic cinema proposed in 1944 and it is available through Psychotherapy.inc. All the techniques devised for self-awareness in psychodrama involve forms of self-objectification: to overcome the "resistance of playing oneself" and bring out a suppressed role, a patient may be asked to act out the role of someone closely associated with him. Mirror techniques should elicit comments from the patient who "may even walk onto the stage and take over his own role from the auxiliary ego." Most relevant of these techniques is reversal, in which case the patient must "react toward himself in the way he thinks someone else would." Moreno, *The Essential Moreno: Writings on Psychodrama, Group Method and Spontaneity*. Edited. Jonathan Fox (New York: Springer Publishing Company, 1987), 74.
43. Pontalis, "Pour un nouveau," 942.
44. Sartre, *Saint Genet*, 55–56.
45. Wolfe, "Extase en noir: le noir comme danseur et chanteur," *Les Temps modernes* 6, no. 59 (September 1950): np.
46. Ibid.
47. Frantz Fanon, *Black Skin, White Masks* (New York: Grove Press, 1967); David Macey, *Frantz Fanon: A Biography* (London: Verso, 2012), 151.
48. Keithley F. Woolward, *Towards a Performative Theory of Liberation: Theatre, Theatricality and Play in the Work of Frantz Fanon*, PhD dissertation, Department of French NYU, 71.
49. Fanon, *Black Skin, White Masks*, 115–116.
50. Woolward, *Towards a Performative Theory of Liberation*, 14.
51. Frederick Cooper, "Decolonizing Situations: The Rise, Fall, and Rise of Colonial Studies, 1951–2001," *French Politics, Culture & Society* 20, no. 2 (Summer 2002): 55.
52. Jean Carta, "La Réalité prise au piège: Shadows, La Pyramide Humaine," *Témoignage Chrétien* 880 (May 1961): 16.
53. Ibid.
54. Jean Rouch, "*La Pyramide Humaine* (Scénario)," *Cahiers du Cinéma* 29, no. 112 (October 1960): 18.
55. Rouch, "Jean Rouch, le bon génie des personnages en liberté surveilé," interview with Jean Grob, *La Technique Cinema*: 50.
56. Rouch, "A propos de *La Pyramide Humaine*," quoted by Jean Carta, *Témoignage Chrétien* 880 (May 1961).
57. Rouch, "La Pyramide Humaine," 16–18.
58. Henley mentions that these were scripted. Paul Henley, *The Adventure of the Real: Jean Rouch and the Craft of Ethnographic Film* (Chicago: University of Chicago Press, 2009), 94.
59. For an exploration of these textual ruptures, see my "The Real In Balance in Jean Rouch's *La Pyramide Humaine*" in *Building Bridges*, 125–133.
60. Ibid., 438.
61. Moreno, "Psychodrama and Therapeutic Motion Pictures," *Sociometry* 7, no. 2 (May 1, 1944) : 238, doi:10.2307/2785414.
62. Ibid.
63. Moreno adds: "Of course the patient himself has to be selected among many who have the same type of problem and chosen because of two attributes: a crucial personal experience touching on all aspects of the syndrome in question, and superior dramatic qualifications." Ibid., 242.
64. Ibid., 236.

65. Moreno insists that the patient is not an actor, that there is no script, and that the director and auxiliary egos (the assistants that articulate the psychological projections for patients and the audience) merely follow a patient left to act on his own spontaneous level. He warns that "action catharsis can never be replaced by spectator catharsis." Ibid., 240–241.
66. Jean Rouch, interview with Marcel Martin, "Comment vivre ensemble?," *Cinéma 60* 51(novembre-decembre, 1960): 51.
67. Morin, "Chronicle of a Film," 233–234. In subsequent interviews, as if foreseeing the interest in self-improvement suggested by the film's therapeutic project, both Morin and Rouch give out information about the characters. Hence we learn that Marilou's happiness is due to her meeting someone (Jacques Rivette), that Marceline married Joris Ivens, that Régis (alias Debray) went to Cuba, and that Angelo was fired from Renault and attempted to organize a strike at Les Éditions du Seuil, where he had been subsequently hired by Morin.
68. Rouch paraphrased in "La Pyramide Humaine," *L'Express* (April 20, 1961). The issue compares *Shadows* and *The Human Pyramid* in exhibition the same week in April.
69. The film's second part opens with a reading of a poem by Paul Éluard, subtitled *La pyramide humaine*.
70. Nadine Ballot mentions this scene was quite shocking for European viewers in Ivory Coast and the film was initially banned there. Nadine Ballot, "La Pyramide Humaine: Nadine Ballot," 135–144. Michel Delahaye disputes the notion that the film's greatest confrontation is with racism. The psychodrama takes place on a sexual plane, shortcircuiting the issue of racism. Delahaye, "La Règle du Rouch," *Cahiers du Cinéma* 120 (June 1961): 8.
71. As Jean Claude reads about youth, loving love itself, and women replacing each other endlessly, the camera solemnly crosses each of the students' faces registering a pensive expectation. "It was after the Human Pyramid that all changed, poetry infected us as poison, love entered our lives." Éluard is an obvious choice for the shift to enchanted territory, for Rouch had associated his own entranced verbal commentaries in *Les Maitres Fous* with the poet's voice, and surrealism in general. Jean Rouch described that while speaking the commentary for Les Maitres Fous "he heard himself speaking in a singular voice (the toneless voice of Éluard or Jean-Louis Barrault reading surrealist poems in the Theater of Champs Élysées in 1937)." Colette Piault, "'Parole interdite' parole sous contrôle . . . " Jean Rouch ou le ciné-plaisir, *CinémAction* 81 (1996): 142. Henley sees this love subtext as a metaphor for the intended relations between Africans and Europeans. Henley, *The Adventure of the Real*, 98.
72. Henley mentions that although Alain and Jean Claude fight for Nadine in a scene at the party, the fight might have broken out because of a scene eliminated from the final cut, in which he is teased for not passing his *baccalauréat*. In any case, if the scene's conceit is to signify fiction its verisimilitude is of minor relevance, and indeed, as Henley reports in his memoirs, Rouch recognized this inconsistency, shrugging it off as a question of the film's production conditions. Henley, *The Adventure of the Real*, 99.
73. Rouch, "La Pyramide Humaine," 25.
74. Henley mentions that Alain went to fight for the French legion and was killed during the Algerian war, while Denise Koulibali eventually became a minister in Ivory Coast. Henley, *The Adventure of the Real*, 99.
75. Dominique says that he sees why France would want to resist meddling in South Africa's internal affairs, since other countries would then bring up the Algerian question.
76. Henley, *The Adventure of the Real*, 99.
77. On this same question see Barbara Bruni, "Jean Rouch: Cinema-verité, *Chronicle of a Summer* and *The Human Pyramid*," *Senses of Cinema* 19 (March/April 2002), accessed March 25, 2004, http://archive.sensesofcinema.com/contents/01/19/rouch.html.
78. Rouch, "La Pyramide Humaine (Scenario)," 18.

79. This was the very film that occasioned Bazin's thoughts on the ontological obscenity of recording death and reanimating the dead through projection. I discuss the implications of death for reenactment in my first chapter.
80. Graham Jones writes on the relevance of the film's intervention at the moment of decolonization. He appreciates Rouch's projective cinema, stating that his camera "was an instrument for liberating the imagination that fit scattered acts of play into a visionary epic of interpersonal and interrracial exchange." Jones, "A Diplomacy of Dreams: Jean Rouch and Decolonization," *American Anthropologist* 107, no. 1 (March 2005): 119.
81. Michel Delahaye, "La Règle du Rouch," 7.
82. While Morin and Rouch see role-playing as an inherent aspect of social interaction, George Herbert Mead's notion of "role-taking" is more germane to their interest in a targeted, pedagogic "donning [of] a mask." Coutu, "Role-playing and Role-taking, a Clarification," 18–181.
83. Rouch, "The Politics of Visual Anthropology," an interview with Dan Georgakas, Udayan Gopta, and Judy Janda, in Jean Rouch and Steven Feld, *Ciné-Ethnography: Jean Rouch* (Minneapolis: University of Minnesota Press, 2003).
84. Morin, "Chronicle of a Film," 264. Rouch wrote all of the footnotes as a sort of running commentary to Morin's text.
85. The discrepancy between the film's original rushes and its final cut is extensively documented in interviews and in Morin's "Chronicle of a Film," to which Rouch wrote the footnotes. For commentary on significant editing interventions, see Di Iorio, "Total Cinema," 34–38.
86. For an earlier version of this same argument see my "*Chronicle of a Summer* (1960) as *Autocritique* (1959): A Transition in the French Left," *Quarterly Review of Film and Video* 21, no. 3 (2004).
87. Lucien Goldmann, "Thoughts of *Chronique d'un été*," *Anthropology-Reality-Cinema, The Films of Jean Rouch*, ed. Mick Eaton (London: BFI, 1979), 65.
88. Ibid., 65–66. It is precisely this nonrepresentative quality that Foreydoun Hoveyda applauds in the film. Hoveyda, "Cinéma Verité ou Realisme fantastique," *Cahiers du Cinéma* 125 (November 1961).
89. Sam Di Iorio, "Total Cinema," 38. For a careful assessment of the elisions and editing maneuvers in *Chronicle*, see pages 34–38.
90. Morin, "Chronicle of a Film," 7–8. Marceline, Jacques Gautrat, Marilu Parolini, Jacques Gabillon and his wife Simone, and Jean Pierre Sergent, Marceline's boyfriend, were Morin's contacts. Modeste Landry and Nadine Ballot had appeared in *The Human Pyramid*. The rest of the interviewees are friends of friends: Régis Debray, a friend of Jean-Pierre, Angelo, and a worker at Renault introduced by Jacques. The credits list the participants along loose categories such as workers (Jacques, Jean); students (Régis, Celine, Jean Marc, Nadine, Landry, Raymond); employees (Jacques, Simone); artists (Henri, Maddie, Catherine); and a cover girl (Sophie); but leave Marceline, Marilou, Angelo, and Jean Pierre unacknowledged.
91. Ibid., 232.
92. Ibid., 252.
93. Di Iorio describes in detail the construction of this scene out of footage shot months apart, a distinction denoted by the different mobile camera movement associated with the later arrival of Michel Brault, intercut with shots filmed with tripod. Di Iorio unravels the political elisions involved in the scene, explaining that the shot by Jean-Pierre's desk was as charged as his depression. If he did not pass his exams he could be conscripted into the military service, and his mood was related to the dismantling of the pro-FLN Jeanson network a few months earlier. Di Iorio, "Total Cinema," 34–35.
94. In Bulgaria in 1947, in Hungary from 1947 to 1949, in Czechoslovakia from 1950 to 1952, and in Romania until 1954.

95. Jean François Sirinelli, "Les intellectuels français en guere d'Algérie," *La Guerre d'Algérie et les intellecuels français*. Eds Jean-Pierre Rioux and François Sirinelli. (Paris: Éditions Complexe, 1991), 19.
96. Sartre's statement that "we may be indignant or horrified at the existence of the camps . . . but why should they embarrass us?" is but one example of an absurd denial of obvious facts. Tony Judt, *Past Imperfect: French Intellectuals, 1944–1956* (New York: New York University Press, 2011), 115. In 1952, Claude Bourdet expressly states his intention to give the crusade against France's colonial wars priority over any investigation into Soviet crimes.
97. In French *Comité d'Action des Intellectuels contre la Poursuite de la Guerre en Afrique du Nord*. James Le Sueur, "Decolonizing 'French Universalism': Reconsidering the Impact of the Algerian War on French Intellectuals" in *The Decolonization Reader*, ed. James le Sueur (New York: Routledge, 2001), 111.
98. Ibid., 107–108.
99. Ibid., 108.
100. For an articulated vision of the Algerian crisis see the June 1958 special issue of *Arguments* entitled "*La Crise Française.*" Morin's essay of the same title joins others in a critique of Gaullist government right after the May 13 coup in Algiers. Morin, "La Crise Française," 9–18.
101. Directed by Morin with Kostas Axelos and Jean Duvignaud, *Arguments* was in constant debate with the group and ideas of Socialism or Barbarism. The *Arguments* 3, no. 4 (June–September 1957) published a small dossier on the group's ideas: Gerard Genette's "Notes sur Socialisme ou Barbarie," and Morin's "Solecisme ou Barbarismes," as well as an answer to Morin's article by Claude Lefort. In 1968 Morin, Lefort, and Cornelius Castoriadis (under the pseudonym P. Coudray), jointly published *May 1968 La Brèche: Suivi de Vingt Ans Après* (Paris: Fayard, 2008).
102. See James le Sueur, "Decolonizing 'French Universalism,'" 110. As Morin stated in *Autocritique*, the event checked the movement's coherence, for it "was not possible to denounce French imperialism in Algeria without denouncing something analogous to what Soviet Union was doing in Hungary."
103. Morin, *Autocritique*, 161–172.
104. Tony Judt mentions Julien Benda's *Les Cahiers d'un clerc, 1936–1949* (1950); Jean Cassou's *La Memoire courte* (1953); and Vercors's *Pour Peendre congé* (1957). Judt, *Past Imperfect*, 32–33.
105. Mark Poster, *Existentialism in Postwar France, From Sartre to Althusser* (Princeton, NJ: Princeton University Press, 1975), 215.
106. Judt, *Past Imperfect*, 32–33.
107. Morin, *Autocritique*, 156.
108. Ibid., 180.
109. Myron Kofman, *Edgar Morin: From Big Brother to Fraternity* (London: Pluto Press, 1996), 18.
110. Ibid., 19.
111. The technological developments associated with *Chronicle* were gradual.
112. Didier Anzieu's "Psychologie des petits groups," a paper presented during the workshop of studies of psychology practitians, cites as a model the American school of group dynamics in Bethel, Maine. Anzieu mentions that the French organizers knew how to adopt for the French spirit and culture the kind of techniques learned at Bethel. Anzieu, "Psychologie des petits groups," *Bulletin du psychology* 10, no. 57 (1956): 567.
113. Tony Judt, *Marxism and the French Left: Studies on Labour and Politics in France, 1830–1981* (New York: New York University Press, 2011), 189.
114. Since his creation of the Theatre of Spontaneity in Vienna in 1923 Moreno uses the term "statu nascendi" to emphasize emergence and presence. See "Foundations of Sociometry: An Introduction," *Sociometry* 4, no. 1 (Feb. 1941), 21; "Psychodrama and Therapeutic Motion Pictures," *Sociometry* 7, no. 2 (May 1, 1944): 238, doi:10.2307/2785414.

115. Karl Schoonover, "*The Cinema, or the Imaginary Man* and *The Stars* by Edgar Morin," *Senses of Cinema* 39 (May 2006), accessed October 8, 2014, http://sensesofcinema.com/2006/book-reviews/edgar_morin/.
116. Morin, *The Cinema, or The Imaginary Man*, trans. Lorraine Mortimer (Minneapolis: University of Minnesota Press, 2005), 147.
117. Morin, "Le Rôle du Cinema," *Esprit* (June 1960): 1073–1074.
118. Ibid.
119. Morin, "For a New Cinema Verité," *Studies in Visual Communication* 11, no. 1 (Winter 1985): 136.
120. Morin, "Chronicle," 260.
121. In a politically charged contingency, the scene fictionally located in Sophiatown had to be filmed elsewhere because the rooms were too small. Rogosin felt it was ironic that those forbidden meetings had to be filmed in an empty mission, a former school that closed by order of the apartheid government.
122. Morin, "Chronicle," 234.
123. Ibid.
124. Arguments (1983), p. xxxi.
125. Another great influence on Morin's interest in depicting working-class daily life is Georges Friedmann, with whom he worked at CNRS. Director of the *Centre d'Études Sociales*, Friedmann favored in situ research and is responsible for giving enormous attention to worksite problems. Céline Béraud and Baptiste Coulmont, *Les Courants contemporains de la sociologie* (Paris: PUF, 2008), 34–35.
126. The film had been seriously criticized for its superficial representation of major issues—the deportation of Jews in France, the Holocaust, and the Algerian War. See Roger Dadoun, "Chronique d'un été: un film projectif de personnalité," *Positif* 49 (December 1962): 10–11. Indeed, there's a marked split between a light approach to the summer and personal experience—halfway into the film the characters go to St. Tropez—and grand issues hovering at the edge. The unresolved differences between Morin and Rouch's approaches to the film, with Morin advocating the heavy hints and silences and Rouch the tourist-as critic perspective, explain these variations in tone.
127. This short text comes from the editorial for "La question Politique (I)" *Arguments* 25–26 (1st and 2nd trimesters 1962), 1. The essay titles in this issue are revealing: Georges Lapassade and Morin's "La Queston Micro-sociale," Jean-Claude Filloux's "Decision collective et Socialisme," Roger Pagès "Marxisme, Anarchisme, Psychologie Sociale," Max Pagès "Pour une Psycho-sociologie politique."
128. Morin, "Chronicle of a Film," 259.
129. Ibid., 235. Jacques Gautrat (Daniel Mothé) wrote constantly for the journal *Socialisme ou Barbarie* and published "L'ouvrier et l'exploitation" in response to Alain Touraine's "Situation of the Working Class Movement," and Serge Millet's "A Working Class in Development." Gautrat, "What Is the French Working Class?" *Arguments* 12/13 (January–March 1959): 21–23. He attacks their sociological approach and uses the Hungarian revolution as an example of workers' re-vindication. See Gautrat, xx, 23.
130. It was eventually cut along with parts of a similar discussion with Angelo.
131. Morin, "Solecisme ou Barbarismes," *Arguments* 3, no. 4 (June–September 1957): 17.
132. For the influence of American approaches on French sociologists during the postwar period, see Céline Béraud and Baptiste Coulmont, *Les Courants Contemporains de la sociologie*, 35–37. In a 1955 work addressing academics, they argue that there was a need to introduce and justify the use of statistics and questionnaires.
133. Mailhiot, *Dynamique et genèse des groupes*, 137.
134. Pontalis, "Reflexions Naives sur quelques experiences de groupe: phénomènes et 'ideologie,'" *Bulletin de Psychologie* (1959): 352. He states that before being a discussion group, an institutional group is "an administrative committee with a specific division of power and conception of social relations." Ibid.
135. *Les Temps Modernes* 108 (1954): 945.

136. Pontalis, "Reflexions," 353. This issue devoted to the pedagogy of group dynamics features articles by *Arguments* contributors Georges Lapassade and Max Pages, among others.
137. Mailhiot, *Dynamique et gènese des groupes*, 134.
138. Pontalis, "Reflexions," 355.
139. Kristin Ross, *Fast Cars, Clean Bodies: Decolonization and the Reordering of French Culture* (Cambridge, MA: MIT Press, 1996), 106–107. Ross's emphasis on the cultural address to the couple and the domestic sphere as an expression of this convergence between the private and commodification has a parallel in *Chronicle*'s interview of a couple about how they live. Maddy and Henri mention their bohemian lifestyle and their consuming habits precisely as proof of their escape from the standard bourgeoisification around them.
140. Cornelius Castoriadis wrote under the pseudonym of Paul Cardan until 1970, when he obtained French citizenship.
141. Castoriadis, *Modern Capitalism and Revolution* (London: Solidarity Press, 1984), 78.
142. Ibid.
143. Pierre Naville, "Note sur la histoire des conseils ouvriers," *Arguments* 1, no. 4 (June–September 1957): 1–4.
144. Joseph Gabel, "*Marxime et dynamique du Groupe*," *Arguments* 25/26 (1962): 30. Gabel warns about the risks of the illusion of overcoming reification in a nonpolitical way. He also links mechanisms of scapegoating proper to group dynamics with the social control dynamics of Stalinist purging sessions. Ibid., 28.
145. Edgar Morin and Georges Lapassade, "La question 'micro-sociale,'" *Arguments* 25/26 (1962): 2.
146. Ibid., 3. The essay mentions that this clandestine cooperation inside the factory is "as repressed as the creativity in work, ideas that follow also from the analyses of Mothé and Chaulieu in the thesis of *Socialisme ou Barbarie*."
147. Ibid.
148. Morin and Lapassade, "La question 'micro-sociale,'" 4. In "Décision collective et Socialisme," Jean-Claude Filloux sees the techniques of group dynamics as models for collective decision-making and real democracy. Only "nondirective" models of management allow individualities to get expressed, questioning their attitudes and evolving in the sense of a truly collective conclusion. Filloux, "Décision collective et Socialisme," *Arguments* 25/26 (1962): 5.

CHAPTER 5

1. Jacques Derrida, "*Demeure*: Fiction and Testimony," in Maurice Blanchot and Jacques Derrida, *The Instant of My Death /Demeure: Fiction and Testimony* (Stanford, CA: Stanford University Press, 2000), 41.
2. Shoshana Felman, in Felman and Dori Laub, *Testimony: Crises of Witnessing in Literature, Psychoanalysis and History* (New York: Routledge, 1992), 204–205.
3. This cinema body and the quandaries of Holocaust representation in cinema have been thoroughly discussed by a number of scholars in the past decades. Joshua Hirsch, Jeffrey Skoller, Janet Walker, and Michael Rothberg's consideration of cinema's address to a posttraumatic historical consciousness; their sharp observations on how the past inheres in the present and their attentiveness to formal strategies modeled on a fragmented or recurring memories have been especially helpful in my reflection on the mediating function of reenactment in post-Holocaust cinema. See Hirsch, *Afterimage: Film Trauma and the Holocaust* (Philadelphia: Temple University Press, 2004); Skoller, *Shadows, Specters and Shards: Making History in Avant Garde Film* (Mineapolis: University of Minnesota Press, 2005); Walker, *Trauma Cinema: Documenting Incest and the Holocaust* (Los Angeles: University of California Press, 2005) and Rothberg's *Traumatic Realism and the Demands of Holocaust Representation* (Minneapolis: University of Minnesota Press, 2000).
4. Derrida, *Demeure*, 45.

5. Rothberg, *Traumatic Realism*, 140. My definition of in-person reenactment, of its flexible temporality and pedagogic instrumentality, is closely aligned with Rothberg's notion of traumatic realism and its emphasis on a performative, future-oriented address. Much like reenactment, a traumatic realist aesthetics is not engaged in a mimetic reflection of a past event but in producing "it as an object of knowledge" pushing the reader [or viewer] "to acknowledge their relationship to post-traumatic culture." Ibid.
6. Ibid.
7. Thomas Elsaesser, "Subject Positions, Speaking Positions: From Holocaust, Our Hitler and Heimat to Shoah and Schindler's List," in Vivian Sobchack, *The Persistence of History: Cinema, Television and the Modern Event* (New York: Routledge, 1996), 174.
8. See Cathy Caruth's work on trauma. Cathy Caruth. *Trauma: Explorations in Memory* (Baltimore: Johns Hopkins University Press, 1995); Gertrud Koch associates Lanzmann's organization of "the experience of the most discrepancy between what there is to see and the imagination triggered by what is seen" with other strategies manifest in early writing on the annihilation which recreated everyday life as "unfamiliar landscapes." Koch, "The Aesthetic Transformation of the Image of the Unimaginable: Notes on 'Shoah'," trans. by Jamie Owen Daniel and Miriam Hansen, in *October* 48 (Spring 1989), 23; Rothberg, *Traumatic Realism*. Ulrich Baer, "To Give Memory a Place: Holocaust Photography and the Landscape Tradition," *Representations* 69 (Winter 2000): 38–62.
9. For an influential collocation of this passage between verité and postverité cinema and its shift towards intervening and performed scenes, see Linda Williams, "Mirrors Without Memories: Truth, History, and the New Documentary," *Film Quarterly* 46, no. 3 (Spring 1993), 9–21. Joshua Hirsch identified significant aspects of Marceline's scene's modernist subjectivity importantly placing it within a genealogy of post-Holocaust cinema, alongside *Night and Fog* and *Shoah*. See *Afterimage: Film Trauma and the Holocaust*, 64–68. Michael Rothberg makes this scene the centerpiece of his discussion in "The Work of Testimony in the Age of Decolonization: *Chronicle of a Summer*, Cinema Verité, and the Emergence of the Holocaust Survivor," PMLA 119, no. 5 (October 2004), 1231–1246. I return to their important insights further below.
10. In the 1990s, Linda Williams, Fredric Jameson, and Bill Nichols identified this work as a new turn in cinema verité, a new kind of documentary that looks for the presence and reverberations of the past in the present. See Williams use of the notion of palimpsestic memory, and reverberation between events, put forth by Mary Ann Doane, to characterize the dynamic mobilization of the past in new contemporary documentary using reenactment. Williams, "Mirrors," 15, 17. Doane, Mary Ann. "Remembering Women: Physical and Historical Constructions in Film Theory." In E. Ann Kaplan, ed., *Psychoanalysis and Cinema* (New York: Routledge, 1990).
11. Rowena Santos Aquino develops a similar argument in her dissertation "Necessary F(r)ictions: Reenactment, Embodied historiography, and Testimony," seeing Marceline's testimony as embodied historiography. PhD dissertation, Film and Television at UCLA, 2011.
12. Derrida, *Demeure*, 41.
13. See Shoshana Felman, *The Juridical Unconscious: Trials and Traumas in the Twentieth Century* (Cambridge, MA: Harvard University Press, 2002).
14. Ibid., 395. This new language and legal space created by the trial will be directly pertinent to my discussion of Rithy Panh's cinema in the next chapter. Given the historical efforts to constitute a proper tribunal to judge the Khmer Rouge, running in parallel to Panh's films on the Cambodian genocide, his work generates through reenactment an alternate, cinematic court of law.
15. Caruth, "Trauma Justice and the Political Unconscious: Arendt and Felman's journey to Jerusalem," in *The Claims of Literature: The Shoshana Felman Reader*, ed. Emily Sun, Eyal Peretz, and Ulrich Baer (New York: Fordham University Press, 2007), 394.

16. Both Felman and Yasco Horsman have importantly expanded the notion of theaters of justice from a restricted legal and judicial context to art and literature as privileged display mechanisms for the enactment of critical, historical, and personal trauma. See Yasco Horsman, *Theaters of Justice: Judging, Staging, and Working Through in Arendt, Brecht and Delbo* (Stanford, CA: Stanford University Press, 2011).
17. This chapter focuses primarily on post-Holocaust cinema, but given Rouch's significant imprint on the aesthetics of the wandering monologue and on the issue of role-playing, I have included the analysis of *Moi Un Noir*'s last sequence to demonstrate the privileged role of such reclamations within films which already were experimenting with alternate forms of confessionals and auto-revision.
18. Felman brilliantly demonstrates the relevance of the Eichmann and O. J. Simpson's trials for enacting traumatic aspects that were not on trial and demonstrating the "indivisibility and reversibility between private and collective trauma." She states: "The Simpson trial starts as a private criminal case but moves from private trauma to collective trauma. The Eichman trial starts as a collective criminal case but it moves to a collective trauma to a sort of liberation of the private traumas, to which it restores consciousness, dignity and speech." Felman, *The Juridical Unconscious*, 7.
19. Dori Laub, "Bearing Witness," in Felman and Laub, *Testimony*, 70–71.
20. André Bazin. "Theater and Cinema, Part One," in *What Is Cinema?* Vol. I. Trans. Hugh Gray, Foreword to 2004 edition, Dudley Andrew (University of California Press, 2004), 92–93.
21. Ibid.
22. Ulrich Baer, "To Give Memory a Place: Holocaust Photography and the Landscape Tradition," *Representations* 69 (Winter 2000): 38–62.
23. Ibid., 43.
24. Ibid.
25. Ibid.
26. Ibid.
27. Ibid., 52.
28. Ibid., 53.
29. Claude Lanzmann, "Site and Speech: An Interview with Claude Lanzmann about Shoah." Marc Chevrie and Hervé Leroux. In *Claude Lanzmann Shoah: Key Essays*, ed. Stuart Liebman (New York: Oxford University Press, 2007), 39.
30. In *Trauma Cinema* Janet Walker engages fully with the quandary of approximating psychic reenactment to textual reenactment. She suggests that "in their textual figuration reenactments offer the film viewer an experience that parallels, without being equivalent to, that of a traumatized person who acts or feels " as if the traumatic event were recurring" and who has a sense of "reliving the experience." . . . Like the psychic impression that an event is recurring, documentary reenactments reexplore and help work through events that are in the past but still refuse to release their grasp on the present." However, she does not separate dramatizations, "reenactments that evoke genuine autobiographical events," and actual, in-person reenactment where the issue of reliving, and its representational nature and impact, may matter more. Her elegant formulation: "reenactments are powerful not just because they ressurect what was but because they constitute something that is not there." Walker, *Trauma Cinema*, 110.
31. Caruth, *The Unclaimed Experience*, 151–152.
32. Thomas Elsaesser, "Subject Positions, Speaking Positions,"174.
33. Janet Walker, "Moving Testimony: Unhomed Geography and the Holocaust Documentary of Return," in *After Testimony: The Ethics and Aesthetics of Holocaust Narrative for the Future*, eds. Jakob Lothe, Susan Rubin Suleiman, and James Phelan (Columbus: Ohio State University Press, 2012), 270.
34. Ibid., 273. See also Felman's influential reading of the scene in "The Return of the Voice, Claude Lanzmann's Shoah" in *Testimony*, 258–268. She describes how the return of Srebnik activates an intervention by Mr. Kantorowski, who animatedly explains that

the Jews willingly accepted their persecution as scapegoats for the death of Christ. In this "substitution of one memory of what happened to the Jews in Chelmno, for another that exculpates the Poles by assigning blame on the Jews, we are made to witness," claims Felman, "the re-enactment of the murder of the witness." 268. The same scene is mentioned by Williams to explain the turn to reenactment in postverité documentary, 17–18.

35. Although the psychic impact of trauma is evident in some of the reenactment scenes discussed here, I analyze in more detail the relations of mimetic and traumatic reenactment in the next chapter. The discussion of reenactment in Panh's *S21: The Khmer Rouge Killing Machine* cannot be split from an analysis of the posttraumatic disorder evident in the reenators affectless behavior, or alternately, manic gesturing.
36. Georges Didi-Huberman. "The Site, Despite Everything," in *Claude Lanzmann's Shoah*, 115.
37. Ibid.
38. Gertrud Koch "The Aesthetic Transformation of the Image of the Unimaginable: Notes on 'Shoah',", trans. by Jamie Owen Daniel and Miriam Hansen, *October* 48 (Spring 1989), 23. Referring to a film made around the time *Shoah* was in production, in the early 1980s *Terrorists in Retirement* (Mosco Boucault), Jim Hoberman states it is not "simply oral history, but a sort of existential documentary. The filmmaker not only interviews these elderly tailors at their workbenches and sweing machines but places them in situ on and under the streets of paris . . . trigger[ing] their recollections by persuading them to engage in stiff-jointed thriller reconstructions." Hoberman, *Village Voice*, April 24, 2006.
39. Ibid., 22–23.
40. Sylvie Lindeperg, *Night and Fog, a Film in History*. Trans. Tom Mes, Foreword by Jean-Michel Frodon (Minneapolis: University of Minnesota Press, 2007), 84–85.
41. Jean Cayrol, "Les rêves concentrationnaires," *Les temps modernes* 36 (September 1948), 529. Cited in Lindeperg, *Night and Fog, a Film in History*, 83.
42. François Niney. *l'Epreuve du réel sur l'écran*, 98. Cited in Lindeperg, *Night and Fog, a Film in History*, 86.
43. Lindeperg, *Night and Fog, a Film in History*, 77.
44. On Marceline's references to *Hiroshima*, see Rouch, in *Jean Rouch. Ciné-Ethnography* (Minneapolis: University of Minnesota Press, 2003), 341.
45. Michel Brault films Marceline from Rouch's 2CV Citroen, while his assistant and Morin push the car. Marceline has the tape recorder slung across her shoulders connected to a lavaliere microphone. Edgar Morin, "Chronicle of a Film," in *Jean Rouch. Ciné-Ethnography*, 240.
46. For inspired investigations of the notion of alienation and modernity in New Wave and European Art cinema, see Mark Betz's chapter "Wandering Women: Decolonization, Modernity, Recolonization," *Beyond the Subtitle: Remapping European Art Cinema* (Minneapolis: University of Minnesota Press, 2009) and James Tweedie's brilliant chapter on New Wave's special relation to a mental, cinematic geography "Walking in the City," in *The Age of the New Wages. Art Cinema and the Staging of Globalization* (New York: Oxford University Press, 2013).
47. Tweedie, "Walking in the City," 119–121.
48. She refers to both films in *Eté 50*, documentary included in the Criterion DVD *Chronicle of a Summer*.
49. See Morin, "Chronicle of a Film," in *Ciné-Ethnography: Jean Rouch*, Ed. Steven Feld (Minneapolis: University of Minnesota Press, 2003), 248–249.
50. This is the topic of my next book, *From Silence of the Sea to the Talking Picture: Extended Speech in Cinema*.
51. See Morin, "Chronicle of a Film," 240.
52. Rouch, "The Camera and Man," in *Ciné-Ethnography*, 39.
53. Ibid.

54. Michael Rothberg had remarked that Marceline's trance-like testimony is actually a kind of "ciné-transe" in Rouch's sense—an event of mutual possession mediated by the presence of the camera. Rothberg, *Multidirectional Memory: Remembering the Holocaust in the Age of Decolonization* (Stanford, CA: Stanford University Press, 2009), 190.
55. Jean Rouch, "La découverte du cinema-vérité," an interview with Jean Rouch and Edgar Morin, by Louis Marcorelles and André.S. Labarthe. *France Observateur* (22 December. 1960), 27.
56. Marla Carlson, "Ways to Walk NY after 9/11," in *Performance and the City*, ed. D. J. Hopkins, Shelley Orr, and Kim Solga (New York: Palgrave/McMillan, 2009), 15–32. Citing Carolyn Christov-Bakargiev. "An Intimate Distance Riddled with Gaps: The Art of Janet Cardiff," in *Janet Cardiff: A Survey of Works Including Collaboration with George Bures Miller* (L.I. City: PS1 Contemporary Art Center) Carlson adds that "the rhythm of walking encourages reverie and specific sound and scenes trigger recollection," 23.
57. Ibid., 16.
58. Rouch, Interview with Enrico Fulchignoni. "Ciné-Anthropology," in *Ciné-Ethnography: Jean Rouch*, 153.
59. Ibid. In an interview with James Blue Rouch emphasizes the involuntary nature of the revelations, calling it miraculous. He also mentions how Marceline after the projection said none of that concerned her, that she was a great actress, capable of acting that. She conveys the same ideas in "The Point of View of the Characters," in *Ciné-Ethnography*, 341–342.
60. Francis Marmande. "*Donc le Taureau*," Presentation of Michel Leiris "*La Course de Taureaux*," ed. Francis Marmande, 23. This phrase is reported in a letter by Andre Schaeffner addressed to Leiris recounting a "fascinating" course by Mauss.
61. Edgar Morin and Jean Carta. "*Les Dangers du 'Cinéma Vérité*," *Témoignage Chrétien* (17 November, 1961), 1.
62. Ibid.
63. Hirsch, *Afterimage: Film Trauma and the Holocaust*, 67.
64. Ibid.
65. Barthelemy Amengual, "*Théatre et Théatre Filmé*," in *Cinéma et Théatralité*, ed. Christine Hamon-Sirejols, Jacques Gerstenkorn, and André Gardies. Cahiers du Gritec, Institut de la Communication et des Arts de la Representation, Université Lumiere-Lyon 2 (Lyon: Aleas, May 1994), 33, 34.
66. Ibid.
67. Ibid., 34.
68. See Rothberg, *Multidirectional Memory*, 228, in particular the chapter "A Tale of three Ghettos: Race, Gender and 'Universality' After October 17, 1961." On January 5, 1960, Le Monde had published an analysis of reports of visits to the internment camps and prisons in Algeria by the International Red Cross committee, and in the November issue of *Image et Son*, as part of its informative dossier on Wanda Jakubowska's *The Last Stage* (*La Dernière Etape*, 1948) on life in concentration camps, one can read extracts of the Red Cross report following other entries such as "The Process of Selection in Auschwitz," "Work in the Commando at Buchenwald," "Resistance at Matthausen," "The Black Market," and "The Gas Chamber in Auschwitz." Didactically the dossier warns that "it would be suitable, after reading this text to show that the Algerian camps are far from being comparable to Nazi concentration camps; still their existence, given the state of war, is very disquieting."
69. Rothberg, *Multidirectional Memory*, 199.
70. Ibid., 236–244.
71. Ibid., 237.
72. Ibid., 237–241.
73. Marceline Loridan-Ivens, *Ma vie balagan* (Paris: Robert Laffont, 2008), 139. This chapter where she tells about her return at a period of heavy silence on the Jewish Holocaust is entitled *Le non-retour*.
74. Derrida, *Demeure*, 30.

75. Joshua Hirsch, *Afterimage: Film Trauma and the Holocaust*, 64–65. I borrow this point from Janet Walker's in her essential essay "Moving Testimony," 286, fn4.
76. See Chapter 4 here. See also "*Chronicle of a Summer* (1960) as *Autocritique* (1959): A Transition in the French Left," *Quarterly Review of Film and Video* 21, no. 3 (2004): 173–185; and "A Sort of Psychodrama," *South Central Review* 33, no. 2 (Summer 2016): 68–79.
77. Rothberg states the story told in Marceline's monologue echoes many camp memoirs, such as the third volume of Charlotte Delbo's trilogy *Auschwitz and After*, but even though Elie Weisel's *Night* and Andre Schwartz-Bart the *Last of the Just* were published two years earlier, only retrospectively they can be seen to form an autonomous discourse on the Jewish Holocaust. Rothberg, *Multidirectional Memory*, 187. See also Michael Rothberg, "The Work of Testimony,"1231–1246.
78. Annette Wievorka, *The Era of the Witness*. Trans. Jared Stark (Ithaca, NY: Cornell University Press, 2006), 81.
79. Rothberg, "The Work of Testimony," 1232. Rothberg's account, especially focused on this scene, is essential to understand the knots activated in reenactment.
80. An earlier scene from Chronicle had ended in a pointed shot showing to us Marceline's camp number. Willian Rothman has analyzed the first time the camera calls attention to Marceline's tattooed numbers in "Chronicle of a Summer," in *Documentary Classics* (New York: Cambridge University Press, 1997), 83. In one of her many illuminating essays on Marceline Loridan's presence in *Chronicle of a Summer*, Frédérique Berthet mentions that in articles coming out on the film, the participants were summarily identified as types, Marceline's captioned as "la déportée" (the one sent to camps). In addition, Berthet relays that Marceline who had gone to Cannes to promote the film participates in "*Reflets de Cannes*," a TV program which opens with images of Oranienburg, Belsen, and Auschwitz, and which thus approximates thematically two of its interviews—Otto Preminger's on *Exodus* and Marceline, interviewed on the Eichman Trial open in Jerusalem. As the commentary states, the films—*Exodus* and *Chronique*—form a postscriptum to the Eichman trial. Berthet, "Sources orales et dispositifs de témoignage: il n'y aura pas de mot "Fin"? In *L'humain de l'archive. Qui trouve-t-on dans les archives?* eds. F. Berthet and M. Vernet, 21–23 (Textuel, Paris Diderot, 2011).
81. Fréderique Berthet, *En direct de l'histoire: les archives sonores de Chronique d'un été, Revue de la BNF*, 2017/2 (no. 55), 173. https://www.cairn.info/revue-de-la-bibliotheque-nationale-de-france-2017-2-page-162.htm
82. Morin, "Chronicle of a Film," 132.
83. Rothberg, "The Work of Testimony," 1231–1232.
84. See Marceline's remarks in *Ma vie Balagan*, 141.
85. As evident for instance in the parallels between the film and the comparative structure of Duras's article mentioned earlier.
86. Like Morin, Marceline leaves the Communist Party after the revelations on Stalinism and it is she who is sent to invite Sartre to join Jeanson in her house. On Marceline Loridan's politics and involvement with the Algerian question, see Hans Schoots's *Living Dangerously: A Biography of Ivens*, trans. David Colmer (Amsterdam: Amsterdam University Press, 2000), 275–276.
87. In the DVD liner notes for *La petite prairie aux bouleaux*, Marceline claims a lot of people reproached her for not having played herself but she said she needed the mediation of actor. "I only used my own memory, departed only from my own memory—for me it was an obsession—it was essential. Since I touched cinema through Jean Rouch and Edgar Morin, I knew I had only one film to make, this one. If I had done it in 1960 it would have been different the situation with Jews was different, there was a plaque of cement on the return of the Jews, it was all about the resistance, . . . only after there was the Eichmann process that we can start talking in the 70s."
88. Debarati Sanyal, "Auschwitz as Allegory in Night and Fog," in *Concentrationary Cinema: Aesthetics as Political Resistance in Alain Resnais's Night and Fog*, ed. Griselda Pollock and Max Silverman (New York: Berghan Books, 2011), 164.

89. Emma Wilson, "Material Remains: *Night and Fog*," *October* 112 (Spring 2005), 95. citing Georges Didi-Huberman, *Images malgré tout* (Paris: Minuit, 2003), 152.
90. Lindeperg backs her analysis on Marie-Laure Basuyaux's study of Cayrol's Lazarean testimonial literature. *"Ecrire après." Les récits lazaréens de Jean Cayrol*, Université Paris IV-Sorbonne, M. Murat ed. Didier Alexandre, Dominique Rabaté, Catherine Coquio. Mention Très honorable avec les félicitations à l'unanimité (2005). See Lindeperg, *Night and Fog, a Film in History*, 118.
91. Basuyaux, 73. Cited in Lindeperg, *Night and Fog*, 119–120.
92. Lindeperg, *Night and Fog*, 120.
93. For a detailed discussion of the film, its production and reception see Claudine Drame " Le Temps du Ghetto ou 'L'Invention' du Temoignage Memoriel." In *Mémorial de la Shoah | Revue d'Histoire de la Shoah* 195, no. 2 (2011): 507–532. Drame mentions that Madeliene chapsal who wrote the narration make ample use of la Chronique du ghetto de Varsovie de Jacob Sloan (best known as Diary of Emanuel Ringelblum), besides other diaries and testimonies edited after the war but lost. Rossif invites her after reading an article in L'Express, amid the Eichman trial in 1961 an article on the filming of *The Time of the Ghetto* called "The Interior Trial."
94. The film starts with a sentimental narration and music over the rubble where the Warsaw ghetto once stood. While one review, titled "Cinema verité has found its model," likened *The Time of the Ghetto*'s manner of interrogating its subjects to *Chronicle*'s, most others found fault with Rossif's overly aestheticized approach. See Jean-Louis Bory, "Le cinéma-vérité a trouvé son modèle," *Arts* 844 (28 novembre 1961).
95. "Frédéric Rossif fait revivre leur tragédie aux survivants du ghetto de Varsovie," interview with Michel Dancourt, *Arts* (6 December 1961).
96. Frédéric Rossif, interview with Michel Capdenac. *Lettres Françaises* (November 15, 1961).
97. Lawrence l. Langer. *Holocaust Testimonies: The Ruins of Memory* (New Haven, CT: Yale University Press, 1991), 2–3. Several testimonies refer to "the context of normality now and the nature of abnormality then, an abnormality that still surges into the present to remind us of its potent influence." Langer, *Holocaust Testimonies*, 22.
98. André Labarthe, "Les Temps du Ghetto," *France-Observateur* (11/30/1961), np.
99. Santos Aquino states: "Marceline's expressive, walking body and its site-specific situatedness not only narrates her own experiences but also remembers and references those of her absent father and the history of the Place de la Concorde's role in deportations." Aquino, "Necessary Frictions," 86, referencing Joshua Hirsch. Aquino, "Necessary Frictions," 85–86. Hirsch, *Afterimage: Film Trauma and the Holocaust*, 67.
100. Aquino, "Necessary Frictions,", 86. Despite all of the references what is most striking, as Hirsch has noted, is the constitution of the scene as a mental internal space. Hirsch, *Afterimage: Film Trauma and the Holocaust*, 67 In a further layering of these passages' significance just two years prior to *Chronicle*'s release, Abdelhafid Khatib put into practice the Situationist notion of psycho-geography with a detailed study of Les Halles region, and that he was arrested in the middle of his study at Les Halles because of a curfew on Arabs in the streets in 1959. See "Attempt at a Psychogeographical Description of Les Halles," Abdelhafid Khatib, *Internationale situationiste* 2 (December 1958). I thank this reference to Katie Model.
101. It was only after Joris Ivens's death and in exchange for accepting to step back into Poland to show her and Ivens's *Tale of the Wind* that Marceline visits Birkenau. It is a fictionalized version of this return that is represented in the film.
102. Without any explanation we see small acts of resistance such as Myriam (Anouk Aimee) entering through a nonofficial gate; crossing out the word "museum" from the plaque at Birkenau and writing "Camp," and peeing by her block in a dramatized scene with a young German who is photographing the camp and to whom she responds aggressively she can do what she wants since this is home.
103. For an elaborate analysis of this relay of presences see Frédérique Berthet's "Il était deux fois une petite fille de quinze ans: *Chronique d'un été* (1961)-*La petite prairie aux bouleaux* in "Inclure (le tiers): Including (the third term)." Eds. Marion Froger,

Djemaa Maazouzi, *Intermédialités: histoire e théorie des arts, des lettres et des techniques* 21, Spring 2013 (Presses de l'Université de Montreal). http://id.erudit.org/iderudit/1020622ar np

104. On the multiple ways *Chronicle of a Summer* suppresses (and foregrounds) Marceline's identity (in order to dramatize her role as deportee), and on the importance of her solo as a creative, unframed gesture see Fréderique Berthet's "Il était deux fois une petite fille de quinze ans."
105. Jean Rouch, "*Moi un Noir*" *L'Avant Scène Cinéma*," trans.by Steven Ungar in "Whose Voice? Whose Film? Jean Rouch, Ouamoru Ganda and Moi un Noir," in *Building Bridges: The Cinema of Jean Rouch*, ed. Joram ten Brink (London: Wallflower, 2007), 116.
106. Ibid.
107. Teshome Gabriel. *Third Cinema in the Third World: The Aesthetics of Liberation* (Ann Arbor: UMI Research Press, 1982), 76.
108. Jean Rouch, "The Camera and Man," in *Ciné-Ethnography*, 40.
109. Ibid.
110. Ibid., 41.
111. Colette Piault, "Parole interdite, parole sous controle," *CinémÁction* 81 (Paris: Corlet Telérama, 1996), 144. Steven Feld states that the limitations of the time, the lack of sync sound were turned into an innovative use of sound track in which the participants are invited to react making their own dialogues and commentaries as an improvised response both to themselves acting and to Rouch's editing. Feld, *Introduction to Ciné-Ethnography*, 17.
112. Piault, "Parole interdite, parole sous controle," 144.
113. Jean-André Fieschi, "Slippages of Fiction: Some Notes on the Cinema of Jean Rouch," in *Anthropology-Reality-fiction: The Films of Jean Rouch*, ed. Mick Eaton (London: BFI, 1979), 73.
114. Ibid.
115. Brecht, *Brecht on Theatre*, 104.
116. See Philippe Dewitte, *Les Mouvements negres en France* (Paris, L'Harmattan, 1985), cited in Christopher L. Miller, *Nationalists and Nomads: Essays on Francophone African Literature and Culture* (Chicago: University of Chicago Press, 1998), 17–18.
117. On Ganda's *Cabascabo* in relation to *Moi un Noir* see Steven Ungar sharp account in "Whose Voice? Whose Film?" 118–119.
118. It is interesting to track Ganda's resentment toward Rouch even as he acknowledges the filmmaker's generosity during the making of *Moi un Noir* and after when pushing him to make his own films. See "*Les avis de cinq cinéastes d'Afrique noire*," interviews by Pierre Haffner, *CinémÁction* 81, 96–99.
119. Gilles Deleuze, *Cinema: The time-image* (Minneapolis: University of Minnesota Press, 1989), 152. This option, he states, also affects the filmmaker, who replaces his fictions by their characters' own storytelling and himself embarks in the continual becoming sparked by their characters' legends and tales.
120. See Fredric Jameson, *Brecht and Method* (New York: Verso, 1998), 47.
121. Jean Rouch, in an interview with Colette Piault, "Parole dominée, parole dominante..." *CinémÁction* 81, 153.
122. Ibid.
123. Ibid., 49.
124. Derrida, *Demeure*, 38.
125. Ibid.
126. According to Remy Besson the interview with Karski may actually have taken place early in 1979. Claude Lanzmann himself cites two different dates: 1978 in Claude Lanzmann "*Jan Karski* de Yannick Haenel: un faux roman" [Yannick Haenel's *Jan Karski*: A False Novel], *Marianne*, no. 666, January 23–29, 2010: 83; and 1979 in "Jan Karski de Yannick Haenel: un faux roman," *Les Temps Modernes*, no. 657, January–March 2010: 3. We know that Lanzmann carried out interviews in New York in November 1978, before filming with Jan Karski in Washington. See Besson's "The

Karski Report, A Voice with the Ring of Truth." Trans. John Tittensor. In *Études Photographiques* 27 (May 2011) (np), an extensive account on the making of *The Karski Report* and its editing process. https://etudesphotographiques.revues.org/3467

127. Hirsch, *Afterimage: Film Trauma and the Holocaust*, 73.
128. Cited in Besson's "The Karski Report, A Voice with the Ring of Truth."
129. On the activities and statements given by Karski as well as Lanzmann, and on the film's relation to the *Shoah* interview, as well as the controversy with Yannick Haenel concerning his portrayal of Karski in his novel *Jan Karski* (translated as *The Messenger*), see the Wikipedia entry *Le Rapport Karski*. Lanzmann's attack on Haenel's was published in the magazine *Marianne* in January 2010. He charged Haenel with quoting from the text of Shoah (which had appeared as a book in 1985) without asking for permission, and with plagiarizing Karski's memoir. Haenel replied that Lanzmann wanted publicity since *Shoah* was about to be rebroadcast on the French TV channel Arte, together with *The Karski Report*. Lanzmann and Annette Wievorka ("Haenel: faux témoignage," *L'Histoire*, January 2010: 30–31) accused Haenel of falsifying the tenor of the report, casting Roosevelt as callous distracted listener. On this controversy see Richard Golsam "L'affaire Karski: Fiction, History, Memory Unreconciled," *L'Ésprit Créateur* 50, no. 4 (2010): 81–96. Introducing the repeat broadcast of Shoah on Arte TV on January 20, 2010, Lanzmann said: 'One final word. A book by Yannick Haenel, which purports to be a novel, has recently been devoted to Jan Karski, the major protagonist of the second part of Shoah. In fact, in 1978 I had already filmed with Karski everything this 'novel' invents. This material will be the basis of a new film titled The Karski Report, to be broadcast in March on this channel. In it the real Jan Karski personally re-establishes the truth." https://fr.wikipedia.org/wiki/Le_Rapport_Karski_(film)
130. See Besson, "The Karski Report, A Voice with the Ring of Truth." Np.
131. The editor had explained that the account was shortened but retained its thrust. As Besson has noted the film strategically edits out a number of references to other figures visited by Karski.
132. Letter from Claude Lanzmann to Jan Karski, dated July 7, 1978, p. 2 of 3 (E. Thomas Wood Archive, online).
133. Ibid.
134. The prologue of the film states: "What is knowledge? What can information about a horror, a literally unheard-of one, mean to the human brain, which is unprepared to receive it because it concerns a crime that is without precedent in the history of humanity? Whatever one may say, once Hitler's war against the Jews had begun, the majority of Jews could not have been saved. That is the tragic side of history, which forbids retrospective illusions that overlook the depth, the weight, of the illegibility of an epoch, the true configuration of the impossible. Raymond Aron, who had fled to London, was asked whether he knew what was happening at that time in the East. He answered: I knew, but I didn't believe it, and because I didn't believe it, I didn't know." *The Karski Report*, supplement to Criterion DVD *Shoah*.
135. Koch, "The Aesthetic Transformation," 20.
136. Ibid., 20.
137. Lanzmann, "Site and Speech," 44.
138. Ibid., 45.
139. Koch, "The Aesthetic Transformation," 20–21.
140. See Chapter 4, "A Sort of Psychodrama: Verité Moments," 58–61.
141. Lanzmann, *"Les Juifs n'étaint pas au centre du monde," L'Observateur* (March 3, 2010). Referring to 1970s studies such as "The Abandonment of the Jews" de David S. Wyman, "The Politics of Rescue" de Henry L. Feingold, and "Terrifiant Secret" de Walter Laqueur and their "retrospective illusions" concerning history he states in the full quote: *"Il y avait, dans ce qu'ils révélaient, beaucoup de vérité, et la tentation était grande d'imaginer une autre histoire que celle qui eut effectivement lieu. Pourtant, rien n'était aussi simple ni aussi ironique que ce qui se dessinait à l'horizon de leurs récits. Il me fallut du*

temps et un travail considérable pour me convaincre que l'illusion rétrospective était à la racine de leur vision des choses. Ils reconstruisaient le passé à la lumière du présent, oublieux des pesanteurs, de l'épaisseur, de l'illisibilité d'une époque. Elevés et instruits dans un monde d'après la Shoah, un monde où un Etat juif existait, où les juifs avaient pris conscience de leur pouvoir neuf, s'étant réapproprié la force et la violence, ils étaient incapables de comprendre les temps qui avaient précédé, ceux d'avant-guerre et même de la guerre, dans lesquels les juifs n'étaient pas le centre du monde, mais y occupaient au contraire une place latérale, sinon marginale."

142. Indeed, the film insists that Poles now live in former Jewish homes.
143. Georges Didi-Huberman states, "This return despite everything, despite the fact that there was nothing left, nothing at all left to see, this return via the agency of cinema, has given us access to the violence of something that I will call the site, despite everything, even if, at one point Lanzmann himself only came up with the expression 'non-site' to refer to it." Didi-Huberman, "The Site, Despite Everything," in *Claude Lanzmann's Shoah: Key Essays*, 115. See Felman, "The Return of the Voice, Claude Lanzmann's Shoah" in *Testimony: Crises of Witnessing in Literature, Psychoanalysis, and History* (New York: Routledge, 1992), 258–268.
144. Georges Didi-Huberman. "The Site, Despite Everything" in *Claude Lanzmann's Shoah: Key Essays*, ed. Stuart Liebman (New York: Oxford University Press, 2007), 115.
145. Shoshana Felman, "The Return of the Voice," 254–262. The scene is mentioned by Williams, xx, 17–18. It is also this scene that Shoshana Felman, sees, in a much replayed comment, a reenactment of the silencing of the witness when, activated by Srebnik's presence in their midst, one of the Poles, Mr. Kantorowski, animatedly explains that the Jews willingly accepted their persecution as scapegoats for the death of Christ. In this "substitution of one memory of what happened to the Jews in Chelmno, for another that exculpates the Poles by assigning blame on the Jews, we are made to witness," she claims, "the re-enactment of the murder of the witness."
146. Lanzmann, *The Patagonian Hare*, trans. Frank Winne (London: Atlantic Books, 2012), 438, 439.
147. Ibid.
148. For an extended discussion of this scene see Michael Rothberg, *Traumatic Realism*, 234–238. Janet Walker uses Rothberg's description of this scene and his defense of it as an indication of his critical view of reenactment. See Walker, *Trauma Cinema*, especially 136–137.
149. Rothberg, *Traumatic Realism*, 235–236.
150. Dominick LaCapra, *History and Memory After Auschwitz* (Ithaca, NY: Cornell University Press, 1998), 100–101.
151. Wood and Nagel suggest the art work "can represent itself either as 'structural object' or as relic. It can represent itself either as magical conduit to other times and places or as an index pointing to its own efficient causes to the immediate agencies that created it and no more." See their *Anachronic Renaissance* (Cambridge, MA: MIT Press, 2010), 14.
152. Ibid.
153. Ibid.
154. As Bill Nichols notes even as the filmmaker is not physically present in the image, he or she is the "one caught up in the sequence of images;" it is his fantasy that these images embody, and even in a de-subjectivized from, he is "present in the very syntax of the sequence in question." Nichols, "Documentary Re-enactments," 176.
155. Ibid.,187.
156. Lanzmann, *The Patagonian Hare*, 484.
157. Ibid., 485–486.
158. Richard Carter-White, "The Interruption of Witnessing: Relations of distance and Proximity in Claude Lanzmann's Shoah," in Paolo Giaccaria, Claudio Minca, *Hitler's Geographies: The Spatialities of the Third Reich* (Chicago: University of Chicago Press, 2016), 315.
159. Ibid., 313–328, 317.

160. Lanzmann, *The Patagonian Hare*, 485.
161. Ibid.
162. James Young, *The Texture of Memory: Holocaust Memorials and Meaning* (New Haven, CT: Yale University Press, 1993), 121.
163. Ibid., 185, 186.
164. Ibid.
165. Young mentioned that the gradual memorialization of the Shoah in Poland involved often less the recuperation of the desecrated polish cemeteries and tombstones than "their reorganization around the theme of their own destruction." Ibid., 188.
166. This is Young's description verbatim.
167. Young, *The Texture of Memory*, 188.
168. Jim Hoberman, "Shoah, the Being of Nothingness," in *The Documentary Film Reader: History, Theory, Criticism*, ed. Jonathan Kahana, 777 (New York: Oxford University Press, 2015).
169. Emma Wilson, "Material Remains: Night and Fog," *October* 112 (Spring 2005), 107.
170. Didi-Huberman, "The Site Despite Everything," 116.
171. Rebecca Schneider, *Performing Remains: Art and War in Times of Theatrical Reenactment* (New York: Routledge, 2011).
172. Ibid., 37.
173. Cathy Caruth mentions this notion in "Trauma Justice and the Political Unconscious," 396.
174. Peter Weiss, *The Investigation: Oratorio in 11 Cantos*, trans. Alexander Gross (London: Boyars, 1996), 10. Cited in Tammis Thomas, "The Gray Zone in Peter Weiss's *The Investigation*" *Modern Drama* 53, no. 4 (Winter 2010), 560. Thomas extensively analyzes the reception of the play, its relations with documentary theater, as well as the allegorical, Marxist key of its intended interpretation. Concerning the preface's antimimetic statement, Thomas refers to Robert Buch observation that this antimimetic poetics "are strongly out of alignment with the play's almost obsessive attention to the concrete details of the camp, particularly to the details concerning the organizational complexity of Auschwitz's structures and procedures," as well as to Gertrud Koch's description of "the misalignment of the play's rejection of mimetic representation and its apparent striving toward that very end as a paradox inherent in the reality of the camp itself." According to Koch (as cited in Thomas), "Weiss's arrangement of documentary material into the form of an oratorio resists the false pathos of symbolization and also opposes attempts to use the alleged incomprehensibility of the camp to exonerate those who either directly or indirectly participated in making it possible." Thomas, "The Gray Zone," 560. Something of the same "misalignment" between factual and antimimetic is apparent in Rithy Panh's *S21: The Khmer Rouge Killing Machine*, as discussed further.
175. I will not expand on *The Investigation*, a controversial play meant to indict the collusion of capitalism and Nazi ideology.

CHAPTER 6

1. Panh explained that he and the cinematographer (Mesa) determined a good distance, and that logically Mesa must follow him at this distance everywhere, so when the guard went in to beat the prisoner he just touched Mesa and he understood he must stop following him. You must have this kind of ethic in your heart . . . I don't know I see people. I see the prisoners. The room is empty but I see people, so I just put a hand on Mesa's shoulder "Don't walk on people, We cannot walk on people who are lying there, who ask for help, who ask for water." Panh, "On a Morality of Filming: A Conversation Between Rithy Panh and Deirdre Boyle," *CineAction* 97 (Winter 2016) : np. Questia, a part of Gale, Cengage Learning. www.questia.com
2. Ibid.
3. For a summary of the controversies surrounding the composition of the tribunal to judge the Khmer Rouge from the moment they were deposed by the Vietnamese up to the creation of the Extraordinary Chambers in the Court of Cambodia, see the lucid article

by Youk Chhang, former Khmer rouge detainee and director of the Documentary Centre of Cambodia, "The Thief of History—Cambodia and the Special Court," *International Journal of Transitional Justice* 1 (2007): 157–172. On April 10, 2017, the New York times reported on the immense expenses in terms of time and money devoted to paltry results in terms of the tribunal's accountability. For a history of the surrounding parajuridical and didactic measures instituted to complement the court's work, as well as a summary view on the constraints in seeking justice, see Manning on the ECCC and the CSD (Centre for Social Development public forums). Peter Manning, "Governing Memory: Justice, Reconciliation and Outreach at the Extraordinary Chambers in the Courts of Cambodia," *Memory Studies* 5, no. 2 (2011) : 166–169. doi:10.1177/1750698011405183
4. Manning., 167.
5. For a comprehensive view on Panh's life and career, see Deirdre Boyle, "Finding the Missing Picture: The Films of Rithy Panh," *Cinéaste* (Summer 2014), 28–32. Boyle mentions that in 1995 Jean Rouch invited Panh to create a Cambodian filmmaking workshop under the auspices of the French Atelier Varan. He trained the crew and the first film resulting from this effort was *The Land of the Wandering Souls* (2000). The Bophana center for Audiovisual Resources was created with filmmaker Ieu Pannakar the former director of the Center for Cambodian cinema and it had, in 2014 over 150 film technicians trained there and working in the Cambodian film industry. The center's name is in honor of the woman who inspired Panh's 1996 *Bophana: A Cambodian Tragedy* (1996). Boyle, "Finding the Missing Picture," 29–30.
6. Rithy Panh states that the missing image's initial idea was a research to know if the Khmer Rouge had hidden or destroyed a reel of film. And it took him two years to get the idea of the nonanimated figurines in clay. He shot for one year and a half using rushes, but he used none of them at the end. Panh, *"L'image manquante,"* interview in *Documentaire et Fiction, Allers-Retours*, ed. N.T. Binh and Jose Moure (Paris, 2015, Les impressions nouvelles), 173, 181. Asked by Deirdre Boyle whether he employed figurines so as not to subject anyone to violence, Panh stated that for him "they are not really figurines. They are something else: a representation of the people, like a soul. An African mask is not a mask. It is a soul, a spirit. . . . With these figurines, I can do things, I can imagine." "Notes from A Morality of Filming," np.
7. For more on the Suramet theater's history and relevance in Cambodian culture, see Robert Turnbull, "A Burned-out Theater: The State of Cambodia's Performing Arts," in *Expressions of Cambodia: The Politics of Tradition, Identity and Change*, ed. Leakthina Chai-Pech Ollier and Tim Winter (New York: Routledge, 2006), 133–149.
8. On the genesis of the film see Annette Hamilton, "Witness and Recuperation: Cambodia's New Documentary Cinema," *Concentric; Literary and Cultural Studies* 39, no. 1 (March 2013), 12.
9. The tortured prisoners were asked and submitted lists of their associates, titled "strings" or "networks of traitors," that sometimes ran to several hundred names. Comparing the ways prisoners were treated under the Nazis and the DK, Chandler states that while both were "removed from any semblance of legal protection," the S21 prisoners were treated almost as if they were subject to a judicial system and their confessions were to provide evidence for a court of law. In this respect they resemble the alleged counterrevolutionaries who went on "trial" in the Soviet Union in large numbers in the 1930s. A number of comprehensive studies on this period detail the Khmer Rouge extermination system, specifically focused on S21: David Chandler's *Voices from S-21: Terror and History in Pol Pot's Secret Prison* (Los Angeles: University of California Press, 1999); Michelle Caswell, *Archiving the Unspeakable: Silence, Memory, and the Photographic Record in Cambodia* (Madison: University of Wisconsin Press, 2014).
10. Jacques Rancière. *The Emancipated Spectator* (New York: Verso, 2009), 100.
11. Ibid.
12. Natalie Rachlin, "'En fin de compte, un génocide, c'est très humain': *s21: la machine de mort Khmère rouge* de Rithy Panh," *L'Esprit Créateur* 51, no. 3 (Fall 2011), 28. Rachlin

makes two important points. First, that the effort of understanding entertained by the film involves listening to the ex-perpetrators, judging them. Second, the film refuses to "obey to the interdiction of images related to a discourse on exception. The Cambodian genocide being essentially a genocide without images, Rithy Panh saw his film—and all of its documentary work as an enterprise of construction ex post facto of an audiovisual archive of the genocide." Ibid.

13. Ibid.
14. Ibid., 24.
15. "Scenario" is a fitting term to explore the reactivation of past texts, behaviors, and attitudes in Panh's film. See my reference in the Introduction to Diana Taylor's use of this notion in *The Archive and the Repertoire*.
16. Panh, "Perpetrators' Testimony and the Restoration of Humanity: S21, Rithy Panh," in *Killer Images: Documentary Film, Memory and the Performance of Violence*, eds. Joshua Oppenheimer and Joram Ten Brink (New York: Columbia University Press, 2012), 244.
17. Ibid.
18. Ibid. See also Panh, "Notes from A Morality of Filming," np.
19. Panh, "Perpetrators," 245.
20. Rithy Panh with Christophe Bataille, *The Elimination: A Survivor of the Khmer Rouge Confronts His Past and the Commandant of the Killing Fields*, trans. John Cullen (New York: Other Press, 2014), 91.
21. Mangeot,Philippe. "Une cérémonie." *Cahiers du cinéma*, n. 587, (february. 2004), 18.
22. Caruth, *The Unclaimed Experience: Trauma, Narrative and History* and *Trauma: Explorations in Memory* (1996), 151–152. See also Ernst van Alphen, "Caught by Images: On the Role of Visual Imprints in Holocaust Testimonies," *Journal of Visual Culture* (2002), 160.
23. van Alphen, "Caught by Images," 210, 207.
24. Ibid., 210.
25. Deirdre Boyle, "Shattering Silence: Traumatic Memory and Reenactment in *S21: The Khmer Rouge Killing Machine*," *Framework* 50, no. 1 (2007): 95–106.
26. Karen Beckman (Redrobe) has smartly theorized the ways art critically appropriates the iterability of military training through reenactment. Beckman, "Gender, Power, and Pedagogy in Coco Fusco's *Bare Life Study #1* (2005), *A Room of One's Own*, and *Operation Atropos* (2006)," *Framework* 50: 125–138.
27. Mieke Bal, *Acts of Memory: Cultural Recall in the Present*, eds. Mieke Bal, Jonathan Crewe, and Leo Spitzer (Hanover, NH: Dartmouth, 1999), ix.
28. For a similar confirmation of one's crimes through reenactments based on "muscle memory," see Saira Mohammed's account of the prideful reenactment by Benzien's methods of torture by suffocation during the TRC. Mohammed, "Of Monsters and Men: Perpetrator Trauma and Mass Atrocity," *Columbia Law Review* 115, no. 5 (June 2015): 1184–1185.
29. Rancière, *The Emancipated Spectator*, 101.
30. Panh stated that it was Khan, speaking in slogan-like manner, that alerted him to the way gestures followed orders ingrained as an indissociable body-mind unit.
31. Anne Rutherford, "Film, Trauma and the Enunciative Present, in *Traumatic Affect*, eds. Meera Atkinson and Michael Richardson (Cambridge: Cambridge Scholars Publishing, 2013), 80–83.
32. Sylvie Rollet, *Éthique du regard, le cinéma à l'epreuve de la catastrophe: D'Alain Resnais à Rithy Panh* (Paris: Herrmann, 2011), 238.
33. Jean Starobinski, "The Style of Autobiography," in *Autobiography: Critical and Theoretical Essays*, ed. James Olney (Princeton, NJ: Princeton University Press, 1980), 74.
34. According to Peter Brooks,"the practice of confession creates the metaphors of innerness that it claims to explore: without the requirements of confession, one may overstate the issue—there might be nothing inward to examine." Brooks, *Troubling Confessions: Speaking Giult in Law and Literature* (Chicago: University of Chicago Press, 2000), 162.

35. Van Alphen, "Caught by Images," 206–220. Many of these traits were dealt with in the last chapters. The key writing on the issue of literalness is Caruth, *The Unclaimed Experience;* Felman and Doris Laub, *Testimony Crises of Witnessing in Literature, Psychoanalysis and History* (1992).
36. Sylvie Rollet. *Une éthique du regard: le cinéma face à la catastrophe, D'Alain Resnais à Rithy Panh* (Paris: Broché, 2011), 240.
37. Ibid.
38. Ibid., 240, 241.
39. Cornelia Visman, "In judicio stare: The Cultural Technology of the Law," *Law and Literature,* 23, no. 3 (Fall 2011) : 309–323.
40. Ibid., 310–311. Visman makes ample use of Michel Foucault's distinction between the shape of a tribunal and that of a trial based precisely on this notion of triangulation.
41. Ibid., 313.
42. Rithy Panh, *"Mon entreprise dépasse celle d'un cinéaste,"* interview with Nicolas Bauche et Domique Martinez, *Actualité,* 37.
43. Rachlin discusses how the photos are silent on the fate of the victims while the paintings show what happened but without the ability of proving. What allows the proof is Houy's confirmation. Rachlin, "'En fin de compte," 25.
44. The description of the film combines information from the close viewing of the film and Rithy Panh's " Bophana: A Cambodian Tragedy," a translation into English of the documentary in Panh's "In the Shadow of Angkor: Contemporary Writing from Cambodia," *Manoa* 16, no. 1 (Summer 2004): 108–126.
45. Stephanie Benzaquem "Looking at the Tuol Sleng Museum of Genocidal Crimes, Cambodia, on Flickr and YouTube," *Media, Culture & Society* 36, no. 6 (2014), 793.
46. Rancière, *The Emancipated Spectator,* 101.
47. Bill Nichols, "Documentary Reenactments," 176. Describing a memorable scene in Patricio Guzman's *Chile Obstinate Memory,* Nichols reflects on an image of contact, the close-up image of the hand of one of the guards who used to protect Allende, as it touches the half-open car window traversing a space, but without the engulfing crowd that followed the Chilean president then.
48. During the Democratic Kampuchea (Khmer Rouge) era, it had been designated by the code name S21. The "S," it seemed, stood for sala, or "hall," while "21" was the code number assigned to Santebal, a Khmer compound term that combined the words *santisuk* (security) and *nokorbal* (police). See David Chandler's *Voices from S-21: Terror and History in Pol Pot's Secret Prison* (Los Angeles: University of California Press, 1999), 3.
49. As Rachel Hughes reports, despite the country's emergency state after the liberation, with no medical facilities or government bureaucracy, the new authorities (KPR) pursued detailed investigation of the S21 facility, preparing it as soon as possible for visitors for international delegations and journalists. In addition to the work on S21 and its transformation into a museum from 1979 to 1989 under the rule of the People's Republic of Kampuchea PRK following the genocidal years of Democratic Kampuchea, they conducted in 1979, a trial in absentia of Pol Pot and Ieng Sary; they created a genocide research committee investigation involving exhumation of mass graves in 1981–1983; they established a local memorial—people were encouraged to place victims "remains" May 20 annual day of remembrance (Day of Anger)—and built a large shrine at the Choung Ex Killing fields on Phnon Penh's outskirts in 1988. Hughes, "Nationalism and Memory at the Tuol Sleng Museum of Genocide Crimes, Phnon Penh Cambodia," *Memory History Nation: Contested Pasts,* eds. Katharine Hogkin and Susannah Radstone (New Brunswick, NJ: Transaction Publishers), 177. In their super 8 film *Cambodia 80* archeology professor Jacques Ellul mentions that he had the strange impression, the same he got watching *Night and Fog,* that the vegetation, the plants and the trees in the courtyard of S21, seemed to have conserved the sense of pain, having witnessed an incredible pain. As he shows the film (in the video *Cambodia 80 Projection* by Lucas Vernier), he apologizes to the Cambodians for

showing them such insufferable things. The context is of the projection of whatever documents and testimonies there are, the eliciting of new testimonies galvanizing the sense of justice.
50. Some 32,000 people visited the museum in the first week it was open to the public. By October 1980, over 300,000 Cambodians and 11,000 foreigners had passed through the facility. Reporting on the visitors in the early days of the museum, Judy Ledgerwood states that "a visit would not have been an easy task; people who went through the museum in the first year said that the stench of the place was overwhelming." Ledgerwood, "The Cambodian Tuol Sleng Museum of Genocidal Crimes: National Narrative," *Museum Anthropology* 21, no. 1 (1997), 89.
51. Judy Ledgerwood, cited in Hughes, "Nationalism and Memory at the Tuol Sleng,"181. Mai Lang traveled to various countries and in particular to East Germany "where 'death camps were memorialized as monuments to socialism and Soviet liberation.'" The current director of the museum Chey Sophieu reported visiting East Germany with the then director Ung Pech by official invitation in 1982. See Hughes, "Nationalism and Memory," 181.
52. Benzaquem, "Looking at the Tuol Sleng Museum," 793. Citing Ledgerwood, Benzaquem mentions a report from the Ministry of Culture, Information and Propaganda dated October 1980 stating that the aim of the museum was "to show the international guests the cruel torture committed by the traitors to the Khmer people." Upon returning to their countries, the visitors would tell what "really" happened during Pol Pot's reign of terror. Ledgerwood, *Cambodia Emerges from the Past: Eight Essays* (Dekalb, IL: Southeast Asia Publications, Center for Southeast Asian Studies, Northern Illinois University, 2002), 108, 110. Benzaquem, "Looking at the Tuol Sleng Museum," 791.
53. Stephanie Benzaquem mentions the elimination from view of the "skull map" made by Mai Lam. She also compares recent material with old photos to reveal the changes of the museum since it opened. Photos of the behind-the-scenes rooms, where discarded armchairs, old prints, shackles, even boxes containing human remains are stored, show how much was deselected in the process. Benzaquem, "Looking at the Tuol Sleng Museum," 792, 793.
54. The Tuol Sleng Genocide Museum Archives are the single surviving documentary collection from a nationwide prison system. Besides the documents from the S21 prison, the archives include other documents from Kraing Ta Chan prison in Takeo. Although probably only covering one-third of the prisoners who were incarcerated at S21, the archives give an overall and integrated picture of the institution.
55. For more information on the documents on the Cambodian genocide as part of the memory of the world register, see http://www.unesco.org/new/en/communication-and-information/flagship-project-activities/memory-of-the-world/register/access-by-region-and-country/asia-and-the-pacific/cambodia/
56. Ibid.
57. Manning, "Governing Memory," 166.
58. Manning, "Governing Memory," 168. Manning's essay articulates the ways the composition of transitional justice mechanisms and the accounts of the past they reconstruct tend to favor existing hierarchies of power. He mentions that "the restricted mandate for prosecutions—personally to "senior leaders" and "those most responsible," and temporally to the 1975–1979 period—was a crucial factor in obtaining consent from the Cambodian government and mobilizing international support for the trials. In the first instance, by ascribing blame only to senior leaders, the trials do not jeopardize the domestic politics of reconciliation by stigmatizing large numbers of citizens. Manning, "Governing Memory," 166–167.
59. Saira Mohammed footnotes Duch's repentance during judicial reconstitution. Extraordinary Chambers in the Courts of Cambodia, Compilation of Statements of Apology Made by Kaing Guek Eav Alias Duch During the Proceedings 13–14, available at http://www.eccc.gov.kh/sites/default/files/publications/Case001Apology_En_.

Other important references on file with the Columbia Law Review are Prosecutor v. Kaing Guek Eav alias Duch, Case No. 002/14-08-2006, Notification of Interview to On-Site Visits and Confrontation to Co-Prosecutors (Extraordinary Chambers in the Cts. of Cambodia Feb. 20, 2008), http://www.eccc.gov.kh/sites/default/files/documents/courtdoc/00164248-00164249.pdf and announcing "on-site visits" at Choeung Ek and Tuoi Sleng; Khmer Rouge Leader "Enacts Role," BBC News (Feb. 26, 2008, 7:45 a.m.), http://news.bbc.co.Uk/2/hi/asia-pacific/7264203.stm describing Duch visit to Choeung Ek). The Court justified the visit as "a normal part of judicial investigation." ECCC Media Alert: Public Notice of OCIJ On-Site Investigation, Extraordinary Chambers in the Courts of Cambodia (Feb. 22, 2008), http://www.eccc.gov.kh/sites/default/files/media/Public_Notice_of_OCIJ_On-Site_Investigation.pdf.

60. Maben's film imparts great information. Besides following the early life of Duch as a math professor, it interviews and identifies many of the staff who are not specifically introduced in Panh's film such as Hom Hoey—the driver who took the prisoners to Cheung Ek, 25 miles away from Tuol Sleng; the photographer who took the identity pictures of all the dead; one of the children saved by the Vietnamese army when they discovered S21.

61. The journalists were accompanied by a three-man patrol from the Vietnam People's Army and the Front (a mix of Khmer Rouge defectors and Hanoi-trained veterans of the historical Communist Party of Kampuchea) victoriously entered the capital city. Benzaquem, "Looking at the Tuol Sleng Museum of Genocidal Crimes," 791.

62. http://www.d.dccam.org/Archives/Films/pdf/Investigative_Inertia_During_the_ECCC_Trial_Phase_Spencer_Cryder_DC-Cam_Eng.pdf provides an elaborate description of the fate of the S21 video shot by Ho Vann tay, as evidence in the ECCC trial.

63. Michelle Caswell, "Archiving the Unspeakable," 28.

64. Ibid.

65. Ibid., 126. Caswell's chapter "Making Narratives," cogently argues for the ways these silent photos (representing silent voices) are reactivated in multiple, present situations and narratives. She also briefly discusses how *S21*, among other documentaries, uses the photos as a way of sparking memories—including feelings of lust on the part of the former staff. Caswell, 106–116. For an earlier assessment of the circulation of the mug shots in art work, see Stéphanie Benzaquem, "Remediating Genocidal Images into Artworks: The Case of the Tuol Sleng Mug Shots," *Re-bus* (2010).

66. "Special Report: Truth, Justice and Reconciliation," *The Guardian* 24 (July 2014).

67. Rithy Panh, Statements to Pascal Mérigeau, *Le Nouvel Observateur* (May 1, 2012), 1.

68. Ibid. Rithy Panh with Christophe Bataille, *The Elimination: A Survivor of the Khmer Rouge Confronts His Past and the Commandant of the Killing Fields*, trans. John Cullen (New York: Other Press, 2014), 17.

69. Kristen Fuhs calls juridical documentaries "nonfiction films whose primary discursive focus is on judicial proceedings or the administration of the law." "Re-imagining the Nonfiction Criminal Narrative: Documentary Reenactment as Political Agency," *Concentric: Literary and Cultural Studies* 38, no. 1 (March 2012), 53. See also her study on how this form of self-representation in juridical contexts fits within the broader panorama of personal voice in documentary. Fuhs, "The Whole Truth and Nothing but the Truth: Documentary Film and the Socio-politics of Justice," PhD dissertation, USC, 2011.

70. The South African Truth and Reconciliation commission explicitly used therapeutic vocabulary to refer to this process. The chairman of the commission, Bishop Desmond Tutu, described its goal as the laying to rest "the ghosts of the past so they may not return to haunt us . . .[thereby] healing a traumatized and wounded nation." Cited in Yasco Horsman, *Theaters of Justice: Judging, Staging and Working Through in Arendt, Brecht, Delbo* (Stanford, CA: Stanford University Press, 2010), 6.

71. Jennifer Mnookin and Nancy West, "Theaters of Proof: Visual Evidence and the Law in *Call Northside 777*," *Yale Journal of Law and the Humanities* 13, no. 2 (2001), 385.
72. Fuhs, "Re-imagining," 53.
73. Ibid., 52. Fuhs cites Errol Morris, "Re-enactments, Part One," *NY Times*, April 2008.
74. Ibid., 54.
75. Mnookin, "Reproducing a Trial: Evidence and Its Assessment in *Paradise Lost*," in *Law on Screen*, ed. Austin Sarat, Lawrence Douglas, and Martha Merril Umphrey (Stanford, CA: Stanford University Press, 2005) 154.
76. Fuhs, "Re-imagining," 59.
77. Mnookin's essay "Reproducing a Trial," revolves around the films *Paradise Lost: The Murder at the Robin Hood Hills* (Joe Berliner and Bruce Sinofsky, 1996) *and Paradise Lost 2: Revelations* produced by HBO. The filmmakers carry their own investigations on the trial of Damiel Echols, Jason Baldwyn, and Jessi Miskelley for the killing of three eight-year-old boys in West Memphis. In " Re-imagining," Fuhs discusses Emilio de Antonio's *In the King of Prussia* (1982) and *Strange Culture* (Lynn Hershman Leeson, 2007), films that "give an opportunity to men and women who have been accused of crimes against the state to speak about their actions outside of (and separate) from the institutions that officiate legal speech." Fuhs, "Re-imagining," 56.
78. I owe this latter observation to film scholar Katherine Model. Model has mentioned that Martha Umphrey pointed out that the phrase "perpetrator testimony" announces the difference—and change in temporality—between documentary testimony and the actual trial since in court the perpetrator is always referred to as "the accused."
79. Lanzmann, "Site and Speech," *Claude Lanzmann's Shoah: Key Essays*, ed. Stuart Liebman (New York: Oxford University Press, 2007), 45.
80. On the rise of expectations around narratives of suffering and catharsis in human rights and Truth and Reconciliation contexts see Christopher J. Colvin, "'Brothers and Sisters, Do Not Be Afraid of Me': Trauma, History and the Therapeutic Imagination in the New South Africa," in Katharine Hodgkin and Susannah Radstone, *Contested Pasts: The Politics of Memory* (New York: Routledge, 2003), 153–167; Julie Stone Peters, "'Literature,' the 'Rights of Man,' and Narratives of Atrocity: Historical Backgrounds to the Culture of Testimony," *Yale Journal of Law & the Humanities* 17, no. 2, article 3; Tim Kelsall, "Truth, Lies Ritual: Preliminary Reflections on the Truth and Reconciliation Commission in Sierra Leone," *Human Rights Quarterly* 27, no. 2 (May 2005): 361–391. Kelsall, writing in the mode of a participant observer registers his slight disappointment that the stories of the victims, although "pregnant with affect, rarely delivered emotionally," 369.
81. Stephanie Benzaquem, "Witnessing and Reenacting in Cambodia," *AI & Soc*, doi:10.1007/s00146-011-0325-7.
82. Ibid.
83. For an excellent articulation of the therapeutic ethos informing Truth and Reconciliation commissions, see Colvin, "Brothers and Sisters, Do Not Be Afraid of Me." The cited portion is from Hodgkin and Radstone's reference to the article in their introduction to *Contested Pasts*, 9.
84. In a brilliant historical and theoretical analysis of the prevalence of narratives of suffering in the late twentieth century and twenty-first centuries, Julie Stone Peters tracks some of the antinomies structuring such emphasis to eighteenth-century rights culture and literature. Peters, "'Literature' the 'Rights of Man.'"
85. Wole Soyinka, *The Burden of Memory, the Muse of Forgiveness* (New York: Oxford University Press, 1999), 34.
86. Ibid., 14–15. It is in fact an imagined Cambodian case that best figures for Soyinka the perversity of reconciliation: "Let us . . . superimpose the face of Pol Pot over any one of these public applicants for remission in a parallel process in Cambodia. Is it really given to the human mind to accommodate, much less annul, such a magnitude of man-inflicted anguish? The logic of Truth and reconciliation, however demands that the

mind prepare itself for the spectacle of a penitent" Pol Pot, freed, morally cleansed, at liberty to go about his business in a humanely restored milieu!." Ibid., 28.
87. Bill Nichols describes Anwar Congo's experience on rooftop as Anwar's "idea of how a movie should end, with the hero showing his vulnerable side and winning some measure of sympathy from an incredulous audience." He suggests Anwar "is concocting a deluded, conveniently troubled image for himself." Nichols, "Irony, Cruelty, Evil (and a Wink) in the Act of Killing," *Film Quarterly* 67 (Winter 2013), at 25, 27. Oppenheimer claims that Anwar felt genuine remorse. See Joshua Oppenheimer, "Production Notes, The Act of Killing," http://theactofkilling.com/background/ (on file with the Columbia Law Review) (last visited March 11, 2015) (characterizing Anwar's experience of watching film-within-the-film as "provok[ing] feelings of remorse" and noting that reenactments "le [ft] him full of doubt about the morality of what he did."
88. Panh in conversation with Boyle, "Notes from A Morality of Filming," np. See also Panh, "Perpetrators' Testimony and the Restoration of Humanity," 246.
89. Panh clearly states "my project goes beyond that of a filmmaker: it is crucial to be also a documentarian, a historian, and even if I don't like that one treats History this way, be part of a judiciary police. I did not know that cinema should include the work of the police. I search for proofs, verify the calligraphy of writings, the facts authenticated by experts." Panh, *"Mon entreprise dépasse celle d'un cinéaste,"* interview with Nicolas Bauche et Dominique Martinez, 37.
90. Rithy Panh, "Sou um Agrimensor de Imagens," in Catálogo Rithy Panh, ed. Carla Maia e Luis Felipe Flores, 70. Published originally in *Cahiers du Cinéma* 587 (January 2004).
91. As Katherine Model has commented, Panh's approach is a fascinating turn on the practice of both Lanzmann and Ophuls of confronting the perpetrator with their own statements where the responses range from adamant, obstinacy—verbally "resigning"—to disassociation. Panh's work provides a different version of splitting the self and trying to separate the past from the present or maintain a continuity of the speaking I.
92. The minimal judgement element is the table—or desk. In Danielle Arbid's *Alone with War* (2000) a man paid by the filmmaker to guide her through places where people were murdered and tortured is filmed demonstrating at those sites through gestures and description what happened during the Lebanon civil war. As he comes close to a carbonized container, he points through the door: "Here is where they were judged, look, you can still see the desk."
93. Bophana was the subject of Rithy Panh's second film, based on the letters between Bophana and her husband killed by the Khmer Rouge.
94. Katherine Model, "Documenting Denial: Atrocities Perpetrators and the Documentary Interview," PhD dissertation, Cinema Studies, New York University, 2016. Saira Mohammed interestingly contrasts the representation of perpetrators in *Shoah* (Suchomel hidden description of the operations of the concentration camp) with Oppenheimer's flaunting of Anwar's self-representation, which he perceives as a "way of exposing impunity." Mohammed, "Of Monsters and Men," 1195.

CHAPTER 7

1. Jacques Derrida. *Specters of Marx: The State of the Debt, the Work of Mourning and the New International*, trans. Peggy Kamuf (New York: Routledge, 1994), 16.
2. Uirá Felipe Garcia, anthropologist and scholar of the Awá Guajá, spells Carapiru as Karapiru. I have chosen the spelling used in all other less specialized references. His help in clarifying various contemporary and ethnographic dimensions of the Guajá was essential in writing this chapter.
3. Tonacci discusses in detail his technical and conceptual choices in "Conversas na Desordem: Interview with Tonacci by Evelyn Shuler Zea, Renato Sztutman and Rose Satiko G. Hikiji," *Revista do Instituto de Estudos Brasileiros* 45, editora 34 (September 2007): 257.

4. Rebecca Schneider, *Performing Remains: Art and War in Times of Theatrical Reenactment* (New York: Routledge, 2011), 53.
5. Wood and Nagel suggest the art work "can represent itself either as 'structural object' or as relic. It can represent itself either as magical conduit to other times and places or as an index pointing to its own efficient causes to the immediate agencies that created it and no more." See their *Anachronic Renaissance* (Cambridge, MA: MIT Press, 2010): 14.
6. Ibid.
7. The Guajá had to become nomadic foragers in the 1800s to escape decimation and are at present reduced to around 360 members, 60 of whom live in a dwindling forest pressed by multiple corporate interests, in particular the mining company Vale do Rio Doce. The remaining Guajá live in the Caru, Jurity, and Tiracambú reservations.
8. Tonacci mentions that he reconstructed the setting, making the Aires family home look older as well as clearing out piles of garbage to show the past site. As for the acting, he only used two takes, often keeping the first for spontaneity. Rather than documentary, he prefers to see his shooting as an intentional selection of the image, with all prepared ahead of time, "using the spontaniety and the knowledge these people have after having lived that situation, accepting and trusting in reenacting reliving that." "Conversas na Desordem," op. cit., 254.
9. Rodrigo de Oliveira, "Um outro cinema pra uma outra humanidade," in *Serras da Desordem*, 71.
10. Ibid., 73.
11. Luis Alberto Rocha Melo, "O Lugar das Imagens," in *Serras da Desordem*, 25–42.
12. Ibid., 37.
13. Ibid., 34.
14. Andrea França, "O Cinema entre a Memória e o Documental," *Intertexto* 2, no. 19 (Porto Alegre: UFRGS, July–December 2008): 7.
15. See Fernando Tacca, "Luiz Thomas Reis: etnografias filmicas estratégicas," *Documentário no Brasil: Tradição e Transformação*, ed. Francisco Elinaldo Teixeira (São Paulo, Summus Editorial, 2004): 313–370. The Service of Indian protection was initially called SPI and Location of National Worker.
16. See Samuel Paiva, "Ao redor do Brasil–cinema como apropriação?" in *Estudos de Cinema*, ed. Rubens Machado Jr., Rosana de Lima Soares, and Luciana Correa de Araujo (São Paulo; Annablume; Socine, 2006; Estudos De Cinema Socine VII): 229.
17. Russell, *Experimental Ethnography*, 6.
18. Joel Fineman, "The Structure of Allegorical Desire," *October* 12 (Spring 1980): 52.
19. Ibid.
20. Luis da Rocha Melo, "O Lugar das Imagens," op. cit., 30–31.
21. The railroad construction started in 1985 to facilitate the export of iron to the coast of São Luis by the Companhia do Vale do Rio Doce, and it brought in its wake illegal invasion, disease, and development, with devastating consequences for the Guajá territory and reserves. See Loretta A. Cormier, *Kinship with Monkeys: The Guajá Foragers of Eastern Amazonia* (New York: Columbia University Press. 2003), xvii
22. Andrea França, "O Cinema entre a Memória e o Documental," op. cit., 8.
23. The years 1984–1985 were important ones in which the transition to democracy initiated in 1979 and full political amnesty took effect after twenty years of military dictatorship. In *Twenty Years Later*, though those who suffered massive repression because of their involvement with the Peasant leagues could finally speak, the precariousness of this moment was revealed in the need felt by the son of the assassinated leader to address the camera to thank President Geisel, the general who "brought us to this moment of democracy."
24. For a trenchant reading of the relation between *Twenty Years Later* to the original film, see Jean Claude Bernadet's "A Vitória da Lata de lixo da história," in *Cineastas e Imagens do Povo*, 227–242. Julianne Burton, "Transitional States: Creative Complicities

with the Real in *Man Marked to Die: Twenty Years Later* and *Patriamada*," in *The Social Documentary in Latin America*, ed. by Julianne Burton (Pittsburgh: University of Pittsburgh Press, 1990): 373–401.

Henri Arraes Gervaiseau, "Entrelaçamentos: *Cabra Marcado pra Morrer* de Eduardo Coutinho," in *Historia e Cinema: Dimensões Historicas do Audio-visual*, ed. Maria Helena Capelato, Eduardo Morettini, Marcos Napolitano, and Elias Thomé Salitá (São Paulo, Alameda, 2007): 220.

25. Julianne Burton's early account and analysis of the film are invaluable. See "Transitional States," op. cit.
26. Jean Claude Bernadet, "Vitória sobre a lata de lixo da história," in *Cineastas e Imagens do Povo* (São Paulo: Companhia das Letras, 2003 [originally published in *Folha de São Paulo*, 24 March 1985]): 235–256.
27. Ibid., 236.
28. Roberto Schwartz, "Culture and Politics in Brazil," in *Misplaced Ideas:Essays on Brazilian Culture* (London: Verso, 1996), 134–135.
29. Ibid., 135.
30. "Real entre Aspas: Uma conversa do cineasta Eduardo Coutinho com Ana Maria Galano, Aspasia Camargo, Zuenir Venura, e Claudio Bojunga." Originally published in *Revista Filme Cultura*, edição (Abril-Agosto 1984): 4.
31. In a 2003 note to his article "A vitória da lata de lixo da História," Bernadet adds: "If the cinema novo films delayed action (pointing to vague utopian hopes), *Man Marked to Die* filmed it. [*Man Marked to Die*] does not address public powers, nor does it depict apathetic peasants. On the contrary they are organized, they form the Peasant leagues and concretely confront the agrarian structure and the landowning system . . . ." Bernadet, "Se . . . " in *Cineastas e Imagens do Povo*, op. cit., 240, 242.
32. Gervaiseu makes an important remark about the scene in which a photo of João Pedro's dead body is shown to his wife Elizabeth and Coutinho remarks "they were never punished," after which Elizabeth holds a long silence, that the condensation of filmic duration stresses the fact that this photo and its framing scene constitute a "photographic archive [that] sums up a historical moment." Gervaiseau, "Entrelaçamentos," op. cit., 224.
33. Burton, "Transitional States," op. cit., 393.
34. Ibid.
35. Both Consuelo Lins and Roberto Schwartz have beautifully commented on this same scene. See Consuelo Lins, *O Documentario de Eduardo Coutinho: Televisão, Cinema e video* (Rio de Janeiro: Zahar, 2004), 52; Roberto Schwarz, *Misplaced Ideas: Essays on Brazilian Culture* (London: Verso, 1996).
36. In another essay praising the film, Roberto Schwartz remarks that "there is nothing more moving than retying a broken thread, regaining a lost identity, resisting terror and surviving it." These are "basic desires of the imagination and paradigms exploited in sentimental fiction. If *Man Marked to Die* were only that, it would not be much more than melodrama or tragedy." Schwartz, "O Fio da Meada," *Novos Estudos CEBRAP* 12 (São Paulo: Junho, 1985), 32.
37. Eduardo Coutinho, "Real entre Aspas," op. cit., 5.
38. Ibid.
39. Vincent Carelli starts *Corumbiara* with an impressive account of his video in the villages' power to cathartically reconnect Indigenous groups to their own culture and traditions. A summary of his activist engagement is in order: after living in various Indian villages, he joined FUNAI, but soon grew dissatisfied with the paternalistic care of FUNAI, which he saw as a highly pernicious jurisdiction of the state over the Indian. He then turned to an alternative indigenism. He and some other college friends founded the CTI (Center of Indianist Work) to fight for basic rights such as independent lawyers in Indian disputes with the state. Later, many of these rights were incorporated in the 1988 constitution. In that same decade—the late 1970s–80s—he started working on an image bank for the publication "Indigenous Peoples

of Brazil." "*Moi un Indien*" biblioteca videonas ladeias. Video nas Aldeias, http://www.videonasaldeias.org.br/2009/biblioteca.php?c=19 Viewed 1/20/12.

40. Eve Kosofsky Sedwick cited in Rebecca Schneider, *Performing Remains: Art and War in Times of Theatrical Reenactment* (New York: Routledge, 2011), 35, fn7.

41. Ibid.

42. Ruy Gardnier, "Julio Bressane makes his *Voyage around Brazil*, in three parts and Rogerio Sganzerla makes a film on old manuscripts and archeology, *The Abyss* and Elyseu Visconti had already a career of films based on rite and religiosity." In Gardnier, "Tonacci, O eros e o Zero," in *Andrea Tonacci: A Volta do Gigante Discreto, Contracampo* 70 dossier on Tonacci. http://www.contracampo.com.br/79/artigos.htm.Viewed12/21/11.Np.

43. The details of this intertribal communication project are fascinating and the results await the funding to transfer the various 1970s video gauges to current formats. In 1978, Tonacci got two Guggenheim fellowships and he started shooting in several reservations in North Central and South America. After *The Araras* in 1982–1983 and until he learned of Carapiru's story in 1993 from Possuelo, he filmed with the Krao, with the Guarani at the frontier with Paraguay, and on fictional films following some Indian myths. He wanted to tell a story "that has been erased—from our ethnocentric Western history, the equivalent of our Greece, Rome." Tonacci, "*Entrevista*," in *Serras da Desordem*, op. cit., 109. He claims he moved between villages and official forms of representation. He shot a number of projects in various American countries—United States, Mexico, Peru, Bolivia, and Brazil—and he showed this material so his subjects would tell him what was significant. "Entrevista com Tonacci," by Daniel Caetano, Francis Vogner, Francisco Guarnieri, and Guilherme Martins in *Contracampo* 70, op. cit. np.

44. Tonacci, "Entrevista," *Serras da Desordem*, op. cit., 97–98.

45. He relates two such experiences. The first with a super-8mm camera given to the Canela results "in off-framed realities—heads, upside down images, just the top of trees. The second experience was with the Araras an Isolated group (and these images remain unedited). They never saw their own image, except when he shows to an Indian Piput the cumulative recordings of several past weeks and he sees images of Indians who had died from colds, and he retreats from the camera." "Conversas na Desordem," op. cit., 244–245.

46. Ibid., 243.

47. Ibid., 245–246.

48. Tonacci, "Entrevista," in *Serras da Desordem*, op. cit., 100.

49. His proposal to hand cameras to the Indians, submitted initially to CTI (Centro de Trabalho Indigenista) avowedly inspired Vincent Carelli's to use video camcorder in his well-known "Video nas Aldeias" project of self-ethnography. Carelli describes his trajectory in the autobiographical essay "Moi un Indien," op. cit.

50. See Tonacci's presentation of the film. In "Palavras de Tonacci," *Contracampo* 70, op. cit. In a longer text in this same online issue, he states: "Notwithstanding the fact that in this work the eye, through the camera, more than *showing* tries to *see* the cosmic vital relation in the Canela universe, this work has the objective intention to make, as wished by the community, a documentary/document of revindication of its rights to land, directed to the Brasilia Authorities. This partial demand, verbalized, contained in sound whose clear listening allows one to understand the motivation of the conflict and the territorial occupation of the physical space traditionally occupied by the group, is obstructed by the lack of subtitles translating what is said in Ge and in Portuguese in some sequences. However its broad meaning is clearly expressed, visible and sensible through the image that offers a vision lacking in exotic nostalgia and which does not transform the Indians in mere objects, nor the film in simple document political-ideological. They are there as individuals, full of integrity, carriers of a Knowledge and experience of a Totality whose meaning, in our cultural massified formation already escapes us, and the images recover, accessing their vision."

51. Ruy Gardnier, who notes that *Conversations* avoids the mutual ratification of discourses and dialectical oppositions common to documentaries intent in instituting a totality. "Os Araras e *Conversas no Maranhão*," in *Contracampo* 70.
52. "Palavras de Tonacci," *Contracampo* 70, op. cit.
53. Tonacci tells how years later a group of Canela who were children at the time of the film, came to his place and, after watching *Conversations in Maranhão*, revised key narratives about their history. "Conversas na Desordem," op. cit, 251.
54. Clarice Castro Alvarenga, "A camera e a flecha em Corumbiara," *Devires* 9, no. 1 (2012), 124. In this key essay Alvarenga rethinks a number of questions related to the contact as well as first contact between indigenous groups and the cinematic apparatus.
55. Only in 1987 after an encounter among several NGOs in 1986—CMI, the Indigenist Missionary Council, OPAN (Operação Anchieta/today Operação Mata Nativa), UNI, Cedi—FUNAI officially changed its compromised policies of contacting Indians, in order to free the area for building roads and hydroelectric plants. "Isolados: Historico" http://pib.socioambiental.org/pt/c/no-brasil-atual/quem-sao/isolados:-historico.
56. See Tonacci's anecdotes around his North American tracking of Indigenous groups in "Entrevista com Tonacci," *Contracampo* 70, op. cit.
57. Tonacci states they were paid, they talked about who wanted to participate and what they wanted in exchange. "Conversas na Desordem," op. cit., 251–252.
58. Ibid., 128.
59. As Andrea França points out, Tonacci brings to bear in his Great Brazil sequence the connotations of fiction, irreverence, and profanity attached to the roles played by Paulo Cesar Pereio. França, "O Cinema entre a Memória e o Documental," op. cit., 7–8.
60. The title *Iracema uma transa Amazonica* can be roughly translated as *Iracema*, an Amazonian fuck. *Transar* in Portuguese means to have sexual relations or any other form of exchange. Iracema is also the quintessential Indian mythical name.
61. Ismail Xavier, *Allegories of Underdevelopment: Aesthetics and Politics in Modern Brazilian Cinema* (Minneapolis: University of Minnesotta Press, 1997), 237. With a title that refers both to the region of Carapirú's wandering and to a nation in a state of disarticulation, *Serras da Desordem* (*Hills of Chaos*) constitutes a significant addition to Brazilian cinema's allegorical tradition.
62. Ibid., 240. For a definitive discussion of *Iracema*, see Ismail Xavier, "Iracema: Transcending Cinema Verité," in *The Social Documentary in Latin America*, op. cit., 361–372. On the insight of the character's double subjection—at the level of plot and cinema's material reality and process—see p. 370.
63. Luis Carlos Oliveira Jr., "Iracema, uma transa Amazonica," in *Contracampo* 77. http://www.contracampo.com.br/77/dvdvhsiracema.htm
64. França, "O Cinema entre a Memória e o Documental," op. cit., 10.
65. Tonacci, "Entrevista," 135.
66. Rodrigo de Oliveira, "A caça do Rinoceronte," *Contracampo* 79, np.
67. Xavier, *Allegories*, 221.
68. Ibid., 219–231.
69. Ibid. In "O Cinema Marginal Revisitado ou o Avesso dos anos 90," Xavier discusses the Marginal movement's resistance to Cinema Novo's program to "turn cinema into a ritual of national identity," its aesthetic violence an oblique reference to "the context of urban guerrilla answering the darkest hour of the dictatorship." Xavier, in *Cinema Marginal Brasileiro e suas Fronteiras: Filmes Produzidos nos anos 60 e 70*, ed. Eugenio Puppo (Brasilia: Centro Cultural do Banco do Brasil, 2004), 23–24.
70. Rodrigo de Oliveira, "*A caça do Rinoceronte*," np.
71. Tonacci, "Entrevista: Territorio da Ambiguidade," in *Teorema* 50.
72. Ibid., 49.
73. Ibid.
74. Tonacci, "Entrevista," *Serras da Desordem*, op. cit., 114.
75. http://www.youtube.com/watch?v=R4LhfieciNQ, viewed on 12/21/11.
76. Tonacci, "Entrevista," op. cit., 113–114.

77. Ibid., 104.
78. Alexander Nagel and Christopher Wood, *Anachronic Renaissance* (Cambridge, MA: MIT, 2010), 14.
79. Eduardo Viveiros de Castro, *Eduardo Viveiros de Castro*, Coleção Encontros, ed. Renato Sztutman (Rio de Janeiro: Azogue, 2008), 150.
80. Importantly this is "not a conception of individual either for one cannot determine who "is Indian" independently from the self-determination work done by indigenous communities, founded themselves in an enlarged concept of kinship admitting affinity, adoptive filiation, religious and ritual kinship." Ibid., 152–155.
81. Ibid., 150.
82. They could not reenact the encounter because Carapiru had an accident in Brasilia and they had to interrupt the filming for six months. "The two sit down, stay silent for a long time then one speaks for one hour the other speaks for two hours, then it seems both chant something and that is it. There are no hugs, no crying." See Tonacci, "Conversas na Desordem," 248.
83. Interview with Tonacci, "Conversas na Desordem," 248.
84. Loretta Cormier, "Decolonizing History: Ritual Transformation of the Past among the Guajá of Eastern Amazonia," *Histories and Historicities in Amazonia*, ed. Neil L. Whitehead (Lincoln: University of Nebraska Press, 2003), 126.
85. Ibid., 127. Cormier explains further that: "the Guajá notion of the self is complex, as individuals are believed to be manifested in multiple states with alters with semi-overlapping consciousness with each other. Three basic modes of being exist: the earthly bodies of the living, the earthly bodies of the dead and the multiple sacred bodies in the sky. The latter can be considered a form of ritualized remembering. For the Guajá these are not merely mental imagery but they have independent existence from the Guajá." Cormier, "Decolonizing History," 127.
86. Ibid., 132.
87. Loretta A. Cormier, *Kinship with Monkeys: The Guajá Foragers of Eastern Amazonia* (New York: Columbia University Press. 2003), Hunter College ebrary 75.
88. Ibid., xx, 65. In "Decolonizing" (op. cit., 130), Cormier states they manifest a profound genealogical amnesia: "Although encounters with dead ancestors are central to their religious life the Guajá have difficulty recalling the names of their dead after several years have passed, they even have difficulty recalling the names of their own parents."
89. Cormier, *Kinship*, 75.
90. This, in contrast to several other Amazonian groups, in contrast to several other Amazonian groups.
91. Eduardo Viveiros de Castro, "Exchanging Perspectives: The Transformation of Objects into Subjects in Amerindian Ontologies," *Common Knowledge* 10, no. 3 (Durham, NC: Duke University Press, 2004), 465. This implies a "perspectival multinaturalism," Viveiros de Castro's concept for an indigenous theory "according to which the different sorts of persons—human and nonhuman (animals, spirits, the dead, denizens of other cosmic layers, plants, occasionally even objects and artifacts)—apprehend reality from distinct points of view." Ibid., 466.
92. Ibid., 89.
93. See Cormier, *Kinship*, Chapters 6 and 7.
94. Nancy Bentley, "The Fourth Dimension: *Kinlessness* and African American Narrative," *Critical Inquiry* 35 (2009): 283.
95. Ibid., 276.
96. Ibid., 270–271.
97. Ibid., 281.
98. Ibid., 288.
99. Tonacci, "Entrevista," in *Serras da Desordem*, ed. Daniel Caetano (Rio de Janeiro: Azogue Editorial, 2008): 120.
100. Xavier, "Artimanhas do fogo," op. cit., 18.

101. Xavier, "As Artimanhas do Fogo, para além do encanto e do mistério," in *Serras da Desordem*, ed. Daniel Caetano (Rio de Janeiro: Azogue Editorial, 2008) : 11–24.
102. Ibid., 23.
103. Tonacci's apposition follows the same logic described by Robin Bernstein in her analysis of photos in which people pose with cut-out objects. Objects, she claims, introduce a different register of textuality scripting a person's body. See Bernstein, "Dances with Things: Material Culture and the Performance of Race," *Social Text* volume 27 number 4 (winter 2009): 67–94.
104. Loretta Cormier, *Kinship*, 6.
105. Rebecca Schneider refers to Richard Schechner's known definition of peformance as restored or "twice-behaved" behavior. Schechner, *Between Theater and Anthropology* (Philadelphia: University of Pennsylvania Press, 1985), 36. She significantly complicates his collocation showing the flaws of Schechner's attempt to separate restoration (of the past and done with acts) from actualization. See Schneider, *Performing Remains: Art and War in Times of Theatrical Reenactment* (New York: Routledge, 2011), 218, n. 39.
106. Schneider, *Performing Remians*, op. cit., 37.
107. Bliss Cua Lim, *Translating time: Cinema, the Fantastic and Temporal Critique.* (Durham, NC: Duke University Press, 2009), 27.
108. Ibid., 32–33.

CONCLUSION

1. Awá-Guajá scholar Uirá Felipe Garcia, in conversation. I thank Eduardo Viveiros de Castro for the suggestion I contact Felipe Garcia.
2. Ibid.
3. Uirá Felipe Garcia mentions that the village is exactly as Tonacci filmed it. For an extended analysis of the Guajá relation with monkeys, see Cormier, *Kinship*, op. cit. chapters 6 and 7.
4. Cristina Amaral, the editor of *Serras*, comments that there was a real effort to recreate that reality prior to the massacre, an entire attentiveness to rhythm, silence to another temporality.
5. Jean-André Fieschi, "Slippages of Fiction: Some Notes on the Cinema of Jean Rouch," in *Anthropology-Reality-Cinema: The Films of Jean Rouch*, ed. Mick Eaton (London: BFI, 1979), 70.
6. James Clifford, "On Ethnographic Surrealism," in *The Predicament of Culture: Twentieth-Century Ethnography, Literature, and Art* (Cambridge, MA: Harvard University Press, 1988), 146.
7. Réda Bensmaïa, "A Cinema of Cruelty," in *Building Bridges: The Cinema of Jean Rouch*, ed. Joram ten Brink, preface by Michael Renov (London: Wallflower, 2007): 78.
8. Citing Daney, Charles Tesson says: "Bunuel's humanism is rather that of honesty (the morality) of a man that accepts to be in direct contact with his contradictions, without imagining too much he can resolve them . . . a rigorous artisan that once he declares war knows he cannot do differently, nor can he win. But who knows always differentiate between what is secondary and the betrayal of what is the main thing." Tesson, *Luis Buñuel* (Paris: Cahiers du Cinéma, 1995), 193.
9. Roberto Schwartz, "Cinema and *The Guns*," in idem., *Misplaced Ideas: Essays on Brazilian Culture* (London: Verso, 1992), 161. He continues: "This distance is the contrary of philanthropy; short of transformation there is no possible humanity; or from the perspective of the plot, short of transformation there is no difference that matters."
10. Ibid.
11. Tesson, op. cit., 90.
12. Giorgio Agamben, *The Coming Community*, trans. Michael Hardt (Minneapolis: University of Minnesota Press, 1993), 1. See also Karen Shimakawa, "The Things We Share: Ethnic Performativity and 'Whatever Being,'" *Journal of Speculative Philosophy* 18, no. 2 (2004): 149–160.

13. From reenactment to repurposed archives of national media Tonacci's approach is one at a remove. Evident in his ethnographic documentaries *Conversas no Maranhão* and *Araras* and in the reservation scene in *Serras* is a very particular way to rhetorically underline the significance of what he sees. Through slight spatial and temporal syncopations performed via editing and reframing he steers certain images to function performatively, as *address* and *acta*.
14. Alice Rayner, *To Act, to Do, to Perform: Drama and the Phenomenology of Acting* (Ann Arbor: University of Michigan Press, 1994), 13.
15. Ibid., 15.
16. Christopher Prendergast, *The Order of Mimesis: Balzac, Stendhal, Nerval and Flaubert* (Cambridge: Cambridge University Press, 1986), 5.
17. Ibid., 12.

INDEX

Figures are indicated by an italic *f* following the page number

Abada, Roger, 146
Abel, Richard, 273n8
activism and in-person reenactment, 4, 7–9, 13–15, 156, 206, 229, 269n5, 315n39
The Act of Killing (Oppenheimer, 2012), 11, 206–208, 208*f*, 215
actual actor. *See* real protagonists
actualization of in-person reenactment, 5, 11–13, 18, 21, 78, 172, 177–178, 220
a-filiation, 36, 219–220, 245–249
Agamben, Giorgio, 32, 260
agency
　actor as agent, 241–244
　authenticity and, 12
　in-person reenactment and, 4, 10, 12–13, 206, 231, 240, 250, 260
　real protagonists and, 5, 20, 167
　testimony and, 250
Aida (Fracassi, 1951), 86, 87*f*
Aimée, Anouk, 160, 160*f*, 162, 302n102
Algeria
　Holocaust compared to, 154, 156, 295n126
　independence movement in, 133, 153
　torture use in, 116–117, 156
　war in, 131 133, 153, 300n68
Algeria 62 (Loridan-Ivens and Sergent), 156
Ali, Muhammed, 32, 81–82, 82–83*f*
Alida Valli (Franciolini, 1953), 14, 40, 71, 71*f*
alienation and in-person reenactment, 3, 48, 66, 122–123, 130, 150, 188–192, 243
All About Eve (Mankiewicz, 1950), 89
Alliston, April, 8–9
Alone with War (Arbid, 2000), 313n92

Alvarenga, Clarice, 238, 317n54
Amaral, Cristina, 319n4
Amendola, Anna, 70–71, 283n132
Amengual, Barthélemy, 52, 153, 282n111
Amet, Edward Hill, 19
L'Amore in Città. *See Love in the City*
anachronic quality of in-person reenactment, 18, 174, 221, 245, 248
anachronistic, critical use of, 22, 174, 221, 236, 258
Andrew, Dudley, 23, 285n26
Andrew, Vanessa, 269n7, 270n15
Anna Magnani (Visconti, 1953), 14, 38, 39*f*, 40, 72–75, 74*f*
Antelme, Robert, 133
Antonioni, Michelangelo. *See also Attempted Suicides*
　aesthetics of, 58–60, 65, 67, 281n96, 282n104
　critiques of, 65
　development of, 59, 66
　ethical approach of, 59, 64–65, 282n122
　existential approach of, 64–65, 116
　in-person reenactment and, 64, 66
　neorealism and, 65, 283n125
　nonactors used by, 69
　phenomenological approach of, 281n96
　on suicide, 57–58, 60, 62–65
　theatricality of, 40
Anzieu, Didier, 134, 294n112
Aran Islanders, 21–22
The Araras (Tonacci, 1980–1982), 236, 238–240, 239*f*
　first contact in, 238
Arguments (journal), 133, 136, 138, 294n101
Aristarco, Guido, 45, 63–64, 281n85, 287n77

Aristotle, 8, 260, 270n19, 280n68
Aron, Raymond, 170, 304n134
Around Brazil (*Ao redor do Brasil*) (Reis, 1930), 226
Arranged Marriage (Fellini, 1953), 278n22. See also *Siamo Donne*
Arruza, Carlos, 102
The Artists of the Burnt Theatre (Panh, 2005), 185–186, 186*f*
atonement and in-person reenactment, 2, 52, 204, 207, 215
Attempted Suicides (Antonioni, 1953), 57–67
 agency in, 64
 alienation in, 57, 66
 authenticity in, 63–69
 casting in, 69, 71
 cinema verité in, 59, 63
 closure in, 63
 confessions in, 66
 criticism of, 58, 64, 282n123
 ethical dimensions of, 66
 existential dimensions of, 14, 58, 64–65
 film techniques in, 61, 69
 first draft of, 58–60
 images from, 57*f*, 61–63*f*
 in-person reenactment in, 57, 61–63, 66, 69
 realism in, 14, 39–40, 65–66
 real protagonists in, 64, 67–69
 repetition in, 60, 67–69
 social and collective portrait in, 60
 talking cure in, 63
Auschwitz concentration camp, 142, 148, 156, 160, 177, 306n173
Auschwitz War Crimes Trial, 178–179, 179*f*
authenticity
 agency and, 12
 cinema verité and, 14
 existential dimensions and, 58, 108
 in-person reenactment and, 12, 14, 19, 21, 63, 88, 103, 221
 real protagonists and, 6, 92, 105
Autocritique (Morin), 130, 133, 134, 289n18, 289n19, 293n86, 294n102, 294n103, 294n107, 301n76.
autonomization, 166
Axelos, Kostas, 294n101

Baer, Ulrich, 142, 144–145
Ballot, Nadine, 292n70, 293n90
Bang Bang (Tonacci, 1970), 236, 242–243, 243*f*
Barbachano Ponce, Manuel, 15, 84, 98, 104–105, 286n69, 288n79

Barbaro, Umberto, 287n77
Barthes, Roland, 261
Basuyaux, Marie-Laure, 156–157, 302n90
Bateson, Gregory, 273n11
Battisti, Carlo, 38
Battle of Orgreave (Deller, 2001), 7
Bazin, André
 on *The Bullfight* (Braunberger and Myriam, 1951), 96–97
 on Chaplin, 93, 94
 on cine-mythographies, 92–95
 on death, 93, 94–97, 108, 293n79
 on existential dimensions of cinema, 92, 94
 on *The Great Dictator*, 93–94, 94*f*
 on in-person reenactment, 52, 78, 95
 in Jury Award for *Torero!*, 7, 104
 on *Limelight*, 93
 on ontology, 93, 110
 on realism, 94, 97
 on recursivity, 108, 110
 on Stalinist cinema, 93–95
 on *The Story of Caterina*, 51–52, 95
 on temporality, 94
 on theatricality, 144, 153
 on *Torero!*, 15, 84, 95, 96*f*, 97, 99, 285n43
 on witnessing, 144
Beckman, Karen, 89, 284n19, 308n26
behavior in in-person reenactment, 4, 9–11, 13, 20, 22, 34–35, 63, 273–274nn11–12
Beijing Bastards (Zhang, 1993), 276n44
Bekele, Gebrselassie, 29, 31*f*
belatedness of in-person reenactment, 5, 12–13, 142, 167, 198, 209, 228
Bellissima (Visconti, 1951), 75
Belzec concentration camp, 167, 170
Benamou, Catherine, 26, 28, 275n29
Bentley, Nancy, 248
Benzaquem, Stephanie, 194, 199, 207, 310nn52–53
Bergman, Ingrid, 69, 72–73, 72*f*, 92
Berliner, Joe, 7
Bernadet, Jean Claude, 230–231, 315n31
Bernstein, Robin, 319n103
Berthet, Frédérique, 155, 301n80
Besson, Remy, 303n126, 304n131
Betz, Mark, 150
Bicycle Thieves (De Sica, 1948), 48, 56, 280n76
biopics, 7, 10, 32, 86. See also celebrity biopics
Bishop, Claire, 270n15
Black God and White Devil (Rocha, 1964), 242

[322] Index

Black Skin, White Masks (Fanon), 122
Blackton, Stuart, 272–273n1
Blue, James, 310n59
body doubles, 27, 102, 110
Bogart, Humphrey, 80, 93
Bogen, Wilhelm, 179
Bomba, Abraham, 145–146, 175–176, 206
Bonitzer, Pascal, 53
Bophana: A Cambodian Tragedy (Panh, 1996), 192–194
Bophana Audiovisual Resource Center, 185, 307n5
Borgien, Angelo, 119, 136–137, 137f, 139–140, 140f, 292n67
Borinage (Ivens, 1933), 271n36
Borowski, Tadeusz, 191
Boyle, Deirdre, 190, 307nn5–6
Brault, Michel, 136, 293n93
Braun, Ritza, 86–87
Brazil and Brazilian cinema
    activism in, 229
    allegory in, 317n61
    Brazilian "Miracle," 220, 227
    Cinema Novo films in, 230, 240, 242
    coup d'etat and, 242
    identity in, 245–246
    indigenous persons in, 12, 18, 220, 245–246, 254
    Marginal Cinema in, 18, 317n69
Brecht, Bertold, 9–10, 48, 165–166, 190
Bressane, Julio, 236
Brooks, Jodi, 90
Brooks, Peter, 308n34
Brunetta, Gian Piero, 38, 69, 73, 90, 92, 277n6, 283n129
The Bullfight (Braunberger and Myriam, 1951), 96–97, 108–110, 109f, 288n92
bullfighting, 15, 32, 84, 94–97, 106–107, 285nn40–47, 286n48, 286n51, 286n57, 286n52, 288n93, 293n79
Buñuel, Luis, 258, 286n65, 286n68
Burns, Elizabeth, 289n11
Burton, Julianne, 232
Butler, Hugo, 98, 104, 106–107, 286n52, 286n65

Cabascabo (Ganda, 1968), 165–166, 167
Cadava, Eduardo, 284n19
Camarade Duch, Bienvenu en enfer (Maben, 2012), 201–202, 203f
Cambodia. *See also* Khmer Rouge; *S21: The Khmer Rouge Killing Machine*
    accountability efforts in, 17, 185, 193, 199–204, 206, 310n58
    Choeung Ek (killing fields), 195, 200–201
    cinema in, 307n5
    culture of, 185–186
    genocide in, 185, 199, 254, 297n14, 308n12
Cambodia Genocide archive (World Memory Archive), 199
Canela tribe, 237, 316n45, 316n50
Carapiru, 221–228
    a-filiation of, 245–249
    agency of, 240
    background of, 219–220
    first contact by, 18, 221, 234
    identity of, 244
    images of, 220f, 222–223f, 255f, 259f
    in-person reenactment of, 18, 219–229, 250–252
    as real protagonist, 240, 249
    revisiting by, 221, 222–223f
    subjectivity of, 18, 245
    temporality of, 221–228, 254
    voice of, 228, 240, 243, 249
Carelli, Vincent, 233, 236–239, 245, 315n39, 316n49
Carlson, Marla, 151
Carta, Jean, 123, 152
Carta, Rosana, 60
Carter-White, Richard, 175
Caruth, Cathy, 142–143, 189
casting
    conceptions of, 20
    in-person reenactment and, 4–5, 92
    lineage, 24
    miscasting and, 92, 95
    psychodrama and, 124, 272n1
    real protagonists and, 19, 270n15
    of relatives, 4, 13, 19, 20–21, 23–24, 26, 28, 29, 30, 32
    of social actors, 20, 21, 24
casting test, 67, 81
Castoriadis, Cornelius, 138, 296n140
Caswell, Michelle, 204
Catholic Church, intervention in Italian cinema, 44
Cayrol, Jean, 148, 156, 178
celebrity biopics
    aesthetics of, 82
    aging in, 15, 77, 85, 90–93
    allure of stardom, 70–73
    development of, 82
    exemplarity in, 81
    existential dimensions of, 79
    fading star subgenre in, 88–90
    in-person reenactment and, 15, 53, 77, 79–82, 87, 90, 92
    mortality in, 15, 82, 92, 94–95
    phenomenological dimension of, 15, 32

Index [323]

celebrity biopics (*Cont.*)
  presence in, 82
  redemptive promise in, 81
  repetition in, 80
  representation in, 32, 71, 73, 79, 284n19
  self-reflexivity of, 80
  sports biopics, 15, 30, 32, 78, 80, 87
  teleology of, 79
  temporality in, 77, 79, 81–82, 89, 92, 94
  tropes in, 81–82
Center of Indigenous Work (CTI), 236, 315n39, 316n49
Cerdan, Marcel, 95
Chandler, David, 307n9
Chaplin, Charlie, 93, 94*f*
The Chicken (Rossellini, 1953), 14, 72–73, 72*f*
Chile Obstinate Memory (Guzman, 1997), 309n47
Chinese cinema, 34, 276n43
Chisholm, Anna, 27, 102
Choeung Ek (killing fields, Cambodia), 195, 200–201
Chronicle of a Summer (Rouch and Morin, 1961), 130–136
  aesthetics of, 145
  alienation in, 130, 150
  authenticity in, 114, 116, 119, 130
  autocritique in, 14, 113, 130, 133, 154
  casting in, 132, 137, 292n67
  cinema verité in, 15, 113–114, 130, 134, 139–140, 272n47
  closure in, 125
  confessions in, 130, 139
  criticism of, 154, 295n126
  deleted scene from, 114
  ethical dimensions of, 15, 136, 140
  exemplarity in, 134
  existential dimensions of, 15, 114, 116
  film techniques in, 114, 130–131, 134, 137, 148–149, 153–155
  images from, 115*f*, 131*f*, 135*f*, 137*f*, 149*f*, 155*f*
  in-person reenactment in, 15, 136, 153, 159–160, 289n14
  making of, 114, 137, 150–151, 293n93, 295n121
  mise-en-scène in, 149, 154, 302n100
  monologue in, 153–154
  phenomenological dimension of, 116, 138, 153
  psychodrama in, 7, 113–114, 117, 119, 134–139
  racism in, 12, 155–156
  realism in, 132, 134, 152

  reception of, 131
  self-awareness in, 14, 113
  social and political context of, 15, 116–119, 131–132, 134–139, 153–154, 296n139, 301n80
  sound in, 114, 125, 148, 154, 164, 167, 303
  subjectivity in, 136, 138, 152, 153, 157
  temporality in, 160, 303n111
  testimony in, 15–16, 148–150, 152, 154, 159, 162
Chum Mey, 187, 201, 202*f*
Cinema Novo films, 230, 240, 242, 317n69
Cinema Nuovo (journal), 45
cinema verité
  agency in, 7
  authenticity in, 14, 75
  closure in, 125
  confessions in, 66, 113, 140
  consciousness-raising in, 16
  existential dimensions of, 113, 116
  psychodrama in, 136, 139
  reconciliation of therapy and dramaturgy in, 125
  screen personae in, 114
  self-performance in, 16
  statu nascendi in, 134, 139, 140
  subjectivity in, 15
  testimony in, 66, 142
  therapy and dramaturgy in, 125
  verité arc, 7
  voice in, 272n47
cine-transe (film technique), 151, 164, 170
ciné-verdad, 204–212
Cliff, Montgomery, 80
Clifford, James, 258
Close-Up (Kiarostami, 1990), 1–4, 2–4*f*, 253
closure and in-person reenactment, 7, 13, 63, 119, 124–130, 216
Cocody Lycée (high school in Abidjan), 114, 120
Cocteau, Jean, 151
Cold War effects on cinema, 38, 44, 133, 137
colonialism, 15, 118–120, 122, 130, 133
The Colonizer and Colonized (Memmi), 122–123
Colvin, Chris, 207
Come Back Africa (Rogosin, 1959), 135
Commission on Community Interrelations, 119, 289n22
Committee of Intellectual Action Against the War in North Africa, 133
Commoli, Jean Louis, 78, 81

confessions and in-person reenactment, 5–6, 15–16, 43, 52, 113, 191, 216, 308n34
consciousness-raising in films, 5, 9, 13, 16, 66, 119, 124, 217
Contest: 4 Actresses and 1 Hope (Guarini, 1953), 67, 67–68f, 69, 70f, 71–72
Conversations in Maranhão (*Conversas no Maranhão*) (Tonacci, 1977–1980), 236–237, 239–240, 316–317nn50–51, 317n53
conversion and in-person reenactment, 5–6, 11, 39, 191, 269n7
Cooper, Frederick, 122
Cormier, Loretta, 247, 251, 318n85, 318n88
Corumbiara (Carelli, 2009), 228, 233–239, 235f, 238f, 245, 315n39
  first contact in, 228, 233–235, 237–238, 317n54
The Courage of the People (also known as *The Night of San Juan*) (Sanjines, 1971), 11
Coutard, Raoul, 136
Coutinho, Eduardo, 18, 228–233
  Twenty Years Later: A Man Marked to Die (1964–1984), 18, 228–233, 230f, 233–234f, 314n23, 315n32
Crawford, Joan, 88–89
CTI (Center of Indigenous Work), 236, 315n39, 316n49
Cuba Mia (proposed film), 105
Cui Jian, 276n44

Daney, Serge, 139
Daniel, Zé, 232
Danieli, Emma, 70, 283n132
Davis, Bette, 88–90
A Day in Court (Steno, 1954), 86, 87f
de Antonellis, Rafaella, 105, 287n71
de Antonio, Emilio, 7, 312n77
death and in-person reenactment, 15, 26–29, 92–97, 110, 126, 129, 141–142, 293n79
"Death Every Afternoon" (Bazin), 96–97
Death in the Afternoon (Hemingway), 106
de Cassia, Edna, 241
de Certeau, Michel, 8
de la Colina, José, 104
Delahaye, Michel, 130, 292n70
Delbo, Charlotte, 154, 191
Deleuze, Gilles, 166, 303n119
del Fra, Lino, 45
Deller, Jeremy, 7, 270n15
Democratic Kampuchea (DK), 199–200, 309nn48–49. *See also* Cambodia; Khmer Rouge

Denning, Michael, 106, 288n85
de Oliveira, Rodrigo, 225, 314n9
de Rochemont, Louis, 104
Derrida, Jacques, 141–142, 219
de Santis, Giuseppe, 45
des Forets, Louis-René, 133
de Sica, Vittorio, 37–38, 40–41, 44, 84–85, 105, 277n17, 280n75
de Souza, Jerônimo André, 25
de Vincenti, Giorgio, 72, 281n96
Dewitte, Philippe, 165
Didi-Huberman, Georges, 16, 146, 178, 305n143
Di Iorio, Sam, 132, 293n93
Dmytrik, Edward, 150
Doane, Mary Ann, 19–20, 297n10
Documento mensile (film magazine), 41–42
Dubois, W. E. B., 248
Duch (Kang Kek Iew), 185, 194–201, 197–198f, 202–203f, 204, 205f, 311n60
Duch: Master of the Forges of Hell (Panh, 2011), 185, 204, 205f, 311n60
Duras, Marguerite, 148, 154
Durkheim, Emile, 65
Duvignaud, Jean, 294n101

East West Palace (Zhang, 1998), 276n44
ECCC (Extraordinary International Chambers in the Courts of Cambodia), 185, 194, 200, 206
Eichmann, Adolf, 143, 154, 204, 214–215, 298n18, 301n80, 301n87
Eisenstein, Sergei, 27, 104
The Elimination (Panh), 188–189
Ellul, Jacques, 309n49
Elsaesser, Thomas, 146
Endurance (Woodhead, 1999), 24, 29–33, 30–31f
Epstein, Jean, 1, 3, 16, 274n13
Eté plus 50 (Dauman, 2011), 114, 116–117f
ethnographic documentaries, 4, 8, 18, 21, 22, 29, 30, 151, 165, 226, 228, 243, 245, 248, 251, 320n13
Europa '51 (Rossellini, 1952), 73
execution films, 20
Execution of Czolgosz, with Panorama of Auburn Prison (Porter, 1901), 20
exemplarity, 8–11, 270–271nn20–22
  in-person reenactment and, 4, 7–10, 16, 28, 80, 269n5
  named individuals and, 53
  redemptive, 16
  self-embodiment and, 80
Exemplum (Lyons), 8
Exile (Panh, 2016), 185

Index [325]

existential dimensions
  arena of, 94–97
  authenticity and, 58, 108
  in-person reenactment and, 12, 16, 39, 82, 92, 103
  psychodrama and, 119, 122
  race and, 122
  sociality and, 122
  temporality and, 93
  tropes of, 122
Exodus (Preminger, 1960), 301n80

Fabrizi, Aldo, 38
The Fall (Guerra and Xavier, 1974), 230
Fame and the Devil (*Al Diavolo la Celebritá*, Monicelli, Steno, 1949), 95
Fanon, Frantz, 122–123
Farrebique (Rouquier, 1944), 23, 23f
Fast, Omer, 6, 270n16
Feld, Steven, 303n111
Fellini, Federico, 42, 279n44
Felman, Shoshana, 141, 143, 298–299n34, 298n16, 298n18, 305n145
Fernandez, Miguel Anxo, 284n12, 286n54, 287n71
Ferreri, Marco, 41–42
Fieschi, Jean-André, 165, 258, 303n113, 319n5
Fighting Near Santiago (Lubin, 1898), 273n1
Finis Terrae (Epstein, 1929), 274n13
Fink, Guido, 59, 282n122
Firestone, Shulamith, 6
"first contact"
  in *Araras* (Tonacci), 238
  in cinema, 228–236
  in *Corumbiara* (Carelli), 228, 233–235, 237–238, 317n54
  in *Serras da Desordem* (Tonacci), 18, 219, 236, 243
Flaherty, Robert, 18, 21–22, 257–258
Flatley, Jonathan, 269n3
Fore, Devin, 22, 275n26
Foucault, Michel 276n48, 309n40
Four Men on a Raft (*It's All True*, Welles, 1942–1993), 25–29, 25–28f
França, Andrea, 242, 317n59
France
  autocritique in, 14, 113
  colonialism of, 118
  discrimination in, 156, 165
  fascism in, 156
  "French community," 114
  identity in, 15, 117–118
  Indochina, military involvement in, 166
  intellectuals in, 133
  Ivory Coast independence from, 114, 120
  Jews in, 140, 156, 295n126
  psychodrama in, 117–118, 122, 294n112
  racism in, 118
  torture use in Algerian War, 116–117, 294n96
Franciolini, Gianni, 14, 40, 71
Frankfurter, Felix, 142, 168–171, 169f
Freire, Paulo, 231
Freud, Sigmund, 63, 121
Friedmann, Georges, 137–138, 295n125
From Nuremberg to Nuremberg (Rossif, 1989), 181, 204
Front of National Liberation (FLN, Algeria), 132
Fuentes, Carlos, 106, 286n68, 288n79
Fuhs, Kristen, 205–206, 269n5, 311n69, 312n77
FUNAI (The National Foundation of Indigenous Aid), 219, 222, 227–229, 237, 239, 245, 315n39, 317n55

Gabel, Joseph, 138, 296n144
Gabin, Jean, 93
Gabriel, Teshome, 163
Gadamer, Hans-Georg, 271n24
Gamboa, Fernando, 287n69, 287n71
Ganda, Oumarou (*Moi un Noir*), 162–167, 164f
  in-person reenactment of, 142, 144, 162, 165
  monologue of, 16, 123, 140, 163–167, 169
  as real protagonist, 147, 303n118
gaps in in-person reenactment, 5, 65, 92, 158, 171–172, 177, 191, 260
Garbo, Greta, 86
Garcia, Uirá Felipe, 247, 254, 313n2, 319n1, 319n3
Gardnier, Ruy, 317n51
Gautrat, Jacques, 137, 295n129
Gebrselassie, Haile, 29–30
Gebrselassie, Shawanness, 29
Genet, Jean, 118, 122
Gente del Po (Antonioni, 1947), 59, 65, 282n118
Germany Year Zero (Rossellini, 1947), 56, 59, 151
Ghione, Riccardo, 41–42
Goffman, Erving, 273n11
The Golden Coach (Renoir, 1953), 73
Goldmann, Lucien, 131–132
The Gold of Naples (De Sica, 1954), 84–85, 87–88, 88–89f, 91

Gomes, Mercio Pereira, 245
Goulart, João, 231
Grande, Maurizio, 48, 56
Grandjaquet, Francesco, 38
The Greatest (Hellman and Gries, 1977), 30–31, 80–81, 82–83f, 284n10
Grierson, John, 7, 104
Griffith, Alison, 20
Griffith, D. W., 224
group dynamics, 15, 117, 119, 134, 136–139, 294n112, 296n148
Guajá tribe, 224–226, 246–251, 255, 258, 314n7, 314n21, 318n85, 318n88
Guarini, Alfredo, 40, 67, 70
Guerra, Rui, 230
Gundle, Stephen, 90
The Guns (Guerra, 1964), 230
Gurvitch, Georges, 117
Guss, Nathan, 107

Haenel, Yannick, 168, 304n129
Haile, Tedesse, 29
Hamon, Philippe, 33
Hampton, Timothy, 8, 53, 270n21, 271n24
Hansen, Miriam, 19, 273n2, 297n8, 299n38
Harlem riots (1943), 119, 290n32
Hemingway, Ernest, 106–107, 110
Henley, Paul, 126, 291n58, 292nn71–72
Herzog, Werner, 10
Hiroshima mon Amour (Resnais, 1959), 148, 150, 299n44
Hirsch, Joshua, 16, 143, 152–154, 159, 296n3, 297n9, 300n63, 301n75, 302n99
Ho Vann Tay, 202–204
Hoberman, Jim, 299n38
Hobsbawm, Eric, 106, 288n83
Horsman, Yasco, 298n16
Huang, Nicole, 276n45
Hughes, Rachel, 309n49
The Human Pyramid (Rouch, 1959), 7, 14, 113–118, 120f, 121–130, 127–128f, 139, 164–165, 290n37, 292n70, 292n72, 293n80
  racism and, 12, 15, 117–118, 121, 122, 124, 129, 292n70
The Human Voice (Rossellini, 1948), 73, 151
The Huron Project (Tribe), 7
Huyghe, Pierre, 6, 271n35

identity and in-person reenactment, 2–3, 6–7, 14–15, 29
Ieng Sary, 200, 309n49
Ieng Thirith, 200

Il Grido (*The Cry*) (Antonioni, 1957), 58–59, 281n96
impersonation and in-person reenactment, 1, 3, 30, 47, 77–78, 86, 90, 272n1
Infante, Guillermo Cabrera, 98, 286n53
in-person reenactment
  activism and, 4, 7–9, 13–15, 156, 206, 229, 269n5, 315n39
  actualization of, 5, 11–13, 18, 21, 78, 172, 177–178, 220
  a-filiation and, 36, 219–220, 245–249
  alienation and, 3, 48, 66, 122–123, 130, 150, 188–192, 243
  anachronic quality of, 18, 174, 221, 245, 248
  atonement and, 2, 52, 204, 207, 215
  behavior in, 4, 9–11, 13, 20, 22, 34–35, 63, 273–274nn11–12
  being and acting in, 32, 35, 40, 46, 53, 73, 92, 124
  belatedness of, 5, 12–13, 142, 167, 198, 209, 228
  casting and, 4–5, 92 See also casting
  celebrity biopics and, 15, 77, 79–82, 87, 90, 92
  closure and, 7, 13, 63, 119, 124–130, 216
  confessions and, 5–6, 15–16, 43, 52, 113, 191, 216, 308n34
  conversion and, 5–6, 11, 39, 191, 269n7
  death and, 15, 26–29, 92–97, 110, 126, 129, 141–142, 293n79
  definition of, 4, 10, 17, 296n5
  'enactment,' meaning of, 12, 271n38
  estrangement and, 14, 35, 143, 151, 234
  ethical dimensions of, 5–6, 18, 32, 48, 220
  exemplarity and, 4, 7–10, 16, 28, 80, 269n5
  existential dimensions of, 12, 16, 39, 82, 92, 103
  gaps in, 5, 65, 92, 158, 171–172, 177, 191, 260
  identity and, 2–3, 6–7, 14–15, 29
  impersonation and, 1, 3, 30, 47, 77–78, 86, 90, 272n1
  judicial and, 5, 140, 142, 193–194, 200, 205–209
  limits of, 15, 62, 66, 69, 220–221
  mimesis and, 9, 35, 118, 142, 190, 253–254, 260–261, 274n12
  monologue and, 114, 140, 142, 144–145, 147, 149–150, 153–154, 156, 165, 168, 170–172, 184, 192, 198n7, 289n14, 301n77
  participatory reenactment, 205, 206, 208, 269n5

Index [327]

casting and (*Cont.*)
  phatic, 171–178
  physiognomy and, 2, 22–24, 27, 35, 76, 86, 106
  post-Holocaust cinema and, 17, 141–143, 145–146, 172, 174, 178, 296n3
  posttraumatic cinema and, 141–146, 206
  postwar cinema and, 14, 20
  real protagonists and, 5, 53, 159, 167, 253
  redemptive promise of, 4, 7, 11, 13, 81, 146, 191–192, 261
  relatives as surrogates and, 4, 19–20, 29–30
  representation and, 2, 5, 11–14, 21, 30, 82, 166, 261
  revisiting original sites and, 16, 39, 132, 141, 145–146, 159–160, 170–172, 221
  social actors and, 10, 13, 16, 20–21, 39, 48, 147, 191
  substitution and, 13, 19, 27, 97, 99, 174, 221, 251
  surrogacy and, 19–20, 27–30, 43, 52, 108, 240, 245, 270n15
  temporality and, 5, 11–18, 20, 23, 82, 88, 174, 224
  testimony and, 11, 15, 141–143, 167, 269n7
  transformative power of, 5, 7, 13, 18, 56, 254, 271n36
  transmission and, 5, 18, 24–25, 35, 249–252
  trauma and, 10, 16–18, 190, 297n5, 299n35
In the King of Prussia (de Antonio, 1982), 7, 312n77
The Investigation: Oratorio in 11 Cantos (Weiss), 179–181, 180f, 306nn173–174
Iracema: uma transa amazonica (Bodansky and Senna, 1974), 227, 240–243, 241f, 317n60
Isa Miranda (Zampa, 1953), 14, 40, 71
Italia Mia (Zavattini, unfinished film), 40, 43, 105, 278n26
Italy and Italian cinema
  break from fascist model in, 38–39, 44
  celebrities in, 69, 82, 90, 91
  censorship in, 44
  Cold War, role in, 44
  critical self-reflection and stardom in, 91
  development of, 287n77
  image of, 44
  neorealism in, 44–45, 59, 279n44, 283n129, 287n77
  nonactors in, 14, 37–38, 69, 75
  normalization in, 45
  political dimensions of, 44–45
  postwar period in, 44–45
It's All True (Welles, 1942–1993), 25–27, 25–28f
It's a Wonderful Life (Capra, 1946), 86
Ivens, Joris, 21, 108, 274n13, 292n67, 302n101
I Vinti (The Vanquished) (Antonioni, 1952), 67, 283n124

The Jackie Robinson Story (Green, 1950), 80, 81f, 284n7
Jaguar (Rouch, 1968), 166
Jameson, Fredric, 166, 297n10
Janie's Janie (Ashur and Varton, 1971), 9
Jasen, Sylvie, 10–11, 21, 271n36, 274nn20–21
Jeanson network (pro-FLN group), 116, 132, 156, 292n93, 301n86
Jews and Judaism
  deportation of, 140
  extermination of, 142, 167, 169f, 170
  in France, 140, 156, 295n126
  Holocaust cinema and, 16, 168
  identity of, 155, 168
  leaders in, 167
  persecution of, 299n34
  in Poland, 177
  as scapegoats, 299n34, 305n145
  survivors, 144, 154
Joan of Arc at the Stake (Rossellini, 1954), 73
Jones, Graham, 293n80
Joselito (bullfighter), 102, 103f, 107–108
Journal d'un ouvrier (Diary of a Worker) (Gautrat), 137
The Journals of Knud Rasmussen (Kunuk and Cohn, 2006), 21–22
judicial in in-person reenactment, 5, 140, 142, 193–194, 200, 205–209

Kahana, Jonathan, 12, 271n38
Kang Kek Iew (Duch), 185, 194–201, 197–198f, 202–203f, 204, 205f, 311n60
Kanoe tribe, 229, 234, 235f, 245
Kaput (Malaparte), 232, 233f
The Karski Report (Lanzmann, 2010), 167–171
  aim of, 170–171
  authenticity in, 170–171
  belatedness of, 168, 171
  cinema verité in, 170–171

[328] Index

existential dimensions of, 170–171
images from, 169f
in-person reenactment of Jan Karski, 142, 167–171, 304n129, 304n131
making of, 168
monologue in, 142, 145, 167–171
prologue of, 304n134
representation in, 170
structure of, 168
temporality in, 171
Khatib, Abdelhafid, 302n100
Khieu Samphan, 200
Khmer Rouge, 12, 17, 18, 185, 187–190, 199–200, 202, 306–307n3
Khrushchev, Nikita, 133
Kiarostami, Abbas, 1–4
Koch, Gertrud, 142, 146, 170, 297n8, 306n173
Kofman, Myron, 133
Korczac, Janusz, 177
Koulibali, Denise, 292n74

Labarthe, André, 158–159
La Capra, Dominick, 174, 305n150
The Lady Without Camelias (Antonioni, 1953), 64, 69
La Gare du Nord (Rouch, 1965), 129
La Grande Renuncia (The Great Renunciation) (Vergano, 1951), 67
Lainé, Rémi, 200
The Land of the Wandering Souls (Panh, 2000), 307n5
Landy, Marcia, 73, 84
Lanzmann, Claude
 aesthetics of, 177
 on Haenel, 304n129
 images of, 175f
 in-person reenactment and, 146–147, 170, 174–175, 206, 297n8, 313n91
 interviews with, 303n126
 on *The Karski Report*, 168, 170, 171, 304n129
 on *Shoah*, 170, 173–176, 206
 temporality and, 146–147
 theatricality and, 168, 170–171, 206
 witnessing and, 174
Lapassade, George, 138–139, 296n136
La Petite prairie aux bouleaux (*The Little Meadow with Birch Trees*) (Loridan-Ivens, 2003), 159–160, 160–161f
"La Pyramide Humaine" (Éluard), 126
The Last Stage (*La Dernière Etape*) (Jakubowska, 1948), 300n68
Lattuada, Alberto, 42, 44
Laub, Dori, 144

La veritàaaa (*The Truthhhh*) (Zavattini, 1980), 46
L'Avventura (Antonioni, 1960), 59, 116, 150–151, 281n96
Le Amiche (*The Girlfriends*) (Antonioni, 1955), 58, 64–65
Lefebvre, Henri, 138–139
Leiris, Michel, 106–110, 118, 288n92
Lemonde, Marcel, 200
Les Belles Lettres (Deblo), 154
Les Parents Terribles (Cocteau, 1948), 144
Les Temps Modernes (journal), 118
le Sueur, James, 133
L'Europeo (magazine), 42
Levin, Mikael, 144–145
Levinas, Emmanuel, 214
Lewin, Kurt, 117–119, 137–138, 290n24
Lim, Bliss Cua, 251
Lima, Raimundo "Tatá" Correia, 25
Li Maoje, 33, 34f, 35
Lindeperg, Sylvie, 148, 156, 302n90
Little Dieter Needs to Fly (Herzog, 1997), 10
Lizzani, Carlo, 42–43, 54–55, 279n44
Loren, Sophia
 career of, 69, 84, 90
 as embodiment of Italian cinema, 84
 images of, 78f, 85f, 87f, 91f
 in-person reenactment of, 15, 77–78, 82, 84–87, 90–91
Loridan-Ivens, Marceline, 153–162
 on casting, 301n87
 cinema verité and, 151
 ciné-transe and, 300n54
 images of, 115–117f, 149f, 155f, 160f
 in-person reenactment of, 114–116, 148–149, 153–154, 160–161, 289n14, 301n80, 301n87
 interviews of, 131, 137
 monologue of, 16, 140, 142, 144–146, 150, 152–153, 155–156, 172
 political activity of, 156, 301n86
 subjectivity of, 297n9
 sync sound in monologue scene, 134, 145, 148, 154
 tattoos of, 301n80
 testimony of, 154–155
 as witness, 143, 145
Los Pequenos gigantes (*The Perfect Game*) (Butler, 1957), 106
Love for Pay (Lizzani, 1953), 43, 54, 55f, 56
Love in the City (*L'Amore in Città*) (various episodes, 1953). *See also Arranged Marriage; Attempted Suicides; Love for Pay; The Story of Caterina*
 authenticity in, 92
 celebrity in, 76, 90

Index [329]

Love in the City (*L'Amore in Città*)
    (various episodes, 1953) (*Cont.*)
  collective filmmaking spirit in, 277n11
  criticism of, 42
  ethical dimensions of, 278n22
  exemplarity in, 84
  as film manifesto, 42, 272n47
  realism in, 39–40
  score in, 280n64
Lukács, György, 45
Lyons, John, 8, 53

Mad Masters (Rouch, 1955), 113, 118, 258
Maggiorani, Lamberto, 38, 56
Magnani, Anna, 38, 39*f*, 69, 71–75,
    74–75*f*, 90, 92
Mai Lam, 199, 310n51, 310n53
Makhmalbaf, Mohsen, 1–3, 2*f*
Mama (Zhang, 1990), 276n44
Mancini, Liliana, 75
Manning, Peter, 310n58
Man of Aran (Flaherty, 1933), 21–24, 22*f*,
    29, 286n64
Manolete (bullfighter), 97, 102, 103*f*, 107–
    108, 109*f*, 110, 111–112*f*, 129
The Man with Clay Hands (Mathot,
    1949), 95
Marceline. *See* Loridan-Ivens, Marceline
March of Time (newsreels), 104, 272–273n1
Marcus, Millicent, 90, 281n102
Marotta, Giuseppe, 87
Marrosu, Donatella, 61–63, 62–63*f*,
    66–72, 67–68*f*
Marxism, 55, 119, 133–134, 136–138,
    306n173
Mascolo, Dionys, 133
Maselli, Francesco, 37, 42, 48, 279n44
Mauss, Marcel, 152
Ma vie Balagan (Loridan-Ivens), 154
Mead, George H., 118, 289n11, 293n82
Meira, Manoel Olimpio "Jacaré," 25–29, 26*f*
Meliès, Georges, 250, 273n8
Memorandum (Brittain and Spotton, 1965),
    178–180
Merimee, Prosper, 73
"The Messenger" (Haenel), 168
Mexican ciné-verdad, 104–112
Mexico Mio (unfinished film), 105–106,
    287n71, 287n74, 287n77, 288n78
Micciché, Lino, 75, 281n98
Michel, Henri, 147
Miller, Christopher, 165
mimesis, 9, 35, 118, 142, 190, 253–254,
    260–261, 274n12
Miranda, Isa, 69, 71
Miskelley, Jessi, 312n77

The Missing Picture (Panh, 2013), 185
Mnookin, Jennifer, 205–206, 312n77
Model, Katherine, 215, 302n100,
    312n78, 313n91
Moi Un Noir (*MUN*) (I a Black Man) (Rouch,
    1958), 123, 142, 153, 162–167,
    163–164*f*, 298n17
Monicelli, Mario, 44
monologue. *See* in-person reenactment
Moravia, Alberto, 42
Moreno, Jacob L. *See also* psychodrama;
    sociodrama
  on cinema, 125
  criticism of, 122, 138
  patient as actor, 124, 291n63, 292n65
  psychodrama, development of, 113,
    117–119, 122–124, 290n32
  reception of, 117–118, 137–138
  role-reversal use, 121–122
  "statu nascendi" and, 134, 294n114
Morin, Edgar
  on autocritique, 113, 130, 133–134, 154
  on cinema, 134
  cinema verité and, 14, 125, 130, 139
  commensality approach of, 135, 135*f*
  confessions and, 136
  existential approach of, 122
  phenomenological approach of, 132
  political activity of, 132–133, 136–137,
    294nn101–102
  psychodrama and, 113, 118–119, 122,
    134, 136, 138–139
  role-play and, 15, 113, 130
  self-enlightenment program of, 122
  on stars, 82
  subjective approach of, 133
  therapeutic frame of, 14–15, 117
  trials and, 133–134
Morris, Errol, 6, 205, 312n73
mortality. *See* death
Muller, Filip, 173–174
Mulvey, Laura, 77
Mussolini, Benito, 38, 44
My House Is Full of Mirrors (*La Mia Casa
    è Piena di Specchi*) (Sindoni, 2010),
    84–85, 85*f*

Nagel, Alexander, 18, 174, 221,
    305n151, 314n5
Nancy, Jean Luc, 2
Nanook of the North (Flaherty, 1922),
    21, 221
Nardi, Lilia, 60–61, 61*f*, 66
Naremore, James, 80, 284n3
Nascimbene, Mario, 48, 54, 280n64
Nath, Vann, 187, 192–197, 196–198*f*

The National Foundation of Indigenous
    Aid (FUNAI), 219, 222, 227–229, 237,
    239, 245, 315n39, 317n55
neorealism
  aesthetics of, 84, 88
  as antifascist, 44–45
  authenticity in, 38, 45
  celebrity biopics and, 15, 40, 82, 84–85
  cinema verité and, 5, 7, 14, 16, 66,
    113, 272n46
  core traits of, 14
  crisis of, 45, 278n32
  critiques of, 45, 279n46
  definition of, 7
  documentarism in, 59
  exemplarity in, 8–9
  international influence of, 54, 84, 104
  non-actors in, 14, 37–38, 75–76, 88, 277n2
  oppositional quality of, 44
  reconstruction and, 90–91
  redemptive promise in, 13, 16, 45
  repetition and, 45
  representation and, 66
  signifiers of, 15
  social and political context of,
    44–46, 53, 93
Nettezza Urbana (Antonioni, 1948), 65
New Wave cinema, 14–15, 129,
    150, 299n46
Nichols, Bill, 5, 10, 66, 174, 197,
    215, 275n24, 297n10, 305n154,
    309n47, 313n87
Night and Fog (Resnais, 1956), 147–148,
    156–157, 172–173, 177–178
Niney, François, 148
nonactors in cinema, 14, 37–39, 69,
    102, 274n13
Nuon Chea, 200
Nuremberg trials, 181, 204

Oppenheimer, Joshua, 11, 313n87
original sites and in-person reenactment,
    16, 39, 132, 141, 145–146, 159–160,
    170–172, 221

Pagès, Max, 295n127, 296n136
Pagliero, Marcello, 38
Panh, Rithy
  The Artists of the Burnt Theatre, 185, 186f
  Bophana: A Cambodian Tragedy, 193
  Duch: Master of the Forges of Hell,
    204, 205f
  evidence and, 200
  Exile, 185
  in-person reenactment and, 188, 199–
    200, 204, 217

life of, 307n5
  The Missing Picture, 185
  on *S21*, 206, 208, 216, 313n91
  Site 2, 185
Pannakar, Ieu, 307n5
*Paradise Lost: The Murder at the Robin Hood
    Hills* (Sinofsky, 1996), 7, 312n77
Paradise Lost 2: Revelations (Sinofsky,
    2000), 312n77
parajudicial. *See* judicial in in-person
    reenactment
parajuridical films, 205, 206
parajuridical processes, 200, 206, 208
Parma Convention (1953), 45, 279n44
The Passenger (Antonioni, 1975), 64
Peasant Leagues, 229, 232
pedinamento approach, 38, 56
pedovision (Jean Rouch film technique),
    16, 136, 147–153
Pedro, João, 230, 232
Pereio, Paulo Cesar, 240–244, 241–243f
Pereira da Silva, Manuel "Preto," 25
Peters, Julie Stone, 207
physiognomy and in-person reenactment,
    2, 22–24, 27, 35, 76, 86, 106
Piault, Colette, 164, 292n71, 303n111
Pickpocket (Zhangke, 1997), 272n45
Plato, 261
Pol Pot, 197–198, 200–201, 309n49,
    310n52, 312n86
Pontalis, J. B., 122, 138, 290n31, 295n134
Ponti, Carlo, 85–86
Possuelo, Sydney, 219, 223, 223f, 225, 229,
    233, 243, 246–247
Poster, Mark, 133
post-Holocaust cinema
  aesthetics of, 145–146, 178
  Algerian War and, 154, 300n68
  ascetic mise-en-scène in, 142, 144, 145,
    147, 149, 151, 152, 154, 159, 253
  camp memoirs in, 301n77
  cinema verité in, 178
  evidence in, 177
  in person reenactment and, 17, 141
    143, 145–146, 172, 174, 178, 296n3
  Jewish status in, 16
  juridical mise-en-scène in, 16, 140, 206
  realism in, 174, 178
  scholarship on, 296n3
  testimony in, 16, 155, 157,
    206, 302n97
  theatricality in, 142, 144
  trauma in, 254
  traumatic realism in, 297n5 *See also*
    Rothberg, Michael.
  witnessing in, 143, 184

Index [331]

posttraumatic cinema. *See also*
　post-Holocaust cinema
　absence in, 142, 206
　aesthetics of, 142
　catharsis in, 146
　cinema verité in, 17
　exemplarity in, 13
　identity in, 144–145, 147
　in-person reenactment and,
　　141–146, 206
　mise-en-scène in, 16, 151
　paradox of, 146
　parajudicial, 205
　real protagonists in, 147
　redemptive promise in, 146
　temporality in, 141, 145, 147
　testimony in, 16, 141–144, 147, 152
　"working through" in, 145–146, 152
posttraumatic conditions, 16, 17, 141–146, 173–174, 189–191, 206, 296n3. *See also* traumatic realism
Power and Land (Ivens, 1940), 21
Prak Khan, 191, 195, 196*f*, 212, 213*f*, 214, 216
Prandi, Carlo, 46, 52
Prendergast, Christopher, 261
Procuna, Luis
　images of, 79*f*, 98*f*, 100–101*f*, 103*f*, 111–112*f*
　in-person reenactment of, 15, 79, 92, 97–99, 102–103, 105–108, 110, 288n90
psychodrama. *See also* Moreno, Jacob L.; sociodrama
　aim of, 118
　casting and, 124, 272n1
　existential dimensions and, 119, 122
　film techniques of, 122, 291n42
　France, reception in, 15, 117–118
　history of, 117–118
　limits of, 124
　mise-en-scène in, 147
　as model for cinema, 119
　race and, 122
　race and sociodrama, 117–119, 290n31
　role-reversal in, 122
　social and political dimension of, 137–138
race and racism, 12, 15, 80, 117–122, 129, 155–156, 292n70. *See also The Human Pyramid; Moi Un Noir (MUN)*
Rachlin, Nathalie, 187–188, 307–308n12, 309n43
racism and sociodrama, 117–119, 290n31
Raengo, Alessandra, 80–81

Raging Bull (Scorsese, 1980), 80
Raíces (Alazraki, 1953–1954), 104–105
Rancière, Jacques, 187–188, 190, 195
Raoni (Kayapo chief), 228
Rayner, Alice, 32, 260, 275n39, 275n40, 275n41, 320n14
real protagonists (real/actor)
　agency and, 5, 20, 167
　authenticity and, 6, 92, 105
　body of, 10, 25, 29, 32, 35, 52, 80, 93, 156, 246
　casting and, 19, 270n15
　conversion of, 5–6
　as critical agent, 18
　existential dimensions of, 88
　in-person reenactment and, 5, 53, 159, 167, 253
　prevalence of, 6
　temporality of, 5, 7
　testimony of, 20
Red Desert (Antonioni, 1964), 64
reenactment. *See also* celebrity biopics; in-person reenactment
　contemporary art and, 6, 7, 270nn14–17, 271n35
　early cinema and, 19–20, 272n1, 272–273n2, 273nn4–8
　as event (Jasen), 21, 271nn36–37
　historical, 269n7, 272nn1–2
　social documentary and, 6, 21–23, 25, 27
Reinartz, Dirk, 144
Reis, Luiz Thomaz, 225–226
relatives as surrogates, 19–36
　bloodlines, 29
　casting of, 20–21, 24–25, 32
　family portraits, 276n45
　importance of, 24–25
　in-person reenactment and, 4, 19–20, 29–30
　resemblances, 30
Renoir, Jean, 73
Renzi, Renzo, 44, 279n46, 282n104
representation and in-person reenactment, 2, 5, 11–14, 21, 30, 82, 166, 261
Resnais, Alain, 147–148, 156, 177
responsibility. *See* atonement
Retour à Auschwitz (Cristobal, 1967), 146
revisiting original sites and in-person reenactment, 16, 39, 132, 141, 145–146, 159–160, 170–172, 221
Ricci, Antonio, 38
Riglioso, Caterina, 7, 37, 46–48, 49*f*, 51, 53, 56
Risi, Dino, 42, 278n22
Riva, Emmanuelle, 148, 150

[332]　Index

Rivette, Jacques, 73, 92, 292n67
Robinson, Jackie, 80–81, 81*f*, 284n4, 284n7
Rocha Melo, Luis Alberto, 225, 314n11, n20
Rogosin, Lionel, 135, 295n121
Rohdie, Sam, 51, 59, 64, 289n16
role-play
  Epstein and, 274n13
  in *Human Pyramid* (Rouch), 120–121, 130, 140
  in *Iracema* (Bodansky and Senna, 1974), 241
  psychosocial techniques, 118, 119, 122–123, 142, 289n11, 293n82
  reenactment and, 7, 11, 15
  Rouch and, 15, 113–114, 118, 120–121, 130, 298n17
Rollet, Sylvie, 191–192
Roma città aperta (Rome, Open City) (Rossellini, 1945), 38, 39*f*
Roosevelt, Franklyn Delano, 142, 168, 304n129
Ross, Kristin, 138, 296n139
Rossellini, Roberto, 72–73, 92, 105, 151
Rossif, Frédéric, 157–158, 302n93
Rothberg, Michael, 16–17, 142–143, 153–156, 174, 296n3, 297n5, 300n54, 305n148
Rothman, William, 301n80
Rouch, Jean
  cine-fictions of, 165
  cine-transe and, 151, 170, 300n54
  criticism of, 152
  death and, 124, 126, 129
  enlightenment program of, 122
  ethno-fictions of, 165, 258
  existential approach of, 122
  gesturing and, 164
  on *The Human Pyramid*, 123–125, 165, 292n71
  images of, 155*f*
  influence of, 298n17
  in-person reenactment and, 123, 272n46
  interrogatory approach of, 116
  on Loridan-Ivens, 150, 151, 300n59
  on mise-en-scène, 152
  pedovision of, 16, 136, 151–153
  psychodrama and, 117–118, 121, 124–125, 134 (*see also* sociodrama)
  realism of, 258
  role-play and, 15, 113, 121, 298n17
  surrealism of, 129, 150–152
  therapeutic frame of, 14–15, 117–118, 292n67

Rouquier, Georges, 23
Rousseau, Jean-Jacques, 5
Rouverol, Jean, 286n52
Rules of the Game (Renoir, 1939), 126
Russell, Catherine, 129, 226, 248

S21: The Khmer Rouge Killing Machine (Panh, 2003)
  aesthetics of, 190–192, 194, 201, 209
  agency in, 209, 212, 214, 216
  alienation in, 190
  atonement in, 204, 206, 214, 216
  catharsis in, 188, 206
  closure in, 192, 200, 204
  confessions in, 187, 205–208
  confrontations in, 193–195
  consciousness-raising in, 217
  conversion in, 205, 208–209
  ethical dimensions of, 183, 194, 207, 209, 215
  evidence in, 199–200, 209, 214
  evidentiary mise-en-scène in, 192–194, 209–210, 213*f*, 214
  film techniques in, 183–184, 187, 191–193, 197–198, 214, 216
  gestural memory in, 188–191, 197–198, 200, 308n30
  images from, 184*f*, 189*f*, 193*f*, 195–196*f*, 198*f*, 203*f*, 211*f*, 213*f*, 215*f*
  in-person reenactment in, 18, 183–184, 187–191, 198, 205–210, 211*f*, 212–217, 253
  making of, 209, 306n1, 307n6, 307n9, 309–310n49, 309n48, 311n65
  parajuridical context for, 200, 206, 208
  parajuridical scenarios, 188, 193–194, 205, 209, 308n15
  performance in, 185, 191, 209, 212
  setting of, 208
  social and political context of, 185, 190, 199, 206
  structure of, 184, 187, 188–189, 192–193, 197–198, 201, 215–216
  subjectivity in, 191–192
  testimony in, 191–194, 205, 206, 208, 209
  trauma in, 189–192, 200, 206, 207, 299n35
  traumatic reenactment and, 190, 299n35
  trials in, 187, 194, 204, 206, 208
Sabzian, Hossein, 1–4, 2–4*f*
Sachs, Albie, 204
Salazkina, Masha, 287n77
salvage paradigm, 220, 226, 248

Salvatore Giuliano (Rosi, 1962), 278n25
Samphan, Khieu, 204
Santos Aquino, Rowena, 10, 159, 297n11, 302n99
Sartre, Jean-Paul, 118, 122–123, 170, 294n96, 301n86
Schechner, Richard, 20, 251, 319n105
Schneider, Rebecca, 12, 178, 220–221, 271n39, 319n105
Schoonover, Karl, 134, 277n2
Schreiber, Rebecca, 106, 288n81, 288n85
Schwartz, Louis George, 17
Schwartz, Roberto, 231, 315n36
Sedgwick, Eve Kosofsky, 236, 316n40
Sensitivity Training Experiment (Lewin), 119
Senso (Visconti, 1954), 45
Sergent, Jean Pierre, 114, 116, 116–117f, 132, 289n14
Serras da Desordem (Tonacci, 2006), 236–240
　aesthetics of, 220, 257
　a-filiation in, 219–220, 247–249
　agency in, 240, 242, 244, 249
　authenticity in, 18, 221, 245, 249, 257
　autonomy in, 224, 244, 248–249
　casting in, 242–245
　circumstantial indianness in, 243–244
　film techniques in, 220, 222–225, 255
　firebrand in, 248–249, 251
　first contact in, 18, 219, 236, 243
　identity in, 18, 242, 244–251, 258, 260
　images from, 220–227f, 254–257f, 259f
　in-person reenactment in, 118, 219–221, 224–225, 228–229, 244–246, 249–252, 260–261
　language in, 237, 246
　making of, 219–220, 225–227, 236, 243, 316n43
　mimesis in, 253–255, 260–261, 274n12
　montage sequence in, 220, 221, 221f, 228, 240
　performance in, 221, 222, 244, 249, 251
　social and political context of, 226–228, 236, 245–248
　structure of, 220, 228
　surrogates in, 240, 245
　temporality in, 18, 222–226, 229, 245, 248, 250–252, 260, 261
　testimony in, 228, 244, 251
　trauma in, 246, 254
Settimana Incom (newsreel), 41
Sganzerla, Rogerio, 236
Shadows (Cassavetes, 1958), 123
Shoah (Lanzmann, 1985)
　aesthetics of, 177–178
　atonement in, 206
　cinema verité in, 16, 170
　criticism of, 174
　ethical dimensions of, 173–175
　film techniques in, 147, 153, 173–176
　images from, 172–173f, 175–176f
　influence of, 7, 17, 140, 306n165
　in-person reenactment in, 6, 145–147, 153, 168, 171–172, 174–177, 253
　making of, 145–146, 173, 176
　mimesis in, 145
　realism in, 174
　real protagonist in, 16–17
　revisiting in, 16–17, 145–146, 168, 171, 178
　singularity in, 176–177
　testimony in, 16, 145, 172–173, 206
　theatricality in, 168, 170, 171, 206
　trauma in, 17
Shulie (Subrin, 1997), 6
Shutzenberger, Ann, 117
Siamo Donne (*We, the Women*, episode film, 1953), 14, 40, 67–71, 70–72f, 74f, 84, 92. *See also* Alida Valli; Anna Magnani; *The Chicken*; *Contest: 4 Actresses and 1 Hope*; Isa Miranda
The Silence of the Sea (Melville, 1947–1949), 151
A Simple Question of Justice (Lainé and Reynaud, 2011), 200, 201–202f
Simpson, O. J., 143, 298n18
Site 2 (Panh, 1989), 185
Sitney, P. Adams, 65, 280n75
Skoller, Jeffrey, 296n3
Small, Pauline, 69, 90
Smith, Albert, 272–273n1
social actors, 10, 13, 16, 20–21, 39, 48, 147, 191
Socialisme ou Barbarie (group), 137, 294n101
Socialisme ou Barbarie (journal), 133, 138, 295n129, 296n146
sociodrama, 113, 117–119, 121, 124, 134, 166, 288n2, 290n27, 290nn31–32. *See also* psychodrama
Sofer, Andrew, 198
Sons (Zhang, 1996), 13, 24, 33–36, 34f, 36f, 253
Sophia: Her Own Story (Stuart, 1980), 15, 77–81, 78f, 84–92, 91f
sound
　direct sound, 114, 125
　sync sound, 134, 145, 148, 154
Soustelle, Jacques, 133
Soviet cinema, 93
Soyinka, Wole, 207, 312n86

Spanish Earth (Ivens, 1937), 108
The Spectator (magazine), 41–43, 41–43f
Spielberg's List (Fast, 2003), 6, 270n16
sports biopics, 15, 30, 32, 80, 275–276n41
The Square (Zhang, 1994), 276n44
Srebnik, Simon, 16, 146, 171–173, 172f, 175, 298–299n34, 305n145
Stalin, Josef, 45, 93–95, 117, 132–133, 136, 296n144
stardom. *See* celebrity biopics
Starobinski, Jean, 5–6, 191
Steimatsky, Noa, 59, 278n25, 281–282n104
Stewart, Garret, 288n94
Stewart, Jimmy, 86
The Story of Caterina (Maselli and Zavatiini, 1953), 7, 14, 37, 39–40, 47–55, 47f, 49–50f, 66
Strand, Paul, 43, 278n26
Straw, Will, 29
Streible, Dan, 19, 273n2
Stuart, Mel, 88
Subrin, Elisabeth, 6
substitution and in-person reenactment, 13, 19, 27, 97, 99, 174, 221, 251
Suharto, 11
Suramet Theater, 185, 185f
surrogacy and in-person reenactment, 19–20, 27–30, 43, 52, 108, 240, 245, 270n15

Tale of the Wind (Ivens, 1988), 302n101
talking cures, 7, 63, 142
Tarde de Toro (Vajda, 1956), 97
Taylor, Diana, 12, 274n20
Teixeira, João Pedro, 229
Teleproducciones (company), 104
temporality and in-person reenactment, 5, 11–18, 20, 23, 82, 88, 174, 224
Terrorists in Retirement (Boucault, 2001), 299n38
Tesson, Charles, 258, 319n8
testimony
  agency and, 250
  cinema verité and, 142
  in-person reenactment and, 11, 15, 141–143, 167, 269n7
  irreplaceability and, 141–142
  monologue and, 11, 16, 114, 140, 142–145, 147, 150, 154, 156, 163–165, 166, 171
  in post-Holocaust cinema, 143, 145, 174, 184
  therapeutic dimension of, 207
  trauma and, 16–17
  trials and, 204
theatricality, 11, 13, 14, 15, 40, 63, 73, 76, 122, 168, 170, 171, 198, 206, 209, 215, 289n11, 291n48

The Thin Blue Line (Morris, 1987), 6, 206
The Third Memory (Huyghe, 1999), 6, 271n35
The Time of the Ghetto (Rossif, 1961), 157–159, 157–159f
Tinnazi, Giorgio, 281n97
Titanus Studio, 69
Tonacci, Andrea
  aesthetics of, 220, 242
  on *Araras*, 240, 316n45
  on circumstantial indianness, 240, 242–243
  on *Conversas*, 240 (*see also Conversations in Maranhão*)
  ethics of encounter of, 237, 240, 242
  identification with characters, 243
  on indigenous self-record, 236–237
  influence of, 236–237
  in-person reenactment and, 224, 242, 320n13
  on *Serras*, 240, 243, 249, 314n8
  trajectory of, 229, 236, 316n43
Torero! (Velo, 1956), 79f, 94–112, 100–112f
  awards for, 104
  death in, 27, 79, 94–97, 102, 107–108, 110
  existential dimensions of, 99, 108, 110
  film techniques in, 84, 95f, 98–99, 102–104, 286n55
  influence of, 92
  in-person reenactment in, 15, 82, 94, 97–98, 103–104, 108, 110
  realism in, 97, 102, 104, 105, 284n12
Tou Zi, 33, 35
Trans-Amazonian Highway, 240
transformative power of in-person reenactment, 5, 7, 13, 18, 56, 254, 271n36
transmission and in-person reenactment, 5, 18, 24–25, 35, 249–252
trauma and in-person reenactment, 10, 16–18, 190, 297n5, 299n35. *See also* posttraumatic cinema
traumatic realism, 17, 296n3, 297n5, 305nn148–149
traumatic reenactment, 17, 18, 190
Treblinka, 147, 170, 174–176, 176f, 177
trial films, 143, 204–207, 297n14, 298n18. *See also* parajuridical films;
Tribe, Mark, 7
Truth and Reconciliation commissions, 7, 142, 200, 206, 208, 311n70, 312–313n86
Tu, Maggiorani (Zavattini, unmade film), 56

Index [335]

Tuol Sleng Genocide Museum, 193–194, 199–201, 310nn50–54, 311n61
Tuol Sleng prison, 190, 200, 202
Tupi-Guarani tribes, 221, 246
Tutu, Desmond, 311n70
Tweedie, James, 150, 299n46
Twelve Angry Men (Lumet, 1957), 138
Twenty Years Later: A Man Marked to Die (Coutinho, 1964–1984), 18, 228–233, 230f, 233–234f, 314n23, 315n32. *See also* CoutinhoEduardo
Duda (son of Zé Daniel), 232–234, 234f
Two Nights with Cleopatra (Mattoli, 1954), 86, 87f
Two Women (De Sica, 1960), 84, 90, 91f

Umberto D (De Sica, 1952), 40–41, 44, 48, 51, 277n17
Under the Sun of Rome (Castellani, 1948), 75
Ungar, Steven, 165
Ung Pech, 310n51
Uwemedimo, Michael, 116

Valli, Alida, 54, 69, 71, 71f
Van Alphen, Ernst, 191
Vargas, Getúlio, 25
Velo, Carlos, 15, 84, 98–99, 104–106, 286n55, 286n64, 287n71, 287n74
Vernani, Shabnam, 9
Vertov, Dziga, 40, 105, 287n77
Viaggio in Italia (*Voyage to Italy*) (Rossellini, 1954), 73
Vierny, Sacha, 148
Viguier, Jean-Paul, 132
Villani, Romilda, 15, 77, 78f, 86, 90, 91f
Virginio, João, 232
Visconti, Luchino, 7, 40, 45, 69, 72–73, 75, 92, 104
Visman, Cornelia, 192, 309nn 39–40
Vitti, Monica, 116, 150
Viveiros de Castro, Eduardo, 245–248, 318n91, 319n1

Walker, Janet, 17, 146, 296n3, 298n30, 305n148
Wang Xiaoshuai, 276n44
Warsaw Ghetto, 167–168, 170
We, the Women. See Siamo Donne
Weiss, Peter, 179, 180f, 181, 306n174
Welles, Orson, 25–29, 275nn29–30
West, Nancy, 205
Whatever Happened to Baby Jane? (Aldrich, 1962), 89

When Women Unite: The Story of an Uprising (Virmani, 1996), 9
Whissel, Kristen, 20, 273nn8–9
Wiesel, Elie, 167
Wievorka, Annette, 154–155, 304n129
Williams, Linda, 17, 297n10
Wilson, Emma, 177–178
Wilson, Richard, 26, 26–28f. *See also Four Men on a Raft* and *It's All True*
witnessing. *See* testimony
Woloch, Alex, 29–30
Wood, Christopher, 18, 174, 221, 305n151, 314n5
Woodhead, Leslie, 29
Woolward, Keithley, 122
World Memory Archive, 199
Wormser, Olga, 147
The Wretched of the Earth (Fanon), 123
Wu Wenguang, 272n45

Xavier, Ismail, 242, 250–251, 317n69
Xavier, Nelson, 230

Yesterday, Today and Tomorrow (De Sica, 1963), 84–85
Young, James, 177, 306nn162–165

Zampa, Luigi, 71
Zavattini, Cesare
 alienation and, 45, 48
 atonement and, 52
 Christianity of, 51–52, 280n76
 cinegiornali projects of, 281n92
 cinema verité and, 15, 84
 critiques of, 45–46, 52–53, 279n46
 enlightenment program of, 53
 ethical approach of, 43, 52, 278n22
 on *film-lampo*, 47
 on film techniques, 46
 influence of, 84
 in-person reenactment and, 14, 40–41, 46–48, 52, 90
 on *Italia Mia*, 40, 43, 105, 278n26
 on *Mexico Mio*, 105, 287n69, 287n70, 287n71, 287nn74–77, 288n78
 naturalism of, 45
 nonactors and, 37–39, 69
 Parma address of, 45–46, 53
 pedinamento approach of, 38, 56, 105
 realism of, 44–45, 51–53, 105
 repetition and, 41, 46
Zhang Yuan, 33, 261, 276n44
Zhang Zhen, 272n45, 276n43